GLOBAL TRENDS IN LIBRARY AND INFORMATION SCIENCE

GLOBAL TRENDS IN LIBRARY AND INFORMATION SCIENCE

Subhas C. Biswas

GYAN

GYAN PUBLISHING HOUSE

New Delhi 110 002

Global Trends in Library and Information Science

(Library and Information Science)

ISBN :- 81-212-0494-1

Published 1995 in India by
Gyan Publishing House
5, Ansari Road
New Delhi-110 002

Printed at Mehra Offset Press, New Delhi-110 002

Dedicated
to
Bābā and Mā

Introduction

An editor's introduction should offer the reader some focusing elements and an overview of the contents of the book. The focus here is on the current trends in all the major facets of library and information science. Comparative librarianship as a topic has drawn considerable attention within the profession over the last few decades. But there are not many publications which deal with the state-of-the-art scenarios on the topic with its multiple dimensions, from all the corners of the world.

One of the main objectives of publishing this anthology is to bring out the anguish and concern for the gaps which exist between the developed and developing countries and to focus on the efforts being consistently made by the professionals belonging to the less developed world over the last decade. The significant results obtained are all recorded here for everyone to notice. The criteria was to have a global coverage, of the trends of development of the discipline under different heads and sub-heads, providing an overview and reflecting the situation in the developing countries. Coverage of the topics relevant to India, in terms of the number of articles, is substantial. A sizable number of authors are specialists in the academic sense, on South Asia, which makes the coverage slightly tilted towards this geographical area. However, the application of the ideas contained in this volume is intended to transcend national boundaries. The other papers are also of considerable importance and quite a few able and informative contributions have been presented. A glance at the contents page will surely reveal that the contributors represent a wide variety of institutions, working contexts and levels of experience.

The volume contains 41 contributions on various aspects of library and information science from 45 authors. For convenience, the contributions have been grouped under six broad headings : (1) Access to information, Resource sharing and Network; (2) Information sources and services; (3) Bibliographical data and Standardization; (4) Libraries and Information systems ; (5) Management and Training, and (6) Information Technology and Databases.

Under section 'Access to information, Resource sharing and Network', authors have presented various programme and planning issues. A few articles also focus on the implementation of some specialised information systems within a region or country. Abdelaziz Abid gives a detailed outline of the various Unesco-PGI sponsored programmes on access to information on science and technology in the developing countries. Abhijit Lahiri, on the other hand, focuses on the causes of non-availability of information on science and technology to the user group in India; suggests remedial measures to overcome the situation and highlightes some of the steps that are being put into action. Tony Leisner in his paper '*Why won't you accept my order ? Global acquisition solution*' has brought up some issues in the process of procurement of a variety of material which are being produced, not necessarily in book form or published and distributed through the accepted trade links. He presents some useful examples which could allow the ultimate users to have direct access to the information that may only be available in electronic format. These changes will inevitably bring conventional library acquisition practices into question. George Baumann deals with the acquisition and processing problems of European libraries, having large South Asian collections of literature. He discusses the procedures followed by the libraries in general, with suggestions for centralization of processing by adopting some standards. This problem could have been partly solved if the current national bibliographies produced by the copyright libraries of South Asia could be brought out regularly and in machine-readable form based on international standards. James Nye of the University of Chicago is steadily building up an all-comprehensive South Asian collection through various programmes. In his paper one finds an exposition of the systematic approach to collection development and its intricacies, for a late starter in the field.

Ramos de Carvalo and Ta'lamo provide a comprehensive coverage of Latin America's various information services and systems that are gradually joining together as part of networks to provide more effective access to information by sharing resources through regional cooperation. They have recorded in definition and use of terms, network, information system, etc. The details of the existing networks and databases in Latin America may be useful to many. Khoo Siew Moon in her paper, explains Malaysia's National Information Clearing House on Women in Development — an area of high priority in social science research in all the developing countries. It has the primary objective of collocating and sharing information on the topic amongst the participating institutions within Malaysia and join the ASEAN regional main-stream through regional network. A national network on Women in Development (WID) established recently comprises national, academic, research and governmental organisations and institutions. The planning and implementation strategies are described in detail which could be of use to others in the field.

Papers grouped under Information Sources and Services have a wide range of coverage from manuscript collections to audiovisual material. Graham Shaw's *History of Printing in South Asia* is a review article throwing open the field to the librarians and historical bibliographers to face a big challenge to locate the missing pieces of the jigsaw and complete the map of the history of printing and publishing in the subcontinent. He sounds an alarm with a plea that, 'the historical pattern of publishing in the subcontinent inevitably cuts across modern state boundaries ... the national libraries of South Asia should cooperate closely - to their mutual benefit - in improving retrospective bibliographical control for the region. The sooner this process is set in hand the greater its chances of success will be.'

Due to historical reasons a few academic and national libraries in the United Kingdom are still jointly having the largest collections of research material on South Asia outside the subcontinent. Barry Bloomfield in his thought-provoking paper expresses concern on the condition of Asian studies and its reflection on the library provision in the United Kingdom. He stresses the need to consider these studies from the South Asian point of view. In the recent past there has been a slow growth and lesser studies on South Asia in the United Kingdom due to lack of sufficient official support. This brief investigation attempts to surmise the past trends and how it may affect the South Asia Library Group in the UK and library provision for South Asian studies.

Libraries do not always contain only printed documents as books, periodicals, etc. Joshi in his brief paper describes the significance of the collection of one of the world's largest sound archives of the All India Radio, Delhi. Prajapati has brought out a short historical sketch of Indian manuscripts—their origins, distinctive features and factors that are to be taken into account while dealing with their identification, processing and storage. Whereas, Shamim Akhtar in his paper deals with traditional manuscript collections in India, with special reference to the National Library. One major information source is serial publications. Libraries spend substantial part of their acquisitions budget on serial publications — their procurement, bibliographical control, documentation, storage and preservation. Pawan Gupta gives an up-to-date comprehensive description of serial publications in India — their growth and status with statistical data. He also brings out the significant issues in dealing with serials in India from the librarian's point of view, such as, legal deposit, guides, union catalogue, indexing and abstracting services. Aina deals with the same topic from the African librarian's point of view. Journals constitute the principal medium for the exchange of ideas for librarians in the region. Authors in the library profession rarely discuss theoretical problems but deal mostly with local library issues which are generally not applicable to the librarianship environment in the region. References cited are mostly dated, thus they hardly contribute to new knowledge. Readers, rarely read local journals as a result of which, the editors do not get any feedback. This situation is very common in most of the developing countries, hence the recommendations made are worth considering.

The Indian Parliament Library by Malhotra is a detailed account of all its collections and services. Much of its special services to the legislators are modelled on the Congressional Services of the US Library of Congress. Recently there has been a lot of discussion on national policy on libraries in various countries. Mastini Hardjoprakoso in her paper on Indonesia's rural library development programme gives an account of the country's national library system. This could help as a model to others who are in the process of formulating a national library policy.

In most developing countries, areas like children's education, adult literacy and public library development programmes do not get much political and financial support from official sources. The lack of commitment on the part of the policy makers and little involvement of public libraries in literacy programmes for children or adults in the third world countries, are being raised by Dennis Gunton with an appeal to move fast to find a way out from this calamity. Barbo Thomas stresses the same idea with facts and figures in the global context.

What goes on behind the scene — the conflicting views, tension, technological innovation, traditionalists and protagonists — in setting up an international standard, is well reflected in Richard Christophers essay on ISBD. It may help the senior professionals who are involved in similar activities. Neelameghan's paper would surely help the large group of information analysts working on designing data processing systems or looking for a conceptual approach to system designing. Kalpana Dasgupta tries to focus on the issues that require special consideration in dealing with multi-lingual publications. She gives examples from National Library, Calcutta where the creation of a machine-readable bibliographical database is now in progress.

There are hundreds of research papers and several monographs which have come out over the last two decades on Intery-Library Loan providing divergent views. British Library's Document Supply Centre, since its inception, brought in a different dimension to the whole issue. Perhaps it is due to these conflicts and confusions — both at the conceptual level as well as in practice — that IFLA is trying to bring some order into this chaos by producing a standard on ILL. Swain and Talim of IFLA's UDT Core Programme have described the progress made in this research work. This would help every library engaged in data exchange in this rapidly changing environment of communication technology. National Bibliography is national memory i.e. it should be complete in recording all types of publications irrespective of their social or academic value. Robert Holley in his survey found several types of gaps in coverage in the OCLC — the largest bibliographical database — for American publications. Is it really possible to get hold of a copy of everything published in a country and then record it in the national bibliography ? And should it be really necessary to take such steps at all ? Whom should we address these questions to ? It may sound an ideal proposal but next to impossible to implement. Holley's survey and analysis may help someone to draw the line accurately.

Much has been written on the role and objectives of national libraries; perhaps equally on its function and services. Most of these are from the pens of library professionals of developed countries. Stephney Ferguson gives a different picture which is more close to the actual condition in most of the developing countries. It is evident from her presentation that much of it is a reflection of her own experience.

Political will of the policy makers, social drawbacks and most important of all limited financial resources determine the type of library a nation would have. Where there is no clarity regarding the purpose, role and function of a national library, it will be difficult to attract resources required to perform effectively. The process of strategic planning, though a difficult and time consuming exercise, can secure far-reaching benefits for the library. On the same topic of national library Kishin Navalani presents a well documented paper on historical perspectives of a national library system and services. One cannot have a standardized national policy on library development for the developing countries. Her views on Indian national library and information policy are positive and thoughtful.

Suseela Kumar's article gives a bird's-eye view of the current Indian library and information science scenario. One would find it very useful for a first hand knowledge on Indian librarianship. Very closely related to this is Davis' and Mohamed Taher's paper reviewing the historiographical studies made so far of Indian librarianship. They feel that a final picture is yet to emerge as studies made so far, are scanty and incomplete. Coordinated efforts may produce a better result.

The impact of Information Technology in academic libraries in the United Kingdom brought big changes in the approaches of the users of libraries. This has also affected the services and demands on the library in a big way. Anthony Evans is perhaps right in saying that online searches made by the user without visiting libraries is becoming more and more a fact of life. This allows the user direct access to a large number of bibliographical sources. But to identify and obtain only the relevant documents out of online searches would depend on the actual holdings of the library and the user would need to seek the assistance of the library staff to help in getting them from other centres. He feels that with the introduction of IT there may not be much of a change in the relationship between library and academics in the 21st century also, at least in Britain. The only difference will be more online searches, more citations, longer time to be spent in locating them, more I-L Loan requests, more documents to look through and more waste of time and energy. Isaac's paper is a description of university libraries in India with some suggestions for improvement of services. The ongoing modernization programme of the Indian academic libraries would help in resource sharing and better access to information sources. It indicates the wide gap between the present condition of an Indian university library and that of a developed country in the West, though one may not consider librarianship in India as underdeveloped.

While education and training are accepted as essential components for growth of every vocation, trade or profession the concept of management as part of librarianship education and training is a recent addition. Maurice Line has discussed staff motivation — a behavioural phenomenon — in library management. He is right in saying librarianship is 'deskilled'. Some of us were always suspicious of the so called "professional" skills of librarianship, which wrapped what were or should have been fairly simple and easily learnt skills in a cloak of obscurity.... which mystified some library practitioners almost as much as it clearly did many users. Automation, in particular the ability to take catalogue records off remote databases, has changed all that. What is required to be learnt is managerial skills which are not taught much in library schools. He suggests how some of the recent management concepts could be adopted to be more effective in getting positive results in these days when every library is facing a budget crunch.

Theory of probability and other statistical methods of analysis are valuable management tools. Basu, in his paper, has demonstrated with examples from the library situation a few areas of applications of probability modelling and statistical methodology in analysing and planning better library services. Examples cited here would help many librarians in understanding the varied usefulness of this tool in library management. Peter Underwood on the other hand brings in several logical approaches in the decision making process of the managers, for consideration within the library systems environment. It would be worthwhile for some library managers to attempt, initially as projects, to verify some of these concepts. Library schools may use these techniques and concepts as part of their graduate training programme.

In a large number of libraries all over the world the catalogue—the most valuable reference tool — is in a transition stage from conventional card to machine-readable magnetic tapes and diskettes and then to multi-access online databases. In that context Barbara Ford's suggestion for training of non-cataloguing staff in a library — who are helping the users continuously—may be worth considering in a large library system. Sharon Hogan's approach to educate and train the users in exploiting the online catalogues has always been accepted as part of user education programme. Research on users' behaviour using an online catalogue may lead to improving cataloguing codes and practices. Mike Freeman has highlighted the need to bring some changes in librarianship education and training programmes, that could allow librarians to face the challenge of the new 'information society'. The latter with its far reaching developments is forcing reappraisal and radical changes upon the profession in all its branches. There is a fast growing feeling that more wide-spread use of technology will tend to weaken the position of the traditional librarian or information scientist. His concluding optimistic note may bring some cheer to a section of the profession — 'as knowledge continues to multiply, the need for expertise will also multiply'. There is not much awareness of the fast changing scenario within the profession as a whole. This is what Pradeepa Wijetunge has observed. The reasons for this short-sightedness or late response, she points out, are poor economic condition affecting the process of modernization, language barrier and distance between the generators of information and users in developing countries.

Those who wish to get a better idea on information technology and databases may study the literature published on these two topics during the last decade. Scope and application of these topics in the field of librarianship are growing fast both at macro and micro levels. There are several periodicals now coming out regularly on these topics alone. A few articles chosen for this volume are exemplary in nature and primarily to demonstrate their use and application in the developing countries.

CD-ROM technology is now being accepted by the library and publishing world for storage of large amount of bibliographical, full text and other data. The retrieved data can be printed or transferred to magnetic media without great difficulty. It provides enormous flexibility for making searches and compactness in storage. Several authors have referred to this technology in different context. The two major disadvantages of this technology are that it is yet to be standardized and life span from archival storage point of view, is yet to be established. Prohibitive cost of library software packages is one of the main causes of slow progress in computer application in libraries of the developing countries. Unesco sponsored CDS/ISIS package, distributed free of cost to non-profit making organisations of the member countries has helped many librarians. It is useful for medium range libraries which happens to be the size of the majority of libraries in these countries. Peter Borchardt has given a detailed note on the use of IT in general and CDS/ISIS in particular, based on his first hand experience in African socio-economic background. Several libraries may find this library software very useful to begin with. Again a microcomputer based software OSIRIS sponsored by IFLA with Unesco support is another package, complementary to CDS/ISIS. It would allow small and medium size projects to take advantage of automation for those who wish to maintain serial bibliography and even support union catalogues. Institutions dealing with less than 30,000 records can find OSIRIS a very handy package provided one keeps in mind the physical limitations of the hardware.

There are presently very few indigenously developed bibliographic databases in India that are accessible to users in general. These are however, limited mostly to English language publications acquired by libraries. Creating a database of the full text of the epic, the Mahabharata (Sanskrit) in original Devanagari characters, coding every metre by punctuating each verse according to Sanskrit grammar and poetics, is the first attempt by Biswas and Daga in India. This machine-readable text will help in developing a software for interpreting Sanskrit grammar which should open up the scope for bringing in the entire range of Sanskrit literary works to the computer environment. There are thousands of manuscripts still waiting to be catalogued, edited and published. The software will help in deciding the originality, text variation, linguistic and grammatical issues of Sanskrit language and literature. Anton Pierce deals with the application of computer technology for similar kinds of material procured by the US Library of Congress from Africa, Asia and South America. It gives an insight into the planning process for automation, introduction, selection, development and implementation of new technology, staff training, etc., simulataneously in all the centres for acquisition and processing of material in hundreds of different languages and scripts. The nature of complexity is enormous but the solutions are there—this is his message.

Majority of the articles are derived from the authors' first hand knowledge and experience. This would add more value to the topics they have individually dealt with. Choice of contributors and the topic they each cover was the sole responsibility of tne editor. Nevertheless, an editor is entitled to his own views and where there are omissions, you may be cognizant of individual circumstances, and my own personal characteristics and eccentricities.

Global Trends in Library and Information Science

LIST OF CONTRIBUTORS

Abdelaziz ABID :

Joined Unesco, General Information Programme (PGI) Division, Paris in 1985, in charge of projects related to libraries and access to scientific literature. Earlier he served as Secretary-General of the National Library of Tunisia. Contributed articles/ papers in Arabic, English and French.

Lenrie Olatokunbo AINA :

Associate Professor, Department of Library & Information Studies, University of Botswana ; formerly Senior Lecturer, Department of Library, Archival & Information studies, University of Ibadan, Nigeria ; Editor-in-chief of African Journal of Library, Archives and Information Science.

Md. Shamim AKHTAR:

Library & Information assistant, National Library, Calcutta. Contributed articles / papers in English.

Sujit K BASU :

Professor, Indian Institute of Management, Calcutta. Specialization in mathematical statistics. Fellow, West Bengal Academy of Science & Technology ; Member, International Statistical Institute. Contributed journal articles/ papers.

George BAUMANN :

Director, Oriental Section, University of Tuebingen Library since 1979; Education: Universities of Heidelberg and Cologne; several publications and journal articles /papers.

Subhas C BISWAS :

Project Director, MIP Project, U. S. Library of Congress Office, New Delhi, since 1990. Formerly worked in various capacities in British Museum, London, Indian institute of Advanced Study, Shimla, British Council, Central Secretariat Library, New Delhi, India; former President, Indian Library Association. Contributed journal articles/papers.

B C BLOOMFIELD:

Former Director, Collection Development, British Library; Director, India Office Library & Records ; Librarian, SOAS, University of London. Professional involvement : various committees of LA ; Vice-President Bibliographical Society; various committees of IFLA. Several publications and journal articles/ papers. Address : Brambling, 24 Oxen Turn Road, Wye, Kent, England.

Peter BORCHARDT:

Chief Librarian and Dèputy Director, Amerika - Gedenkbibliothek, Berlin since 1993 ; formerly Librarian, Deutsches Bibliothekinstitut for 11 years ; conducted continuing education training courses for African librarians ; Secretary, IFLA-Section for Public Libraries; several journal articles/papers.

R A CHRISTOPHERS :

Head, 20th century British Collections, British Library, London. Contributed journal articles/papers.

Sheela DAGA :

Research Assistant, Mahabharat Project, Central Secretariat Library, New Delhi; formerly Lecturer in Sanskrit for Non-collegiate Women, University of Delhi.

Donald G DAVIS, Jr. :

Professor, Graduate School of Library & Information Science, University of Texas at Austin, USA. Contributed journal articles/papers.

Kalpana DASGUPTA :

Principal Library & Information Officer, National Library, Calcutta since 1983. Formerly served Botanical survey of India, Calcutta, Indian Council of Agricultural Research, New Delhi, National Council of Applied Economic Research, New Delhi and Indian Institute of Mass Communication, New Delhi. Education : Universities of Patna, Jadavpur and Syracuse (USA) ; several publications and journal articles/ papers.

Anthony J. EVANS :

Professor, Department of Information & Library Studies, Loughborough University of Technology ; Formerly Librarian of the University ; several publications and journal articles / papers. Address : Alumni Office, Rutland Hall, Loughborough University of Technology, Loughborough, Leicestershire LE 11 3 TU, UK.

Stephney FERGUSON :

Senior Lecturer, Department of Library Studies, University of the West Indies, Kingston, Jamaica. Formerly Director, National Library, Jamaica, WI. ; past President COMLA. Contributed several publications and journal articles/papers.

Barbara J FORD :

Director, University Library Services, Virginia Commonwealth University, Richmond, Virginia 23284-2033, U.S.A. Formerly employed at Trinity University and the University of Illinois at Urbana-Champaign and Tuft University ; served as President of the Asson. of College and Research Libraries of the ALA from 1990-91; several publications and journal articles/papers.

Mike FREEMAN :

Library and Information Consultant ; researching at the Centre for the Study of the Professions, Aston Business School, Aston University, Birmingham, UK ; Previous employments : Chief Librarian, Head of Learning Resources and Tutor Librarian posts in seven Further and Higher Education Institutions' libraries ; National Councillor of the Library Association.

Ilona GLASHOFF ;

Librarian, Hamburger Offentliche Bucherhallen since 1976. Head of the national "Committee for Children's Libraries, Young Adults and School Libraries" Germany ; Member, Standing Committee for Childeren's Libraries in IFLA.

Dennis GUNTON:

Served for the British Council in Nigeria, Malaysia, India and Yugoslavia and also as the Director of the Council's Books, Libraries and Information Services till 1988. Several publications and journal articles/ papers. Address : Drayton Farm Cottages, Wendens Ambo, Saffron Walden, Essex, CB 11 4JX UK.

Pawan K GUPTA :

Deputy Librarian, University of Rajasthan, Jaipur, India since 1982. Formerly Assistant Professor, Department of Library Science, University of Rajasthan ; Acting Director, University of

Rajasthan Library ; Editor, Index India ; Several publications and journal articles / papers.

Mastini HARDJOPRAKOSO :

Director, National Library of Indonesia, Jakarta. Contributed several publications and journal articles/papers.

Sharon A HOGAN :

University Librarian and Interim Director of the Academic Computer Center, University of Illinois at Chicago. Taught in Library Schools at the University of Michigan, Drexel University and Louisiana State University. Co-founding and co-editing of *Research Strategies : a Journal of Library Concepts and Instruction* (1982-1990) ; active member of the American Library Association.

Robert P HOLLEY :

Associate Dean of Libraries, Wayne State University, Detroit, USA. Contributed journal articles/papers.

K A ISAAC :

Formerly University Librarian and Professor and Head of the Department of Library & Information Science, University of Kerala, Trivandrum, India till 1985. Served as visiting Professor, University of Calicut ; Special Officer (Library), Mahatma Gandhi University, Kottoyam, Kerala ; served as member of several national organisations. Contributed several publications, journal articles/papers.

H M JOSHI :

Chief Engineer (Planning), All India Radio since 1986. Joined AIR in 1965 and served at Radio Stations and Project Offices of AIR in various capacities.

Khoo SIEW MUN :

Project Coordinator, National Information Clearinghouse on Women in Development, Ministry of National Unity and Social

Development, Kuala Lumpur, Malaysia. She was with the University of Malay for 33 years, out of which she was the University Librarian for ten years. Several publications, journal articles /papers.

Suseela KUMAR :

Former Regional Librarian, British Council, Madras, India. President, Madras Library Association. Several publications journal articles/papers.

Tony LEISNER :

Group Strategic Planner, Dawson Group. Formerly Vice-President, Quality Books, Inc. Adjunct Professor of Marketing, J. L. Kellogg Graduate School of Management, Northwestern University. Several publications, journal articles/papers. ALA Council member.

Abhijit LAHIRI :

Joint Advisor (NISSAT) , Department of Scientific & Industrial Research, Govt. of India, New Delhi. Several publications, journal articles/papers.

Maurice B Line :

Information & Library Consultant; formerly Director General, Sc. Tech. & Industry, British Library ; Director General. British Lending Library. Former President LA ; Visiting Professor, Loughborough & Sheffield Universities. Editor, *Alexandria* ; Contributed several publications and journal articles/papers. Address : 10 Blackthorn Lane, Burn Bridge, Harrogate, Yorks, England.

G C MALHOTRA :

Director LARRDIS, Parliament Library, New Delhi.

Kishni NAVALANI :

Professor & Dean, Dept. of Library & Information Science, Punjabi University, Patiala, India ; formerly, Deputy Librarian, University of Rajasthan ; Contributed several publications and journal articles /papers.

A NEELAMEGHAN :

Information & Library Consultant. Formerly Consultant, Unesco-PGI ; Professor & Head DRTC, Indian Statistical

Institute, Bangalore ; Project Coordinator, Post-Graduate Training Course for Sc. Inf. Specialists in SE Asia, Inst. of Library Science, University of the Philippines ; Chmn. FID/CR. Several publications and journal articles/papers. Address : C/o DRTC, Bangalore, India.

James H NYE :

Bibliographer for South Asia, University of Chicago, USA since 1984- ; Vice President and Editor/Publisher, Musicdata, Inc. Contributed several publications and journal articles/papers.

Anton R PIERCE :

Automation Planning & Liaison Office, Library of Congress, Washington, DC. Contributed journal articles/papers.

M K PRAJAPATI :

Librarian & Head, Department of Library & Information Science, North Gujarat University, Patan, Gujarat ; formerly Assistant Director, Central Secretariat Library, New Delhi.

Elizabet Maria RAMOS DE CARVALHO :

Consultant, COLLECTA, Processo, Produto e Coleta de Dados since 1991. Formerly Senior Librarian, Petroleo Brasileiro S. A. In-charge of IFLA Regional Office for Latin America & the Caribbean ; President of the Federacao Brasileira de Associacao de Bibliotecarios (1987). Several publications, journal articles/papers

Suzanne SANTIAGO :

Director, ISDS International Centre, Paris. Chair, IFLA Standing Committee on Serial Publications. Formerly, Head, Science section, University of Picardie Library, France ; Director, French Books in Print and French ISBN Agency.

Graham W SHAW :

Deputy Director, Oriental & India Office Collections, British Library, London. Contributed several publications, journal articles/papers.

Leigh SWAIN :

Manager (Acting), Information Analysis & Standards, Inf. Tech. Services, National Library of Canada ; Director, IFLA's UDT core programme since 1988.

Mohamed TAHER :

Deputy Librarian, American Studies Research Centre, Hyderabad, India. Contributed several journal articles/papers.

Ivone TA'LAMO :

Supervisor of the Documentation and Inf. Center of Sao Paulo State Official Press, Brazil, 1980. Formerly, Consultant, Culture Secretariat of the State of Sao Paulo ; Consultant, Library of the Order of the Economist of Sao Paulo ; Head Librarian, State Company of Environmental Technology ; Professor, Library School of Fundacao Escola de Sociologia e Politica of Sao Paulo. Contributed several publications and journal articles/papers.

Paula TALLIM :

Asst. Library Network Specialist, Inf. Tech. Services of the National Library of Canada, Ottawa; Programme Officer, IFLA's UDT core programme since 1987.

Barbro THOMAS :

Head, Dept. of Libraries and Literature, Swedish National Council for Cultural Affairs, Stockholm, 1984. Executive Officer, IFLA Section of Public Libraries. Several publications, journal articles/papers.

Peter G UNDERWOOD :

Professor & Director, School of Librarianship, University of Cape Town, S. A. Formerly, Lecturer, Dept. of Inf. & Library Studies, College of Wales, Aberystwyth UK. Several publications, journal articles/papers.

Pradeepa WIJETUNGE :

In charge of the Library of the Faculty of Graduate Studies, Acquisition Section and Automation Project of the University of Colombo Library, Colombo, Sri Lanka. Several journal articles/papers.

ACKNOWLEDGEMENT

I am indeed grateful to the contributors for their overwhelming positive response. The hard work, professionalism, inspiration and any success achieved, belongs to them. I am most thankful to IFLA for allowing me to reproduce some of the papers presented at the 58th Annual General Conference (1992), of which a few were published in IFLA Journal. Thanks are also due to my colleagues in the U S Library of Congress Office (MIPP) Meena Sivarajan and S. Vasu who continuously supported me at various stages of editing ; to Geetha Balasubramanian, who was coerced into reading a variety of scripts and provided so much support and valuable unbiased opinion. Above all I am grateful to my wife Atreyi for her patience, forbearance and enduring support all the time.

CONTENTS

III - BIBLIOGRAPHICAL DATA PROCESSING AND STANDARDIZATION

PART I
Access to Information, Resource Sharing & Network

Improving Access to Scientific Literature in Developing Countries : A Unesco Programme Review

ABDELAZIZ ABID

Scientists in developing countries have a special need for documentation and information services because 1) they generally benefit less than their colleagues in developed countries from scientific colloquia, "invisible colleges" and other important alternative means of access to information and 2) they must make more prudent use of limited scientific facilities and manpower by not repeating experiments which have already been conducted elsewhere.

Despite having greater needs, however, scientists in developing countries have less easy access to the scientific information than their colleagues in developed countries because 1) the local library and information systems are generally poorly developed and 2) international publications and information services are relatively more costly in developing countries, both in absolute terms due to mailing and handling costs and in relation to the local budgets for scientific research.

As a result, the gap in access to information between users in developing countries and the rest of the world increases each year.

Libraries in many developing countries rarely have enough money to subscribe to journals or to buy books ; they remain libraries in name only and are unable to perform their vital role — that of providing ready access to critical information and knowledge. This serious shortcoming has another less obvious, but, unfortunately, even greater negative result. Because users know their libraries will not be of much value, they do not even try to find information that might be useful. Resignation among users because of lack of help from libraries further undermines the services libraries might be able to provide.

As a result of this situation, scientists and scientific institutions in developing countries are understandably concerned, and recent years have seen an increasing number of pleas and proposals made to ensure equitable access to scientific information. Unesco has been working for many years in this area and is uniquely equipped to make an even greater contribution in the future, thanks to its mandate, accumulated experience and on-going programmes in the areas of science and technology, higher education, book promotion and copyright and library and information science.

Access to Literature as One Aspect of a Larger Problem

Basic science is by nature international, and scientific results published in the "traditional" international literature form the foundation for scientific advancement. Many other types of information are also needed, however, particularly for applied research relevant to the problems of developing countries. In this context one can cite patent literature, which often announces discoveries which are only later, or never, published in scientific communications, and the so-called "grey literature" of research reports, which are not published at all in the formal sense. The research results of developing countries often form part of this grey, or uneasily identifiable, literature, in that they may be published in reports and journals which are not systematically abstracted or disseminated. One must also consider the need for information which may never be published, but which can be identified in scientific gatherings, in informal communications, and through specialized databases describing research in progress, products and processes, sources of expertise, etc.

"Value-added" information services, such as critical analyses tailored to the needs of specific users, as much as and perhaps more so than simple access to published works, are particularly important for scientists in developing countries if they are to take advantage of all available information and knowledge in solving developmental problems.

It is clear in this context that the access of libraries in developing countries to books and journals is only one link, although a very important one, in the overall information transfer chain. These materials can only be utilized effectively if the library and information infrastructure is able to manage and disseminate them, and to process and analyze them according to user needs.

All efforts to improve the access of developing countries to scientific literature, even if based on the ideal of equal access, must, of course, pay special attention to economic realities, and particularly to the cost and effectiveness of the various options for programme action. In practice, any solution will, of necessity, be imperfect and will have to be clearly defined in terms of national and international budgets, users to be reached and services to be rendered.

User Needs—The *"Core" Literature*

The concept of a core list of journals or journal articles, i.e., a grading of items in terms of the priority and frequency of the users' need for them, offers in theory an attractive approach. It has been known for many years that a very small number of journals or articles account for a very large number of user requests (for example, according to the empirical Bradford's Law, if 1000 journals will satisfy all user requests in a given field, about ten journals will satisfy one-third and about 100 will satisfy two-thirds). These core journals should naturally be accorded priority in deciding on library acquisitions and on the organization of information services; the satisfaction of the rarer requests for other information sources should, of course, also be ensured, but for practical organizational and economic reasons they will take longer and be more expensive to satisfy.

A major problem with the above strategy is that there is no clear, unique method by which a core list can be defined. Within any given scientific discipline, there are three basic methods which can be used (singly or in combination) for this purpose: peer evaluation, citation analysis and coverage by major international indexing and abstracting services.

In 1979 Unesco, within its General Information Programme, sponsored the preparation of core lists of journals in the life sciences (document PGI/79/WS/12) and engineering (PGI/79/WS/13) by the Abstracting Board of the International Council of Scientific Unions (ICSU/AB). The criterion proposed by this body was to select the journals which collectively accounted for 80% of the coverage of the major indexing[1] abstracting journal in each area (chosen as *Biological Abstracts* and *Engineering Index* respectively). This approach yielded 1333 journals in the life sciences and 732 journals in engineering. Each list also included a subset of 100 journals of particular relevance to scientists in developing countries on the basis of their subject coverage and practical, more "development-oriented" orientation.

These lists were extensively distributed and greatly appreciated. But it was suggested that the criteria for selection of core journals should be more flexible to account for diverse user needs. Based on this experience in 1986 Unesco/PGI published a core list of journals in the earth sciences (PGI-86/WS/25) prepared by the International Council for Scientific and Technical Information (ICSTI) the successor to ICSU/AB. This list contained a total of 1300 journals, including 700 selected on the basis of productivity (contribution to the Geo Ref and PASCAL-GEODE data bases), 250 less productive journals which are nevertheless important to general research activity, and 350 journals which are mainly descriptive and regional in nature, and which are particularly important for centres involved in regional studies. A special effort was made to ensure that the list contained titles of interest to scientists in developing countries, including 393 journals published in those countries.

From the above discussion it can be seen that, out of about 50,000 scholarly scientific journals, several thousand can be considered "core journals", including at least several hundred in each major discipline area. Other journals can be considered as being of medium importance and still others as fringe journals in a given discipline (although these same publications may be core journals in another discipline).

Library Networking and Resource Sharing as the Basis for Document Delivery

Scientists should have ready access to the core journals in their discipline, if not in their own institution at least in a major library in their city or country. This is only possible through interlending and other cooperative arrangements.

It is clear that international assistance in document delivery can only be effective if appropriate local document delivery mechanisms are established. The steps to be undertaken in this context include:

— agreement on objectives among the cooperating libraries and information centres, within the framework of a national information policy or other basis for common interest;

— definition of the target users and their literature needs;

— division of responsibility among the cooperating centres for acquisition and provision of the core literature; compilation of a union catalogue identifying their holdings and establishing a system of inter-library loans and reprographic services to satisfy user requests for this literature;

— arrangements with external document delivery services to provide literature not included in the core holdings.

Review of *Unesco* Efforts

Unesco activities to promote library and information services, notably within the framework of UNISIST and the *General Information Programme*, have always included a strong effort to improve the access of scientists and engineers to information and documentation. Efforts in this area have included:

— advice on national information policies and the development of national library and information systems;

— development and promotion of standards and methods for the transfer of information, such as CDS/ISIS and the Common Communication Format;

— support for the development of scientific libraries and information centres, and of regional and international scientific information networks;

— promotion of the training of information specialists and of users of scientific and technological information.

One specific Unesco effort designed to improve access to publications has been the work undertaken with the scientific community on the preparation of the core lists of journals described above.

The overall objective of access to publications has been advanced through the UAP Programme, which was initiated jointly by IFLA and Unesco in 1982. Under this programme guidelines have been published and a number of training seminars and pilot projects undertaken. Among the guidelines one should cite the *Model Handbook for Interlending and Copying* (PGI - 89/WS/2), *Measuring the Performance of Document supply systems* (PGI-87/WS/21) and *training Modules for Interlibrary Lending and Document Supply* (PGI-91/WS/7)/. The most extensive pilot project, through which more than USD 100,000 has been provided for training, equipment, advisory services, and financial support, has been undertaken in Senegal with a consortium of three cooperating institutions — the Library of the University of Dakar, the National archives and the Institut fondamental d'Afrique noire (IFAN); a number of subscriptions to international scientific journals have been defrayed within the overall project designed to provide better access of library users to national and foreign publications.

International Provision of Entire Scientific Journals

This is a major problem, but one about which Unesco has to exercise particular caution because:

— The needs for journals and the costs in satisfying them are very high, and Unesco's contribution could thus only be a small one. The minimum number of journals required in each country in each broad scientific discipline (like the life sciences or the earth sciences) is several hundred and the minimum number in all disciplines at least a thousand. Of course, the majority of users' requests will involve a smaller number of journals, but scientific progress cannot be ensured without ready access to at least the core journals in each field. Thus the minimum total journal budget for 1000 core journals for about 100 developing countries will exceed USD 30 million annually (at an average subscription price of USD 300, including delivery).

— Decisions on what assistance to provide and to whom it should be provided are difficult. Journal subscriptions are only one part of the overall national scientific research budget of developing countries. International subsidies for journal subscriptions should therefore be evaluated on the same basis as subsidies for other parts of the research budget requiring convertible currency expenses, such as research equipment or training; as in all types of international assistance, a necessary condition should be that the national authorities themselves accord the concerned activities an adequate budget and priority.

— Long-term subsidies run counter to the approach of Unesco's action, which aims at helping countries to help themselves through advice, training and catalytic support. A large-scale

> diversion of funds to operational support for journal subscriptions would reduce the very limited resources available to carry out the essential role of the Organization.

Pilot projects were, however, designed but did not succeed in mobilizing the necessary funds from extrabudgetary sources.

In 1984, following a proposal by the Scandinavian Unesco National Committee, a study was prepared within the UAP framework concerning the establishment of a literature assistance programme. This study recommended that provision be limited to periodicals and that about 500 core titles be identified by monitoring and evaluating requests for journal articles through existing channels. Initially, a fund to defray charges for loan and photocopy services of major international document suppliers was recommended, along with wide publicity in developing countries to stimulate demand for such services. Gradually, starting in the second year, subscriptions to the identified core journals would replace the provision of interlibrary loans and photocopies and it was felt that the core demand would largely focus on a few priority disciplines, enabling a solid coverage with a relative limited injection of funds. The scheme was proposed for implementation as a seven-year pilot project in three countries in differing development situations, to be coordinated at the national level by a major national information centre in each country. The cost per country was estimated at about USD 1 million over the duration of the project. Attempts to find the necessary financial resources to implement this project were not successful — not even in the Scandinavian countries which had proposed the study. Unesco accepts, however, under its Participation Programme and within specific extra-budgetary projects, requests for journal subscriptions, while trying to ensure that the requesting Member States are prepared to continue these subscriptions after short-term international assistance has been provided.

International Provision of Copies of Scientific Articles

When scientific articles are not available through national and regional journal holdings, a request is normally made to an international document supply centre such as the British Library Document Supply Centre (BLDSC). This procedure is generally used as a last resort because it is expensive (USD 5.00-10.00 per standard article, normally to be paid in convertible currency) and involves relatively long delivery delays (unless telefax is used, which adds to the expense and is not yet practical in many developing countries). One fruitful approach could be to negotiate with one or more such centres a bulk rate for provision of these service to institutions in developing countries, which would be designated in consultation with Unesco. It would appear essential to expect a financial participation from the requesting centres in order to work towards self-sufficiency and to avoid frivolous requests, but an international subsidy greatly helps to develop such an activity, at least during a pilot period.

A pilot project for literature delivery was initiated in 1989 within the Regional Network for the Exchange of Information and experience in Science and Technology in Asia and the Pacific (ASTINFO), which is a cooperative framework for development of information systems and services in the region established under Unesco auspices in 1983. The pilot project involves assistance through the National Library of Australia which provides photocopies of needed scientific articles to the 12 developing countries who are members of ASTINFO over a period of three years. Each of the countries has received partially prepaid request forms, to be administered by selected major scientific and technological information centres. Photocopies of articles are provided by the Library at a cost of AUD 6.00 each, of which AUD 2.00 is paid by the requester and AUD 4.00 is defrayed by Unesco. The pilot project has been financed initially by a Unesco contract for USD 11,000 with the National Library of Australia, which has ensured the provision of about 2500 articles. A similar contract has ensured the provision of another batch of about 2500 articles and a third contract for an amount of USD 15,000 will extend this pilot project to the end of 1993. A proposal for a five-year document delivery project is being prepared for possible extrabudgetary funding.

Unesco, through its General Information Programme, has also contracted the British Library Document Supply Centre (BLDSC) and the French Institut national d' information scientifique et technique (INIST) to conduct a pilot project to assess the literature supply and demand patterns in more than 30 developing countries.

This project, subsidized by Unesco, enables scientific libraries and research institutions in a selected number of developing countries to make requests for photocopies of articles from science and technology publications held at these institutions. Reports will monitor and analyze the volume and type of material requested. It is hoped that the reports will enable each country to improve its library collections and document delivery services and, as a result, a more effective information exchange network will develop within the countries and between them, using the technical guidelines issued by PGI. It is also hoped that this data could be used to design at a later stage projects on using CD-ROM and other optical media to increase the flow of scientific literature in developing countries.

Book Donation Coordination

Hundreds, if not thousands, of book and journal donation programmes exist in the world. Under such schemes, institutions and individuals with surplus documentation are encouraged to make them available to needy information centres, particularly in the developing countries. A major problem with such schemes is the cost of shipping the selected materials. Another problem is that they are usually more relevant to general needs than those of science and technology which, by definition, require the most recent information as a priority. Thus, for example, although back issues of journals are often donated, it is difficult to organize donation schemes for current issues of scientific journals which represent the greatest needs. Recent evidence suggests that many of the book donation schemes are less effective than expected. The most obvious reason is that the overwhelming majority of such schemes are operating on donor-led basis only.

One of the most successful of the scientific literature donation programmes is that of the International Centre for Theoretical Physics (ICTP) and the Third World Academy of Sciences (TWAS). This scheme was initiated by ICTP some years ago to provide universities in developing countries with books, journals and proceedings. The publications are normally donated to ICTP on a regular basis by libraries, publishers, international conferences and international organizations. For example, an agreement has been established with North-Holland Publishing Company, the World Scientific Publishing Company (Singapore) and the Physical Society of Japan to provide ICTP with 150 surplus copies of each of their publications for distribution to libraries in developing countries.

Special reference also should be made to the book donation programmes operated by the Canadian Organization for Development in Higher Education (CODE), the American Association for the Advancement of Science (AAAS), the German Foundation of International Development (DSE), the Australian Centre for Publications Acquired for Development (ACPAD), the Swedish Agency for Research Cooperation with Developing Countries (SAREC), the International Campus Book Link, ICSU Press, professional associations, scientific unions, AUPELF/UREF (French speaking universities).....

The only way for existing book donation schemes to overcome some of the problems they are facing is for them to be recipient or request-led. This presupposes that potential recipients will have a knowledge of what is available and from what sources and that donors will have some awareness of, and sensitivity to, the needs of the recipients.

A database has been established by TWAS under a Unesco contract. This database records the available publications (about 150,000 books, journals and proceedings) and both donor and recipient interest by subject and level against which requests can be matched. The list of recipients contains 2,256 addresses, whereas the list of donors is limited to ten addresses of the major donors. The inventory of available publications is automatically updated on the basis of the shipments made.

Another database on book donation programmes is being established by ICSU under another Unesco contract which records at present more than 100 donors.

These databases would facilitate direct connections between partners. In the long run, shipping costs will be reduced and book donation schemes more requested.

In October 1988, ICTP/TWAS organized a workshop in Trieste on "Increasing the Flow of Scientific Literature to Third World Institutions" which was attended by representatives of ICSU, Unesco and several other concerned organizations. This workshop issued a recommendation to create a cooperative network on scientific and technological literature for developing countries which would coordinate and provide information on existing donation programmes and the materials they provide, to explore additional sources of literature for developing countries and to help to identify funding to expand the scope of existing distribution programmes and to launch new ones. As a long-term objective, the network will seek to support scientific publishing in the South and dissemination of the resultant publications.

The lack of a network means that the same work of establishing contacts is being done over and over and that many potential donors become overwhelmed by the logistics involved.

A meeting of librarians, participants in donation programmes and representatives of ICSU and Unesco was held in Paris, on 11-12 March 1991, to examine the guidelines for the proposed network. The participants foresaw a system where an interested donor could get in touch with the network and send in a list of the material available. The network would put the donor in touch with the most appropriate participating programme to handle the donation, to store the material, to find a recipient and to ship the material.

It was stressed that all the donations should be specifically asked for by the recipients. The purpose of these programmes is not to turn the libraries of the developing countries into dumping grounds for obsolete or unwanted material. The donated literature should be selected according to strict criteria, in order not to waste money on shipping useless material.

The network has now been launched by ICSU in cooperation with Unesco. It has been named INASP, the International Network for the Availability of Scientific Publications.

INASP plans to run a seminar on the appropriate provision of scientific and technical materials at the Conference on Donated Book Programmes to be organized jointly by Unesco, the Canadian Organization for Development through Education and the International Book Bank in September 1992, in Baltimore, Maryland (USA), "Dialogue of Partners".

Promoting CD-ROM Publishing and Use

CD-ROM could help libraries in developing countries, provide quick access to at least some of the critical literature needed by practitioners, researchers, educators, students who could become productive users.

Several conditions prevent the immediate widespread use of CD-ROM in developing countries. These include the lack of knowledge about the technology; reluctance of some publishers to allow republication of printed material on CD-ROM; and the cost of maintaining subscriptions to journals published on CD-ROM.

Market forces are working to reduce these factors. Prices are declining and can be expected to continue to do so. And, as the medium gains popularity, publishers will be more willing to allow republication in this form. CD-ROM will help libraries in developing countries to leap ahead into the 21st century.

PGI has published a *Guide to CD-ROM* which is a practical source of information on CD-ROM hardware, software, services, products and related training opportunities. Also in 1989, PGI began to explore with the Japanese authorities the possibility of an extrabudgetary document delivery project mainly for the countries of Asia and the Pacific using modern information technology. The project would aim at the publication of core journals on CD-ROM, to be provided to libraries in developing countries according to their needs. It would be hoped that, after an initial injection of capital and a subsidy for operations over a period of about five years, the publishing system would be self-supporting, and the model could be extended to other developing regions. During a second phase of the project, vehicles for publication of scientific results from the region itself could be initiated.

The most notable attempt at publication of scientific journals on CD-ROM has been the ADONIS project which involved the dissemination of about 219 journals in the biomedical field on this medium for a two-year trial period. The aim was to demonstrate a technical solution which could ultimately be more efficient and less costly than photocopying journals for users, while providing some royalties to publishers who have felt that widespread photocopying by libraries is unfairly reducing their revenues.

The results of the trial have been sufficiently encouraging for the ADONIS Board to decide to introduce a commercial service in 1991 covering some 400 titles.

The journals offered are based on the list of titles taken on subscription by major pharmaceutical companies. The subject distribution is biology 19%, chemistry 11%, medicine 47%, pharmacology 16%, physics 2%, veterinary medicine 1% and general science 1%.

An annual subscription fee of DFL 22,000 (about USD 12,000) is charged and royalties are to be paid depending on whether a library subscribes to the printed version of the journal. Royalties are based on the automatic recording for articles printed or transmitted over a network (but not for items displayed on screen).

A conference, held in Khartoum in 1990, illustrated the appropriateness of CD-ROM to developing countries. Two hundred persons, from 16 countries, participated in this first International Conference on the Use of CD-ROM in Developing Countries organized by the Sudan-American Foundation for Education, with Unesco assistance. The verdict of participants was clear : CD-ROM services offer the single best solution to the "information gap" or "book famine" besetting users in developing countries. This view was not only expressed by librarians, who would be expected to embrace CD-ROM as a solution to gaining access to at least some current information, but it was held even more strongly by end-users, who comprised the majority of the participants.

Several training workshops were held in different regions to promote CD-ROM use in library and information work.

An international seminar on the use of CD-ROM and other optical compact media for the transfer of scientific literature took place in The Hague in 1991. This meeting was intended to lay the conceptual basis for pilot projects (USD 18,000). The main working document, prepared by the International Federation for Information and Documentation (FID) discussed the technological, economic and copyright aspects of CD-ROM publishing. The meeting recommended that:

— Unesco prepare a comprehensive study and a companion database on CD-ROM sites, equipment and local mastering initiatives;

— Unesco explore with existing image-based products and services the possibility of collaborating in the provision of scientific literature on CD-ROM to developing countries with a view to launching a pilot project;

— In the longer term, a programme based on the findings of the pilot project involving as many developing countries as possible be designed in cooperation with development agencies and national governments.

The study and database are being prepared under a Unesco contract. Negotiations of bulk subscription rate are under way with ADONIS and other similar services to provide CD-ROM products to selected sites in developing countries. As to the long-term programme, it will be designated progressively on the basis of the results of the other actions.

Concluding Remarks

All these efforts have a convergent aim — improving access to scientific literature in the South. Other initiatives include promotion of scientific publishing in developing countries and twinning arrangements between libraries in order to provide advice, training, channels for information access and, possibly, equipment and information materials.

Emphasis on helping Member States to develop and manage their own document delivery services particularly through the publication of guidelines, advisory services and training activities should be continued.

Extrabudgetary support should continue to be actively sought for national projects to develop information infrastructure, including subscriptions to journals. However, it should be noted that funding sources like UNDP are very wary about including journal subscriptions in the projects they sponsor since, unless the national institution is able to continue the subscriptions, such international assistance is unlikely to have any appreciable development impact.

About the author

Abdelaziz Abid is Programme Specialist, Unesco General Information Programme, Unesco, 7 Place de Fontenoy, Paris 75700, France.

[Mr Abid's paper was delivered during the 58th IFLA General Conference, Delhi, 30 August — 5 September 1992.]

Why won't you accept my order ? Global Acquisitions Solutions

TONY LEISNER

Why is there so much information, yet it is so hard to acquire certain types of products ? Book and serials dealers, agents and wholesalers often seem confused by your requests. Material that is thought to be in print and available cannot be easily acquired from your traditional supplier. Orders for the same material are placed several times with various sources and the item never seems to arrive. Is this the fault of the publisher? The dealer, or the librarian? Or is this the result of a fundamental and structural change in the information industry ?

To understand the current situation and make preparations for the future, we must first visit the recent past. Only ten years ago a fundamental and radical change took place in the publishing industry. Manuscripts, which had always been prepared in paper form and then entered into computers for the typesetting and composition in readiness for printing, were now created directly on the computer. The era of desktop publishing had begun with the invention of the Apple Macintosh Computer and the introduction of laser printers. It was now possible for an author to be also the publisher. The available software would enable the author to create actual page layouts, spell check the document and design its format. Printing technology improvements followed. Which enabled the new "self publisher" to economically produce a small quantity of finished books at a cost far below that of a traditional publisher. It is estimated that in the United States, as many as 20,000 of these new small publishers came into existence in the years 1982, 83 and 84. The Small Press Group of Britain lists over 2,000 members. This is a number greater than the total number of publishers that existed in the UK before the advent of desktop publishing.

Prior to the start of desktop publishing, the flow of information about new books and journals was very orderly. Publishers were traditional in their method of promotion, announcement and distribution of new titles. Reviewers received copies and standard library sources carried both reviews and advertisements to inform librarians.

Book and serial dealers were made aware of new titles and could arrange to carry stock so that library orders would be filled. Very little imagination was required on the part of the industry in order to sell product or to acquire it for a library.

The new small presses lacked the experience and the money to promote their new books and journals in the traditional method. Reviewers were reluctant to print their comments about books and journals from publishers and authors they had never heard of and librarians were unable to obtain reliable information about these new presses. Yet these new publishers became successful. It is widely believed that the first bound book ever published about AIDS came from a new self publisher in Palo Alto, California (USA). This was in 1982 when little was known about AIDS. Even so, Quality Books (a USA small press supplier to libraries) reportedly sold over 5,000 copies to USA libraries. More than 50,000 copies in total were sold during the next two years.

Clearly this was not the so called "grey or fugitive" literature that so much has been written about. Still, it was similar to grey literature as far as acquisition librarians were concerned because it was not easily available through their regular supplier. These new publishers were often not listed in directories, their names were unknown and they relocated their growing businesses with an astounding frequency. What was needed was a new distribution service for these beginning publishers. In Great Britain, the Small Press Group of Britain was founded and in the United States Publishers Marketing Association began in order to provide marketing services for the new presses. Specialized dealers to libraries focused service on the promotion and distribution of small presses. So the industry responded to this structural change in publishing by providing sources for librarians to obtain these new titles. Librarians have been somewhat slower than the industry in their response to these changes. Many still prefer the traditional review and known publishers and feel uncomfortable purchasing from lesser known sources. While this is understandable, the large publishers are reducing the number of new titles they produce and the small presses keep growing so that eventually there will be situations where the only source of information on a topic will be a small press. Librarians will need to seek out these specialized distributors of small and new publishers to consolidate ordering and establish an ongoing business relationship. Otherwise they will be sending large numbers of small orders direct to unresponsive publishers who have little desire to sell single copies to a distant library.

This background brings us to the present time and the conditions in the publishing industry that affect acquisitions librarians. In times of economic recession, which is happening world wide, the pressures on information providers are intense. Each weeks industry news reports yet another old name publisher going out of business. The prices of journals and monographs are still climbing and library budgets are not. Libraries are in a never ending struggle for adequate funding and many are cutting hours and purchases. The supply of new sources of information continues to grow and your customers want even more than you can provide.

The writer of this paper, as he often does, visited the professional library of the American Library Association to research the topic of the paper. The problem of acquiring difficult material is not new to librarians and much has been written on the subject. A C-D-ROM search of a Wilson Data Base revealed such diverse sources of information as New Zealand Libraries, Pakistan Library Bulletin, a Seminar on the Acquisition of Latin American materials and Government Publications Review (USA). *Understanding The Business of Library Acquisitions*, published by The American Library Association was another source of information and it covered the topic of non-traditional formats very well. However, even this fine publication frequently stated that solutions are very difficult for acquiring little known publications or those from government offices. The next step was to interview librarians. From these interviews one answer came up constantly. Ask a librarian. Often times, the information, documents, books or serials you seek have already been acquired by another library in your own community or country. There is a reluctance on the part of many librarians to ask their colleagues for assistance in fulfilling requests unless some formal information sharing system exists. In some cases as much as 50% of the material needed is provided by other libraries, particularly those with specialized collections. National Libraries, Professional Associations and corporate libraries frequently are underused and willing to share their solutions for obtaining unusual kinds of materials.

Elements of Fundamental Change

Why has acquisitions become so difficult ? Why can't the traditional sources of supply fill all acquisition needs ? Why is it sometimes easier to obtain needed materials from another library rather than the original source ?

Libraries and the entire information industry are in the midst of a structural change in their fundamental business. This change is as great as it was when the automobile was introduced. Some businesses hung on to the horse with a passion. But the auto carried more people, was faster, more convenient (ultimately) and changed the transportation industry forever. So it is with the information industry. For years customers had to go to the possessor of the information. The library, the publisher, the researcher. The information was only available in controlled form, usually a book, article, paper or journal. Desktop publishing changed that forever as surely as the auto changed the transportation industry. All information has time value. Old time, that is historical value, current time or must know now, and leisure time are some of the ways we can classify time value. Books and journals can provide for two of these categories but not the third.

A New Concept in Information

We are used to thinking of the book, journal or paper as the product that we are purchasing. However, with the intellectual base now residing in the desktop computer, it becomes the product and every other form of output is simply a by-product. This is important to the acquisition and collection building process. It means that ordering information is now far more complicated and flexible than in the past. The book form of output may be "out of print", never printed or printed on demand. Or you may be able to direct access the data base and just get the answer without actually purchasing any product in the traditional sense. The information can be acquired on disk, as a document by fax or mail, through E-Mil, or in its entirety. All of these are by-products of the original intellectual property, the data base. This data base can be up-dated at will and all by-products previously produced become dated and the new by-product is current. The implications for libraries are enormous. One of the major costs of libraries has been the storage, access to and management of hard copy information. Money has been invested in larger buildings to store more hard copy and more staff to access the stored materials. This has often meant less money was available to purchase new materials. Money libraries have adopted C-D ROM technology as a way of addressing the storage and access issues. C-D ROMs, however, are more like microforms. They are a by-product which compacts the information and make it more accessible but tie the user to a machine much like a micro film reader. In terms of progress they still require the user of the information to go to the possessor of the information just as in the past. The C-D ROM is also dated as soon as it is produced. It is a by-Product of a moving intellectual data base and as such has value mostly for its historical time value, ease of access and lower storage cost. The user can't update CDs.

Like the small presses, C-Ds have been ignored by most traditional book dealers. They have been distributed by major serials agents and available direct from the producer. Because the C-D requires constant updates it is more like a journal than a book and serials agents are better able to handle this type of acquisition.

What is Ahead ?

Globally, libraries vary considerably in their role in the country, funding, locations and usage. In most countries the purchasing power of libraries is a small percentage of the total information volume. In Germany and the United Kingdom it is about 5% of total book sales (turnover). In U.S.A. the estimate is closer to 15% and in many poorer countries it is less than 1%. Individual libraries have little financial power. In the old system of hard copy only information, many specialized dealers were willing to comply with a libraries complex purchasing requirements. The dealer supplied many of the services that the library needed such as MARC cataloging and processing of the books. This will still be the situation for a portion of the by-products that the library purchases such as traditional books and journals. However, just as with the introduction of the automobile, a whole new industry has been created and the role of libraries must change or they will be left as a barn where horses are kept. Government policy in much of the world is by-passing the library as an important part of the dissemination of information. Large new entrants into the field of information provision are by-passing the library. IBM, national and local telephone companies, cable and satellite TV as well as SONY and their electronic book are going around the library directly to the end user. Tomorrows acquisition librarian will not just work to purchase by-product to be stored on a shelf. Rather the job will be to evaluate the costs, time value, alternate sources and appropriateness of the selected material to the overall role of the library in information provision. Acquisitions librarians will seek out the new companies entering the information industry and lead the way to change so that libraries can have choices about the form of product or by-product that they purchase. Acquisitions departments will have to examine requirements that vendors meet the standards of the library rather than the standards of a changing industry that is far larger than just libraries. It is possible in most of the world to pick up a telephone and call anywhere. That system enables all of us to communicate with one standard yet seldom do two neighboring libraries have the same standards for acquisitions. This raises the costs for vendors and libraries alike and may be cause for a source of important information to say "I can't accept your order".

GLOSSARY AND DEFINITIONS

C-D ROM A compact disk with acread only capacity which must be used in a special device connected to a computer.

Desktop Publishing Utilizing a personal computer and specialized software to create a manuscript, edit, design, layout the pages, number then and in all ways produce a book ready to go to the printshop.

Self Publisher One who uses desktop technology. Also small press, independent publisher.

Structural Referring to the way in which an industry and its various components interact. Encompasses technology, competition, current suppliers, new entrants, political environment, economic conditions and customers.

Recent South Asia Projects at the University of Chicago Library and the South Asia Microform Project

JAMES NYE

During the past seven years, several programmes related to South Asia have been undertaken at the University of Chicago Library and the South Asia Microform Project. These are projects of bibliographic description, collection development, and preservation. The following notes describe each briefly.

1. University of Chicago

South Asian Books in Series

The bibliography *South Asian Books in Series : Sanskrit, Prakrit, and Pali* will be published next year. It is a guide to texts published in South Asian monographic series in the classical languages, as well as to translations and studies included in those series published from 1849 through 1979. The bibliography is arranged alphabetically by series title and sub-arranged within each series by series number. An index, in addition to the main entries with their full bibliographic descriptions of each individual volume, provides access by name (author, editor, commentator, and publishing institution), title (uniform title and published title), and, in subsequent editions of the bibliography, subject (both for individual volumes and for series, where appropriate). Scholars in a variety of disciplines will find the guide useful for its inclusion of translations and studies, many of which are in English. *South Asian Books in Series* provides çoverage of both original publications and reprints produced in the South Asian subcontinent. Approximately 1,820 series encompassing some 31,490 individual titles arc currently in the working files. The first edition will contain descriptions of 620 series encompassing more than 14,500 volumes. Funding for the bibliography was provided in part by two grants from the National Endowment for the Humanities (NEH) in 1986 and 1988.

The large and significant tradition of series publishing in India began in 1849 with the first volume of *Bibliotheca Indica* by the Asiatic Society of Bengal. The practice spread, and major academic centers throughout the subcontinent continue to this day to publish such series, which occasionally run to hundreds of volumes, covering comprehensively what was considered "formal learning" - philosophy, poetics, grammar, music, art and architecture, astronomy and astrology, sectarian religion, law, scripture, literature, history and medicine.

Series from South Asia vary widely in scope and character. In addition to containing almost everything considered worth knowing by the cultures from which they spring, they also act as mirrors of those cultures. For example, the first volume published in *Bibliotheca Indica* the oldest of the series, was the *Rgveda,* the oldest Sanskrit text. This series continued not only with works in Sanskrit, but also works from such South Asian cultures as the Islamic and early regional language traditions. Some series are the products of important intellectual organizations, such as the Ānandāśrama in Pune and the Lalbhai Dalpatbhai Institute in Ahmedabad. Other series may reflect government sponsorship or the efforts of private individuals. The *Kashmir series of texts and studies* is of the government-sponsored variety, exhibiting an interesting development over the duration of series publication from classical texts in the early period to more modern studies after Independence, while maintaining the theme of Kashmiri identity. Some series celebrate or commemorate a prominent individual, such as the *ŚrīĀtmānanda svargavāsa arddhaśatābdī sīrīa* (memorializing the fiftieth death anniversary of the prolific nineteenth century Jain scholar, Ātmarāmajī) or the *Śrī Ātmānanda janma-śtābdi-smāraka granthamālā* (commemorating the centenary of his birth). Other series, such as the *Vishveshvaranand Vedic Research Institute publication* or the *Śata-pitaka series,* are monuments containing the work of individuals, such as Raghu Vira. In many cases, the series contain texts of scholarly value published by leading universities and research institutes in South Asia. *Tañjapurī Sarasvatīmahālaya granthamālā* is an example of a series specializing in the publication of important texts from the Tanjore Sarasvati Mahal collection of more than 50,000 manuscripts.

The decision to arrange the bibliography by series was made, among other reasons, because many of the series are organized on topic-specific or sect-specific basis. Examples include the *Kṛṣṇadāa Āyurveda Sīrīja* which containing Sanskrit texts on Indian medicine and

and the *Srī Mahāvīra Jaina Granthamālā* with religious texts from the Jain tradition. Consequently, collecting books by series creates an arena within which readers may serendipitously uncover related works of interest.

The bibliography's scope is defined by the following characteristics; publications of value for research; printed in a monographic series; published in the South Asian subcontinent; and within the subject areas of ancient or classical India, except classical Tamil publications. Excluded are purely pedagogical series such as the *Sanskrit Study Made Easy Series,* a series of texts and English translations published as language teaching aids in Palghat, Kerala, and the *Dayanand High School Series,* a set of Vedic readers prepared for instruction at the high school level.

Some limitations placed on the bibliography's scope were the result of external constraints of time and funding. In its original conception, the bibliography was to encompass Indological series without respect to the locus of publication. During the first two years of the project there was dramatic success in uncovering important but little-known series. After reflection and correspondence with Indologists, we chose to take series originating from South Asia as the exclusive focus. A major reason for this decision was that books from the subcontinent were under considerably less adequate bibliographic control than books from Europe and North America.[1]

Within this bibliographic arena it was necessary to further restrict coverage by date of imprint. Only those series whose first volume appeared prior to 1980 are included. This date was chosen because in late 1979, the Library of Congress began preparing romanized machine-readable bibliographic records for books from South Asia, providing good bibliographic control for the publications. Series entirely published after 1979 are described in an appendix to the bibliography with summary information. Series begun prior to 1980 but continuing into the 1980s or later are described with complete bibliographic records only for those books published through 1979.

Another important restriction in scope, the exclusion of classical Tamil series, became necessary during the second year of the project. A preliminary and partial exploration of Tamil monographic series led to discovery of more than 160 series predominantly in that language, most of which contain at least some literature or studies related to classical or ancient topics. These series were excluded because coverage of this large body of monographic literature would have significantly extend the time required to complete the project. In addition, it appears that thorough work with Tamil series might well identify twice as many series as our initial investigation uncovered.

Many books, while not completely meeting the criteria for inclusion, are nearly within scope. These were given the benefit of doubt and included with full entries in the bibliography and complete indexing. These publications include texts and studies, often in regional languages, built upon classical traditions in medicine, religion, mathematics, architecture, astronomy, and other similar subjects. Archaeological publications are also included in this category.

A relational database houses information in interconnected files on series, publishers, books, and index headings in *South Asian Books in Series*. The series file, now in excess of 2,390 records, contains detailed descriptions of 1,820 individual series from South Asia and the variant forms of series titles. These records contain the series title, dates of publication, number of the last known published volume, publisher, series subject, and links to series which share titles. In addition, the records contain the numbers of volume for which we have either no information or partial information, the status of work on a particular series, sources from which data was drawn to construct the file, a narrative statement describing unusual characteristics of the series publisher or the series itself, and added entries for series editors.

Two Preservation Projects

Preservation of Indological publications was an immediate corollary to the preparation of *South Asian books in Series*. It became painfully apparent while examining volumes to describe them for the bibliography that many of the books would survive use by only a few more readers, no matter how gentle the handling. We recognized that books acquired through careful collection development needed both to be preserved and made more easily accessible for research. Further, many of the series described in the bibliography are important scholarly resources, little known outside of India only because they were not held by any American or European research library. As a consequence, proposals were made to the U.S. Department of Education and the National Endowment for the Humanities to support two complementary projects for preservation microfilming of selected older series publications from the bibliography.

The project which was proposed in 1988 to the Department of Education under Title II-C was to acquire and preserve 3,500 important books cited in the bibliography but not held by a research library in the United States. Books were filmed in British and Indian libraries or purchased from book dealers in India. Microfilm and books acquired during the project included Indological series published in India, Sri Lanka, Nepal, Pakistan, and Bangladesh which deal with classical and ancient India.

A second complementary project was submitted jointly by the University of Chicago and Harvard University to the NEH Office of Preservation in 1988. Under the funded collaborative effort, nearly 4,000 brittle titles cited in the bibliography and held by the two libraries have been microfilmed.

A printed list of titles filmed and institutions holding master negatives is under preparation. These projects, along with the bibliography will assure scholars throughout the world of bibliographic access to the Indological publications and physical access through interlibrary loan or the purchase of microform copies.

The Adyar Library/University of Chicago Library Program

The Adyar Library of the Theosophical Society located in Madras and the University of Chicago Library are being supported by a grant in a collaborative pilot program to ensure that publications and manuscripts from the Adyar collections are available for continuing use of scholars and to augment the collections of both institutions. Specifically, under this program, 2,000 important early books, journals, and pamphlets and 500 manuscripts from the Library in Madras are being microfilmed over 3 years, begun in 1990. Also, 2,000 microfilmed volumes from the University of Chicago are being added to the Adyar Library.

The major reason for this effort is that the significant scholarly collections at the Adyar Library contain early publications, manuscripts, and archival resources which are endangered because they are in fragile condition and not available elsewhere. These resources are crucial for a more complete understanding of South Asian cultural history and the development of Theosophy along with related institutions such as Kalakshetra.

South Asia Serials Project

The aim of the South Asia Serials Project is to identify the variety of vernacular newspapers which were printed in India during the nineteenth century. South Asian scholars both in India and the United States have realized the importance of newspapers in the languages of India as essential sources for a variety of information. Historians interested in alternatives to imperial histories need access to these early sources for a fuller understanding of the colonial period. Scholars of Indian literatures need these serials in order to fill out the history of writing in various languages. It was often in newspapers and journals that new literary genres first appeared and important writers initially published their work. Political writings within vernacular newspapers are important for political scientists' interpretations of this period. A potential of rich information for all scholarly disciplines, from anthropology to the history of science, exist within these serials, if only they can be identified, located, and filmed for preservation and scholarly access.

The Bombay Presidency was set up as a test area for the project, using funds from the University of Chicago's Committee on Southern Asian Studies. The database that was established incorporates not only title and publication information but also circulation figures and the cost of individuals issues when known. In addition to being a bibliographic database, the file also can serve as an economic database from which figures for cost and production can be contrasted and compared. The fortnightly *Report on Native Newspapers* published in the Bombay Presidency was used as a source for identifying newspapers as well as supplying important circulation, cost, and publication information. Additional information on serials was taken from such sources as : Sisir Kumar Das's *The History of Indian Literature*, v. 7; J. Natarajan's *History of Indian Journalism;* and N.K. Murthy's *Indian Journalism.*

Nineteenth Century South Asia Short Title Catalog

A pilot project has been proposed to test the feasibility of creating short title catalog of nineteenth century publications from the South Asian subcontinent and to estimate requirements for creation of a database covering monographs published during the period 1867-1900. The pilot project is awaiting approval by the Government of India. A machine-readable database will be created in four months by entering information for 2,000 randomly-selected records from the several listings entitled *Catalogue of books printed in the ... Presidency during the quarter ending...* (abbreviated as *Quarterly reports.*) The Sahitya Akademi, in conjunction with the Library of Congress and the Southern Asia Department at the University of Chicago Library, will conduct the work in New Delhi.

Documentation of these early Indian imprints will extend the work begun by Graham W. Shaw as *The South Asia and Burma retrospective bibliography (SABREB).* Shaw's publication is a significant addition to the bibliographic knowledge of printing and publishing in India from the first printing in 1556 through 1800. In his bibliography he describes phases two and three of *SABRED* as including, respectively, coverage of the years 1801-1866 and 1867-1900. Preparation of *SABREB* at the British Library has been suspended for both fiscal and personnel reasons.

Uses for the machine-readable file of India's publishing record are numerous. A few examples include :

> **Cultural History.** Prof. Ravinder Kumar has referred to the late nineteenth century as a vital period in the "construction of Indian consciousness." This may be most clearly manifest in the published literature of the period, especially those publications in the regional languages of South Asia. The Nineteenth Century South Asia Short Title Catalog bibliographic database will be an invaluable tool for access to this literature.
>
> **Preservation.** The database will enable systematic and intelligent selection decisions for a national preservation program. It will be possible to identify the published works of an author, editions of a text, or the works of a particular

publisher and to allow this more comprehensive view to inform the choices made in preserving an important part of India's cultural heritage.

History of Publishing. Studies of publishing culture in South Asia will profit enormously from the database. The amassed information will, for example, assist scholars studying the spread of publishing into the countryside and into smaller languages, investigating the output of specific publishers, and assessing changes in pricing over time and geographic region.

This project will be related to other regional efforts to describe the output of presses in India. For instance the Bangiya Sahitya Parishad is preparing a bibliography of Bengali publications from the nineteenth century. Information on publishing will be shared with the Parishad and other similar efforts. It is important, though, for optimal usefulness that the information be prepared in machine-readable form rather than merely as a typeset bibliography. However, the database could also be used to generate a printed publication with indexes, such as by region, by date or by size of print-run, which would be beyond the capabilities normally associated with bibliographies complied manually.

The pilot study for nineteenth century Indian publications will encompass the following objectives : 1) determine if the methodology of entry from the *Quarterly reports* is practicable and, if not, to make recommendations on possible alterations to the methodology; 2) assess performance potential of data-entry contractors; 3) refine the definition of funding requirements for a larger project to enter all data for 1867-1900 from the *quarterly reports* as the first phase of a nineteenth century short title catalog; 4) enter 2,000 records for books; and 5) explore possible formats for dissemination of the compiled data in South Asia and elsewhere .

2. South Asia Microform Project

The South Asia Microform Project (SAMP) is a cooperative organization created in 1967 to acquire and maintain a readily accessible collection of materials in microform on South Asia for the common use of subscribing institutions. SAMP, an affiliated organization of the Association for Asian Studies, is supported and governed by twenty-six institutional members, each of which contributes an annual membership fee. The Project is administered by the Center for Research Libraries in Chicago. Over the twenty-six years of its existence, SAMP has devoted more than $250,000 of its collected annual membership dues to the preservation microfilming of books and serials, many of which are held by the British Library.

Between 1986 and 1989, under the leadership of Profs. N. Gerald Barrier and Kenneth Jones, SAMP commissioned the systematic microfilming of the nineteenth century Panjabi holdings of the India Office Library. Nearly 1,000 volumes were encompassed in the project, expenses for which were borne by the membership. Subsequently, proposals were submitted to the National Endowment for the Humanities (NEH) to extend that work over publications in Hindi and Hindustani. NEH made awards of $69,000 in 1991 for Hindi and $140,000 in 1992 for Hidustani microfilming. 2,000 Hindi titles and nearly 3,000 Hindustani publications are included in the projects. In making the grants, the Endowment recognized the importance of these materials for scholars in the humanities and social sciences, the fragile condition of the imprints, and the paucity of holdings in the United States. Further, members of SAMP have found that by making early published materials available to scholars on microfilm for reading in this country, students and faculty are better able to use research time abroad for consulting unique resources such as those in archives.

All reformatting to microfilm under these NEH grants is taking place at photo duplication facilities of the Oriental and India Office Collections in London according to internationally accepted standards for preservation microfilming. Master negatives are retained by the British Library under their copyright and stored in their archival storage facilities. A positive microform use-copy of each reformatted title is deposited by the South Asia Microform Project at the Center for Research Libraries in Chicago (CRL). Machine-redable cataloging records are being created for each microfilmed book.

The paucity of holdings in these languages in the United States is a central reason for these activities. As a example, a systematic sample of titles from the Hindustani section of the *Catalogue of the Library of the India Office* showed that United States research libraries hold virtually no original editions of nineteenth century Hindustani publications and only rarely have reprint editions. Not a single book from the sample was found in the *National Union Catalog (NUC)* in the same edition as that in the IOL *Catalogue.* searching further in the *NuC* and the Online Computer Library Center (OCLC), we found only 5.9 percent of the titles available in reprint editions. One of those found was an edition of the famous and frequently reprinted *Bahar*. Remarkably, only 10.1 percent of the authors from the sample and an entry for any work at all in the NUC and of those with entries, nearly half were British authors.

An important motive for SAMP's concentration on nineteenth century books is that many of the most significant publications in Indian languages from the early twentieth century are being acquired through a complementary program of preservation, acquisition, and cataloging in India. The project, begun in 1990, is administered by the Library of Congress using rupee currency available in India under the U.S.- India Fund. Because of the early twentieth century focus for the Library of Congress program there is no overlap with these SAMP projects. B.S.Kesavan's *National Bibliography of Indian Literature: 1901-1953* is being used as a guide to preservation of books in the languages of India. As an example, the sections on Urdu and Hindi in Kesavan's *Bibliography* include more than 12,6000 titles which will complement the titles acquired under the microfilming at the Oriental and India Office Collections. Underlying the division of location for microfilming is a knowledge that Indian books from the last century are not only more easily available in London, but also their physical condition, while still precarious, is generally better than that of volumes found n Indian and Pakistani libraries. In other works, there is an economy of scale working in a single British library, saving the expensive work of locating rare older titles and the simultaneous advantage of microfilming nineteenth century Hindustani books and tracts from well-preserved copies.

REFERENCES

1. Jain religious publications comprise a particularly noteworthy example of the benefit derived from consolidating efforts in the area of South Asian imprints. In 1986 the series file contained 61 Jain series. There are now more than 265. These series encompass more than 5,240 primary texts (mostly in Prakrit and Sanskrit) and secondary works (many in regional languages, especially Gujarati and Hindi). Holdings of many Jain series by libraries outside of India, even at the British Library, are slight when

compared to the sum of publications. Also, holdings in Indian libraries are highly fragmented. Thorough coverage of Jain series has begun to fill a lacuna in Indic studies.

The principle of exclusion by locus of series publications is significant in that it removes from the purview of the bibliography at least 300 series published in Europe, North America, Japan, and Australia, many of which are highly esteemed vehicles for publication of critically edited Indic texts.

2. Interrelationships among series are frequently complex and require explication. Quite often a single book was published with more than one series attribution on the title page. For instance, volume 143 of the *Anantasayanasamskrtagranthavalih* is simultaneously volume 32 of the *Sri Citrodayamañjar iś*, and volume 1 of *University Series (University of Kerala)*, both of which are wholly subsumed series under the *Anantasayanasamskrtāgranthavalih*. Books originally published in a series were also often reprinted in another series or in the same series. For instance, *R āyacandrajainasāśtramālā*, a series which began as a bimonthly serial and later converted to a monographic series, includes many texts which were reprinted in the *Srimad Rājacandra Jaina Śāstramālā*. Both the series record and the entries for individual books depict these types of relationships.

Malaysian Information Clearinghouse on Women in Development: National Network Within a Regional Strategy

KHOO SIEW MUN

When business firms engaged in the same kind of activity have extensive dealings with each other, it is an obvious convenience and economy to establish an institution to enable them to offset one transaction with another, thus limiting payment settlements to net balances. Such mutual institutions are called clearinghouses and they may be established in many branches of industry.

I. Clearinghouse

Clearinghouses are commonly associated with the banking sector. 'The first modern bank clearinghouse was established in London 1773, although the clearinghouse idea had been applied in various forms of trade in such places as Tokyo, Japan, Florence, Italy and Lyons, France, many centuries earlier.'[1]

It has been graphically illustrated that where there are three banks or more, a clearinghouse is more efficient as a mechanism for clearing or settling monetary balances outstanding amongst the three, than if each bank were to transact with the others.[2]

Information Clearinghouses

Taking the idea from trade clearinghouses, information clearinghouses have been established in order to minimise the number of wild searches for information. Information clearinghouses can aggregate and accumulate information from a group of organisations with similar interests and information. They will, in pursuance of access of information, make all such information in the pool available to all users on a continuing basis. Thus, the activity of information clearinghouses does not strictly correlate with that of financial clearinghouses on all counts. No information is 'owed' to anyone; and 'net balances' of information are purveyed to all.

In the process, they effectively tap resources within the chain; and will 'switch' information queries to relevant sources. Like trading clearinghouses, they may also implement other service-oriented activities demanded by members in the information chain (such as document exchange, information updates, establishing specialised databases of common interest, etc.). Thus, in their function, they emulate the efficiency of commercial clearinghouses, as information needs are 'cleared' or settled, with a minimum of time-consuming, messy, criss-cross transactions.

Information clearinghouses may take as their models, such famed clearinghouses as the US Department of Commerce Clearinghouse for Federal Scientific and Technical Information, now known a the National Technical Information Service. Established in 1964, it annually distributes millions of copies of scientific and technical documents to thousands of users. Like other clearinghouses:

> The Clearinghouse is designed to complement, and not replace, the information services of the more mission-oriented agencies... The Clearinghouse serves as a central starting place for inquiries... and thus is a resource to the more specialized information centers as well as to the public directly.
>
> (*Encyclopaedia of Library and Information Science,* 1971, Vol. 5, p. 192)

Other examples would include the American National Clearinghouse for Mental Health Information, the National Clearinghouse for Poison Control Centre; National Clearinghouse for Restoration Child Life; the Educational Resources Information Center (ERIC) Clearinghouses; the American Library Association's Social Responsibilities Roundtable Clearinghouses. The philosophy, functions and concerns of these clearinghouses are so diverse that one must remember that:

> Clearly... the word clearinghouse does not identify the specific functions of that information activity nor does it describe the kind of products or services it generates. The word has been used so often and in so many different contexts, one must look

further than the title to find what a clearinghouse is for or what it really does.

(*Encyclopaedia of Library and Information Science,* 1971, Vol. 5, p. 197.)

Within this context it behoves each clearinghouse to conceptualize its own philosophy; to define its own role; and implement its own functions—all in consonance with the dictates of the times and the social imperatives for which it was established.

II. WID Clearinghouse Network in Asean

Women in Development (WID)

In the past illiteracy, economic dependence, cultural traditions and social taboos were some of the factors that had served to relegate women into a subordinate position. For a while Asian movements for feminine development lagged behind. The latter decades have seen tremendous changes and Asian women have begun to take a closer look at themselves, and organize themselves as a force for progress. Moves have been made for integrating women into national development and linking such movements on a worldwide basis. Details on these changes are evident in the literatures, and indicate the wide-ranging activities which have been undertaken both by governments and by non-governmental organisations (NGOs) in the region to bring women into the mainstream of development. In ASEAN,[3] the decades of the '70s and '80s have seen positive feminism come into its own with an unprecedented enthusiasm which shows no evidence of abating.

The UN Decade for Women (1975-1985) provided the initial impetus. The Resolutions taken, at Nairobi in 1985 with the conscious need for 'Forward Looking Strategies'; at the Heads of Commonwealth Governments (Nassau, Bahamas, 1985); Vancouver, 1987; and the 1987 Harare Conference further spurred activities in ASEAN, and strengthened the search for ways and means to integrate women within development. The concept, and the phrase, of women as 'Equal partners in development', have come into common usage. Within ASEAN, WID issues were treated almost immediately as a regional concern and against a regional perspective.

AWP Proposals

In 1980, the ASEAN Women's Programme (AWP) was

established in conjunction with the mid-term UN Decade for Women. The programmes are under the purview of a standing ASEAN Committee on Social Development (COSD). In 1981, country representatives of AWP met in Jakarta for the first time with the primary objective of exploring methodology for cooperation in furtherance of WID.

Regional Resolution

The AWP Meeting of 1981 resolved that a regional network be established based upon national focal points, to be styled national information clearinghouses on women in development. These national clearinghouses would build up national collections and information databases to service WID information needs. They would join in a bibliographical sorority to collect, generate and disseminate information to support research on WID, and act as catalysts for WID policy formulation. They would be the foci for meeting national regional and international needs on WID and WID-related information.

ASEAN Clearinghouses[4]

In the wake of the AWP proposals, a string of national clearinghouses have been established, enhanced and expanded.

Indonesia (1979-). In actual fact Indonesia had preceded the AWP proposals.[5] In 1979, a Clearinghouses for Information on Women in Development had already been established in he National Scientific Documentation Centre at Jalan Jend. Gatot Subroto.[6] By the time of the AWP proposals, the Clearinghouse had already a good collection and initiated services. The Centre itself was in the process of being computerised.

Philippines (1976;1981-). The Philippines were also way ahead. The Philippines has a long bibliographical tradition,[7] and by 1976 had established a Special Library and Data Bank on Women.[8] 'In 1981, the Special Library on Women was expanded to become [the] Clearinghouse and Information Center on Women' (CIC),[9] based at the National Commission on the Role of Filipino Women (NCRFW).

Thailand (1979; 1981-). Thailand also has a very long history in bibliographical research and activities.[10] Its information centre on women had been established in 1979, and thus, as with Indonesia and the Philippines, had pre-dated the AWP proposals.

> [The Center] came into being in 1979, under the National Economic and Social Development Board, as an information center for the preparation of the 5th National Economic and Social Development Plan 1982-1986 in which emphasis was placed upon women as a special target group with 4 main areas: labour, education, public health and opportunities for social and political participation.
>
> (Country Paper, Experts Meeting Report, Jakarta, 1992, p.1)

In 1981, the responsibility for women's affairs was transferred to the National Council of Women of Thailand (NCWT). From 1981, the National Women's Information Center (NWIC) Library has assumed the role of the national clearinghouse, which is now under the National Commission on Women's Affairs, established in 1989.[11]

Brunei , Malaysia and Singapore established their clearinghouses after the AWP proposals. All were effected in the 1980s.

Brunei (1987-). Brunei established its Clearinghouse on 1 February 1987, at the Social Affairs Division of the Ministry of Culture, Youth and Sports. Bibliographic control in Brunei is a relatively recent activity, but the Clearinghouse has begun collection-building and services, and has participated in regional meetings and activities.[12]

Malaysia (1983;1987-). In 1983 a Secretariat for Women's Affairs was established at the Prime Minister's Department. In 1987 the National Clearinghouse was established at the National Population and Family Development Board. In July 1990 the Clearinghouse became the responsibility of the Women's Affairs Division at the Ministry for National Unity and Social Development.

Singapore (1982-). Singapore established it Clearinghouse in 1982. 'From 1982 to June 1984, the former Ministry of Social Affairs carried out thefunctions of the Clearinghouse in Singapore'.[13] In 1984, the National Library of Singapore took over this responsibility.

> The National Library was chosen to be the Singapore Clearinghouse on Women in Development (WID) because it already had a ready-made infrastructure to carry out the role of the Clearinghouse effectively in the collection, organisation

and dissemination of relevant information and data on women in development.

(Country Paper, Experts Meeting Report, Jakarta, 1992, Para. 1.2.)

Objectives of ASEAN Clearinghouses

The purpose of the clearinghouse in each ASEAN country is to improve information service capabilities in order to serve as a substantial input towards the goal of the sharing and exchange of information for decision-making processes and other programmes related to women in development.

(Workshop on Thesaurus Construction Report, Jakarta, 1986, Annex III, p.[1].)

The immediate objectives of the clearinghouses include:

(a) acting as a national resource for WID information;

(b) acting as the regional/international focus for dealing withe WID information queries; and

(c) supporting women's programmes through information activities.[14]

III. Emphases for Regional Cooperation

Cooperation is not new to ASEAN. Ever since its formation in August 1967, and even under the preceding ASA (Association of Southeast Asia) in 1954, cooperation has been effected in fields as diverse as Culture, Education, Sports, Trade and many others.

Bibliographic cooperation. In the Bibliography and Information sector, regional cooperation has spanned over thirty years. This has resulted in specialised regional bibliographical publications; better bibliographical control; standing professional conferences and continuous interaction between the region's information personnel.[15] It is not surprising that issues and questions concerning information exchanges and standardisation of bibliographic standards are continuing concerns.

Cooperation on WID

There has been much consensus on areas of cooperation among

ASEAN WID clearinghouses. For convenience, strategies and emphases for bibliographic regional cooperation may be grouped under the following:

1. Bibliographic control of WID materials
2. Organising of WID materials
3. Exchange of WID information.

1. Bibliographic Control of WID Materials

Each national clearinghouse is envisaged to build up collections which would effectively meet the needs of diverse groups of users. Of relevance would be collections of textual, statistical, graphic and audiovisual, and other materials related directly or indirectly to WID.

A fundamental activity of the national clearinghouse would certainly be a comprehensive collection of the national literatures, which it must be expected to vigorously collect. Grey and fugitive materials, not generally kept in main academic and even specialist research libraries should be sought out by the national centre, and made available to the region, whenever needed.

2. Organising WID Materials

It is in this sector that ASEAN clearinghouses have made much significant progress. In 1984, the Second Meeting of the Expert Group on Clearinghouse for Women in Development discussed useful methodology for organising WID materials for regional use. It was observed in the Meeting that traditional library methods for organising information and collections are not suitable, and general library schemes are inadequate for information retrieval.

The Meeting adopted a resolution to construct a special thesaurus for organising WID materials in ASEAN clearinghouse. Subsequently, spearheaded by the Centre for Scientific Documentation and Information at Jakarta, ASEAN Clearinghouse representatives met at two Workshops (Jakarta, 1986 and 1987). The thesaurus was jointly developed; and published in 1991. It is currently being tested by the regional clearinghouses as a tool for organising and retrieving WID materials using standardised thesauri terms.

3. Exchange of Information

This is the hub of all cooperative efforts. A strong and continuing emphasis for regional cooperation is information exchange. Various wayand means have been explored.

In 1992, when the Expert Group met in Jakarta, it was pronounced that:

> In the spirit of cooperation amongst ASEAN clearinghouses on WID, the Meeting agreed to embark on an exchange programme of databases which are in a machine readable form. These databases are to be made available with the use of CDS/ISIS.
>
> (Report, Annex P, [p.4].)

CDS/ISIS has been chosen owing to its popularity in Southeast Asia, in libraries ranging from big academic collections to small, specialised institutions. CDS/ISIS is maintained and enhanced by UNESCO, and is distributed free to accredited libraries in the developing world.[16]

Other Strategies

Regional forums have also emphasized Publishing, Training and Networking.

Publishing. Exchange of publications, and national information via regional publications has been mooted.[17]

Training. Institutions and organisations in the region have played training hosts to different levels and types of personnel for many decades. Clearinghouses have proposed that training, especially of trainers, be emphasised. Disseminating knowledge on the use of CDS/ISIS, which is not a particularly user-friendly tool at grass-root OPAC level for users, has been mooted for 1994.

Networking. As has been stressed above, national clearinghouses will form part of a regional Chain. The network will assist each other to provide information and services to users of information, such as policy-makers, researchers, activists and executives. Regular meetings of Clearinghouse representatives keep each other updated on developments, and provide a spur for progress.

IV. Pusat Sumber Wanita Dalam Pembangunan: Information Clearinghouse on Women in Development, Malaysia

History, 1983—1993

In the early days of 1983-6, officers from the secretariat of Women's Affairs, Prime Minister's Department, participated in regional Clearinghouse forums and deliberations. Such participation established an identity for the Malaysian Secretariat, both within the country and within ASEAN programmes. With the formal establishment of the National Clearinghouse at the Population and Family Development Board between 1987-90, an active period of development followed. A small library collection was built up, and their bibliographic details entered into the Board's computer database. A publications programme produced some useful titles; and the Board's officers continued to contribute to ASEAN clearinghouse activities.[18]

When the Clearinghouse moved to the Bahagian Hal Ehwal Wanita or Women's Affairs Division (abbreviated in Malay as HAWA), in July 1990, their officers continued to be responsible for Clearinghouse activities, which became, in a sense, merged with those of the Division's undertakings.

Progress

By the end of this ten-year period, substantial progress had been made. The collection of monographs and periodicals had grown at the margin, and now totals about 2,000. Main roles and functions had been identified, and services prioritised. An impressive list of nearly 50 women's associations in the region and abroad had been contacted to initiate linkages. In addition, various types of socio-economic data had been identified for data capture to initiate specialised databases.[19] A quarterly newsletter, the *Beritanita* (Vol. 1 - 1987 -) together with various useful directories and bibliographies were published; seminars, workshops and meetings sponsored and held. Participation within the ASEAN Clearinghouse scene continues.

More important, by the early 1990's the Women's Affairs Division, which is under the Ministry of National Unity and Social Development, had drawn up a realistic and necessary budget, which also included both professional and non-professional support posts for staff.

Vigorous requests by all quarters, including those from NGOs for substantial funding, happily coincided with the Government's commitment to encouraging WID. The Sixth Malaysia Development Plan, 1991-5, allocated a generous RM20 million to support WID programmes.

Shortcomings

Despite all these efforts, the Clearinghouse was relatively unknown. None of the big academic institutions in the country used the Clearinghouse. Its collection was even rarely used by those who were specifically associated with HAWA on HAWA-funded or sponsored research projects. A similar picture existed with regards to the special, research and bigger public libraries.

Reasons. There were two main reasons for this situation:

(1) The lack of trained library professionals to process and manage the collection and give services from the Clearinghouse.[20]

(2) More important, the Clearinghouse operated as an individual, self-contained library-unit. In all aspects, it was constituted as a small government departmental library, without the necessary resources to give the services needed of it.

Like most government department libraries elsewhere, nearly all other government departmental libraries in Malaysia are closed to the general user. The library public at large could be forgiven for assuming that this was also the case with the Clearinghouse collections and services. In any case, for lack of suitable accommodation, the collection was stored in a small area, and stacked without any order, making it inconvenient and unsuitable for reading and reference.[21] Lacking trained staff also meant that no publicity could be given; and no library services of even a basic professional nature could be entertained.

The Ministry and the Division had felt very strongly that steps must be taken, and taken swiftly, to remedy this situation. In March 1993, two librarians with considerable teaching and practical experience between them, were engaged as the Project Coordinator and as the Technical Manager, to help the Clearinghouse function better both as a national resource centre, and as a node within the ASEAN network of clearinghouses.

National Network, April 1993

The most fundamental change recommended was that the Clearinghouse itself should be conceptualised as a network. Instead of operating as a single, small unit, trying to be all things to all users, it was felt imperative that the bigger, and other more established institutions should somehow be formally inked to the Clearinghouse. This would mean that the big collections on WID at these institutions, be they national, archival, academic, special or official, would together form a bigger and more formidable resource pool.

Role. The Clearinghouse role was redefined. While its own collection-building would be enhanced to add to its credibility, it would not seek primarily to duplicate holdings better held elsewhere (e.g. theses materials at the universities). It would, as a matter of priority, seek out and acquire those materials not easily obtained by other libraries and institutions, for one reason or another. At the core, its role would lean heavily towards centralising and consolidating WID information on a national union basis. This centralised information would in turn be purveyed back to users and the nodes.

Consensus. In April 1993, top policy-makers representing 16 institutions and organisations, academic, national and official and the National Council for Women's Organisations, representing some 60 women's groups and organisations, met Clearinghouse personnel at a Meeting, which was chaired by the Deputy Permanent Secretary to the Ministry.

At close of the Meeting, all institutions agreed to give the idea a try. They agreed that a national WID Network be established, and that they would participate in it.[22] Network members are indicated in Annexure A.

Bases for Participation by Network Nodes. The Meeting took fundamental cognizance of the fact that all Network nodes will have their own priorities, unremitting tasks and unique targets which will extend institutional resources such as staff time, funding and infrastructures to the limit. Thus institutions would expect to participate at a pace that is realistic to them. For the moment, therefore members in the Network with computerised systems will find ways and means to download their data on WID to the Clearinghouse. Others will furnish information (in hard copies, etc) to permit manual input. Efforts will be directed towards establishing a union database on WID.

Benefits

It was also recognised that no sensible institution will participate in any scheme merely to contribute to yet another superstructure that will only add greater burdens to their staff and offers nothing in return. For a Network to work, there must be real benefits to all parties, although some of the benefits may be only realizable in the future. Benefits that are expected to accrue to different parties are as follows:

To Clearinghouse. Continuing benefits will accrue to the Clearinghouse is being able to realize its role as a national Clearinghouse with access to information on WID held in organizations/institutions within the country.

To participating institutions/organisations. Participating institutions will be able to obtain updated information on WID within the network. As institutional resources are restricted, institutions may prefer to channel their WID bibliographic needs to the Clearinghouse to fulfil. Focussed service can be given by Clearinghouse staff and collections that are geared to only attending to WID-related queries. Resource savings effected by network participants can be used for other purposes.

Individual scholars and users of WID information. Anyone with a need for WID information, whether associated with big research, academic institutions, or researching on an individual basis, will be able to resort to a one-stop information agency. This saves time and energy, and ensures information is given to those with or without funding for WID-research. This adds to greater and more equal access to WID information.

All this may not be possible overnight; but will have to be phased according to progress of the Clearinghouse, to a stage when it can efficiently and expeditiously deal with queries and services needed by users.

Plans for Future Development

Staff. Besides the Project Coordinator and Technical Manager, the

Clearinghouse currently has five posts for permanents staff: one professional and four support posts. Additional requests for five more professional (contract) officers have been made for 1993. For 1994, posts requested include those for a systems analyst, a programmer, two more library professionals, and support staff.

Collection. A target collection of 10,000 volumes has been set for the end of 1995. It is hoped that a strong feature of the collection will be 30-40 journal title subscriptions on women's issues, which local universities are unable to take, as few offer women's studies as distinct, formal courses; and all have heavy demands for their journal allocations. Another feature will be the collection of official reports, and NGO publications which the other Network nodes often face difficulties in locating, acquiring and maintaining. Audio-visual materials, such as photographs of women in Malaysia at their work and leisure, of which the Clearinghouse holds some 700 items, will be useful for a variety of purposes: in displays, publishing, etc.

Databases. From June 1993, the Clearinghouse will be subscribing to a variety of national and international databases which will yield information on women. DIALOG has been taken; POPLINE on CD-ROM, and WIS have been requested; and WISTAT is now available.

A local database, LOL (Library-Online) marketed by the New Straits Times Press (NSTP) giving on-line access to newspaper articles in key English and Malay dailies, has been taken. This database is being retrospectively built up to cover relevant newspaper features on women (issues, associations, personalities, news) published in the NSTP group of papers and magazines.

Specialised databases. The Clearinghouse will in future attempt to create specialised Malaysia WID databases. Initially three are being planned, being:

(a) Personalities (women as resource)

(b) Socio-economic indicators on women

(c) Women's organisations.

Work has already begun to collect and update data; and information capture can be effected once the Clearinghouse is computerised.

Computer System. To cope with all these demands for information storage, retrieval, database creation and networking, computerisation has been planned. An integrated library software in an open system seems indicated to cope within—house operations. CD-ROM facilities; PC networking; graphics technology; data capture, are some of the features incorporated in the plans. Records stored and disseminated will be in standard MARC format, to permit easy information exchange.

Expansion of the Network. For the future, as the Clearinghouse gains in experience, and more resources are acquired, the Network will attempt to reach out to all libraries, information centres, women's associations and political auxiliaries that are interested in joining the network.

VI. Parallels in National and Regional Planning

The Malaysian Clearinghouse has consciously sought to emulate the regional structure, and has deliberately incorporated features in its planning to facilitate fulfilling regional requirements. There are therefore many parallels between features in the national and regional clearinghouse structures.

Collection-building

National Clearinghouses do collect significant materials on other countries (within the region and abroad). However, they make no conscious effort to duplicate all holdings held in other clearinghouses, especially preferring to let each clearinghouse specialise in locating and acquiring their national literatures on WID.

In like fashion, the Malaysian Clearinghouse within its own network, will not seek to duplicate all that is held in its nodes, but would prefer to let specialist literatures be held by the nodes. All significant WID materials, however, will be duplicated. This concept is in line with both economic dictates and bibliographic realities.

Standards for Bibliographic Description

Since the collection held will not be comprehensive of everything in the region, or even within the country, the union database of information for the country is an important feature. To be useful, this information must be recognisable when exchanged. The use of standard, acceptable formats is a prerequisite. Within ASEAN, major libraries have adopted the MARC format, but with variations. Similarly, in Malaysia, while major libraries have all adopted MARC there are variations and different versions (AUSMARC, MALMARC, USMARC, etc.). The conversion of all entries to a common version will be an imperative, and a challenge.

Current dictates within ASEAN also make it necessary for the Clearinghouse database to be available in CDS/ISIS format. Within Malaysia, it is also clear that many libraries will continue to use this package to organise their collection. Clearinghouse is therefore initiating its database on CDS/ISIS. In this context, an excellent start has been made with the generous donation of the total CDS/ISIS database of Malaysian WID by the Library, University of Malaya.[23] Network nodes have also begun to contribute records in both CDS/ISIS and MARC formats.

In addition, the MALMARC consortium has also kindly agreed to make available all records on WID held by the MALMARC consortium of libraries.[24] These records will begin the MARC database. The MALMARC consortium existed from 1977-1990, but records date from much earlier, as most of the members in the consortium had begun retrospective conversion of their catalogues, and a few had completed this exercise by 1990.

Exchange of Information

At the moment, operations at the Clearinghouse are extremely hampered by the lack of computer system. This is expected to be available by the end of 1993. When this comes on stream, it will be expected that the union database will continue to be available in two formats: (a) a MARC database; (b) a CDS/ISIS database.

Dial-up access will immediately be available to the MARC database. The CDS/ISIS database will be distributed to those libraries (in the country and within the region) operating on CDS/ISIS, for information. In this fashion, national, regional and international dictates may be fulfilled.

Publications and Publicity

Publications. A regional concern has always been that developments in clearinghouse should be made known to each other.

Similarly, the Malaysian Clearinghouse feels a need to update the Malaysian network on developments and achievements by network nodes. It is hoped that a publication, *Network Notes* will be published twice or three times a year to fill this need. In addition, the quarterly newsletter of the Women's Affairs Division, *Beritanita* will also carry news items related to the Clearinghouse.

Publicity. Women's Day is celebrated in Malaysia in August. The 1993 celebrations will include an Exhibition by network members, to be held in the brand-new building of the National Library of Malaysia which has kindly agreed to lend its Exhibition Hall for this occasion. The theme is on 'Information, Research and Women in Development'. Members will have an opportunity to display their WID projects; the human expertise who contributed/are contributing to WID research; their institution's research projects, activities and findings; and library/information resources that have been build up to support these projects and programmes. The Exhibition, therefore, is expected to be an exercise in updating knowledge on a national scale, and will effectively publicise activities in a more consolidated fashion.

Training

The training of WID personnel is another regional concern. The Malaysian Clearinghouse is conscious of this need. At the moment, the Clearinghouse Library Officer is being sent to a CDS/ISIS course, organised by the National Library. When trained, she will offer training to those attached to smaller library units e.g. at women's groups and associations, etc. (whose resources may be too limited to permit them to attend the formal courses), and will assist them in organising their materials along bibliographically acceptable lines. This will be the requirement for other professional staff later recruited into the Clearinghouse.

Networking

ASEAN Clearinghouses work as a regional network. Each national node is a centre of excellence on national WID. the chain concert is a regional resource to support WID programmes and activities.

The Malaysian Clearinghouse, in operating as a national network, recognises the individual excellence of each node. Cooperatively, a better information system is established, both to support national and regional activities.

Most important, the Malaysian WID Clearinghouse is part and parcel of the Malaysian Bibliographic Network, coordinated by the National Library; with each academic library; specialised research and government library; and public libraries recognised as individual units of excellence within their specialised networks, within a national chain. Within this context, the National Library has designated the Clearinghouse to be the focus on WID. As elsewhere, therefore, there are many concentric rings within this networking concept.

IV. Concluding Remarks

The difficulty of any project lies not in its initiation, but in the ability to realise all its potential, and bring the project to full fruition. In network-building, the natural instinct is to include all and every relevant element, as quickly as possible, regardless of the state of preparedness of individual or coordinating units. The watchwords for the Clearinghouse are therefore 'Sustainability' and 'Practicality'. Expansion there must be, but at a rate that can be coped with, to ensure that there is sufficient perceptible progress along the way.

Initial success in establishing the national network, though euphoric cannot count for anything, if resources (of finance, infrastructures and human expertise) are not available to sustain the Clearinghouse to maturity. Plans will remain just so.

There is much truth in the saying; success breed success. Everyone wishes to participate in a successful network; but for it to be so, benefits must not only be envisaged, but they must be delivered. The Clearinghouse has so far been fortunate in gaining the enthusiastic support and cooperation of many organisations and institutions, nearly all of which are older than it. But they did not get so old without some degree of wisdom, and they will wisely withdraw from the network if it is in fact, not able to deliver. The Clearinghouse, therefore, will have to rather quickly proceed from its initial launching stage to a full-blown operational one.

Finally, one must remember the dynamics of change. In particular, changes in technology can be expected to be of paramount importance in bringing about the need for changes. Perhaps the most successful network witnessed in Malaysia was the MALMARC consortium, begun in the days when telex was new, and participating libraries had to use this 'latest' in technology to communicate with each other and the coordinating/processing centre at Universiti Sains Malaysia. In time, 'faxes' phased the telex out; and yet later, developments in software and hardware industries made it economic, and possible, for each consortium member to computerise inhouse. With CD-ROM technology and the appearance of databases such as Bibliofile, the massive joint-cataloging consortia of the past became unnecessary. MALMARC dissolved in 1990, but with the satisfaction that it was successful, and that while it lasted, it was a useful networking operation and necessary at a time when no other technology was available to offer alternative solutions.

So it is envisaged with the Clearinghouse on Women in Development. In time to come, better communications nationwide will permit all libraries and organisations to be 'hooked up'. Dial-up access or online access, as already exists in Singapore, may be available. Downloading of records will no longer be necessary. In time, all of ASEAN maybe linked up communications-wise, and the current plan of maintaining dual databases will no longer be necessary.

That day is yet a little way off. In the meantime, the Malaysian Clearinghouse will hope to fill a useful niche in the national and regional information chain on WID. To do so, even half successfully, it will have to look to the Government to provide the funding; to network nodes for goodwill and cooperation; and to itself, to get its own act together, to play the role chartered out, reasonably effectively and well.

FOOTNOTES

1. *Encyclopaedia Britannica*, 1970, Vol.5, p.894.
2. *Encyclopaedia Americana*, 1992, Vol.3, p. 181-2.
3. The Association of Southeast Asean Nations or ASEAN, currently comprises six countries, being : Brunei, Indonesia, Malaysia, the Philippines, Singapore and Thailand.
4. For this paper, it suffices that only thumbnail sketches be provided. For more details on the history, directions and current activities of the national Clearinghouses, see Reports of annual AWP Meetings, 1981-1993; Reports of Experts Meeting on Clearinghouse on Women in Development, 1982-.
5. Indonesia has long paid attention to national bibliographic control. Its *National Bibliography* began in 1953.

6. Workshop on Thesaurus Construction Report, 1986, Annex III, p.[2].
7. The Philippines' *National Bibliography* starts from 1974; and a *Retrospective National Bibliography 1523-1699* and subsequent listings, have been published.
8. Country Paper, Experts Meeting Report, Jakarta, 1992, p.1.
9. Workshop on Thesaurus Construction Report, 1986, Annex III, p. p[2].
10. Royal and religious libraries go back a few hundred years; legal deposit was effected as from 1941; and the *Thai National Bibliography* has been published from 1958.
11. Country Paper, Experts Meeting Report, Jakarta, 1992, p.1.
12. 7th AWP Meeting Report, Annex H.
13. Country Paper, Experts Meeting Report, Jakarta, 1992, para 1.2.
14. Workshop on Thesaurus Construction Report, Jakarta, 1986, Annex III, p. [1].
15. As witness he many activities and publications of the Southeast Asian Branch, International Council on Archives (SARBICA); standing Conference of Southeast Asian Librarians (CONSAL), etc.
16. The designation of national distribution centres, such as the National Library of Malaysia for Malaysia, has made the acquisition of the CDS/ISIS software an easy process.
17. See for example, Experts Meeting Report, Jakarta, 1992, Annex P.
18. Fatimah Saad, 1990.
19. Women's Affairs Division, Clearinghouse Progress Report, 1991, Annexes B1-E.
20. The Project Coordinator and the Technical Manager only joined the Clearinghouse as consulting contract personnel from 15 March 1993; and the single permanent professional officer came on board from 7 June 1993.
21. In late June 1993, the library collection was sorted out by the library officer, and though not yet processed, is now available for reference in a specially designated library area within the Women's Affairs Division. While awaiting processing, books are arranged on the shelves under broad subject headings.
22. One other organisation, the Malaysian Women's Advancement Institute, although not represented at the Meeting, had earlier on agreed to join the Network.
23. The information is published in the bibliographical essay on *Status and Role of Malaysian Women*, by Khoo *et al.*, 1992.
24. The MALMARC consortium was essentially a shared cataloguing project. Participants consisted of the National Library and six academic libraries. Much literature is available on this project.

GLOSSARY OF TERMS USED

ASEAN	Association of Southeast Asean Nations, August 1967-
ASA	Association of Southeast Asia, 1954-1967.
AWP	ASEAN Women's Programme
CD-ROM	Compact disc; read-only memory
COSD	ASEAN Committee on Social Development

CIC	Clearinghouse and Information Center on Women, Thailand
CONSAL	Conference of Southeast Asian Librarians
HAWA	Bahagian Hal Ehwal Wanita [Women's Affairs Division, Ministry of National Unity and Social Development.]
LOL	Library On-line [A newspaper database retrievable online, by the NSTP.]
MARC	Machine-readable catalogue
NCRFW	National Commission on the Role of Filipino Women, Philippines.
NCWT	National Council of Women of Thailand
NGO	Non-governmental organisaion(s)
NSTP	New Straits Times Press
NWIC	National Women's Information Center, Thailand
OPAC	Open public access catalogue (online)
SARBICA	Southeast Asian Branch, International Council on Archives
WID	Women in Development
WIS	Women's Information System database Division for the Advancement off Women, United Nations Office at Vienna.
WISTAT	UN Women's Indicators and Statistics database Division of Statistics, UN Office, New York.

REFERENCES CITED

1. ASEAN Women's Programmes (AWP), *Report*, 7th Meeting, Manila, 13-15 April 1988.
2. *ENCYCLOPAEDIA Americana*, International edn., Danbury Grolier Incrop., 1992. 30 vols.
3. *ENCYCLOPAEDIA Britannica*, Chicago, 1970. 23 vols.
4. *ENCYCLOPAEDIA of Library and Information Science*, New York, Marcel Dekker, In., 1968-.
5. EXPERTS Meeting on Future Cooperation among ASEAN Clearinghouses for Information on Women in Development, Jakarta, 6-8 October 1992 *Report*, [Jakarta], Centre for Scientific Documentation and Information, Indonesia Institute of Sciences, [1992].
6. FATIMAH Saad, 'Projek Pusat Sumber Maklumat Wanita dalam Pembangunan: National Clearinghouse on Women in Development', Paper presented at the Bengkel Sistem Maklumat Wanita [Workshop on Women's Information System], Genting highlands, 5-7 February 1990.
7. *STATUS and Role of Malaysian Women in Development: a Bibliographical Essay* by Khoo Siew Mun, Shaikha Zakaria, Norehan Ahmad, Noriyah Md Nor and Kristin Cheah, Kuala Lumpur, Faculty of Economics and Administration and National Population and Family Development Board, 1992.
8. WOMEN's Affairs Division, Ministry of National Unity and Social Development, Laporan Kemajuan Pusat Sumber Maklumat Wanita Dalam Pembangunan [Progress Report on the Information Clearinghouse on Women in Development], 14 October 1991[In Malay.]
9. WORKSHOP on Thesaurus Construction for the Clearinghouse for Women in Development, Jakarta, 6-10 January 1986, *Report*.

ANNEXURE-A

NETWORK PARTICIPATION-PHASE I: 1993

Stage	Institution/Library
I	Asian & Pacific Development Centre
	Arkib Negara Malaysia [National Archives of Malaysia]
	Dewan Bahasa & Pustaka [Language and Literary Agency]
	Institutes Kemajuan Wanita Malaysia [Institute for Women's advancement Malaysia]
	Institute for Strategic and International Studies
	Institute Teknologi MARA [MARA Institute of Technology]
	- Library School
	- Library
	Lembaga Penduduk & Pembangunan Keluarga Negara [National Population and Family Development Board]
	National Council of Women's Organizations
	Perpustakaan Negara Malaysia [National Library of Malaysia]
	Universiti Islam Antarabangsa [International Islamic University]
	Universiti Kebangsaan Malaysia [National University of Malaysia]
	Universiti Malaya [University of Malaya]
	Universiti Pertanian Malaysia [Agricultural University of Malaysia]
	Universiti Sains Malaysia [Science University of Malaysia]
	Universiti Teknologi Malaysia [University of Technology of Malaysia]
	Universiti Utara Malaysia [Northern University of Malaysia]
II	Libraries and Organisations and Sabah & Sarawak

Notes:

(a) The stages for implementation are not inflexible. They may be implemented sooner (or later) depending on the rate of success encountered.

(b) All 17 libraries/organisations indicated above have expressed support for, and agreement to participate in the Network.

(c) Phase I coincides with computerisation period for the Clearinghouse.

South Asian Literature : Acquisition and Processing in West European Libraries

GEORGE F. BAUMANN

Abstract

Various universal and specialised libraries in Europe have extensive area collections of South Asian Literature. These special collections began as early as the 16th century and although originally mostly classical literature in the form of manuscripts were collected, for the past 100 years mostly printed material has been bought. Today the acquisition profile was been widened to include literature in all of the humanities and indigenous natural sciences and medicine.

In all these institutions discussed here acquisitional policies in recent times have been very similar to each other although the situation at the University Library in Tuebingen tends to be a bit different due to the long and regular financial support this South Asian collection in Germany has had through the auspices of the German Research Soceity. In general, these acquisition policies are (1) individual purchases; (2) exchange and gifts; (3) legal deposit copies. The first mentioned category can again be subdivided into (1) buying trips; (2) conventional books orders; and (3) blanket - order agreements. A short description of these methods has been given.

Book processing has been discussed, particularly the question of a uniform internationally recognised transliteration system for all South Asian languages. Another important aspect is the need for a name's authority file to be implemented in present and upcoming data-banks. The multi-cultural situation in South Asia demands such a guide which will have to be accompanied by a comprehensive commentary.

A supra-national effort on the part of all of these European libraries is necessary in order to rationalise acquisitions and guarantee that processing can be done with a minimal amount of personnel. The growing balance between new and traditional South Asian studies has to be reflected in the growth of the South Asian collections.

Introduction

The geographical term **'South Asia'** used in this paper refers to the Indian Subcontinent and the surrounding islands. It includes the countries of Bangladesh, Bhutan, India, Maldive Islands, Nepal, Pakistan and Sri Lanka. In addition, at the India Office Library (IOL) and the School of Oriental and African Studies (SOAS), both in London, Afghanistan and Burma are also traditionally included in the region of South Asia due to colonial administrative boundaries in the past. At the University Library in Tuebingen Tibet up to the loss of its autonomy in the 1950's is also included in that special area collection on South Asia.

In spite of the seemingly numerous cultural strata today within this region there is a strong overlapping common cultural 'blanket' giving these countries a certain homogeneity. Its long oral and written library history covering more than 2,500 years is comparable to similarly long cultural developments in the Middle East and in China. South Asia is also the birthplace of two great Oriental cultures, the Hindu and the Buddhist, and has been for many centuries the home of the third, Islam.

During the literary movement in Europe at the end of the 18th century called the Romantic Period there was a great fascination with Indian culture upon discovering that there was a common, if distant, linguistical connection between Sanskrit and European languages. These linguistical studies, along with research in Hinduism, particularly Vedism, and later in Buddhism, became known as **indology.** This term has become synonymous with classical Indian studies which have dominated research on South Asian topics throughout Europe until recently. In Great Britain there always has been a more pragmatic approach to such studies since the colonial administration had to be trained in every-day affairs and instruction in the vernaculars began much earlier. In Germany and France, however, there was more emphasis on research in historical linguistics and comparative religion. Until the middle of the 19th century very few printed texts were available in Europe, most literary sources being manuscripts lying in Paris or London. In fact, Professor Rudolf von Roth (1821-1895), who held the first chair for Sanskrit established in 1854 at the University of Tuebingen, had to travel to London and Paris to copy manuscripts to collect material for his famous Sanskrit-German dictionary, published from 1852 to 1875, and completed in co-operation with Professor Otto Boehtlingk (1815-1904) in St. Petersburg.

After most countries in South Asia had achieved independence towards the middle of this century there has been a noticeable change in the emphasis of South Asian research in Europe. Today, of course, research on classical subjects like Sanskrit, Pali and Prakrit, is still dominant, particularly in Germany, but a growing emphasis on sociological, economical and political questions can be discerned. Indigenous medicine, e.g. Ayurveda, is becoming a very important field of research, too. Usually these so-called modern studies are not offered in the classical indological institutes, but rather in the various faculties or institutes at the respective universities where, sometimes just for a limited period, doctorate and other advanced research on South Asian topics is done. For some aspects of modern South Asian studies even specialized institutes have been founded, e.g. the Südasien-institut (SAI) in Heidelberg, or the various institutes in Paris and, of course, the School of Oriental and African Studies in London.

An enumeration of the main libraries in Europe having important holdings of South Asian literature should include the following institutions, but this list is by no means exhaustive. They are : in Great Britain—the India Office Library (IOL) of the British Library, the Library of the School of Oriental and African Studies (SOAS), both in London; in France — the Bibliothéque Nationale, the Bibliothéque de l'Institut de Civilisation Indienne, the Bibliothéque de la Centre d'Etudes de l'Inde et de l'Asie due Sud, the Bibliothéque de l'Ecole des langues Orientales, all in Paris; in the Netherlands — the Bibliothek of the Kern-Instituut, Leiden; in Italy — the Biblioteca Apostolica Veticana, Rome; in Germany — the Südasien-Institut (SAI), Heidelberg, and the Tuebingen, the Universtätsbibliothek. Most of these libraries are government supported and most maintain general Oriental collections, of which literature concerning South Asian is only one major aspect.

Several of these libraries mentioned here have a very long history, beginning with the European voyages of discovery in the 16th century. Due to the ever-pervading presence of the East India Company from the 17th to the early 19th century, whose motives were predominantly commercial, little or no effort was made in Great Britain to officially collect literature from the region. However various employees of the Company had gathered literature privately and had taken it back to Great Britain upon retirement. Gradually it became obvious that these specialized collections needed a common home, as their owners or the inheritors of the original owners later began to offer these legacies to the East India Company for preservation. The necessity of a national repository for such material became obvious. Therefore the **India Office Library** was established in 1827, mostly through the efforts of Charles Wilkins (1749 ? - 1838). Soon after its establishment several important donations and war trophies like the Tipoo Sultan's library were added. This library and even earlier, the **Bibliothèque Nationale** in Paris employed agents, who were already residing in South Asia, to purchase books and manuscripts for them. The Bibliothéque Nationale even employed various well-known Englishmen living in India to supply it with literature. Professor Roth, in Tuebingen, requested the English colonial authorities in Kashmir to search for a possible different version of the Atharvaveda and in 1874 they were able to trace the so-called Paippalada version, written on birch-leaf. It is now one of the rare manuscripts in the Tuebingen collection.

The **University Library in Tuebingen** is not just a special area collection library but rather a universal library, collecting literature in all subjects. Its Oriental collection, or more specifically, the South Asian collection is only a part of its total collection of more than 2,00,000 volumes, the special Oriental collection on South Asia containing about 2,00,000 volumes. This library is financed by the State of Baden-Wuerttemberg, in which it is situated, but the greater portion of the budget for the Oriental special collections is given by the German Research Society in Bonn, a body financed in part by the Federal Government. This special area collection in Tuebingen is part of an extensive nation-wide programme to collect foreign academic literature. The **German Research Society** began its activities in the 1920's and various types of libraries—16 university libraries, 2

State libraries and 2 specialised libraries — presently participate in its special subject and area collections' programme. This idea of a national programme for special area and subject collections in existing libraries has also gained supporters during the past decade in Great Britain and France, where similar nation-wide programmes are being developed. Each participating library in Germany agrees to use the special funds provided by the German Research Society and the local State government to collect foreign academic literature (i.e., literature published outside of Germany) on a wider scale than an academic library would normally do. This responsibility also requires the respective library to make its collection known to potential users, be it through the publication of accession lists, publication of library catalogues, etc. Such accession lists are published by the IOL and the SOAS and the University Library in Tuebingen, all having an international distribution.

The idea of a national programme for special subject and area collections has been taken up and implemented in France and Great Britain also.

The **Sudasien-Institut (South Asia Institute)** in Heidelberg was established in 1962 as an inter-disciplinary institute concentrating its research on South Asia. Its library has grown very rapidly during the past 30 years and now contains approximately 2,00,000 volumes, mainly recent literature on South Asian studies. Apart from some antiquarian purchases and various legacies it does not have the historical holdings of the 19th and early 20th centuries as the older libraries in Europe have.

The **Biblioteca Apostolica Vaticana in Rome** was a very important centre for collecting manuscripts in the early period, mostly during the 16th and 17th centuries. In the 15th century Pope Nicolas V (Tommaso Parentucelli, 1447-1455) had his emissaries search in the Orient for important manuscripts for this library. With the help of Catholic missionaries, particularly the Jesuits, during the next three centuries it probably had the best stocked library in Europe and its Oriental material, mostly manuscripts, is of great importance, even today.

The **Kern-Institut in Leiden, the Netherlands,** was founded in 1926 and named in honour of the first professor of Sanskrit in that country, Hendrik Kern (1833-1917). For many years, from 1926 to 1984 it published the well-known 'Annual Bibliography of Indian Archaeology'. This publication was the basis for an active international exchange programme over the years adding valuable works to this library. It now contains approximately 30,000 volumes and the former South Asian holdings of the University in Utrecht are soon to be assimilated into this collection, increasing its value considerably.

Some of these libraries have produced alphabetical catalogues of some or all of their holdings, and in the case of the SOAS and the IOL, we also have subject catalogues.

Acquisitions Policies

Book production in South Asia varies in intensity from country to country. On the one hand India ranks about 8th in world publishing and even 3rd if we only consider English-language publications, closely following the United States and Great Britain. Its book trade is highly organized and efficient. In the context of the multilingual situation in India the individual linguistic regions have also developed extensive book publishing industries. Countries like Sri Lanka and Pakistan have growing publishing industries but as a rule they are not as well organised and fiscal red-tape makes exporting a rather tedious affair. In Nepal and Bangladesh the book trade is mostly concentrated in the respective capitals, Kathmandu and Dhaka, although some publishing is done in outlying areas. Bhutan and the Maldive Islands have as yet practically no book trade to speak of, although a few government offices produce some relevant literature.

In spite of the proverbial high illiteracy rate in South Asia the absolute number of literates, particularly in India, is greater than in Europe. Therefore the demand for literature in the local market is very intensive, leading to a high production rate. In India we can assume that approximately 12,000 to 15,000 new titles of academic interest are published each year. The annual book production in Pakistan and Sri Lanka is approximately 1,000-2,000 relevant titles and in Nepal and Bangladesh between 500-1,000 relevant titles annually.

Acquisitional policies can be divided into three basic categories : (1) individual purchases, both for manuscripts in the earliest period as well as for current purchases of antiquaria and contemporary literature; (2) exchange and gifts; and (3) legal deposit copies. The first-mentioned form — individual purchases — can be further sub-divided into the following categories : (1) buying trips; (2) conventional book orders; and (3) blanket-order agreements.

The earliest acquisitions were, of course, mainly manuscripts as there was no printing in the subcontinent until Portugal set up the first printing press in about 1556. Whereas mostly classical literature was collected up to the middle of the 20th century, during the past 50 years there has been a noticeable increase in the acquisition of modern South Asian literary texts and contemporary subjects in the humanities and the social sciences. Interest in indigenous medicine is growing rapidly.

The growth of the South Asian collections was, however, by no means always systematical. During the two centuries, from 1600 to 1800, growth of South Asian literature collections was haphazard and relatively slow in all Western European libraries. Since there was hardly any commercial book trade in South Asia the Europeans had to rely on emissaries for purchasing manuscripts and lithographed works.

In the 18th century the King of France, Louis XIV, sent out emissaries to collect manuscripts and printed books for his Royal Library, which later became the basis for the Bibliothèque Nationale. These **buying trips** might seem similar to our present-day buying trips. However, in earlier times the lack of an organised book-trade meant that the searchers had to rely on chance and guidance from local officials and on accidental discovery. The French also used in the auspices of the Compagnie de Jésus (Jesuits) and the Compagnie des Indes Orientales founded by Jean Baptiste Colbert (1619-1683) in 1664. Because of the interest shown by Abbott Bignon who had become librarian of the Royal Library in 1718, acquisitional efforts gained momentum.

Contemporary buying trips have to be seen in the light of unsatisfactory conventional bookseller relationships, or for the purpose of purchasing antiquaria. Experience shows that buying antiquaria on the basis of printed catalogues from South Asia can be a delicate matter. The condition of the books is usually not sufficiently described and many times the actual condition is so bad that the book can no longer be used. The only alternative then is to have a film made of the original book and dispose of the original. The average South Asian bookseller also has little sensitivity to the problem of authors' names when he puts his catalogue together. Hence a certain amount of experience on the part of the European academic librarian is necessary in order to judge the correct main entry for a particular name in the European library catalogue. For these reasons selection of antiquaria should be made on the spot, i.e. through autopsy. Due to the poorly organised book trade in other parts of South Asia, outside of India, acquiring titles from such areas through the local book trade can prove to be unsatisfactory. Therefore during such buying trips one should also try to locate publications which have escaped one's attention previously. This presupposes a good knowledge of one's own stock, of course, and also awareness of unfulfilled requests from researchers in the past. One must also be constantly on the look-out for more efficient booksellers. A personal visit and detailed discussions of the needs and methods of acquisition prove to be very important in South Asia.

Contemporary **convensional book-ordering** should be familiar to everyone, although book-ordering can be done in two different ways—through local agents where the library is situated or directly with booksellers in South Asia. The former possibility, however, is likely to be impractical as the multi-lingual literature and the numerous scripts cannot be handled by the average European bookseller who has little or no knowledge of Oriental literature. The more specialized a collection is the greater the necessity to have direct contact with reliable booksellers in the region. In those South Asian countries where the book trade is well organized there is certainly no need to depend on local European booksellers. Booksellers in Great Britain, particularly in London, do have an advantage over booksellers on the Continent as they can more easily communicate in English concerning reclamations, etc. and can rely on the assistance of many emigrants from South Asia, if there be need to. My long experience, however, shows that a direct relationship with booksellers in the region is more beneficial for both sides.

Today we have to depend on the local booksellers in South Asia and a library having a special subject collection will find it necessary to engage more than just one book supplier. The multi-lingual situation, particularly in India, generally demands three or four different booksellers, distributed throughout the different linguistical areas—at least one in East India for Bengali and Oriya and other northeastern languages and literatures, one in Delhi for English-language publications, Hindi, Panjabi and other north Indian varnaculars. In West India there will be need of a supplier for Marathi and Gujarati, and finally one or two in South India for the four Dravidian languages and literatures.

Turning now to the practical side of ordering there are, as a rule, order-forms for individual book-orders. The ordering process is not yet computerised in Europe. One copy or more of the conventional order-forms are sent to the respective bookseller who returns one copy with the relevant book. The bibliographical data on the order-forms will, as a rule, be transliterated into the Roman alphabet, either because the bibliographical source was already transliterated or because the ordering library has transliterated the relevant data since typewriters for most South Asian scripts are a rarity and proper personnel in Europe to operate them is also scarce. If, in turn, the bookseller in South Asia submits his invoices in one of the regional scripts and languages then there shall have to be experts in the recipient library who can transliterate such invoices. In the larger European cities where most of the above-mentioned libraries are located there are many times well-trained South Asians who can be employed for many of the routine needs of such a specialised library. Otherwise the academic librarian in these specialised area or subject collections have to become involved in such daily routine processes which is very counter-productive to building up such collections.

The third type of conventional book ordering is the so-called **blanket-order agreements** with very specific profiles. Such agreements have existed at the India office Library and still exist at the Universitaetsbibliothek in Tuebingen. In the latter library we have a continuous experience with this acquisitional method for the past 15 years. This arrangement is usually justifiable only when the budget allows for extensive collecting. As we all know the stock of most libraries reflects the fluctuations of budgetary reality. In order for such an agreement to be successful, however, a library must have previous long-standing experience with a particular bookseller and be convinced of his reliability. In the case of Tuebingen the agreement covers only English and Sanskrit-language publications of the last three consecutive years. The library must create a very exact profile of its literature needs, both in regard to subject as well as to formal literature categories, e.g. the question whether printed dissertations, periodicals, ephemeral literature, etc. are to be included. Such literature profiles need regular revision due to possible financial restrictions on increases. The possibility to reject literature must be included in any such agreement as experience shows that there will be many border-line cases, where, in spite of a detailed profile, the booksellers will still be in doubt. The Tuebingen we have, in fact, agreed to have the bibliographical data of such doubtful cases sent to us so that we can take a decision before the literature is mailed. This data is sent on our own blank order-forms, which we supply to our bookseller regularly.

Gifts and exchanges played a very important role in building up the collections in the older institutions discussed here. We have already mentioned the legacies which led to the establishment of the IOL in the early 19th century. Private bequests were received, e.g. from Henry Colebrooke (1765-1837), the Maharaja of Baroda, Sayajirao III (1864-1939), the William Jones Collection and the Georg Buehler (1837-1898) legacy. Various donations increased the number of books considerably during the late 19th century at the Bibliothèque Nationale in Paris. Through the efforts of the well-known librarian, Charles Schefer (1820-1898), the library of the present Ecole des langues orientales grew rapidly and contained approximately 50,000 volumes by 1883. 'Cette collection de livres orientaux est unique au monde et accessible á tous les savants.' (Meuret, p. 4030). 'Enrichie principalement par les largesses des gouvernments étranger, par les échanges internationaux et les heureux hasards des ventes publiques...' (Meuret, p. 403).

Many European countries created **legal depository laws** for literature published in their own countries or even in their colonial territories. In Great Britain the Indian Press and Registration of Books Act (Act XXV of 1867), paragraphs 9 to 11, stated that one copy of every printed or lithographed book issued in India was required to be forwarded to the Secretary of State for India. The IOL became in consequence vested with the nature of a copyright library for Indian publications. In 1877 at Reinhold Rost's (1822-1896) insistence, who was the librarian at IOL, a new procedure was sanctioned whereby only a selection of such copyright literature was ordered to be transmitted, such a selection, being made at the Librarian's discretion. For facilitating this process, quarterly catalogues were issued and continue to be issued by the various provincial governments, listing all publications which may appear in each respective province during the relevant three months. Act XXV was later amended in many particulars. France had already created a **dépot légal** in 1537, which covered works published in its colonies also. It, too, was modified in 1943. Multiple copies, no matter how they had come about, were often used for exchange or gift purposes amongst the libraries of Europe. Professor Roth in Tuebingen meticulously recorded such gifts in his yearly reports during the middle of the 19th century.

In all the libraries discussed here there has been a widening of the literature scope in the 19th century in all fields of study except the natural sciences, technology and modern law. Indigenous medicine and sciences have always been included as a rule.

Book Processing

Over the past centuries since these collections were established normal access to each collection has been through the usual alphabetical card catalogue or book catalogue. Some catalogues in recent years have been printed also. I need not go into detail about such conventional catalogues as all of you are most likely familiar with these type. As a rule there are only alphabetical author-catalogues, subject catalogues usually being less common and of more recent date.

Although in some libraries alphabetical catalogues in the original Oriental scripts are in use, it is generally the rule that these scripts are transliterated for cataloguing purposes. The history of the **transliteration** systems shows variations, but as a rule in Europe and North American a common system of transliteration for South Asian languages is used among academic libraries. There has always been a tendency to transcribe and not to transliterate in academic circles, thereby bringing phonological and phonetical influences into the system. Since the middle of this century, however, there has been a growing attempt to unify all European systems into an internationally recognized system. Due to the growing importance of interchangeability of electronic data the urgency of an international standard is obvious. The use of the original Oriental script in the library catalogues presupposes that sufficient staff is available to process such material. Cataloguing data in transliterated form, however, can be handled by all staff members.

Firstly, the question of transliteration of the original Oriental sources is of upmost importance from the very beginning of the processing activities. If the book offers are in South Asian scripts then this information has to be transliterated for internal processing in the library. Secondly, as one copy of the order-form will be entered into an order-file there has also to be uniformity of the author's name. Thirdly, ordering activities are still done conventionally and not with computers. A very important step for such special area or subject collection is to be able to offer the bibliographical data of such ordered works on-line to library users. If such information is available on-line then the potential borrower will know that that particular book will soon be available. He could then enter his name on a waiting list.

As a rule the bookseller in South Asia will submit his invoices in Roman script, so the employees of the accessions department are able to process these without any outside help. If, however, invoices should be submitted in South Asian scripts then those academic librarians having knowledge of that particular script will have to assist the accessions department. Sanskrit books, a part of the South Asian collection in Tuebingen selected by blanket-order, are generally sent in transliterated form, done by the bookseller himself. This accommodation by the bookseller is of immense benefit for a library having limited qualified academic personnel.

The cataloguing of literature in South Asian scripts has to be prepared by the academically trained librarian in such a manner that this data can be entered into the data-bank by a trained cataloguer in the cataloguing department, who then determines the formal cataloguing.

Extensive data-banks have grown up in England, France and Germany during the past decade. Compatability of data is still an unsolved problem, not just internationally, but even within individual European countries, including Germany. Each book added to a collection needs to be catalogued within the respective data-bank only once. The various participants in the data-bank, each of whom benefits from this co-operative cataloguing, can make suggestions to correct existing data. An interesting aspect of the data-bank for the academic libraries of my region, the State of Baden-Wuerttemberg, in the Southwest of Germany, is a names' authority file. Any one familiar with South Asian names knows how complicated a matter this is. Due to the numerous alphabets used for the innumerable languages of this region and the fact that an author may write in as many as three of these regional languages, libraries are confronted with different forms of the name of the same person in its transliterated form. We all know how important it is to make catalogue entries only under a single form of the author's name, using cross-references for all other known forms. This names' authority file can only function well, of course, if there is a central co-ordinating office having a good knowledge of name-giving in South Asia. What is urgently needed is a guide to name-giving in South Asian cultures with a detailed commentary. This task is a very difficult one and there will be innumerable exceptions to any rules as the use of one's name is certainly a personal right and cannot always be defined in terms of a rigid rule. The experience gained in large collections is a good teacher. Various incompatible data-banks also exist even in a comparatively small geographical region like Paris. Tübingen has been cataloguing into its regional data-bank since 1986, which is not yet compatible with other data-banks in Germany either.

We have cursorily described here the two most important aspects when cataloguing South Asian literature. These are : (1) an internationally accepted transliteration system for all South Asian languages; (2) acceptable rules for defining the main name entry for the alphabetical catalogue. Cataloguing of vernacular language material will, as a rule, have to be done by academically trained South Asian experts. These experts in the specialised libraries will, of course, set standards for other libraries having only limited material of this sort and not having academically trained personnel for Oriental literature. The cataloguing of European language literature is less difficult, although even here the standardisation of name entries is very important. As a rule in Tuebingen with its large collection of almost 2,00,000 volumes the form of the author's name chosen for the main entry is that which he uses most. This may mean that he predominately writes in English. This form will be the main entry form and the transliterated form gained from any other South Asian language he may use will be entered as a cross-reference. The data-bank in which Tuebingen participates allows for easy change of the main entry form, if this should be necessary. Each author has an identity number and the computer automatically makes the correction for all entries under this identity number. This data-bank also has a cooperate-body authority file. This is one of the most difficult cataloguing questions for South Asia where we have numerous cooperate bodies and languages. In which language should the main entry for the cooperate body be made ? Even the question wether a cooperate body is involved or not is not always easy to decide.

In rent years a new medium of publishing, **microform,** has been increasingly put on the market. Although some specific cataloguing rules have been developed this type of document still has no internationally recognised standard for cataloguing. In many cases the institutions mentioned here have to protect their older material because of deterioration and can only offer the researcher a microfilm or microfiche copy. Due to the condition of antiquaria in South Asia the question of making microfilm facilities in South Asia available is gaining in importance. The long journey to Europe in many cases would damage delicate antiquaria to such an extent, that it is only sensible to reproduce them in advance in microform on the spot. This medium could then be sent to the requesting library in Europe. The Library of Congress Office in Delhi has been doing this for a number of years now.

Conclusion

Many of you may be familiar with the acquisition activities of the Library of Congress in Washington, D.C. and its office in New Delhi. The aim of this programme is to procure South Asian literature for interested academic libraries in the United States. The literature is bought, catalogued and forwarded to the individual participating libraries in the USA. When we consider the increasing difficulties we have in

Europe to find qualified personnel and to have sufficient personnel at all, we too, in these times of a fascinating political development in Europe should seriously consider, either participating in this LOC-programme, if this is possible for non-American academic libraries, or even better, establish a common European procuring office in South Asia to supply interested academic libraries in Europe with the desired South Asian literature. Each library would be responsible for the formulation of its own literature profile. The cataloguing data could be delivered in the form of magnetic tapes or discettes. The recipient libraries would then only have to integrate the data into its own data-bank and after having given each book its individual call-number add the book to its stock. I estimate that there would be at least 20 such libraries in Europe which would be interested in such a processing centre in South Asia. It is time we give serious consideration to such possible rationalisation methods.

When one studies such wide-spread special collections one cannot overlook the fact that co-ordinated international efforts are necessary to make this material uniformily available. Although acquisitions may in many cases be duplication still there is a great amount of material available only in one particular library collection. Through documentation of these collections the researcher will have quick access to them and know where special collections are located.

Our ability to keep our special subject collections alive, vital and relevant, to keep them in the new discourse of teaching and research, to integrate them into larger contexts wherever possible will be the key to our successes. The relative costs and benefits of building and maintaining special collections in times of dwindling resources are very much a part of our scenario and closely related to matters of management and organisational culture.

The management culture of the 90's — with us already — values speed, flexibility, opportunism, entrepreneurship. This is the culture of high technology. Therefore we should look to co-operative collection development and management programmes for South Asian literature.

There can be no doubt that the role of South Asia in world research will grow. Its population is immense, its economic development of great importance. The European Common Market has begun to realize the importance of this region and seems to believe that co-operation in its development will benefit both the region and Europe.

Our academic institutions dealing with South Asia must however try to keep a balance between new and traditional studies. A true understanding of the contemporary situation can only be obtained through a thorough knowledge of the past.

These remarks have been primarily from the standpoint of research in Europe, but our colleagues in South Asia should strengthen their efforts to preserve and enlarge their own collections. Many weaker cultural areas of the region will surely disappear in this modernizing age and without any contemporary documentation these cultures will be inevitably lost to posterity. After independence there have been traditional relationships between the former English colonies of South Asia and England, mainly due to the common English language, but it certainly will be a duty in the future of all members of the European Community to train librarians and support efforts to develop publishing, the book trade and librarianship throughout the region.

SELECTED BIBLIOGRAPHY

(1) Arberry, A.J.: The India Office Library — a historical sketch. London: Commonwealth Office 1967. 108 p.

(2) La Bibliothéque de I'Ecole Nationale des Languages Orientales Vivantes. Paris: Imprimerie nationale de France. 1948. in: Cent-cinquantenaire de I'Ecole des Langues Orientales.

(3) Datta, Rajeshwari: Guide to South Asian materials in the libraries of London, Oxford and Cambridge. 2nd ed. Cambridge: University. 1966. 18 1.

(4) Debout, Marion: La Bibliothèque de I'Ecole des Langues Orientales. pp 26-38.

(5) Les imprimes indiens à la Bibliothèque Nationale.

(6) India Office Library and Records. Guide to the European printed book collection. London: India Office Library. n.d.

(7) Mémoires de la Société de l'histoire de Paris. 1893.

(8) Mémoires de littérature.... de l'Académie Royale des Inscriptions. T. xliv. (1808).

(9) Meuvret, Colette: La Bibliothèque de l'Ecole Nationale des Langues Orientales Vivantes. Paris: Imprimerie Nationale de France. 1948. pp 395-408.

in: Cent - cinquartenaire de l'Ecole des Langues Orientales.

(10) Omont, Henri: Missions archéologiques francaises en Orient aux xvii-e et xviii-e siécles documents publiés par.... 1.2. Paris: Imprimerie Nationale 1902.

(11) School of Oriental and African Studies. University of London. Library catalogue. Boston, Mass.: Hall. 1963.

28 vols. (author, title and subject)

Suppl. 1: 1968. 16 vols.

Suppl. 2: 1973. 16 vols.

Suppl. 3: 1979. 19 vols.

Suppl. 4: Zug. ca 1986. 363 microfiches.

(12) Shaw, Graham: The South Asia and Burma Retrospective Bibliography (SABRAEB). STAGE I: 1556-1800. Compiled by Graham Shaw.

London: The British Library 1987. 554 p.

Networks of Specialized Information Services in Latin America

ELIZABET MARIA RAMOS DE CARVALHO and IVONE TÁLAMO

1. INTRODUCTION

Due to socioeconomic problems in underdeveloped countries, we have to increasingly endeavour in order to integrate their cultural, scientific and technological potentialities so as to produce an *articulation* that may ensure a coherent and well balanced development of the Region.

Devices that can ensure a better awareness of these potentialities and types of information *exchange* should be set up so as to maximize the available resources and disseminate broadly this data, which should always reach the users in proper form and especially be available when decisions have to be made either by public or private organizations protecting the social, cultural and economic interests of our countries. We should make the best out the developments achieved in this field, rationalize the use of resources and cooperation and should introduce new information technologies in such a way that information may be taken as a *resource* and so that, in each country, it will be acknowledged both as regional offer and demand.

In Latin America and in the Caribbean, networking is increasingly expanding itself, because it is through resource sharing that we may have access to the information we need, avoid unnecessary duplications and grant access to existing available information in the region, in due time and at reduced costs.

In this study, we first define networks and information systems, because these terms are often used interchangeably. We deal with the advantages of networking and its structure, leading to the description of networks found in Latin America and in the Caribbean. However, this study is neither exhaustive nor intends to be seen as pioneer, but may stimulate other studies to go perhaps deeper.

Since we are fully aware of the importance of knowing about, having access to and making use of the services and products of networks found in the Region, we are including an annex containing their addresses, so as to facilitate the indispensable approach for supplying the needed informational resources in Latin America and in the Caribbean.

2. INFORMATION NETWORKS OR INFORMATION SYSTEMS ?

Relying on a revision of literature made by Baldúino and on studies of Araújo and Paula, we are led to the conclusion that, usually, the terms "networking" and "system" are used interchangeably. The SLA Networking Committee defines network as "a formal arrangement according to which several libraries and other organizations engage in a common standard for information exchange, materials and /or services, having as target a functional purpose."

Gray of the British Library gives the following definition : "An information network is essentially a means of joining a large variety of users. This definition departs from the idea that each source is based on certain resources and that these resources, even if possibly elaborated for a specific purpose, should be shared by all that can profit from them."

On the other hand, Von Bertalanffy, in his *General Theory of Systems*, defines a system as a "complex of interacting elements".

According to Paula, as a good example we can take the INIS - International System of Atomic Energy, which is called a *system*. Also the ISONET - the ISO network, which is called *net*. In both cases, however, the model of organization and performance is practically the same, for example : decentralized information gathering, centralized processing and integration of information, and decentralized use and distribution. This example shows that both the terms indicate same meaning.

For further clarification, we reproduce here the chart "Basic differences between the concepts of 'network' and 'system'", taken from Balduíno's dissertation:

NETWORKS	SYSTEMS
— Interconnected elements	— Integrated elements
— Common objectives	— Specific objectives (of the system)
— Autonomous components	— Interdependent components

— Individual characteristics	— Standardization
— Cooperation	— Intercomplementarity
— The lack of one component will not endanger the attainment of the network aims as a whole	— The lack of one component will endanger the attainment of the system aims as a whole

A full account of the application of these basic differences is specified in the above mentioned dissertation. Balduíno arrives at the following conclusions regarding the definition of networks and systems :

- — The network is formed for the attainment of a common purpose when the components agree to comply with conventions, attributions, etc.
- — The system is conceived, philosophically, as a definition of attributions of each element of a set designed to attain a pre-determined objective;
- — Whereas the network components interact and reach effective communications, producing mutual exchanges of influence and so configuring a king of interdependence, the system consolidates and enlarges itself. Thus the network components may also become parts of a system;
- — It is impossible for a network to exist completely deprived of a system, even if it is present only as a philosophical concept of the network as a whole; and
- — The system, on the contrary, can exist independently from a network.

This verification allows us to conclude that the two realities under study - "network" and "system" - may co-exist in the same structure and the name chosen, be it network or system.

In Latin America and the Caribbean also these terms are used interchangeably to designate programs of cooperation aiming at a common purpose.

Taking the above into consideration, we will use the term "network" in the present study.

3. INFORMATION NETWORKS

The ultimate objective of networking is to offer wider and better services to the users, at reduced unit costs and on time. It is the isolated units would get ready to become integrated and share services and collections, constituting a "common fund" from which every user may get support.

Among the advantages of networking, we can emphasize some aspects such as: better utilization of information, allowing broader information sharing by an increasing number of users aware of their requirements. Also as an advantage, there is the non-duplication of services and products, which avoids costs with unnecessary duplication. Prompt service is another benefit of networking, since the alternative methods in formulating search strategies for information are broadened. Sharing the development of common services and products allows economy of costs, which will benefit the participants of the network.

3.1 Configuration of the Information Networks

Among several studies on the structure of information networks, we have singled out Linstone and Shoene's suggestion that the following factors deserve consideration : function, scope, large number of clients, organizational basis, availability of workmanship, degree of centralization of authority and production of imported technology as compared to domestic.

The same authors, while examining factors and conditions prevailing in Latin America, concluded that the model tending to centralization is the most adequate for the Region.

On the other hand, Grolier considers that according to their territorial extension, networks comprise :

a — Infranational level (local and regional)

b — National

c — Supranational (regional and world-wide)

a — Infranational level : local and regional networks

As an example, we can quote the networks of public, university and other libraries which, as a rule, are co-ordinated by a central library and constitute the most representative models of local networks.

b — National level

It comprises national information systems or networks, planned and structures so as to meet the information requirements of a certain country. In Latin America, these networks cover mostly science and technology fields. A typical example of this kind of network is the Mexican Scientific and Technical Information System developed by the National Council for Sciences and Technology [Conselho Nacional de Ciencias Technologia (CONACYT)].

c — Supranational level

It covers multinational firms and international or regional information systems as well as international networks sponsored by UNISIST (World System of Scientific Information).

Examples of this kind are networks directed toward information requirements existing in Latin America and in the Caribbean.

4. OVERVIEW OF INFORMATION NETWORKS IN LATIN AMERICA AND IN THE CARIBBEAN

In underdeveloped countries, the concept of network, as we have already mentioned earlier is being well accepted, because it is with networking we the economically less favoured countries, find a solution to have access to required information at a reasonable cost.

In a Seminar on the Experiences of the Regional Information Networks in Latin America, in Havana - Cuba, in 1988, observations on the development, handling and utilization of networks were discussed.

As an overview, this shows that the first network established in the Region was designed for data base in technology and science fields, including agriculture (AGRINTER) and health (BIREME). Another example in the field of education is REDUC, which was created in order to facilitate communication among researchers in the field, forming a data base comprising information and resumes.

In the same study, it is said that the failure of some networks is due to the fact that they could not rely on strong support of a regional organization and that of others resulted from the fact that their initial objectives were superseded. The benefits of some networks have not been limited to the participating information units. Their influence has reached other institutions. The focal points of some networks have served to introduce new concepts and methodologies in the field of information, as well as to demonstrate new technologies already in use. The networks also have a decisive role in the organization of national system and specialized information services in a country. This study also demonstrates that there is a strong exchange between networks, especially during their first stages of existence. However, there is no systematic registration and dissemination of these experiences for the networks operating in the region, which could possibly serve to overcome several problems that generally occur.

4.1 General information on networks operating in Latin America and in the Caribbean

In our study the following networks have been reviewed : BIREME, DOCPAL, REDUC, REPIDISCA, RIALIDE, RIBLAC, RICORR, RITLA, SIAMAZ and INFOPLAN.

For each of them a short historical presentation will be given, mentioning its aims, products and services. [respective addresses are given in Annex 1.]

LATIN AMERICAN AND CARIBBEAN INFORMATION CENTRE FOR HEALTH SCIENCES

[CENTRO LATINOAMERICANO Y DEL CARIBE DE INFORMACTIÓN EN CIENCIAS DE LA SALUD (BIREME)]

The Latin American and Caribbean Information Centre for Health Sciences, formerly called Regional Medical Library [Biblioteca Regional de Medicina (BIREME)], was one of the first networks in the region. It was founded in 1967 by means of an agreement between the Pan-American Health Organization [Organizatión Pan-Americana de la Salud (OPS)] and the Brazilian Government.

Its purpose is to establish a regional Information and Documentation System in Health Sciences, and its structure is that of a cooperative network designed to meet the information requirements of health professionals at any level and in any place wherever they may be.

BIREME is the coordinating centre; its structure reckons with domestic co-ordinating centres, an advisers' committee and technical staff.

During its first years, it functioned as co-ordinating and centralizing unit for activities and services, facilitating access to international biomedical literature, especially to texts issued in Latin America and in the Caribbean, and giving training to the participants of the system. Among its responsibilities it also had to create a Latin American data base and to process all the literature to be integrated into the system; later it changed to decentralized co-ordination, allocating specific and precise responsibilities to the participating institutions.

In Brazil, its national co-ordinator, it has 298 libraries, 30 cooperators, 15 collaborators and other participants.

To become a participating unit, the basic requirements are as follows: a microcomputer, a CD-ROM reader and a printer; and for teleprocessing; a modern and a facsimile. Having a modular structure gives the Library the opportunity of developing further inside the network.

It is responsible for supplying information in the fields of human, environmental and public health, nutrition, hygiene, sanitation, environmental contamination and food supplies.

Among its service stand out bibliographical research according to the Medline and LILACs system, bibliographical exchange and Selective Dissemination of Information (LACRIP).

It is responsible for creating the data base LILACs, which includes literature concerning health sciences by Latin American and Caribbean authors since 1980, and publishes the Index Medicus Latinoamericano (IMLA), which includes 150 Latin American periodicals.

DOCUMENTATION SYSTEM ON POPULATION IN LATINAMERICA [SISTEMA DE DOCUMENTACIÓN SOBRE POBLACION EN AMERICA LATINA DOCPAL)]

It was founded in 1976 by the Latin American Demography Centre [Centro Latinoamericano de Demografia (CELADe)] from the CEPAL System of the United Nations with the support of the International Development Research Centre (IDRC) [Centro Internacional de Investigaciones para el Desarrollo (CIID) in Canada. It has been maintained by the United Nations Fund for Population Activities [Fondo de Naciones Unidas para Actividades de Población (FNUAP)] and by CEPAL.

Its objective is to improve the flow of information about population in Latin America and in the Caribbean, to organize and disseminate the documents produced in the region, especially those having significance for its economic and social development. It maintains a bibliographical data base and makes contributions to the collection of the CELADE Library, collection information related to this subject matter.

Information available through this network cover population in general, geographical distribution of migration, fertility and mortality, marriages and family.

Among its products and services, besides the data base initially constituted by the CELADE Library collection with some editions recorded on CD-ROM together with LILACs, it also publishes "DOCPAL: Summaries about population in Latin America, bibliographical research and bibliographical exchange service".

INFORMATION AND DOCUMENTATION NETWORK ON EDUCATION FOR LATIN AMERICA AND THE CARIBBEAN

[RED DE INFORMACIÓN Y DOCUMENTACIÓN EN AMERICA LATINA Y EL CARIBE (REDUC)]

REDUC grew out of the necessity of professionals in the field of education to have access to literature related to their areas of activity produced in Latin America and in the Caribbean.

The main goal of this network is to identify, assemble, summarize, divulge and disseminate documents produced in the field of education in the region.

REDUC is a cooperative, decentralized network constituted by a coordinating centre, and special and national centres - a total of 23 centre at present. Studies are being made in order to transform it into a Non-Governmental Information Organization (ONGI), so as to obtain more funds for its development. Brazil participates in this network through Carlos Chagas Foundation with 80% of the literature on education produced in the region.

The products and services offered by this network are analytical summaries [Resumenes Analiticos de Education (RAE)], in national and Latin America editions, RAE indexes, microfiche carrying the complete text of documents data base in CD-ROM to be issued together with LILACs, national and subject bibliographies, seminars and so forth.

PAN-AMERICAN INFORMATION AND DOCUMENTATION NETWORK IN SANITARY ENGINEERING AND ENVIRONMENTAL SCIENCES

[RED PANAMERICANA DE INFORMACIÓN Y DOCUMENTACIÓN EN INGENIERIA SANITARIA Y CIENCIAS DEL AMBIENTE (REPIDISCA)]

The network started functioning in 1981 and was co-ordinated by the Regional OPS Centre, Pan-American Centre of Sanitary Engineering and Environmental Sciences [Centro Panamericano de Ingenieria Sanitaria Y Ciencias de Ambiente (CEPIS)], with its headquarters in Lima, Peru, and by the International Development Research Centre (IRDC) of Canada.

The purpose for establishing this network was to develop an infrastructure so as to facilitate access to information and documents generated inside specialized institutions in the field of sanitary engineering and environmental sciences, as well as to maintain exchange with the cooperating centres in Latin America and in the Caribbean. The network has a coordination and exchange centre, a library, undertakes information analyses and has a data base in CD-ROM, published together with LILACs data base (BIREME).

Funds are received from 300 regional institutions; only in Brazil there are 31 such cooperating centres. The network is decentralized; in each country there is a co-ordinating unit and several cooperating centres. Brazil, due to its territorial magnitude, owns two co-ordinating centres: one for the southern region, with headquarters at the Technology and Basic Sanitation Company [Companhia de Tecnologia e Saneamento Básico (CETESB)], in São Paulo, another in Brasília, FD, with headquarters at the Brazilian Institute for the Environment [Instituto Brasileiro do Meio-Ambiente (IBAMA)], for the rest of the country. The network has approximately 27.000 documents with annual additions of 3.000. Its services and products are : REPINDEX (Bibliography), TABACONT, Thesaurus of Sanitary Engineering and Environmental Sciences, general catalogue, catalogue of the CEPIS Library and CD-ROM containing a data base and manuals; assistance is given to companies that integrate the network concerning organization and automation of their libraries; bibliographical surveys and reproduction of documents are performed.

INFORMATION NETWORKS OF THE LATIN AMERICAN ASSOCIATION OF FINANCIAL DEVELOPMENT INSTITUTIONS [REDES DE INFORMACIÓN DE ASSOCIACIÓN LATINOAMERICANA DE INSTITUCIONES FINANCIERAS DE DESARROLLO (RIALIDE)]

RIALIDE was founded by the Latin American Association of Financial Development Institutions [Associación Latinoamricana de Instituiciones Financieras de Desarrollo (ALIDE)], in order to the information requirements of financial development institutions in Latin America. It is formed by part of the main libraries and documentation centre of ALIDE member institutions.

The main goal of the network is to strengthen cooperation, operative and technical capacity of the participating libraries and thus make accessible financial and related information to its users to provide support for decisions, studies and research.

To fulfil the goals of the network, three projects have been developed in 1991: Consolidation and co-ordination of ALIDE Information Network, consolidation of ALIDE Documentation Centre and provide technical assistance to the information units of financial development institutions.

The network has a co-ordinating unit and national centres with mini-networks. It supplies bibliographical statistical and legal information concerning capital investment in projects. It supports biblio-graphical data base in legislation and projects in development and financing sources, besides these services Financial and Technological Information about Projects and Investments [Información Financiera y Tecnológica sobre projects y Inversiones (SIFT)], are available upon request.

INFORMATION NETWORK IN BIOSCIENCES FOR LATIN AMERICA AND THE CARIBBEAN [RED DE INFORMACIÓN EN BIOCIENCIAS PARA LATINOAMERICA Y EL CARIBE (RIBLAC)]

RIBLAC was developed with the aid of the General Information

Programme PGI of UNESCO, in order to foster cooperation among institutions specializing in biosciences in Latin America and in the Caribbean.

It is a referral information network and covers the fields of general and molecular biology, biotechnology, biomedicine and related subjects. Its data base has been built with the information supplied by the network participants and it provides information on biosciences, projects in progress, institutions and events related to this field.

The Regional Co-ordinating Centre has its headquarters at the Venezuelan Scientific Research Institute [Instiuto Venezoelano de Investigaciones Cientificas (IVIC)], in Caracas, Venezuela.

In a meeting that took place in Venezuela in April 1992 the following recommendations were made: dissemination of information will be processed semi-annually through supply of disks; the Regional Centre should generate, as a by-product, a bilingual Portuguese - Spanish dictionary having as starting point the information generated in Brazil; e-mail service will be used for any kind of communication; the RIBLAC Bulletin should have information content pages.

IBERO-AMERICAN NETWORK OF TECHNOLOGICAL INFORMATION ON CORROSION [REDE IBERO-AMERICANA DE INFORMAÇAO TECNOLÓGICA SOBRE CORROSAO (RICORR)]

The network was created at a meeting in Medelin, Colombia, in 1991, where the following countries participated: Argentina, Brazil, Colombia, Spain, Mexico, Peru, Portugal and Venezuela.

RICORR integrates the XV Corrosion Sub-program/ Environmental Impact on Materials and the Ibero-American Program of Science and Technology for Development. The objective of the network is to establish and turn operative an Ibero- American Technological Information Network on Corrosion, with special emphasis on dissumination of information related to corrosion, anti-corrosion protection and available technology. The network should be structured so as to strengthen the technological capacity of the participating countries, stimulating innovation, supplying and facilitating the use of information especially to small and medium sized companies.

The methods and procedures for RICORR will be established and it will render efficient service analysing and evaluating information in easy language for the user; the network will contribute to disseminate information and therefore these guides should contain: titles of specialized periodicals in the field published in the network member countries, research centres on corrosion, consulting firms, qualification and specialization courses, information and documentation centre functioning in the member countries and national technical standards in the field of corrosion and protection set up by the countries participating in the network.

The compilation of information for the Guide will be undertaken by the representatives of the Network in each country and will be co-ordinated by Brazilian representatives, who will be in charge of editing and publishing.

Small brochures will present basic information on corrosion and protection against corrosion in simple language so as to make the content easily understandable non-specialists in the field.

The activities foreseen for the future are as follows : preparation of a technical glossary, audio-visual packages publish a bulletin and implementation of a data base which will contain information on Ibero—American production in the field.

LATIN AMERICAN NETWORK OF TECHNOLOGICAL INFORMATION [REDE DE INFORMAÇAO TECNOLÓGICA LATINO-AMERICANA (RITLA)]

The RITLA executive committee was created in 1983 according to a decision of the Latin American Counsel of the Latin American Economic System [Sistema Econômico Latino Americano (SELA)] which, in compliance with a Brazilian request, designated the country as headquarters. In 1990, an act was passed by the Brazilian government, RITLA was formally established in Brazil.

Besides Brazil, the following countries are members of the network: Argentina, Mexico, Nicaragua, and Venezuela.

The main objectives of RITLA are:

(a) To support the development of infrastructures, technological information systems for the member countries and to promote their full utilization by governmental and private support;

(b) To foster permanent co-ordination and cooperation so that the exchange of technological information takes place in accordance with the requirements of the participating countries;

(c) To consolidate national and regional competence in generating their own technologies;

(d) To support and improve the ability of member countries in search for, negotiation, evaluation, adaptation and employment of imported types of technology;

(e) To stimulate the formation and qualification of the human resources required for technological development of the member countries;

(f) To promote exchange of technico - economical information in order to strengthen the link between supply and demand of regional technology;

(g) To extend technological cooperation among member countries by means of dissemination of existing opportunities and other activities which respond to the problems and challenges arising from regional cooperation;

(h) To establish linkages with other international, regional or sub-regional technological information systems or networks. In order to avoid non-productive superpositions RITLA will be integrated with the National Council for Scientific and Technological Development [Conselho National do Desenvolvimento Científico e Tecnológico (CNPQ)], through the National Research Network [Rede Nacional de Pesquisa (RNP)], a project developed by the National Council which will allow an optimization in transmission of data for researchers and research institutions, ensuring compatibility of technological solutions, efficiency in the network connections, and conditions for dissemination of electronical networks for data transmission in the States and regions of the country.

Arrangements are being made with the Brazilian Institute of Scientific Technological Information [Instituto Brasileiro de Informação Científica e Tecnológica (IBICT)], to provide technical support for the utilization of the network and establish contacts between the Brazilian "Nuclei of Technological Information".

UNIDO has recommended close interaction between its Data Bank in Industrial Technology and RITLA to encourage better understanding within the region and sub - region.

AMAZONIAN INFORMATION SYSTEM

[SISTEMA DE INFORMACAO DA AMAZONIA (SIAMAZ)]

The idea of an Information System in the Amazonia Region originated in the recommendations of the First Scientific and Technological Meeting of the countries which signed the Amazonia Cooperation Treaty [Tratado de Cooperação Amazôpnica (TCA)] in 1924, namely: Bolivia, Brazil, Colombia, Equador, Guiana, Peru, Suriname and Venezuela.

In 1988, during the International Seminar on Amazonian Scientific, Technological and Cultural Information and Documentation, which took place in Iquitos, Peru, a proposal was made for the institutionalization of the Amazonia Information System [Sistema de Informação da Amazônia (SIAMAZ)], which occurred in 1990.

This system is a fundamental instrument for efficient Pan - Amazonia cooperation in collecting, processing, recuperating and disseminating scientific, technological and cultural information of the region, interconnecting with the member institutions of the Association of Amazonia Universities [Associação de Universidada Amazônicas (UNAMAZ)], through a computor based information network.

This is a decentralized network and each country has a national co-ordinating centre which is responsible for the operationality of its network for collecting and processing of information generated inside its borders and for incoporating the same into the System.

Among the services and products there is a data base containing bibliographical references, referral information (institutions, experts and researchers, research and development studies), factual information and information on legislation related to the Amazonia Region; bibliographical exchange services, analytical summaries, directories of institutions and experts, events calendar, publication in CD-ROM of research work on the Amazonian Region.

Federal University of Pará, Brazil is, presently, the Regional co-ordinating Centre of the SIAMAZ.

INFORMATION SYSTEM FOR PLANNING IN LATIN AMERICA AND IN THE CARIBBEAN

[SISTEMA DE INFORMACIÓN PARA LA PLANIFICACIÓN EN AMERICA LATINA Y EL CARIBE (INFOPLAN)]

The INFOLAN system was founded in 1979 by the Economical Committee for Latin America and the Caribbean [Comissión Económical para America Latina y el Caribe (CEPAL)], with the financia aid of the International Development Research Centre (IDRC) to meet the information requirements for planning economic and social development of Latin America and the Caribbean.

The INFOPLAN is responsible for bibliographical coordination and cooperation among underdeveloped countries, controlling, analysing and disseminating information generated by these countries. The system consists of a regional decentralized network formed by the participation of cooperative centrés within the region.

The system covers all the documentation generated in Latin America and in the Caribbean written in French, English, Portuguese and Spanish, related to socioeconomic planning, global, regional and local programs and projects.

The INFOPLAN system is the most important project of CLADES and functions as general co-ordinator of studies and researches about the most efficient documentation techniques, provides technical assistance and promotes qualification courses to enable the personnel to operate the system on regional and national levels.

Among products and services of INFOPLAN are:

(a) Publications - EL PLANINDEX, Regional, the first INFOPLAN product, National PLANINDEX, INFOPLAN Series and INFOPLAN Bulletin.

(b) Services - Bibliographical research, data base consultation service, reference services, document distribution service.

5. CONCLUSION

It becomes clear in this study that the networks are quite similar : a database and a bibliography or a specialized index which recompiles the information generated in the region at pre-determined regular intervals.

After analysing several aspects of this study, we come to the conclusion that information networks or systems can be set up and successfully used in institutions. However, to implement, operate and maintain them we should take into account such aspects as infrastructure, human resource and technological factors which have been responsible for their success or failure. Therefore, some basic steps should be followed such as establishing a policy guidelines determining the resources to be demployed and the cost involved in each case.

There is great motivation for implementing networks in Latin America and in the Caribbean due to the similarity in the requirements of these countries, these networks are often cease operation because of the political and economic instability in member countries, which prevent the goals to be fully achieved unless the networks can rely on substantial support from a Regional or International Organization.

And finally we would like to stress the necessity for the networks to undertake systematic public relation work aimed at government agencies institutions and individual users, focuing on the mutual benefits that may be gained from networking such as resource sharing, acquiring a large number of informative materials and offering services at low cost.

REFERÊNCIAS BIBLIOGRÁFICAS

AKHTAR, S. - Las redes latinoamericanas de información; observaciones sobre su desarrollo, manejo y utilizaçãciõn. In : Seminario. Faller sobre experiencias de las redes regionales de informacions en America Latina. Habana, Cuba, out. 1988.

BALDUINO, P. Politica de compartilhamento de recursos informacionais nas redes e sistemas de informação em instituições do poder publico brasileiro. Brinba, UNB, 1988. Dissertação de mestrado em Biblioteconomia.

CENTRO PANAMERICANO DE INGENIERIA SANITARIA Y CIENCIAS DEL AMBIENTE (Peru). Grupo consultivo sobre informações en Ingenieria Sanitária y Ciências Ambientales: informe final. Lima : CEPIS, 14-16 nov. 1977. 32p.

JORGE, Arleti Botlesini. *Rede de informações ambientais:* um projecto que deu certo. São Paulo, CETESB, 1992. (No prelo)

GRAZIANI, Maria Pulcheria Amaral & Stenzel, Norma. CEPAL/CLADES e o Sistema INFOPLAN. *In*: Congresso Brasileiro DE Biblioteconomia E Documentação, 16, Salvador, 22-27 set., 1991. Anais.... Slavador, APBEB, v. 1: 764-777.

DE GROLIER E. - Esquisse d'une ētude comparative des réseaux d' information; introduction. In: RESEAU et systémes de documentation; texts réunis par Raymond Guilloux.

Paris, Gauthier - Villars, 1975. pp. 1-48.

INFORMATIVO IBICT. Brasilia, maio/ junho, 1991.

LISTON JR, M & SCHOENE, M.L. Basic elements of planning and design of national and regional information systems Washington, D.C., OEA, 1971. p.39.

PARKER, T.F. - Resource Sharing from the inside out : reflections on the organizational nature of library networks. *Library Resources and Technical Services*, 19(4): 349-55, Fall 1975.

PAULA, A.C.M. - Redes e sistemas de Informação: elementos conceituais. Rio de Janeiro, 1979. 45p.

PINHEIRO, L.V.R etal. - Estudo de viabilidade de participação de unidades de informação em programa cooperativos de automação. Relaóprio de pesquisa. Rio de Janeiro, UFRJ/ECO, 1989. 84p. (projeto apoiado pelo PADCT).

PRAT Y TRABAL, Ana Maria. Analisis comparativo de las redes de informacion de América Latina y el Caribe. IN: AKHTAR, Shahid, redactor. *Las redes latinoamericanas de información:* observaciones sobre su desarrollo, manejo y utilización. Informe del Seminario-taller sobre experiencias las redes regionales de informacion en América Latina. La Habana, Cuba: 20-22, octubre 1988. Spīndice, p.55.

ANNEX

ADDRESSES OF THE COORDENATOR CENTRES

BIREME
Centro Lationoamericano y del Caribe de Información en
Ciencias de la Salud
Rua Botucatu, 862
04023 São Paulo - SP
Brasil
Tel.: (011) 549-2611

DOCPAL
Centro Latinoamericano de Demografia
Edificio Naciones Unidas
Casilla 91, Santiago - Chile

INFOPLAN
Centro Latinoamericano de Documentación Economica y social (CLADES) Edificio Naciones Unidas
Avda. Dag Hammarskjold, s/n
Casilla 179-D
Santiago-Chile

REDUC
Rede de Información y Documentación en Educatión para America Latina y el Caribe
Erasmo Escala 1825
Casilla 13608
Santiago-Chile

REPIDISCA
Rede Panamericana de Información y documentación en Ingenieria Sanitaria y ciencias del Ambiente
Centro Panamericano de Ingenieria Sanitaria y Ciencia del Ambiente (CEPIS)
Los Pinos 259 Urb. Camacho
Lima 12, Peru
Casilla de Correo 4337
Lima 100, Peru
Tel.: (5114) 37-1077
Fax (5114) 37-8289

RIALIDE
Centro de Documentación, Secretaria General de ALIDE
Paseo de la republica 3211 s.1
Apartado Postal 3988
Lima 27, Peru

RIBLAC
Instituto Venezolano de Investigaciones Científicas
Apartado (POB) 21827
Caracas 1020-A - Venezuela

RICORR
Instituto National de Tecnologia
Centro de Documentação
Av. Venezuela, 82
20081 rio de Janeiro - RJ
Brasil

RITLA

SIAMAZ
Centro Coordenador Regional
Universidade federal do Para
Campus Universitário - Guamá
Caixa Postal 558
66050 Belém - Para
Brasil

Initiatives to Facilitate Access to S&T Information in India

ABHIJIT LAHIRI

Introduction

The imperative to enhance farm productivity to feed the growing millions, the necessity to build an industrial base with up to date technology and the desirability of promoting the services sector to bring about an improvement in the life-style of the population, make it essential for India to be a constant participant in the activities on new and the emerging areas of science and technology (S&T). The need to strengthen information services is therefore not a matter of debate, how it should be done is more important.

Most consumers in a developing country like India are generally accustomed to a poor level of services; information service is no exception. The consumers do not know what to ask for; nor they realize that the services could be or ought to be better. An information user takes a lot of pains to collect information and perhaps he expects that anybody in need of that information should undergo similar troubles and therefore, he does not share information with others. The drudgery involved in the collection process further dampens the initiatives to use information. Such characteristics invariably lead to the dormancy of demand.

On the other hand, Information managers are equally constrained and lack exposure to the variety of modern alternatives and adequate infrastructural facilities. They also need to manage their services with frozen financial inputs. Further, their activities in an institution are viewed as a purely supporting function. However, skills are not lacking and given proper facilities and environment it would not be difficult for them to adopt modern information concepts, tools and techniques.

Science & Technology Scenario

The total R&D expenditure in India, now stands at about one percent of the Gross national Product. In absolute terms, it was Rs. 34.72 billion in 1988-89 in which the share of private industry was Rs. 3.64 billion. As much as 67% of the total amount was spent on applied research and experimental development. It is also interesting to note that 80% of the investments went towards non-defense research which by and large generated information in public domain.

India is well-endowed with a huge stock of S&T manpower. The estimate was 3.4 million in 1990; out of them 81% were economically active. However, only 268 thousand were engaged in research and development related S&T areas. Enrolment of students in the institutions of higher education is equally astounding. As many as 3.8 million were in 164 universities and 6,597 colleges in 1987-1988; 29.5% of them were in S&T faculties. It is also worthwhile to note that there were as many as 242 thousand teaching staff in higher education sector.

The purpose of quoting these gross estimates is to provide an understanding of the order of magnitude of the size and potential STI market and user population.

STI Market

The magnitude of investments in S&T would support the contention that the market is likely to sustain a sizable volume of STI transactions. Precise information is not available on STI investments. A quick estimates puts it at US $ 185 million excluding overhead costs. This is perhaps an underestimate.

Indian institutions have been subscribing heavily to printed copies of databases. Recently several service facilities were created to provide STI and custom search services in batch mode using databases on magnetic tapes and CD-ROM. Facilities for accessing international online datahosts are now available though by and large concentrated in a few metropolitan cities. So far, no datahost for public access has been established.

India has made considerable progress in the recent past in the field of computer communication and networking. Implementation of the PSDN is however, considerably delayed. Several data networks using satellite and microwave communication and ordinary landlines have come to existence and many more are being planned. Besides, an international gateway has also been established.

Two essential ingredients to sustain a viable market already exist viz. a sizable population of consumers and the user capacity to pay for services. However, the situation is rather weak in respect of the development of products and services and their distribution system.

The principle concern is to increase the market share of modern information products and services in relation to the traditional ones. Presently, this share is very small. That is why perhaps, ESA - RS did not pursue the early lead it had gained during the 80's; Maxwell Communications did not bother even to enter the Indian market or DIALOG maintains a low-level of presence. In contrast, all the database publishers have a good business of hard copies; peculiarly, they are not aggressive in marketing their CD-ROM products.

Promotional & Executive Institutions

Role of Government

Private investment is an index to a real demand, while public expenditure is aimed at social well-being. With stable interests like profitability, expansion and diversification, private investments tend to be efficient. With changing social goals, public interest may also result in varied success.

Government efforts or public funding would be welcome to develop the market, but it must be realized that there is a limit up to which it can go. Perhaps, public investment on information (at constant prices) will never be more than that in the last decade. The following courses of action may be explored:

— All information products and services whether generated through public funding or otherwise may be priced to offset the costs in part or full.

— All information on centers may optimize their resources or infrastructural build-up individually and collectively.

— Actions may be taken to attract private investments on information industry. Book publishing excluded, such investments so far have been of low order. The most essential measures in this direction would include:

Recognition of information as an *industry*

Provision of liberalized credit to entrepreneurs by banks

Provision of venture/risk capital to entrepreneurs by financial institutions

Granting of liberal tax benefits in the initial years of operation

— The private enterprises may also be allowed to use information resources and infrastructure of government and government supported institutions on reasonable terms.

— The responsibility of dissemination of government information may also be given to the private enterprises. In this context the initiatives taken by the Department of Trade and Industries, U.K on tradeable government information might be recalled.

Role of Non-profit Organizations

Internationally, non-profit organizations run some of the most successful database ventures e.g. CAS and INSPEC. In India, though non-profit organizations are involved, the growth of the industry has been dismal. This may be attributed to the composition of the sector itself—here the organizations are largely government owned or supported. Such organizations are generally concerned more with meeting the social welfare objectives and not taking a path of self-sustenance. They neither compete among themselves nor face competition from outside. On the contrary, they give unfair competition to the private enterprises from a favourable financial platform and preferential tax benefits. Further these operate in a situation where the demand exceeds the supply. As a result, the services do not improve in response to the needs of users.

Role of Profit Organizations

The low share of private sector to research and development (about 10% of total investment) indirectly indicates the magnitude of their STI infrastructure. In fact, apart from a few centers, most of them draw heavily from public libraries and information centers.

In India, apart from the book publishers and sellers, information companies do not exist. Though information brokers could have a field day by maintaining a line of supply between potentially information hungry customers and passive sources of supply, as yet there has not been many success stories. Few market research and management consultancy organizations offer database services, but only relating to consumer products.

If India is to come out of the library - based information culture and adopt modern information products and services the concept of *marketing* would have to be adopted. The concept includes a wide range of activities such as the understanding of user needs, design of products and services, design of pricing, distribution and promotion systems, all finally geared towards satisfying the users needs. For this, required elements of awareness and motivation are to be generated among key players in the market : Consumers, product developers, distributors and also investors.

The Task

Given the background, the responsibilities of the Indian Information Industry would be :

— to facilitate Indian STI user community access to the global knowledge base,

— to specifically collect, collate and disseminate to national and international community of users, the S&T information generated in India and published in Indian literature, and

— to gain access to the more significant part of the Indian contribution to the world of knowledge recorded in non-Indian publications.

To accomplish the tasks, government, private non-profit and profit organizations will continue to play their respective roles. However, the desirable scenario would be the one in which the present dominant role of government in STI declines progressively in relation to the other two sectors. This may impose some financial burden on the users community no doubt, but they would be assured of the continuity of supplies. Moreover, the users are expected to take on some responsibilities themselves and just not keep looking at the government institutions for non-fee based supplies.

The process of change in work culture, attitude, practices and the like would invariably be slow. Certain policy instruments are required to expedite the change and direct it towards the specific goal.

Strategies for STI Market Development

Accessing the Knowledge Base

Universality of science implies that information support required in pursuit of science both in the developed and developing countries is similar. The fact that scientists in developing countries do not get this much needed support gets finally reflected in their output. Of course, there are other factors.

In order to bring up the information support services to scientists and technologists at par with those available to their counterparts in the developed countries, India should set up facilities and capabilities to access the entire spectrum of knowledge (at least, all that is available in public domain). In this context, the strategy should be limited only to gaining easy access. To have all the information in store is an unrealistic proposition, though strangely enough many pursue such a goal at a much isolated level. For an economically poor country like India, even the access may have to be arranged on a collective basis. This may mean a sacrifice in efficiency, but it could be potentially more cost-effective.

Technologies for Access

A wide range of technological options is available the specific mode and modalities for access may be chosen given the national infrastructural framework and socio-economic conditions. Though one may like to have the most upto date technology, the environmental conditions in a developing country might be a damper to their adoption and absorption.

Further, information industry depends significantly on parallel development of other sectors especially the telecommunications. As in other developing countries, different sub-sectors within the telecom sector compete for a share of the limited budget. In such situations, it is obvious why rural communications should get a dis-proportionately high share *vis-a-vis* digital data networks (considered as esoteric or elitist requirement). However, it is not easy to influence the plan priorities. While one may aspire to have a digital data network, one has to learn to live with such prevailing conditions and try to make the best out of what is available. The philosophy advanced here is that information industry may continue lobbying for a fully blown PDN and links with the national and international data carriers but it should not wait endlessly for such an infrastructure to be in place or make this a precondition for action.

For a resource scarce economy of India, the waiting time could be long. Techno-economic alternatives are now available for useful application during the interim period. Nevertheless, due care should be taken to select a hardware-software system that would allow easy transition from one technology level to the other with minimal modification or replacement.

The state of computer communication facility is due to the country's poor capacity-to-invest (and also a general lack of management). It is in no-way a reflection on the technical work force. The strength of skills available may be utilized for innovating interim solutions to partially cover the gaps in infrastructure.

Safeguarding Access

It has been mentioned earlier that self-reliance in information is not achievable even at the collective level. Indian S&T therefore would become more and more dependent upon the flow of information from exogenous sources. And this is unavoidable. An obvious corollary would be:

— How real is the possibility that the information tap may go dry ?

— What could be the impact of such an event ?

Though not directly related to the field of information, India has already been facing problems in acquiring certain items of high-technology. Restrictions have been imposed on the *alibi* That the product/technology might be transferred to a third country, or it could be used for the purposes other than stated. Therefore, the eventuality of a squeeze (deliberate obstruction to the flow of information) cannot be ruled out but the matter may not be all that serious in real terms.

Even if a squeeze takes place for some geo-political reasons, it may not last for long. Two major forces viz. scientific spirit and commercial motive are expected to defuse the crisis soon. Scientists in all democratic societies are free to communicate so long as that does not go against national interests. Therefore, the *invisible college* will continue to operate; the professional bodies may also exert pressure to neutralize the problem. Since the information business is largely in private sector, the lobbying to safeguard commercial interests is likely to be strong.

A more plausible situation is the breakdown in certain commercial arrangements. A case already exists in which the National Centre for Science Information (NCSI), Bangalore had to discontinue its SDI services based on Chemical Abstracts database because of stringent conditions of payment to CAS. These conditions were not relaxed in appreciation of certain genuine difficulties, and even on the consideration that India buys more than 100 hardcopies of the database at a fabulous cost.

The more interesting cases are those in which the country's own rules and regulations cannot be negotiated. For example, the NTIS database on CD-ROM ordered by the National Aeronautical Laboratory, Bangalore could not be cleared through the customs. The arrangement of Indian Embassies sending (*smuggling* may be more apt an expression) datatapes through diplomatic bag to Indian destinations to avoid delays in consignment clearing is another instance. However, if the case is properly argued, Government can always rationalize such rules.

Whatever way the flow might get impeded, the information industry should be prepared with the alternative means of tapping information. For instance, the CAS case cited could be handled in following ways:

- The NCSI could use SDI facilities available with Online vendors like ESA-IRS or DIALOG at off-peak hours.
- Or the centre could use the STN and avail of the huge university discounts available.
- Or it may explore the feasibility of using alternative databases like PASCAL.

Contribution to Knowledge Base

Long-range sustenance might become a problem if the Indian Industry were acting only as a conduit for flow from exogenous sources. A healthy industry should be able to stimulate and nurture a two-way flow.

Improvement in Primary Publications

Much of the significant output of Indian S&T activities gets published in journals of foreign origin mainly for two reasons -- that foreign publications give more visibility to the work and secondly, Indian periodicals are poor in quality and their timeliness.

Improvement in primary publications alone could result in a long chain of benefits:

- Apart from that Indian materials could be found from sources within India because Indian writers would be more inclined to contribute to Indian literature it would potentially attract foreign authors also to write in Indian journals. As a result, Indian information itself will become a quantity to deal with,
- More Indian publications will then be included by the indexing and abstracting journals (for example, presently the Science Citation Index covers only 18 periodicals of Indian origin).
- Indian publications would become a good instrument of exchange for primary as well as secondary publications.
- Indigenous databases on Indian publications would be more respectable. And foreign hosts may also find these commercially attractive. Further establishment of Indian hosts for generation of national and international database services should also be viable.
- Established database producers would get more interested to work out tie-up or co-production arrangements.

Generation of Databases

Initiatives on following lines may be worthwhile :

- India could create databases in her areas of strength.
- India could adopt areas of database generation for which an indepth treatment is lacking in global databases.
- India could undertake activities of value addition.

— India could produce valued added products in which the addition of Indian information might be of significant interest.

— Besides, it is obligatory for a country to collect, collate and to generate services on certain national information or information of national interest.

Product Development and Delivery

The Indian database producers are likely to come across serious marketing problems abroad and also within the country. The Indian users may depend more upon their personal contacts and their personal knowledge, than refer to a database for Indian information. Whereas, a foreign user may look at Indian databases as too small a segment of knowledge to warrant specific attention.

However, both sets of users may welcome any Indian information that comes along with others through a single search. Such facility would demand that the Indian database segment be merged with a relevant global database. Such arrangements are beneficial to both Indian as well as the international database producers.

Benefits to international Database Generators:

* Decentralization of input preparation reduces the lead time between primary publications and production of indexing and abstracting materials.
* It helps in overcoming the local language barriers and also in understanding the concepts which may be local in nature.
* It obviates the need to build up primary collections and required infrastructure for abstracting, indexing and computer handling at the central processing unit.
* It promotes better dissemination of information at the local level.

Benefits to Indian Input Suppliers :

* The involvement in international ventures helps in standardizing the data compilation efforts at the local level.
* Such collaborations may also involve transfer of software for input preparation, local processing etc.

* Acquisition of international compilation in lieu of inputs implies savings of cash expenditure more often in terms of hard currency.

* Association with international activities may eventually lead to development of comprehensive information system at the local level.

It is likely that in future many database producers, both commercial and non-commercial, may opt for decentralized input arrangement which could work on the basis of payments in kind or may involve cash payments on commercial terms. Similarly a large database like PASCAL may also welcome bilateral collaborations. All such arrangements are however to be worked out on one-to-one basis.

Resource Management

The following three principles are important in the Indian context:

— Reduction of avoidable overlaps in input

— Increase in coverage even at constant input level

— Reduction in use of foreign exchange

It need not be mentioned that these three are inter-related. Rationalization is also one subject which needs very careful piloting as a government move could be mistaken for bureaucratic interference.

The major STI operators often find it difficult to take a realistic view of the demand. Since high sensitivity and impatience characterize the user community, a lot of redundancy is usually built into the system to take care of exigencies. The problems are acute at the institutional level where the information manger tries to satisfy the clientele with a budget that is steadily eroding in real terms. He may reduce the extent of redundancy provided he could be reassured of supplies at the time of his needs. Such guaranties cannot be given to an isolated institution. A mutual assurance scheme is called an *information hinterland* delineated carefully on logistics considerations. Overlaps can be reduced through voluntary adjustments.

Since the measures in the form of directives may not work, government could play a disguised role and try to create conditions conducive to collective decision-making. To start with, a form that facilitates exchange of notes among decision-makers may be established. The extreme scenario to work towards would be the pooling of a common fund for making investments.

The practice of hardcopy acquisitions may be too historically entrenched to break away from. However, information centers and services should coordinate their actions while dealing with other forms of database delivery such as online and stand-alone products on CD-ROM. Multiple imports may be discouraged to the extent possible. Further, in every decision, the trade off between acquiring one *vis-a-vis* the cost of accessing the same through alternative means, may be analyzed. For example, databases in low demand may be accessed online; whereas, oft-used databases could be procured in stand-alone mode, and installed on a host to generate cheaper local online services.

Similarly, when SDI profiles are small in number, the SDI operators could use online facilities (that too availing of concessional rates at off-peak hours).

Aligning with the World

Online services started in North America and Europe through bibliographic databases primarily relevant to the S&T area. Under the UNISIST programme, Unesco had taken major initiatives to introduce the technology in developing countries. In accordance with its charter, the subject coverage was also S&T and Social Sciences.

After an experimental phase, the Online Services provision were quick to adopt other forms of databases as the S&T bibliographic databases lost the market share rapidly. In North America, the STI had only 2.4 per cen market share in 1988, which may decline further. Many factors are responsible for this. Investment on a subject like S&T and activity like R&D do not usually show immediate visible returns and therefore, are easy targets in the event off a budget squeeze.

The question is whether a similar scenario is possible for India. So far, there has not been any movement in the market to allow an inference either way. However, considering that the Indian market is not an isolated entity but part of a world market, and recognizing that it is too small a part to influence the global scene, the plausible conjecture would be that the Indian situation will eventually align with the world trend. The obvious corollaries to be answered are:

— Whether measures should be taken to expedite the change;

— Who should take the responsibility to promote the change ? What role government should play ?

Generation of Internal Strength of STI Market

One has to recognize that the S&T information market lacks an intrinsic financial strength. In a country like India, the consumption is mostly paid for through public funds. And the flow of funds largely depends upon policies formulated by governments. To illustrate the point, in India, in the later part of 70's, the emphasis on high technology shifted to S&T for rural development. The policy reverted to high technology in he 80's until 1990 when the focus once again changed to rural and backward area development, development of weaker sections and the like. These policy shifts usually have impact on budgetary provisions. Further, even within S&T information sector, a balance was not maintained. In other words, long-term dependence on public funds would not be in the best interests of the STI market. And it is time that STI market generates its own strength. For this, there are two alternatives:

— The STI market remains a passive observer of the international market trend, or

— Taking due note o the international trend, STI operators lend their expertise and take initiatives to develop other components of the market.

It is felt that the former alternative would be short-sighted and suicidal. A stunted growth of business and financial information sector would not be in the long term interest of the market of which STI is also a part. Whereas, adoption of the second alternative would ensure a pivotal role for STI operators in the information market place for years to come.

In other words, this would mean that the conventional STI programmes should extend their activities to business and financial information areas as well, by promoting the generation of a whole set of databases and services which the business people also require. The ultimate aim should be to evolve a mechanism whereby revenue surpluses of the business and financial information sector could partially support the STI activities (this might be an idealist's way of viewing a really difficult situation).

Self-Sustenance

The other pertinent issue to be considered is whether an information market in a developing economy could be self-sustaining. It is safe to assume that it would not. Some of the activities taken up in the private sector may earn an independent existence, others would require incubation for a long time.

The international experience is no different. Those which start as a private enterprise, perform better e.g. DIALOG and ISI. Some do well on a collective basis e.g. Maxwell Communications. In yet another case, collateral activities compensate for the poor earning capacity of information services; for example, WEFA's 75% turnover comes from lucrative economic consultancy and information consolidation activities.

In contrast, government subsidies continue to prop up the national host services in West Europe. For example, according to BMFT data (Ministry of Research and Technology of FRG) government subsidies to West German hosts like FIZ Teknik and DIMDI is higher than 50 per cent of expenditure. In fact, the high level of subsidy might be responsible for the delay in attainment of maturity by national information markets in western Europe.

The situation in India will largely depend upon the success in enticing private enterprises in the information market; more it is the better. For that matter, government funds will be better spent in infrastructural development and provision of credit to private enterprises. In any case, the promoters and financiers would need to keep their interest alive for about a decade to observe any perceptible change in the scenario.

Summary

Building up of a modern information market would require active participation of information users, individuals and institutions responsible for product development, distribution and investment. The existing library-based information services would have to go.

The market should facilitate the Indian users to access the world of knowledge and the foreign users to access Indian information. A goal of self-reliance in information should not be pursued. It is necessary to keep abreast of the new developments in the international information market and identify alternative sources for accessing similar sets of information for fall back support.

To generate an intrinsic strength of the market, India should organize indigenous primary and secondary information for national and international consumption. A lot could be achieved simply by improving the quality and timeliness of primary publications, India may also selectively create databases in the areas of her S&T strengths besides exploring the possibilities of value added products. Further, Indian institutions should arrange tie-ups with global database producers for Indian or partial database input support.

Keeping in view the economic conditions in the country, utmost effort is required to be made to optimize investments *vis-a-vis* information resources development especially when foreign ex-change is involved. Though desirable, it is not essential always to have *state-of-art* technology to maintain the market. In an investment-scarce situation of India, one has to innovate appropriate solutions with whatever infrastructure that is readily available.

The scientific and technological information alone is not sufficient to sustain a healthy electronic information market. In keeping with the global scene, other components of the market should also grow simultaneously, and the sooner it does, the better. As the early starters, professionals and institutions involved in developing and managing the STI should take initiatives to effect this change. A mechanism may be evolved to reinvest the surplus of the business and financial information sector for furtherence of the STI.

The proportion of government investments on information activities should decrease. The non-profit organizations and private enterprises should take on increased responsibilities. Even where government investment is involved, the activities should be such designed as to be self-sustaining in the long run.

Acknowledgement : I am grateful to my colleagues Mr. B.G. Sunder Singh for meticulous editing and Mr. M. Sundaram for the personal care in the production of the paper.

REFERENCES

Department of Science & Technology, India (1990). *Research and development statistics*. New Delhi : The Department. iv, 196 p.

Lahiri, Abhjit (1991). *An Indian mode for Database services* [prepared on a senior bursary, EEC]. New Delhi : Department of Scientific and Industrial Research. ix, 94. Appendix I &II. No. NISSAT/SR-005/92.

Lahiri, Abhijit and Sunder Singh, B.G. (1989). *Bibliographic databases and networks : Indian Scenario.* In Bibliographic databases and networks, edited by S.S. Murthy, Anuradha Ravi and A. Lakshmana Moorthy. *Proceedings* of the International Conference, New Delhi, 22-25, February 1989. New Delhi ; Tata McGraw-Hill. pp.1 - 41 -1 - 66

LINK Resources Corporation, USA (1990a). *Current situation and forecast of electronic information industry in Europe, 1989-94*. 148 p.

LINK Resources Corporation, USA (1990b). *Current situation and forecast of electronic information industry in North America, 1989-94*. 149 p.

PART II
Information, Source and Service

The History of Printing in South Asia : The State of Current and Future Research

GRAHAM SHAW

The printing history of South Asia is still imperfectly documented even at the most rudimentary level of gathering facts, let alone their analysis and interpretation. This is all the more surprising in view of India's position today as one of the world's largest publishers, not least of English-language works, and also from the historical perspective when one remembers that India was the first country in Asia proper to which printing technology from Europe was introduced with the establishment of a printing press by Portuguese Jesuits at Goa in 1556. This comparative neglect may be due to a number of factors, not least the 'Atlantic dominance' of Europe and North America as fields of interest in research into printing history. Much more emphasis is now needed on studying the diffusion of printing technologies - typography and lithography - outside Europe and North America from the 16th century onwards. Only when the international and interlocking patterns of book-production and - distribution are fully understood will a truly balanced picture of the evolution of publishing world-wide finally emerge.

At an earlier IFLA venue in Asia, I. R. Willison delivered a paper on *The western view of the history of the book in the East and the south* (Rare and Precious Books section, IFLA General Conference, Tokyo, 1986). In it he observed the transition from the traditionally narrow discipline of *historical bibliography*, preoccupied with the invention and spread of printing and with the aesthetics of the book to the wider *history of the book* approach as an integrated aspect of general cultural history, extending its scope into publishing and book-distribution, patronage and authorship, the interface between literacy and orality, and so on. As Willison pointed out, this wider view was particularly important for documenting the full cultural impact of the printed book in Asia and Africa, on the colonizer as well as on the colonized.

To date, however, in the context of India rather than Japan upon which Willison was focussing, one cannot report much published progress in the wider perspective, and this paper perforce concentrates on the more traditional aspects of printing history. Until an old-fashioned 'bibliographical pioneer battalion' has dug out all the facts, the validity of any overall assessment of stages or trends will naturally be circumscribed. This battalion must be composed principally of Indian scholars (if only for linguistic reasons about which more below) but it must also make use of library and archives collections both inside the subcontinent and outside it, in North America as well as Europe. In the training of librarians in India, the historical bibliography of the region is almost totally ignored, a fact which I have heard vigorously deplored on more than one occasion by a former National Librarian of India. This needs to be rectified urgently to ensure that the future custodians of India's national printed heritage have the knowledge and awareness to fulfil their responsibilities. There are individual examples of excellence such as the Central Library, Panjim, in Goa which proudly preserves a small but extremely important collection of early Indo-Portuguese books. Moreover, in a culture in which the widespread production of manuscripts ceased barely a century and a half ago, leaving perhaps the largest single manuscript heritage in the world, there is a certain 'tyranny of the manuscript' with which those interested in the documentation and preservation of the lesser printed book must inevitably contend, not least in the present age for purposes of fundraising.

Two publications deserve mention for having usefully treated India within the general context of the world-wide diffusion of movable-type technology. Jean Müller and Ernst Røth: *Aussereuropaische Druckereien in 16. Jahrhundert. Bibliographie der Drucke* (Baden-Baden, 1969) includes a succinct summary of the beginnings of printing in India from 1556 (pp. 39-52) but leaves unresolved many of the uncertainties surrounding the earliest printing by the Portuguese at Goa and elsewhere. D.E. Rhodes: *India, Pakistan Ceylon, Burma and Thailand (The spread of printing. Eastern hemisphere)* (Amsterdam, 1969) is all too brief but, although lacking in any significant original research, does contain a pioneering sketch of "early printing in the smaller centres" i.e. non-metropolitan India and Pakistan. The catalogue of the exhibition at the Lilly Library, Indiana University, *Exotic printing and the expansion of Europe, 1492-1840: an exhibit* (Bloomington, 1972), based on the collection of the eminent historian Professor C.R. Boxer, and D.F. Lach: *Asia in the making of Europe. Vol. II. Book 3: The scholarly disciplines* (Chicago & London, 1977) are also useful in setting the context.

The introduction of typography in the mid-16th century as an important instance of technology transfer from Europe is discussed in Ahsan Jan Qaisar: *The Indian Response to European technology and culture (A.D. 1498-1707)* (Delhi, 1982), pp. 58-64. In fact, 16th-century printing in India was very much a 'false dawn'. Right down to 1800 the printing press in the subcontinent remained a coastal phenomenon, and ownership and exploitation of it the preserve of Europeans. It was not until the nineteenth century that printing took firm root in the hinterland of the subcontinent or made any significant impact upon the lives of the vast majority of its population. This theme is explored in G. Duverdier: *Les imprimeries neo-europeennes* in: La Revue francaise d'histoire du livre 16 (1977), offprint pp. 1-30. Indeed, printing in many minor and tribal languages in the remoter areas did not begin until the very end of the nineteenth or the early years of the twentieth. This is revealed in *The Historical catalogue of printed Christian scriptures in the languages of the Indian sub-continent* (London, 1977), an invaluable revision and updating to 1976 by the British and Foreign Bible Society of the relevant portions of T.H. Darlow and H.F. Moule's original Scriptural bibliography of 1903-11.

On present evidence South Asia, with the notable exception of Nepal, seems to have remained immune to the xylographic tradition of printing which was diffused from the Far East as part of the baggage of Buddhism in the middle of the first millenium A.D. *Le livre et l' imprimerie en Extreme-Orient et en Asie du Sud* (Bordeaux, 1986) contains the proceedings of a colloquium which brought together researchers interested in both the xylographic and the typographic traditions in Asia and the interplay between them, 'revisiting' to some extent the theme of that classic work, T. -F. Carter, *The invention of printing and its spread westward* (New York, 1925). It includes K.S. Diehl: *L'imprimerie catholique en Inde jusque'en 1850;* G Duverdier ; *L'imprimerie protestante en Inde (1712-1850);* and G. W. Shaw: *Les debuts de l'imprimerie gouvernementale et commerciale en Inde* (p.

295-330). This last aspect was also dealt with in K.S. Diehl: *The role of government and introduction of type printing to South Asia.* In: *Primary printed and manuscript sources for sixteenth to nineteenth century studies available in Bengal, Orissa and Bihar Libraries* (Calcutta, 1971), pp. 221-231.

Our understanding of the cultural milieu which printing with movable-metal types from Europe penetrated, both as regards traditions of textual transmission and indigenous methods of book production, has been enhanced by several recent works. Ananda E. Wood: *Knowledge before printing and after: the Indian tradition in changing Kerala* (Delhi, 1985) emphasizes the rapidity of India's cultural transformation in the wake of the introduction of printing. *Das Buch im Orient: Handschriften und kostbare Drucke aus zwei Jahrtausenden* (Wiesbaden, 1982), the catalogue of an exhibition at the Bayerische Staatsbibliothek, Munich, contains G. Grönbold ; *Die Bunchkultur Sudasiens* (pp.221-264) which points to the persistence of some characteristics of the manuscript tradition into the era of print. J.P. Losty: *The art of the book in India.* (London, 1982) demonstrates how by the middle of the 19th century printing and photography had combined to kill off the Indian manuscript tradition.

Since 1970 the most significant progress has been made in the field of enumerative bibliography. In August 1982 the British Library announced a new project, the *South Asia and Burma Retrospective Bibliography (SABREB),* with the aim of providing for the first time a comprehensive bibliography of all works printed in the subcontinent up to 1900. The project is now in abeyance but at least the results of *Stage 1: 1556-1800,* compiled by G. W Shaw (London, 1987) have been published, describing 1771 titles printed in 8 European and 19 oriental languages and also listing as many extant copies as could be traced (about 900 locations in well over 100 collections). This now enables us to view the totality of Indian publishing in its formative period, progressing from a solely religious and missionary press output through the early official and government publications into the rise of commercial printing and the beginnings of journalism. The introduction also contains a short *Outline of early South Asian printing* based directly on the findings of the project. Among the most important works discovered by *SABREB* was a copy of the *Khurdah*

Avesta, the Parsee scripture in Pahlavi, printed at Bombay in 1798 - truly a landmark in South Asian publishing as the first work printed *by* Indians (albeit a minority group in the population) without any direct European stimulus or involvement.

The *SABREB* project adopted the three-part chronological division of early Indian imprints (1556-1800), 1801-67, 1868-1900) which the late A.K Priolkar, the doyen of Indian printing historians, defined as "pre-incunabula", "incunabula" and "post-incunabula" (*Indian incunabula.* In: *Comparative librarianship: essays in honour of Professor D. N. Marshal,* ed. N. N. Gidwani. New Delhi, [1973] pp. 129-135). While the application of these terms in this way may infuriate the purist, it does emphasize the extreme rarity of surviving copies of works printed in the subcontinent up to as late as the middle of the last century. 1801-1867 is the least well documented but arguably the single most important period in the whole history of South Asian publishing. It was the heyday of missionary publishing but, more significantly, also saw the growth of Indian-owned presses and the development of vernacular journalism. For the period 1868 onwards, the quarterly lists of publications for each of the provinces of British India as required by the Press and Registration of Books Act (1867) form an embryonic retrospective national bibliography for India, Pakistan and Bangladesh. Their usefulness is described in F. W. Pritchett: *The history of Indian publishing: a note on sources* in: India International Centre Quarterly 10 (1983), pp. 467-471. Recently the Sahitya Akademi, New Delhi, in conjunction with the US Library of Congress New Delhi Field Office, has undertaken a pilot project to test the feasibility of converting the contents of these published lists into machine-readable form. If this important project could be completed, it would open up that vast and invaluable mass of publishing data to much more sophisticated searching than possible while they remain in unindexed hard-copy.

Concerning the first two centuries of printing in India, usually referred to as the Indo-Portuguese period, there has been some significant work published. C.R. Boxer: *A tentative check-list of Indo-Portuguese imprints* in: Arquivos do Centro cultural Portugues 9 (1975), pp. 567-599 describes 38 items printed between 1556 and 1679. Since 1970 a further 7 volumes in the series *Documenta Indica,* edited by Father J. Wicki, collecting together all extant Jesuit letters as far as 1598have been published at Rome. These are an invaluable source of references to early printing by the Portuguese in the Indian vernaculars, particularly Tamil, through the long career of Henrique Henriques who can justifiably be given the title of the first serious European scholar of Indian languages. His translations into Tamil were the mainstay of the Jesuit press at Quilon-Cochin, as discussed in S.J. Rajamanickam: *Padre Henrique Henriques, the father of the Tamil press* in: *Proceedings of the Second International conference Seminar of Tamil Studies.* Vol. 2 (Madras, 1971), pp. 520-527. The earliest work printed in Tamil in India, thought to have been the 1578 Quilon catechism, is now known to have been a similar *Doctrina Christiana* printed at Goa in 1577. A copy, collected by the scholar Joseph Scaliger, survived in Leiden University Library until the beginning of the 18th century but is now lost (G.W. Shaw: *Scaliger's copy of an early Tamil catechism* in: The Library 6th Series 3 (1981), pp. 239-243). A copy of Henriques' *Confessionairo* (Cochin, 1580) has been 'rediscovered' in the Bodleian Library, Oxford, and is described in G.W. Shaw: *A 'lost' work of Henrique Henriques: the Tamil confessionary of 1580* in: The Bodleian Library Record 11 (1982), pp. 26-34. A second copy of Henriques' Lives of the Saints, his longest work, has been identified in the Danish Royal Library by G. W. Shaw — see *The Copenhagen copy of Henrique' Flos Sanctorum* in: Fund og Forskning 32 (1993), pp. 39-50.

Although twice as many works are known to have been printed by the Portuguese in India in the 17th compared with the 16th century, our knowledge of this later Indo-Portuguese printing is far less certain but it will undoubtedly improve as publication of the *Documenta Indica* series continues. The most significant new centre of printing was Rachol, in Salcette south of Goa, where works in Konkani were issued in Roman rather than vernacular types, establishing a tradition that has lasted until today and which may be cited as the most extreme example of European 'influence' upon Indian typography. With Henriques' death in 1600, Tamil printing died out and was only revived in the 1670s at Ambalacatta, near Cochin, when another greater scholar of the language, Robert de Nobili, began to prepare works for the press. Several key questions concerning printing in the 17th century still await resolution. For instance, how extensive was Syriac printing at

Vaipikkotta ? Why was Ignacio Arcamone, a scholar of Konkani-Marathi, printing Tamil works at Ambalacatta ? Did Bhimjee Parekh, the East India Company's broker at Surat, succeed in anything other than a trial printing using 'Banian' or Gujarāti, types ?

Printing in India during the first half of the 18th century was confined to the press of the earliest Protestant mission in the subcontinent at Tranquebar on the Coromandel coast. A detailed discussion of this important press has yet to be written and it is a matter of particular regret that the talented French scholar, Gerald Duverdier, who was working on this theme, has now apparently abandoned his studies of South Asian printing history altogether. The antecedents of Tranquebar, the preparation of Tamil types and Tamil printing in the Lutheran Ostindische Missionsanstalt at Halle, are told in G. Duverdier: *Über die Bedeutung unbedeutender Drucke. Die ersten tamilischen Drucke zu Halle, 1712-1713* in: Wissenschaftliche Zeitschrift der Universität Halle 24 (1975), pp. 103-126. Apart from being the most prolific press in India up to 1800, Tranquebar is also important for the stimulus it gave to the development of printing elsewhere, ending a type-founder Michelsen to prepare a Tamil fount for the fledgling Dutch East India Company (NVOC) press at Colombo, and providing manpower and materials for its Madras offshoot, the Vepery Mission Press. Another by-product of Duverdier's Tranquebar research is his definitive treatment of the missionary Benjamin Schultze's study of Telugu: *L'oeuvre en telugu de Benjamin Schultze* in: Bulletin de l'Ecole Francaise d'Extreme-Orient 63 (1976), pp. 265-312.

During the second half of the 18th century printing reached all three of the Presidency capitals of British India: first Madras, then Bombay and finally Calcutta. The fascinating story of the capture of the French press by the British at the siege of Pondicherry in 1761, its transfer with its printer Charles Delon to Madras to become the East India Company's press under the superintendence of the SPCK-sponsored missionaries at Vepery, and the subsequent independent development of the Vepery Mission Press to outstrip Tranquebar, is fully described in G. Duverdier: *L' apparition de l''imprimerie a Madras et sa disparition á Pondichéry* in: Gutenberg-Jahrbuch (1976), pp. 351-363 *Les debuts de l'imprimerie tamoule à Madras et la fin de celle de Halle, 1761-1772* in Gutenberg-Jaharbuch (1977), pp. 183-194; and

L'imprimerie tamoule de Vepery et les deux dictionnaires de Fabricius in : Gutenberg-Jahrbuch (1978), pp. 189-197. The origin of printing at Madras is also discussed in J. Mangamma: *Book printing in India: with special reference to the contribution of European scholars to Telugu (1746-1857)* (Nellore, 1975).

At Bombay, by contrast, the arrival of the press was due to commercial rather than missionary stimulus, with the 1772 printing of a broadsheet for a patent medicine, *Diogo' drops,* by one James Tod later to be tried by the East India Company and convicted of corruption. Tod's career, the publication of newspapers from 1789 onwards, the surprising range of early Bombay imprints including a little-known account of Tipu Sultan of Mysore, the development of vernacular type-faces at the Courier Press (for Marathi, Gujarati and Malayalam), and the introduction of lithography in 1824, are all covered in G.W. Shaw: *The beginnings of printing in Bombay* in: *India: a pageant of prints,* ed. P. Rohatgi & P. Godrej. (Bombay, 1989), pp. 111-124. It was Calcutta during the last quarter of the 18th century which developed into the first great centre of commercial and government printing and where one can begin to speak, for the first time in the context of South Asia, of a fully fledged book trade: printers, binders, subscription publishing, libraries, etc. G.W. Shaw: *Printing in Calcutta to 1800: a description and checklist of printing in late 18th century Calcutta* (London, 1981) describes in detail the general conditions under which printing operated as well as the particular difficulties encountered by would-be authors, reconstructs the careers of the various printers working there, discusses the products of the press from the staples of newspapers and alamanacs to the rarified heights of pioneering editions of classics of oriental literature, and deals with the vexed question of materials for printing from type-metal to paper. The unsuspected mass - listed in this study - of official documents surviving in Bengali translation from late 18th century Calcutta has led to a re-evaluation of the development of early Bengali prose in Ghulam Murshid: *Kalantare bangla gadya* ["Bengali prose at the turn of the century"] (Calcutta, 1992) — a direct example of how bibliography can stimulate new lines of research. A fascinating account of the rivalry between the earliest printers in 18th-century Calcutta may be found in G. Duverdier : *Deux imprimeurs en proces a Calcutta: Hicky contre Kiernander (1777-1787)* in: Moyen Orient & Ocean Indien 2 (1985), pp. 51-78.

During the 19th century printing 'exploded' in the subcontinent, reaching every major language and almost every large city and town by 1850 or soon after. A balanced and accurate history of printing in South Asia either in English (or any of the major vernaculars of the region) has yet to be written as both Rhodes' account mentioned above and the only previous attempt, A.K. Priolkar : *The printing press in India : its beginnings and early development* (Bombay, 1958) are unsatisfactory. There has been one further attempt since 1970 by B.S. Kesavan, a former National Librarian of India, who has embarked upon a multivolume *History of printing and publishing in India : a story of cultural re-awakening*. To date only 2 volumes have appeared (New Delhi, 1985 and 1988), devoted to the *South Indian origins of printing and its efflorescence in Bengal* and *Origins of printing and publishing in Karnataka, Andhra and Kerala* [i.e. in the Dravidian languages Kannada, Telugu and Malayalam]. This project is best described as a haphazard compilation rather than presenting a coherent narrative and, as the author readily admits in the preface, it is "an exercise in academic parasitology". There is little evidence of original research having been undertaken, its sole and limited virtue being that it brings together many scattered pieces of information otherwise difficult to access. Kesavan's work also illustrates a fundamental and inescapable difficulty facing any attempt to arrive at a balanced history of printing in South Asia - the multiplicity of languages to be covered, not least the 16 languages accorded national status in the Indian Constitution. It is impossible for any one scholar to comprehend and keep abreast of whatever research may be published in each of them. Unfortunately most of this predominantly article-indexing of Indian-language periodicals is lamentably patchy. The linguistic i.e. mother-tongue imperative to compile a vernacular language-based bibliography is very strong in South Asia, the most recent example being Shahbaz Malik ; *Punjabi kitabiat (a bibliography of Punjabi printed books written in Perso-Arabic script)*. Vol 1 (Islamabad, 1991). The results in this field since the 1960s are surveyed in K.M. Govi & P. Govi: *Retrospective bibliographies of Indian literature* in: Libri 24 (1974), pp. 319-323. It is, therefore, curiously enough the English-language output of the 19th-century presses which is at present the more elusive and its overall scale and range impossible to gauge with accuracy. All these considerations surely argue that a balanced history of printing and publishing in India will only be achieved through some collaborative venture, akin to the multi-scholar seven-volume *A history of the books in Britain* now underway, perhaps under the patronage of a major institution such as the Sahitya Akademi.

Although this paper (for want of space and my linguistic competence) inevitably concentrates on Western-language research, I will present a picture of recent research undertaken in one Indian vernacular, namely Bengali, as a sample. Besides, Bengali is, along with Tamil, perhaps one of the two languages in which most interest in printing history has so far been aroused. Tamil interest is exemplified by P.A. Mohanrajan: *Glimpses of early printing and publishing in India* (Madras, 1990). Despite its title it is confined to the history of printing in Tamil only and to the rise of Tamil journalism. His 1979 University of Madras thesis was entitled *The growth of printing and publishing industry pertaining to Tamil language up to 1900: a study of early developments contributing to modern Tamil printing and Tamiliana.*

Several chapters of the first volume of Kesavan's work mentioned above are in fact simply translations of contribution to *Dui shataker bangla mudran o prakashan* ["Two centuries of Bengali printing and publishing"]. Edited by Chittaranjan Bandyopadhay (Calcutta, 1981). This is the most important of a number of works issued around 1978 to celebrate the bicentenary of the first printing in Bengali characters in N B Halhed's *A grammar of the Bengal language* (Hooghly, 1778). Bandyopadhyay's book brought to light a specimen of the Bengali types prepared by the London type-founder Joseph Jackson for the adventurer and would-be Bengal printer and publisher William Bolts in the 1770s, the first ever attempt at a Bengali fount and predating that of Sir Charles Wilkins used in Halhed's grammar. Not the least important chapter of the book is P. Chaudhuri's selective but still impressive bibliography of works (both Bengali and English) relating to the history of Bengali printing. Halhed's famous grammar was reissued in an unabridged facsimile edition (Calcutta, 1980) with an introduction by N. Sarkar.

Among other works published on this anniversary were Atul Sur: *Bangla mudraner duso bachar* ["Two hundred years of Bengali printing"] (Calcutta, 1978); *Du'sha bacharer bangla bai* ["Two hundred years of the

Bengali book"] (Calcutta, [1979]), a useful catalogue of the bicentenary exhibition held on the Calcutta Maidan with an extensive listing of early imprints, mostly Bengali; N. Sarkar: *Yakhan chapakhana elo* ["Once upon a time there was a press'] (Calcutta, 1977), surveying Bengali publishing up to the end of the 19th century; and K. Chaudhuri & P. Chaudhuri: *Kalakatar chapakhana* ["The Calcutta press"] (Calcutta, 1978). A more recent study, Ghulam Murshid: *Bangadeshe mudran o prakashanar adiparba, 1777-1817* ["The first phase of printing and publishing in Bengal, 1777-1817"] (Dhaka, 1985), gives a fuller account of early government, commercial and missionary printing at Calcutta and Serampore. Mohammad Abdul Qayyum: *Abhidhan* ["Dictionaries"] (Dhaka, 1987) is a detailed analysis of early Bengali dictionaries and acts as a companion to his earlier *A critical study of the early Bengali grammars: Halhed to Haughton* (Dhaka, 1982).

Despite its celebrity, the Serampore Mission Press still awaits a definitive treatment of its achievements (and failures) in printing and type-founding. G.W Shaw: *Some thoughts on serampore bibliography* in: Carey Day souvenir (1983), pp. 6-10, traces the history of attempts to document its output, while the most balanced assessment of Serampore to date is still that in E. D. Potts: *British Baptist missionaries in India 1793-1837: the history of Serampore and its missions* (Cambridge, 1967, chap. 5: 'Translation, literature, journalism and printing'). The press at Fort William College, an important early provider of educational works in Indian vernaculars, is dealt with in S.K. Das: *Sahibs and munshis* (New Delhi, 1978), pp. 68-86. John Borthwick Gilchrist, a cantankerous scholar and publisher associated with the College, is discused in N. Ahmad : *A Scottish orientalist and his works* in: Libri 28 (1978), pp. 196-204.

The early history of printing in Bangladesh is now beginning to emerge clearly. Muntasir Mamum: *Dhakar samskrtik itihaser upadan ["Sources for the cultural history of Dhaka"]* (Dhaka, 1991) contains *Dhakar adi mudraner itihas 1848-1900* ["History of early printing in Dhaka, 1848-1900"] (pp. 9-38); *Dhakar battalar khomje* ["Inquiry into popular printing in Dhaka"] (pp. 39-67); *Unisha shatake Dhakar sambadpatra;* ["Nineteenth-century Dhaka newspapers"] (pp. 68-102) and *Dhakar adi kabitapatra* ["Early poetry magazines of Dhaka 1860 onwards'] (pp. 103-122). G.W. Shaw: *printing and publishing in*

Dhaka, 1849-1900 in: *Dhaka past present future,* ed. Sharif Uddin Ahmed (Dhaka, 1991), pp 89-121, uses the evidence of the quarterly lists of publications issued for the Province of Bengal to reconstruct the printing and publishing trade in Dhaka, the movements of printers between presses, their ventures into publishing, the predominance of the school-book market, etc. G.W. Shaw: *The first Bengali book printed in Bangladesh* in: Oriental & India Office collections Newsletter 45 (1991), pp. 42-43, describes a book of Bengali riddles recently 'rediscovered' in the British Library's collection to show that the earliest Kattra Press in the city issued works in Bengali as well as English.

The various reasons or stimuli for the diffusion of printing into the Indian hinterland from the metropolitan centres in the first half of the 19th century are still imperfectly understood. Certainly one important strain is the work of the missionaries, as documented, for instance, in G.W. Shaw's three articles : *Printing at Mangalore and Tellicherry by the Basel Mission* in: Libri 27 (1977), pp. 154-164; *The first printing-press in the Punjab* [that of the American Presbyterians at Ludhiana begun 1836] in: The Library Chronicle 43 (1979), pp. 159-179; and *The Cuttack Mission Press and early Oriya printing* in: British Library Journal 3 (1977), pp. 29-43. Another element was the interest in and adoption of printing by various Indian rulers continuing their traditional patronage but through the medium of the press rather than the manuscript studio. Examples of this are described in K.S. Diehl: *Lucknow printers, 1820-1850* in: *Comparative librarianship: essays in honour of Professor D.N. Marshall,* ed. N. N. Gidwani (Delhi, [1973]), pp. 115-128, which charts the significant switch from letter-press to lithography in the royal press at Oudh, and G.W. Shaw: *The Tanjore "Aesop" in the context of early Marathi printing* in: The Library 5th series 33 (1978), pp. 207-214, on the private press of Raja Serfoji II of Tanjore set up in 1805 and the stimulus that gave to the production of Marathi literature at the royal court. The straightforward spread of printing as a commercial enterprise centred upon the publication of a local or regional newspaper was also to the fore, but this aspect of printing history has regrettably been little documented to date. The example of the *Kurrachee Advertiser,* first issued in 1845, is presented in Allah Rakha Butt: *Origin and development of printing press in Sind* is: Pakistan Library Bulletin 12 (1981), pp. 1-10. One of the most interesting case-studies is provided by the Anglo-Indian Greenway family which, from roots in the Bombay and Calcutta newspaper printing-offices of the 1790s, applied successfully to the Bengal government to establish a press at Kanpur in 1822 and finally built up a network of newspapers and presses in Uttar Pradesh at Meerut, Allahabad, Agra and Secundra — a saga which deserves to be documented in detail.

The history of journalism itself as an opinion-moulding and ultimately political force has, however, received considerable attention recently. R. Parthasarathy: *Journalism in India from the earliest times to the present day* (New Delhi, 1989) is a comprehensive general survey covering both English and vernacular newspapers from 1780 down to 1947. P. Thankappan Nair: *A history of the Calcutta press: the beginnings* (Calcutta, 1987) deals only with the period 1780-1800. T.K. Mukhopadhyay: *Hicky's Bengal Gazette: contemporary life and events* (Calcutta, 1988) considers in detail the short but notorious life of India's first ever newspaper. S. Chakraborti: *The Bengali press (1818-1868) a study in the growth of public opinion* (Calcutta, 1976) charts the rise of vernacular journalism in Calcutta. For 19th-century Dhaka there is Muntasir Mamun: *Unisha shatake Bangladesher sambad samayikpatra* ["Newspapers and periodicals in 19th-century Bangladesh"] 4 vols. (Dhaka, 1985-90), with volume 5 currently in the press. Nadir Ali Khan: *A history of Urdu journalism (1822-1857)* (Delhi, 1991) discusses newspapers published in Delhi, Agra and seven other cities. *Mumbai samachar dorhaso varasani tavarikh 1822-1972* ["A history of the 150 years of the Bombay Samachar 1822-1972"], ed. Rasik Jhaveri (Bombay, 1972) is a beautifully produced and illustrated history of the oldest Gujarati newspaper and its association with Fardunji Marzaban, the 'father' of the Gujarati typography. Chummar Choondal: *The missionaries and Malayalam journalism* (Trichur, 1975) contains a chronological list of 19th-century Malayalam newspapers and periodicals.

Studies of printing by minorities in the population (e.g. Armenians and Jews) who made early use of the technique must not be forgotten. E.N. Musleah : *On the banks of the Ganga - the sojourn of Jews in Calcutta* (North Quincy, Mss., 1975) contains a chapter on "Hebrew printing and printers" and an appendix listing 114 Hebrew-Arabic items printed in the city between 1841 and 1897 beginning with the press of Eleazar Arakie. S.B. Isenberg: *India's Bene Israel: a comprehensive inquiry and sourcebook* (Bombay, 1988) includes in the chapter on "Arts and letters" a history of Hebrew printing in and around Bombay and an appendix of Bene Israel publications from 1842 to 1918 as well as periodicals from 1877 onwards. Short accounts of Hebrew printing in India can also be found in the *Encyclopaedia Judaica* (Jerusalem, 1971) under the names of various towns (Bombay, Calcutta, Cochin, Madras and Poona) as well as under 'Bene-Israel" and "Press". The introduction to Dr V. Nersessian: *Catalogue of early Armenian books 1512-1850* (London, 1980) includes an excellent summary of early printing in that language at Madras and then Calcutta with detailed descriptions of some 36 works printed in India.

The serious study of early Indian typography which began with the Portuguese foundry at Goa in the 1560s is still in its infancy. Bapurao S. Naik: *Typography of Devanagari.* 3 vols. (Bombay, 1971) is a very rambling book but does contain a good deal of information and specimens of various early founts. A shorter account is G.W. Shaw: *Printing in Devanagari* in: The Monotype Recorder New Series 2 (1980), pp.28-32. Jamil A. Naqvi: *Nastaliq - the elegant Urdu script - its origin and progress from the sixth century to the present day* in: The Monotype Recorder New series 3 (1981) pp. 1-4, surveys the most important of the scripts used for the printing of Islamic languages in the subcontinent. The full range of Charles Wilkins' typographical experiments is revealed in F. Ross and G.W. Shaw: *An unexpected legacy, and its contribution to early Indian typography* in: Matrix 7 (1987), pp. 69-79, including his work on the cursive Modi script. The most authoritative study to date of the typographical development of any one Indian script is undoubtedly F. Ross: *The evolution of the printed Bengali character from 1778 to 1978* [1988 thesis, the School of Oriental & African Studies, University of London, shortly to be published in a revised version]. As a consultant to Linotype, Paul specializing in non-roman founts, she brings a designer's eye to the historical analysis of Bengali typography, one of the most calligraphic of all Indian scripts. The *Souvenir: All India Type Founders 7th Conference* ed. Dipankar Sen (Calcutta, 1982) includes Nikhil Sarkar: *Early type-founders of Calcutta.*

There has been a resurgence of interest in the aesthetic qualities of Indian scripts, seen in the formation around 1983 of *CALTIS (Calligraphy, Lettering, Typography of Indian Scripts).* This body has held annual seminars on the historical evolution of the 'family' of Indian scripts with the aim of rediscovering India's calligraphic legacy and taking advantage of modern computerized phototypesetting techniques to produce 'new fount designs from old'. only the proceedings of the 1983, 1984 and 1985 annual seminars have been published, replaced from April 1987 by the far less substantial monthly *Akshar rachana.* The implications of the new technology for Indian type design have recently been explored in F. Ross: *From metal type to digital letterforms - a straightforward transition for Indian scripts ?*in: Matrix 9 (1989), pp. 128-136.

The impact of lithography on printing in South Asia and its mass appeal because of its link back to the manuscript tradition, has not yet been fully appreciated. The earliest use of lithography in India by James Nathaniel Rind at Calcutta in 1823 has been traced in A.S. Cook: *The beginnings of lithographic map printing in Calcutta* in: *India: a pageant of prints,* ed. P. Rohatgi & P. Godrej (Bombay, 1989), pp. 125-134, where its appeal was specifically at the level of easing the office burden of manuscript copying of maps and surveys which had to be sent back to the Company in London. The new process held a particular attraction for the Muslim communities, whose early use of printing has been summarized in G W Shaw: *Maktaba'a 4. In Muslim India.* In: *The Encyclopadia of Islam* (new ed.) Vol. VI. Fascicules 111-112 (Leiden, 1989), pp. 804-806. Lucknow became the preeminent centre of lithographic printing in northern India. Apart from K.S. Diehl's article already cited, Lucknow is dealt with in Abdul Halim Sharar: *Lucknow: the last phase of an oriental culture* (Delhi, 1989), pp. 102-108 ("Scripts - calligraphy and the Urdu press", stressing how the traditional nurturing of the art of calligraphy benefited the output of the Lucknow presses). Syed Jalauddin Haider: *Munshi Nawal Kishore (1836-1895): Mirror of Urdu printing in British India* in: Libri 31 (1981), pp. 227-237, details the career of perhaps the single most influential 19th-century printer and publisher in northern India. A more extensive recent study in Urdu is A. H. Nurani: *Munshi Navalkishor: halat aur khidmat* (Delhi, 1982). Professor M. Twyman: *Early lithographed books: a study of the design and production of improper books in the age of the hand press* (London, 1990) includes scattered references to lithographic printing in Indian scripts not only in Europe but also in the subcontinent beginning with Rind in Calcutta, the Asiatic Lithographic Press, etc. from the 1820s onwards. F. Robinson: *Technology and religious change: Islam and the impact of print* in: Modern Asian Studies 27 (1993), pp. 229-251, deals specifically with the South Asian context and the reaction of various strata of Muslim society to the arrival of lithography.

The study of book illustration and book-binding in India has hardly begun. *Woodcut prints of nineteenth century Calcutta*. Ed. A. Paul (Calcutta, 1983) includes chapters by Nikhil Sarkar and others on the Battala tradition of Bengali book illustration and its relationship with folk art traditions, especially the Kalighat school. S. Sen: *Battalar chapa o chabi* ["Battala printing and illustration"] (Calcutta, 1984) gives an authoritative account of popular publishing (almanacs, etc.) in the Battala district of Calcutta and their famous woodcut illustrations. G. Duverdier: *Tranquebar: un atelier de reliure dans l'Inde tamoule du XVIIIe siecle* [offprint - source unknown] is a meticulous study of the manning, costs and materials of the mission bindery, together with a list of just 13 extant Tranquebar bindings so far identified with certainty. Beyond these, however, there is very little significant research to report.

At the beginning of this paper I mentioned that the history of the book approach had yet to make any impact on research related to India. However, one significant work has recently been published which augurs well for the future, namely S.K. Das: *1800-1900: Western impact: Indian response* (A history of Indian literature Volume VIII) (New Delhi, 1991). Considering factors of change, Das sets the arrival of printing within the entire context of literary creation, showing that as it altered textual transmission so it also brought changes in patronage and readership which in turn can be linked to changes in the themes and forms of Indian literature. The important link with the change in the relative status of languages (Sanskrit and Persian v. English and the vernaculars) and the emergence of literary prose and journalism are also considered. Not the least important part of the book is an enormous chronology (pp. 419-772) of literary events covering the period 1800-1910 and 23 languages, recording the establishment of printing preses, significant publications including newspapers, the foundation of cultural and educational institutions, libraries, etc. — a marvellous 'springboard' for further research in depth.

The impact on printing of the status — official and cultural — enjoyed by various languages at different periods is also considered in B.S. Cohn: *The command of language and the language of command.* In: *Subaltern studies IV* ed. by Ranajit Guha (Delhi, 1985), pp. 276-329; and C.R. King: *Forging a new linguistic identity: the Hindi movement in Banaras, 1868-1914* in: *Culture and power in Banaras: community, performance, and environment, 1800-1980* ed. S.B. Freitag (Delhi, 1989), p. 179-202. K.S. Diehi : *The literary Hussain family of Chinsurah/Hooghly, 1800-1850* in : *Proceedings of the 1978 Southwest Conference on Asian Studies* ed. L.J. Bilsky (Little Rock, 1979), pp. 150-162, traces the earliest known initiative on the part of a group of Indian scholars led by Hakeem Muhammad Hussain to publish in *moffusil* or up-country Bengal.

Attention is beginning to be paid to popular publishing of folk literature, such as K. Hansen's two articles: *Nautanki chapbooks: written traditions of a folk form* in: India Magazine (Jan. 1986), pp. 65-72, and *The birth of Hindi drama in Banaras, 1868-1885* in: *Culture and power in Banaras: community, performance, and environment, 1800-1980*, ed. S.B. Freitag (New Delhi, 1989), pp. 64-67. F.W. Pritchett: *Marvelous encounters: folk romance in Urdu and Hindi* (New Delhi, 1985) includes a chapter on "Qissa and mass printing" (pp. 20-36). R.W. Nicolas: *Sitala and the art of printing: the transmission and propagation of the myth of the goddess of smallpox in rural west Bengal* in: *Mass culture, language and arts in India* ed. M.L. Apte (Bombay, 1978), pp. 152-180, shows how the "inexpensive printed book" can be more important than either manuscript or oral tradition. As part of a multidisciplinary project on popular culture in Pakistan sponsored by the Smithsonian Institution, a survey of chapbook publishing in Lahore, Peshawar and elsewhere was undertaken in 1989 by a team led by W. Hanaway of the University of Pennsylvania. This involved interviewing printers, publishers and booksellers and has resulted in a bibliography of some 950 items covering such genres as traditional and modern romances, religious and secular poetry, film songs, marriage manuals, humorous stories, spells and charms. These results constitute a valuable index of popular taste and deserve to be published as a model for similar field-work in the future in other parts of the subcontinent.

There are many desiderata for the future, some of which have already been hinted at, such as a balanced general history of early printing in South Asia, although the linguistic hurdle to be overcome before that can be written cannot be overestimated. A comprehensive gazetteer of early printing would also be invaluable, particularly for charting the spread of the press in the 19th century, and this I have personally recently embarked upon. An urgent desideratum is to begin a systematic search within South Asia for surviving sets of early type and other printing materials (such as those of the Baptist Mission Press, Calcutta, which recently surfaced) as well as publishers' archives, and to preserve them in suitable institutions in India with full scholarly access. The publication of a centenary booklet by P. M. Bagchi & Company, a leading light in the Calcutta booktrade, *Shatabarsha smarka patrika 1883-1983* ed. Arabinda Bhattacharya (Calcutta, 1983), outlining the firm's development from the manufacture of perfumes via inks to publishing and bookselling, gave a fascinating glimpse of what might lie in store. Another desideratum is the compilation of catalogues of early works preserved in South Asian libraries themselves, and here some advance has been made. Perhaps most promisingly The Bibliographical Society of India has recently been formed and has already produced *The National Union Catalogue of incunabula and early printed books* ed. R.D. Singh (Calcutta, 1986). It lists some 5,000 editions of mainly European imprints in about one hundred libraries in India. Karachi University Library, home of the eminent Pakistani bibliographer Anis Khurshid, has also produced a *Catalogue of rare books* compiled by Sarwar Ahmad Siddiqui. 2 vols. (Karachi, [c. 1985 ?]), again predominantly containing European rather than South Asian imprints. Serampore College has issued *Carey Library books in different languages other than English, Bengali and Latin* [typescript] (Serampore, 1982). The contents of many more such valuable collections, both institutional and private, remain to be fully documented.

A final plea : the historical pattern of publishing in the subcontinent inevitably cuts across modern state boundaries. To cite just one example, with no press in Nepal until the 1850s, all Nepali books, periodicals and newspapers published before that date were printed in India, principally at Varanasi. This kind of cultural unity surely argues that the national libraries of South Asia should cooperate closely - to their mutual benefit - in improving retrospective bibliographical control for the region. The sooner this process is now set in hand, the greater its chances of success will be. For the precious raw material for this study, the books themselves, with their 'built-in obsolescence' of poor-quality paper and the subsequent ravages of climate and pests (human as well as insect), are disappearing from libraries and private collections more quickly than we realise.

The South Asia Library Group from the Past to the Future; Some Reflections on South Asian Studies in the United Kingdom and the Sub-Continent

B.C. BLOOMFIELD

A number of previous articles[1] reviewed the position of Asian studies and their interaction with library provision in the United Kingdom, and attempted to draw some conclusions as to the future. This form of crystal gazing can be useful, but what has previously appeared in print has generally been written entirely from the European point fo view. There is also a need to consider these studies from the sub-continental point of view and this brief investigation attempts to surmise what may then transpire and how it may affect the South Asia Library Group in the United Kingdom and library provision for South Asian studies.

Systematic British studies of South Asia may be said to have begun in earnest with the foundation of the Asiatic Society of Bengal. While they often sprang from a purely academic interest in languages, customs and history, they equally often had clear advantages for the British who undertook them in that they promoted trade, facilitated converse with the peoples of India and generally reinforced a primacy of knowledge and economic interest. "Knowledge itself is power" as Bacon put it and this drove much of the research conducted in India during the time of the British Empire, although such research was often also directed to promote the economic and social benefit of the people. Research into customary law promoted good administration, and research into agriculture and economic products extended the financial power of the country and the well being of the population. Purely academic research was first based in the universities of the United Kingdom, mainly Oxford, Cambridge and London, and often financed by Indian capital and patronage. Such research was slow to take root in the universities of the sub-continent which were largely occupied in providing vocational courses of instruction to supply the steadily growing need for an educated class to govern and run the country in association with the British elite. There were in the United Kingdom few academics who did not have some association with the ruling power either through direct links with government training schemes, or from previous membership of the Indian Civil Service. Their opinions were rarely sought nor were they consulted on political or constitutional questions where the civil servants, the India Office and the power of the Viceroy reigned supreme. Archaeology, for example, was mainly the province of the official Government Archaeological Survey, and academic participation was not sought. A scholar like Sir Ralph Turner was for almost all his career associated with research that was either funded or sponsored by official money. And this was the usual pattern. However after independence in 1947 there were changes. While the Government of India continued to sponsor and use research conducted in Indian universities and official government departments - as do the other countries of the sub-continent - the balance of research began to swing towards the interests of professional university teachers, and so it did in the United Kingdom too. Such professionals owe their prime loyalty to the pursuit of knowledge and the disinterested promotion of their subject of study, and not necessarily to good government, improved administration, and the betterment of their peoples. This change of direction is inevitably reflected in the subjects and research topics pursued, the character of publication and the use of library resources provided to underpin that research. Thus, both the character and the driving force behind research work on South Asia has changed to reflect the independence of the countries in the sub-continent and the status of the persons undertaking that research.

In the United Kingdom and South Asia most academics undertaking research are no longer funded by governments but are driven by their own interests and academic fashion; they no longer regard themselves as part of the governing elite, in fact quite the contrary, they are often regarded as the intellectual driving force behind movements opposing governments. University teachers and researchers see themselves as "professionals" and form themselves into professional associations such as BASAS in the United Kingdom.

Studies in the humanities are frequently based on printed and archival material held in libraries and other depositories and following the publication of the Hayter report in the United Kingdom, Mr. J D Pearson, the Librarian of the School of Oriental and African Studies, took the initiative in calling several conferences of librarians and active scholars, as a result of which the South Asia Library Group (SALG) and a number of other regional library groups were established. SALG held its first meeting in February 1968 and has continued to meet regularly ever since, to publish a newsletter (since 1973), and to sponsor several extremely valuable bibliographical publications, notably *South Asian bibliography: a handbook and guide,* edited by J D Pearson (Brighton: Harvester, 1979); *The bibliography of South Asian periodicals: a union list....,* compiled by G W Shaw and S Quraishi (Brighton: Harvester, 1982); and the *Directory of South Asian library resources in the UK and the republic of Ireland,* edited by S Gunasingam (London: SALG, 1988). Other projects are in course of preparation. However since SALG was founded there has been a decline in participation by academic members of the Group, although the attendance of library representatives has increased slightly over the years. Valuable work has been done and is being planned, but it is likely that the committee will need to review the direction of future efforts and SALG's publication programme.

In 1982 there occurred an event that was significant for South Asian scholarship world-wide, the coming together of the India Office Library & Records with the Department of Oriental Manuscripts and Printed Books under the aegis of the British Library. The joint resources of these two collections are the premier international resource for library and archive based research on South Asia, without any question whatsoever. Whether or not this position was maintained depended, of course, on whether the British Library could provide resources to maintain new and retrospective acquisitions to ensure the currency of the collections and make them available as a resource for all scholars. So far the British Library has managed to achieve this and there has been no discernible slackening either of use or acquisitions since 1982. The projected move at an unstated date—but almost certainly by 1997—to the new building at St. Pancras promises easier and speedier availability of material for readers. But these unparalleled collections still need to be made much more accessible than they are at present. Only a small part of the collections has been microfilmed, some parts are still uncatalogued and no authoritative handlists exist for some of the records groups. The recent award of a major grant from the Getty Foundation will list and index the photographic collections, but there is much more to be done to make the information contained in the collections more easily available for research. And scholars from abroad still occasionally find it difficult to fund their research if it involves a visit to London to use these resources.

In 1986 two significant events occurred for South Asian scholarship in the United Kingdom : the publication of the Parker committee report, "Speaking for the future"; and the foundation of the British Association for South Asian Studies (BASAS) as the main professional association of scholars concerned with those studies. The association has gone from strength to strength and can now be fairly considered to be well-established with its own agenda, conferences, and publications. When previous expansions of Asian studies took place as a consequence of the Scarbrough and Hayter reports, the newly recruited academic staff predominantly reflected old imperial and colonial attitudes, and indeed were often recruited from the ranks of former colonial servants. The new professional academics have none of those associations—for better or worse. The membership and interests of BASAS appear to be concentrated in the humanities and social sciences with little or no representation from the sciences, medicine or technology and industry. The whole ethos of BASAS, judged from its bulletin and publications, is quite different from preceding generations and in this changing tone can be detected a reflection of the changing relationships between the countries of the sub-continent and the United Kingdom, exemplified in the changing generations, the increased maturity of the countries of South Asia, and the shrinking importance of the United Kingdom in the sub-continent. (This takes no account of the influence and role of the immigrant communities here and the enormous and continuing British commercial interests there, both of which will continue to make our mutual links significant.) However there has so far been little formal contact between SALG and BASAS, as, for example, was the case with the Standing Conference on Library Materials on Africa (SCOLMA) and the African Studies Association of the UK (ASAUK) where there was (and may be still is ?) reciprocal committee membership for each organisation.

BASAS has, on the whole, not been very confident of the future for South Asian studies in the United Kingdom. It refers to "...the dwindling band of South Asian scholars...(*Bulletin*, 2, January 1987,

p. [1]) and "The outlook for South Asian studies in this country continues to be grim" (*Bulletin,* 3, June 1987, p. [1]), but, in fact, taking into account the new polytechnic universities the range of studies has widened considerably with film, other media and music being offered as optional courses, while the number of undergraduates entering universities has increased considerably, often overwhelming the teaching and library resources available in universities that are now less well-funded by the government. An article by William Crawley on "South Asian studies and the BBC" (*Bulletin,* 6, June 1988, p [1-2]) reveals the resources and interests of yet another player in the field. And two new centres of South Asian studies have been created in the universities of Hull and Edinburgh, while the Victoria & Albert Museum has at last managed, with the aid of some outside funding, to re-furbish a limited gallery of Indian art in its Nehru Gallery (*Bulletin,* 19, December 1992, p. 3-7) and still wants to plan further enlarged provision for its magnificent collections. There are approximately 1.25 million citizens of South Asian origin now in the United Kingdom, some 2.5% of the total population, to provide some continuing interest in South Asian studies.

It may also now be helpful to re-state a number of factors that are continuing to affect libraries :

(*a*) financial support from central and local government will decline ;

(*b*) the allocation of that support will change with more going to larger units and less to smaller units;

(*c*) the proportion of library budgets available for the purchase of books and periodicals will decline relative to the amount spent on staffing;

(*d*) technical services will become more expensive and more sophisticated;

(*e*) libraries will be asked to support an increased range of studies at widely different levels ;

(*f*) libraries are likely to introduce charges for services, often at quite a high level.

To these factors can be added others particularly affecting SALG and library materials for South Asian studies. The most likely being :

(*a*) a considerable increase in the published output of South Asian countries;

(*b*) an increased demand from scholars and users for much of this increased publication (provided there is adequate bibliographic control);

(*c*) difficulties (for a variety of reasons) in gaining access to this increased publication;

(*d*) difficulties for libraries in deciding and selecting what part of the increased output needs to be acquired;

(*e*) nineteenth and early twentieth century material published in South Asia will become increasingly scarce and difficult to obtain;

(*f*) interlending between libraries will become a subject of increased attention (i.e. demand will increase but so will costs, and conservation restrictions will become more inhibiting);

(*g*) preservation and conservation of existing library materials, whether under threat from deteriorating paper or excessive use, will become increasingly expensive and troublesome problem;

(*h*) microfilming of newspapers, archival groups and similar batches of material will be an essential part of the librarian's strategy in preserving items and making them available for study world-wide; and

(*i*) British libraries, together with SALG, already stronger in older materials for the study of South Asia compared with those in the USA, will find this contract likely to be accentuated in the future.

These points were first adumbrated in 1984 and it is perhaps salutary to realise that almost all of them have come to pass—in varying degrees. What was not then forecast was the fact that in the United Kingdom the government, by reducing funding for universities and discouraging and restricting research studentships in the humanities and social sciences, has encouraged a flood tide of undergraduates without providing the funding for the necessary accommodation and support services for those students. Thus, libraries and other university facilities find themselves under severe stress with inadequate resources, matching the position of most universities in the sub-continent.

Cheap travel has enabled our scholars to travel to the sub-continent fairly freely (in spite of needless reciprocal visa arrangements), but research work in the sub-continent for British scholars is constrained by restrictions imposed by the countries of South Asia, both on scholars themselves and the topics of their research. However scholars from the sub-continent continue to be constrained by the need to fund their research if they want to come to the United kingdom to work on library materials here, and the fact that neither travel nor subsistent is for them cheap.

Having gone so far and having identified some of the factors affecting present and future South Asian studies, we may now turn to some consideration of the possible implications they may have for SALG and its future programme.

First, it might seem profitable if SALG were to consider widening its sphere of interest to include academic disciplines outside the traditional humanities and social sciences, perhaps bringing in medicine and law as a start.

Second, SALG needs to be more outward—looking and to emphasise co-operation with other bodies, first of all perhaps BASAS. Reciprocal membership of committees and the planning of events could be productive. Scholars and librarians are inter-dependent and need to be in constant consultation. There are numerous other societies in the United Kingdom that SALG might consider relations with, e.g. the British Association for Cemeteries in South Asia (BACSA), which is carrying out valuable documentation work and publishing the results; the various ex-Indian associations, ICS, Army, etc.; the numerous immigrant societies; the High Commissions and Embassies of South Asian countries and their cultural representatives; student bodies; and the heads of the centres for South Asian studies in the universities.

Third, the bibliographical work of SALG has up to now been concentrated on the provision of guides to the location of library materials and the strengthening of provision on the basis of identified gaps. The need to provide location guides is much reduced by the ability to consult library catalogues at a distance by means of JANET (and in the future SUPER-JANET), Internet, RLIN, and other bibliographic utilities. SALG might well be advised to carry out more structured consultation with scholars and other users to try to forecast research trends, and gaps identified by users and not simply by librarians.

Fourth, there is the need to fill identified gaps in library provision and to assist in programmes of preservation microfilming to make such rare materials available to other libraries and scholars overseas. Co-operation with, and the use of, schemes like the Mellon Microfilming Project, Newsplan in the United Kingdom, and the encouragement of similar schemes in the sub-continent should form an essential part of SALG's programme to improve library provision. (The British Library's OIOC is co-operating with the University of Chicago in such a scheme to microfilm the major Sanskrit series, funded by the National Endowment for the Humanities in the USA.) Funds should be sought in the United Kingdom to support such schemes for international benefit.

Fifth, SALG need to consider and devise a programme of scholarships to enable scholars to study in United kingdom collections. The Charles Wallace Trust has already made a start in providing funds for similar purposes, but a more structured programme is essential to stimulate the use of the unrivalled collections held in the United Kingdom. Bodies like the Hinduja Foundation might be approached to endow such a programme; and in India the Tata Foundation might be asked for support. The British Council would no doubt be an appropriate body to advise on any such scheme, and eager to help.

Sixth, since the British Library and its OIOC collections is the unrivalled international library collection for the study of South Asia, it must be stimulated to take the lead in bibliographic programmes and initiatives, and the Board of the Library should be constantly reminded that this inheritance needs to be maintained and renewed. The India Office Records microfilming programme should be accelerated, in cooperation with the governments of South Asian countries who all need copies of the records for administrative, legal and cultural purposes. SALG, in co-operation with the International Council on Archives (ICA), should encourage the institution of such a programme funded perhaps by the British government and the South Asian Association Regional Co-operation (SAARC), which was founded to encourage such cultural co-operative projects. The cost would be substantial, but the benefit to the countries of South Asia and the world of scholarship generally would be incalculable.

Seventh, SALG should encourage the British Library to secure funding for and re-start work on the second tranche of the *South Asia and Burma retrospective bibliography (SABREB)* covering the period 1800-1869, planned for some time past in co-operation with the countries of the sub-continent. Volume 1 edited by Mr. Graham Shaw is published and available in ESTC format; volume 2 needs to be funded and started; while volume 3 was planned to be carried through in India itself. The library resources for this period are excellent in United Kingdom libraries and would provide a firm basis for the compilation.

Eighth, SALG need to look more closely, on the basis of what it discovers about possible future research needs from users, at the current acquisition of library materials from the countries of South Asia and their availability to readers. Restraint on budgets for purchase, on the costs of inter-library loans, on scholars' travel costs, on facsimile transmission, will all affect library provision and SALG needs to take some account of these factors.

Ninth, once SALG has a firm programme and has established links with other bodies interested in South Asian studies in the United Kingdom, it should consider links with similar societies in the countries of the sub-continent and internationally, such as the International Federation of Library Associations (IFLA) to bring its concerns and interests to prominence in more general forums. Since it deals with studies affecting the culture of countries with a considerable portion of the world's population there need be no hesitation in bringing its concerns before a wider audience.

Tenth, once SALG has formulated its programmes for the future these should be discussed and publicised widely both here in the United

Kingdom and in the sub-continent. Here again it is likely that the British Council will be able to advise and assist, and the World Service of the BBC might be helpful in gaining more publicity for SALG and its work.

Co-operation with others, both librarians and scholars, is essential to the future health of SALG; and this co-operation must extend to the countries of the sub-continent if scholarship is to continue to be both soundly based and productive in its results. Librarians are the traditional mid-wives of scholarship; long may SALG flourish in this fruitful role !

REFERENCE

1. Notes on library provision for Oriental and Asian studies in Great Britain (*Journal of librarianship*, 8 (2), April 1976, 111-121; Asian studies in libraries (*Asian affairs*, 12 (O.S. 58), pt II, June 1981, 173-190; south Asian studies and libraries in the United Kingdom: now and in the future (*SALNAQ [South Asia Library Notes and Queries]*, 19/20, Fall 1985/ Spring 1986, 1-11; The future for South Asian libraries and studies in the United Kingdom (*SALG newsletter*, 37, January 1991, 1-8.

Illiteracy : The Global Orphan

DENNIS GUNTON

Since the ultimate aim of all writing, publishing, bookselling, information and library activity is reading, it is baffling that so little has been done to eradicate illiteracy; "a want of learning" as defined by Alexander Pope but more readily recognised today as the inability to read or write. In 1930, the U.S. Bureau of the Census considered illiterate any person over 10 years of age who could not read or write in any language. The United Nations in the Demographic Yearbook, 1970, has recommended that "a literate person must be able to read with understanding and to write a short statement on every day life in any one language." When Nigeria undertook a census in 1952-53, illiteracy was recorded in all those over 7 years of age, from these figures United Nations statisticians computed figures based on the U.N.'s minimum age of 15. Doubts about the validity of such variable statistics are inevitable and the United Nations in the same Yearbook anticipates and allays them somewhat by this justification :

> "Lack of Statistics for developing countries and territories, particularly in Africa, is probably a reflection of the fact that illiteracy is estimated to be so widespread in certain areas that the need for remedial action is obvious without detailed statistics."

The definition of an illiterate, his or her age and their numbers has yet to gain universal endorsement. There is, by contrast, far more certainity about the retarding effect of illiteracy on a nation's progress. This was particularly the case in the early 1950's when illiteracy was positively identified as a blight on mankind and a fitting subject for a Unesco campaign. The target was, after all, legitimate, non-controversial and one which could unite the disparate elements of the parent United Nations in common cause for the greater good of humanity. Following Unesco public library seminars in Manchester in 1948, Sweden in 1950 and Brazil in 1951, the sponsors held the fourth in Nigeria and the report published in 1954, indicates Unesco's pre-occupation with the problems of illiteracy. In a foreword, the Director of the seminar wrote :

"In regard to this resolution, which affects the social and economic life of the African peoples, the acquisition of a new technique as essential as reading is of the utmost importance."

The intention of the organisers in the matter of illiteracy is to be clearly seen in the subjects of the papers :

Organisation of public libraries	5 papers
Provision of suitable reading material	7 papers
Training of librarians	2 papers

One illustration, showing a teacher before a blackboard with the letters of the alphabet, is significantly captioned : "Public libraries are needed throughout Africa to support programmes of mass education". Mass education, adult education and fundamental education are used almost synonymously with teaching literacy and librarians are indicated as having a central role to play in the undertaking. The Report goes on :

"Recent developments would seem to indicate a marked trend in the direction of establishing, on a regional basis, services closely linked to library development ... for training fundamental educational leaders. These developments offer suggestive examples for the planning and provision of library training."

What could have been a seminal influence on illiteracy campaigns in Africa and other parts of the developing world—for Unesco intended to expand the programme worldwide—was not followed-up, for two reasons. First because there was a diminishing enthusiasm for illiteracy campaigns as such, and second, a growing belief that universal (or free) primary education held the solution to the problem of illiteracy. The popular solution, which rapidly gained ground, suggested that illiteracy was less a disease and rather more a symptom, an external manifestation of an illness that required curing from within rather than cosmetic medication from outside. Within Nigeria, which was intended as the test-bed for the experiment, national interest became centred upon constitutional issues, the campaign for independence and the struggle for political powers within the new federation rather than upon domestic social concerns. Moreover, there was good economic long-term sense in teaching children rather than adults since the benefits for the nation would be spread over a much longer time-scale. The methodology was orthodox, literacy was part of an existing syllabus and really only amounted to an expansion of a system already in place, a virtue not lost on ambitious officials in Ministries of Education. Unesco, faced with ths rejection of a plan by those for whom it was tailored, endorsed universal primary education as the one true path to enlightenment and in *World Illiteracy in mid-century*, published in 1957, gave their stamp of approval :

> "If all children of school age in any country attended school for a sufficient length of time, there would eventually be no adult illiterates in the population, except those mentally deficient and incapable of learning to read or write. It follows, therefore, that the best means of preventing illiteracy is to provide adequate education for all children."

It is all the more sobering, therefore, to find that a decade after the Unesco publication cited above, the Northern Region of Nigeria recorded that only 11·46% of eligible children were attending primary schools. The poverty, size of region and dispersal of the population prevented any serious consideration of implementing the prescribed policy. If the history of universal primary education in developing countries, as well as anti-illiteracy campaigns, teaches anything it is that the success of such ventures strains resources beyond their limits and depends upon economic developments outside education. There is also the moral dimension involving teaching children and allowing the older generation of illiterates to die out. The issue may not have arisen, either way it is short-sighted since a mass of illiterate adults will—in the nature of things—impede the economic, social, cultural and political progress of developing countries.

It can be said that in some respects the publications of Unesco have the ambiguities and contradictions of the Bible, and their popular citation rather than universal adoption may owe something to their inconsistency. As Voltaire pertinently observed of the medical profession: "Doctors pour drugs of which they know little, to cure diseases of which they know less, into human beings of whom they know nothing."

Looking for Signs

It has been estimated that in eighty five countries of Africa, Asia and Latin America, the illiterate population is growing at the rate of twenty million a year.

Virtually all figures associated with illiteracy, as we have already seen, are more admired for their purpose than their accuracy. In 1919 Lenin signed a decree that the entire population of the USSR must learn to read and write; in 1939 it was announced by Stalin that illiteracy had been eradicated. Cuba carried out a comparable campaign and was declared free from illiteracy in 1960. In 1905, a mass education movement was inaugurated in China but little on the subject comes up subsequently in the literature.

By contrast, the western democracies such as the USA and Britain, from time to time produce horrifying statistics proving that 10% of their populations are illiterate. There usually follows a swift indictment of television, incompetent teachers or indifferent parents and attention is directed towards the need for social reform rather than illiteracy itself. Deflection from illiteracy and its stigma has been helped in the west by the discovery of dyslexia—a reading handicap which may cause semantic errors—such as reading *forest* as trees, or reading *sympathy* as orchestra because of an interfering link with *symphony*. There is also visual dyslexia, for example reading *rib* as ride when whole word recognition is found difficult. If they do nothing else, neuropsychological studies since 1970 into dyslexia have kept the illiteracy bogy alive and well and lucrative in the west. It is however, the mass illiteracy in developing countries that is generally regarded as pernicious and whereas whether or not people could read or write hardly mattered in some societies centuries ago, today this century does not exist for those who are trapped and immovable because they cannot read, write, find their way about, tell the time, know what day it is, what lies beyond the village or defend themselves against swindlers, fakers, bureaucrats and politicians.

Any attempt to discover success with literacy campaigns has, however, reluctantly, to recognise the poineering work of Christian missionaries. In Africa, Asia and Latin America, it was the mission's emphasis on the importance of "The Word" that led to unravelling strange languages and the introduction of printing so as to propagate the Christian message, although it is true some of the messages may currently be embarrassing to the western civilisation which circulated them and the books themselves have become no more than tokens of the past in collections which are rarely consulted. With hindsight, it may be easier to be indifferent rather than impressed by their dedication and commitment to the problem of illiteracy, nonetheless the early missions deserve our respect for their work in breaking down language barriers and demonstrating the value of literacy for whatever ends. At the very least, it must be conceded that written records for some of the 1,300 African languages, spoken by 400 million people, have only existed since missionary activity began on the continent around 150 years ago.

It is not easy to trace anything of comparable merit going on today.

Godparents

Whilst it is difficult to point to any contemporary, productive campaigns against illiteracy, the literature suggests it has not lost all its fascination for visitors to, rather than natives of, those countries with abnormally high illiteracy rates. It may be the missionary's cause lives on as a post-colonial apology and in some ways keeps alive a universal endorsement for the importance of literacy which has outlived the issues abandonment.

It has to be recognised that famine, for example, is more important than illiteracy and far simpler to rectify. Huge shipments of grain may pose problems regarding finance, collections, freighting and distribution but they are nothing compared to the complications associated with literacy campaigns. And as the achievements of Band Aid demonstrate, combatting famine has a media appeal in the west that illiteracy would find hard to emulate. Of almost equal importance is the recognition of the danger of saddling developing nations with the responsibility to maintain institutions beyond their needs and beyond their means. Comparable—in some ways—to the shipment of grain is the donation of books and a variety of donors from western countries have provided books to developing countries. Four factors stand out when considering such programmes :

1. The books are meant for literates.
2. They are usually in the English language.
3. Most books are a random collection and sent unsolicited.

4. Tailor-made presentations are usually directed at tertiary level institutions.

None of which does much for the illiterate except to pose the importance of the problem of the language in which literacy is to be taught. English and French are the official languages in the southern bulge of West Africa where there are 17 million Yoruba speakers, 13 million Igbo, 8 million Akan and 2 million Ewe. In which language should any literacy campaign be conducted ? Moreover, whereas western institutions may have expertise in teaching their own languages, they are less likely to be able to teach in African languages; which effectively rules out seasoned assistance from outside the indigenous community. Finding responsible parents who will adopt the orphan of illiteracy is no easy option.

Who are today's orphans ?

It has been estimated there will be one billion illiterates by the end of the century. Around 75% will be in the five most populous Asian countries : China will be 34% illiterate; India, 60%; Indonesia, 33%; Pakistan, 74% and Bangladesh, 71%. Nigeria has 57% of the population illiterate and Somalia around 88%. Nearer Europe, Portugal has 16% and Turkey 25%.

Some countries have done better than might be expected in recent years. Iraq has only 11%, Chile 9% and Mexico 10% of the population unable to read or write.

Tending to call attention to the validity or relevance of such figures is Saudi Arabia, where 50% of the population are illiterate. Most westerner's first impression of Saudi Arabia is that of visiting a country where everyone in the population has won the national lottery. All the outward signs of prosperity—luxurious hotels and offices—expensive motor-cars—well equipped hospitals and universities—opulent airports—ostentatious shops and supermarkets—suggest an overflowing economy that has only to identify a difficulty and at a stroke, remove it. The world at large may be moved by the problem illiteracy poses in Asia, Africa and Latin America—but in Saudi Arabia ? It may be that women make up most of the 50%. For, a general rule, men are generally more literate in a ratio of 2 : 1 in most countries where illiteracy is endemic. This fact brings into play aspects which concern social and religious perceptions of the importance of literacy among members of a community In many communities women play a very full part—cooking, cleaning, raising children and working on the land. In others, often Muslim communities, women are restrained. Either way, it is obvious there are considerable impediments to eradicating illiteracy and campaigns enjoy nothing like the automatic local support well intentioned westerners might suppose. In Kerala in south India, on the other hand, women have organised anti-illiteracy campaigns with conspicuous success. Birth control, sexual instruction, child care and family health are all cleverly interwoven messages to be conveyed by the newly acquired skills; literacy is not just a goal n itself but a powerful means of improving life within a community.

Contemporary Attitudes

Regarded in the west for a hundred years or more as a scourge on society, it is an attitude towards illiteracy that spills over in evaluations of the importance of reading and writing in developing countries. This frame of mind may be no more than a post-colonial apology and owe a good deal to western ignorance combined with good intentions. Is it irrational to yearn for widespread literacy ? Do the rising numbers of illiterates really matter ? How far is the way of life in Saudi Arabia restricted by the exceptional tally of those who can neither read nor write ? It might seen that whilst no swift eradication policy has been discovered, it has been that much easier for most of us to come to terms with illiteracy as an almost permanent condition for an increasing portion of the world's population. A view reinforced by the divide in the attitude to illiteracy to be found in developed and developing countries.

When examining the tangled web of illiteracy, there are one or two strands that can be unravelled and examined. From the beginning it is possible to question the value that has been placed upon it in the west as well as the figures produced largely by the same source. The problems of literacy in what language and the kind of reading materials which will provide an opportunity for those with newly-won skills to exercise their competence are also central to the issue. In particularly short supply are any valid costings of literacy campaigns or analyses of where those campaigns that failed, went wrong. Silence, in this respect, is as pervasive as it is ominous.

"Reading maketh a full man and writing an exact man" as Francis Bacon recorded, but they are talents which an ever larger percentage of the earth's inhabitants will be unable to exercise in the foreseable future. It would therefore be timely if, fifty years after its pioneering endeavours, Unesco once again gave leadership in a concerted campaign to—at the very least—diminish the numbers handicapped by illiteracy.

From Reading Promotion to Media Literacy - Public Library Services for Children and Young People

ILONA GLASHOFF

The end of reading culture?

Never before, since the beginning of the history of letter press printing has the amount of printed materials been greater than today. At the same time, the public press of the 80 has predicted the imminent end of reading culture - a shocking prediction for all those who are engaged with books, so also for librarians.

What is the reason for such a pessimistic forecast? Is it the fear that marketing laws will dominate and the new technologies and media will replace the book? One fact is certain, the new media have spread to such an extent which the 'book' as a medium never achieved.

Empirical research has meanwhile found out, thus setting our minds at rest, that the book still holds a steady place in the media field[1]. It still has advantages when compared with other media, e.g. the reader can decide himself with what speed and at what time and place he wants to read the book, and for this reason it cannot be simply replaced by any other medium. So is the reading culture not yet at an end? Contrary to the loud announcements of the press based on false interpretation of statistical surveys[1], empirical researches have proved that reading even now-a-days is a fixed part of the daily routine, especially with children and young people. They, in certain phases of their development, spend much less time watching television than adults do[2]. Nevertheless, the time at disposal is distributed differently than twenty years ago: among diverse media, the availability of which depends on the equipment existing in the children's rooms.

But all the same, the growing number of secondary illiterates in the industrial countries is alarming. This leads us to the conclusion, that we are not necessarily heading towards the end of reading culture, but media researchers are warning more and more of the increasing knowledge gap: with the speedy development of new technologies and the increasing presence of media, the gap is broadening between those who can handle these and are thus in a position to obtain every type of information they require, and those who are lacking abilities to do so. Reading, as a cultural technique, is the basis for the active handling of the majority of the media and therefore reading promotion is doubtless necessary.

Reading promotion meanwhile has become a term with inflationary tendencies: numerous institutions use it for their purposes. Now and again one gets the impression that reading promotion is used to support the sales market for literature.

It is time to consider what the results of all well-meant speeches and programmes have achieved for the group of unpractised readers and those with poor reading skills. It is time that the libraries define their own part in supporting reading.

The Part of the Libraries in Promoting Reading

Reading is one of the methods possible to achieve culture, knowledge and information and serves for amusement and relaxation. It is the duty of pedagogic institutions to teach people to read and not that of the libraries. But it is their duty to support people when they acquire the ability to read, to retain this ability and to promote the pleasure of reading. Reading promotion in libraries should start, where the parental home, school and similar institutions do not provide this or not to a sufficient extent.

"Pleasure in reading" is not necessarily the aim of parents in educating their children. In a questionnaire in 1988 among 16 requirements "What should children learn for their later life" [3], 39% answered "Enjoy books, like reading" (multiple answers were possible). Thus this educational aim reached position 11. In the same questionnaire 53% of the people questioned did not remember having had an education in reading worth mentioning in their parental homes.

It is also not the main issue in schools to make children enjoy reading. Achieving the ability to read is on the teaching curriculum, decoding the letters, first of all to produce a word and then a text in order to understand their meaning. Instructions in literature later on are also not intended to make reading a pleasure: when trying to understand the contents of the books read at school, an interpretation in the direction as laid down by the teacher is the aim rather than individual pleasure in reading for the student.[4]

Support of the individual process of learning to read, promotion of the individual reading practice and developing a pleasure in reading must, therefore, be the main aim when libraries want to operate with reading promotion. How do they achieve that?

Children are never too young to make use of a library. Even before the process of learning to read starts, they can gain their first experiences in handling books: looking at picture books together; story hours and picture book cinema are the most popular offers made to the very young in many libraries. Books as part of their games make them curious and permit an active participation of the small listeners in the process. When they first learn to read, reading on their own is a challenge, where a positive or negative experience can influence future reading habits. Here, it is necessary for the libraries to offer a multiple collection of books for the various stages of reading ability of the child: with contents suitable for all ages, with a progressive amount of text, which also makes it possible for poor-skilled readers to have a positive experience. Events like authors' reading hours, fairy tales recitations, childrens' theatre and similar happenings make children feel, that a library is a place in which they can have fun with books and an interesting world of reality and fantasy opens up. In cooperation between schools and libraries it is most important for librarians to make clear that the use of the library and the choice of reading material is of the child's own free will, even if the results are only comics.

The availability of a multiple, comprehensive book stock is the most important criterion to encourage reading, to assist in developing an adequate reading ability, and thus to produce the enjoyment of reading. The wish to read, means the desire to experience the fascination of the reading material and to discover one's own competence to select the reading material.

Encouraging Reading in Libraries - a Political Issue

"No time - no money - no staff" are surely weighty reasons preventing the active implementation of plans promoting reading after it has been realized that these are necessary. This makes promoting reading a political issue. Unfortunately, the general economic recession often makes a reduction of services necessary. But by reducing library work with children and young people the libraries are rendering themselves a bad service. The development of reading habits is based on developing phases in childhood and cannot be measured against a uniform standard but requires continues observation of the reading behaviour of children, their reading habits and the changes in the way they experience their environment (children's culture). Reduced inclination to read in childhood is hardly compensated in adult years.

In this connection, permit me to make a remark concerning staffing level. Especially in library systems in large cities in Germany, the "allround" librarian is increasingly asked for, due to the poor staff situation. The training colleges in the majority of cases offer very little specializing facilities for work in children and youth libraries. Here it is urgently necessary that additional practical training courses are offered, which make the problems of library work with children and young people obvious to all, and make effective work in reading support possible.

Training institutions should aim their courses more than even before at the duties of the libraries to promote reading. It is not enough to pass on knowledge about literature for children and young people. In order to meet the increasing amount of non-readers it is necessary that the present evaluation in building up holdings with the high placed goal of "the good book for young people" should be reconsidered. Literary quality or even pedagogic intentions are not a guarantee for a positive reading adventure. The majority of children and especially young people - even in highly industrialized and technically developed countries with their numerous educational and training systems - are not readers in public libraries or have ceased to be readers some time; possibly because the library did not meet their requirements.

The IFLA Standing Committee, Section of Children's Libraries, has taken up the subject of training schedules for librarians for library work with children and young people. It intends to evaluate the programmes of training institutions and plans to work out recommendations for the special professional subject of library work with children and young people.

Children's and Young People's Everyday Life with Medias, or are Books the better Media?

The reason why I have spoken so far only about work with books in connection with promotion of reading is, that acquiring the ability to read is the primary condition for handling up-to-date technologies and new media. It also cannot be denied that we cannot do without these media in our everyday life. Whereas about thirty years ago the printed media was the only existing and for the child available media, now-a-days children of pre-school age already possess cassette recorders which they can use at random to hear their cassettes with children's songs or stories. Later on, walkman, radio, television and now-a-days a CD player have been added. A simple personal computer today also belongs to the standard media equipment in the child's room. These media enable the child to gain access via vision or sound to the adult world without the precondition of having to be able to read.

In an essay, a German media pedagogue described the everyday media experience of three young people as follows [considerably shortened, slightly changed (4)]:

"After school Thorston retreats to his room to relax. He puts on his earphones, grabs the local daily newspaper, later on a periodical, and enjoys his favourite music. In the late afternoon he goes off to his volley-ball training. When he comes home he meets his father in front of the television set. Thorston joins him, at the same time eating and talking about this and that. The television set does not interfere with these activities. By the by, one gets to know that has happened in the world. At the weekend, especially during the cold season, his father recently brought along some video films. In that way the video recorder replaces the cinema, especially if there is nothing of interest on TV.

His friend Klaus (12) was presented with a personal computer for Christmas. In the meantime he has read most of the introductory manuals, although he generally does not read such "dry" books. He proudly demonstrates his first programmes: an exercise for English vocabulary and statistics about soccer results. He is now working on a programme about electronic music.

His sister Heike (14) is not much interested in her brother's computer hobby, but now and again she makes use of his vocabulary programme. Heike has always read a great deal, and she still does so today. She is engaged in animal preservation and has subscribed to an analog specialized journal. She mainly uses the video recorder to record animal films. She has catalogued them neatly, and she has already written some articles about threatened animal species for her students' magazine."

This is surely a stereotype description, but it makes certain points clear :

1. Making use of all types of media belongs to the everyday routine of children and young people and cannot be done without any more. Printed media are no longer the only source of information, relaxation and acquisition of knowledge.

2. Different types of media are used alongside. "With the development and spreading of new media, the old ones do not disappear, they only change their function: they lose certain functions and at the same time take over new ones (e.g. television - cinema - video)."[5]

   The use of a certain media is governed by its appropriateness and the conditions of the situation (Kubler a.a.o). During the child's development and the biography (here also during the different seasons) the use modem changes, as can be perceived from empiric studies.[6]

3. The children/young people described have grown up with the media and make use of them as a matter of course. But not enough, they are by no means victims of a media flood but have acquired competence in handling them (music and reading for relaxation - computer as an occupation for leisure hours - books and periodicals for entertainment and information - video recorder for entertainment and active documentation).

The media pedagogues of the 80's have uttered urgent warnings concerning the effects the media flood would have on the rising generation (e.g. Neil Postman). It is surprising, how little criticism is allocated to the medium book and how much other media are defamed concerning their effects. The "good book" cannot be compared with a computer game or film. A comparison of media can only be made with contents of equal quality in connection with their respective media processing. The book is not in every case the better medium. "Old and new media can be complementary to one another in a sensible way. The child that read does not need an auriola, the book does not need a museum to protect it"[7]

Making the most of Reading and Media Use as Part of Reading Promotion in Public Libraries

In numerous professional publications which define the activities of the public library it is pointed out, that the change in social development also affects the functions of the library. New technologies and media are already being applied in many libraries, at least in the cities of high-tech countries. Childrens libraries are no exception in this respect. Children are said to be the busiest users, but at the same time also the busiest users of new technologies and media - as far as they have access to them. And that is the point where the problem arises:

When building up holdings, priority still is given to printed media. I have not yet seen an almost equal balance of media in any library in my country. On the contrary, in arguments towards the funding authorities it could often be heard that as there was not even enough money for books, building up media holdings should not be started; or the financing authorities critized libraries for spending public money to buy what they consider "poor quality" media (radio plays, popmusic etc.). The professional staff also expressed reservations concerning the "value" of media. The city state of Hamburg provides a typical (bad) example: videos are so far not available, computer software was first offered in 1991. In many cases holdings were built up in Germany with a view to reaching easily high lending results[8]; a proof of an inconsequent holdings policy.

New technologies and media are not included in the culture which is represented by libraries and therefore their handling is not supported. This is drastically contrary to the development of the market. But where else, when not in libraries, can they be integrated in culture? Where else can people, especially children, get information about the types offered and gain experience in handling them in order to get competent for using them later on.

Here the same applies as for reading promotion: education for reading is not our job, neither is media education, but promotion of reading is and also the support to acquire the ability to handle media: their choice, offers on the market, providing them and advice concerning them; and to apply it, where the parental home and school omit to do so entirely or not in a sufficient manner.

Reading promotion now-a-days must include equally all media. Projects for promoting reading should at the same time support other media which provide children with "knowledge about all media, about appliance measures and the ways they functions" and "show them a way out of passive consumption and so to stimulate their creativeness, phantasy and judgement"[9]. Book fans, computer and video freaks - as kids of their time, they all have to be helped to become competent to make sensible use of all media and to prevent that is only the privilege of a chosen few, who can inform themselves increasingly better by making use of a continuous technical development, whereas the others are left without. It seems to me, that micro-electronics are only at the beginning of is development. Libraries should not miss their connexion to futuristic children's library work.

REFERENCES

1. Eine Marketingkonzeption fur Offentliche Bibliotheken. Berlin, 1987 (dbi Materialien; 71)
2. Kubler, Hans-Dieter: Lesen Jugendliche oder lesen sie nicht? in: Medienrundbrief. Hrsg. Referat Medienarbeit.... Amt fur Schule. Nr. 18. Hamburg, o.j.
3. Lesen. Zahlen, Daten, Fakten... Hrsg von der Stiftung Lesen. Mainz 1990. (Materialien der Stiftung Lesen zur Leseforderung und Leseforschung. 3)
4. Hoffmann, Hilmar: Lesen setzt Orientierungen. in: In Sachen Lesekultur. Hrsg. Budesminister fur Bildung und Wissenschaft. Bonn 1991.
5. Kubler, Hans-Dieter: Lebenswelten, Orientierungsdilimmata und Medienverhalten Jugendlicher. in: Buch und Bibliothek. Jg. 1988. H.
6. Heidtmann, Horst: Kindermedien und Medienverbund. in: Geschichte der Deutschen Kinder - und Jugendliteratur. Hrsg. von Reiner Wild. Stuttgart 1990.
7. Wurster, Erich H.: Gutenberg, Postman und die jungen Analphabeten. in: Buchanzeiger. 1985. H. 3, Umschlagseiten
8. Pawlowsky-Flodell, Charlotta: Technischer Fortschritt ja, aber bitte mit Kultur: neue Aufgabenfelder fur die Offentliche Bibliothek?
   in: Bibliotheksdienst. 25. Jg. 1991. H.1
9. TJW und das Geheimnis der Gummibarchen. Hrsg. Horst Heidtmann in: Informationen Jugendliteratur und Medien. 2. Beih. 1991.

Sound Archives in all India Radio

H.M. JOSHI

ABSTRACT

The paper outlines the status of present sound Archives (Interim set-up) in All India Radio. Plans for the proposed permanent set - up have also been described. In the preservation of sound (aural) documents, unlike printed and written documents, the on-going technological developments play an important role. The factors, which should be taken into consideration while selecting the technology and medium for preservation of aural documents for posterity, have also been mentioned briefly.

1. Introduction

All India Radio (AIR) is one of the earliest broadcasting Organizations in the world, having started broadcasting way back in 1936. This is the sole sound broadcasting organization in our country and acts as a prime carrier for the message of development along with information, news, views, mass education, promotion of national and international understanding. Having started with only one station, it has grown into a major broadcasting organization, with 133 stations at present, increasing to 205 after the completion of all the 7th plan schemes. About 85.4% area of the country and 95.9% of the population have already been covered by AIR network.

India is a very vast country with unmatched diversity in the way of life of its people. It has a very rich and ancient cultural heritage and is endowed with great traditions in almost every walk of life. Classical and folk music has been an integral part of this heritage. Apart from this, India has produced eminent personalities in other fields who have made great contributions towards enrichment of human life. AIR, as the sole sound broadcasting organization, had the unique privilege of acquiring a large number of sound recordings pertaining to the great Indian personalities of the 20th century as well as recordings of various phases of social transformation undergone by the country during the Independence struggle and in the post Independence era. It would not be out of place to add here that, before the development of audiovisual media/ sound recording techniques, the link with the past would have been only through the printed and written medium, but now it is a great boon to the people of this generation and future generations that they can have these great people come alive right in their living rooms or at any other place, whenever desired, through the audio-visual media and provide them with feelings and sensation, unmatched through any other form of communication available to mankind so far.

2. Background of air archives, its present collection and system of storage/retrieval

The Transcription and Programme Exchange Services (TPES), of which the sound archives presently forms part, began its activities in April, 1954 with the record processing plant for making copies of specially produced light songs then known as 'Prasar geet'. The archives itself began with the transfer of about 7000 presto-discs to tapes in the early fifties. Now, recordings of all important programmes broadcast over AIR and which are worth preserving for posterity are acquired by the DTPES for preservation.

Presently, the archives is located temporarily in Akashwani Bhavan, New Delhi, which is AIR's Headquarter. The sound recordings in the archives are preserved on 1/4" analogue audio magnetic tapes (1.5 mil mylar) conforming to internationally accepted standards and gramophone discs. It currently holds around 40,000 tapes which contain recordings of speeches and reminiscences of eminent leaders and personalities of the past and the present.

The country's musical heritage in AIR's collection are the recordings of memorable, soul-stirring music recitals by master musicians who are either no more or have passed their prime. Some of the artistes who are no more and whose recordings are available include Abdul Karim Khan, Allauddin Khan, Amir Khan, Bade Ghulam Ali Khan, Hirabai Barodekar, Begam Akhtar, Faiyaz Khan, Pannalal Ghose, Hafeez Ali Khan, Ariyakudi Ramanuja Iyengar, Madurai Mani Iyer, Dwaram Venkataswamy Naidu, Onkarnath Thakur, D.V. Paluskar, Rajab Ali Khan, Rassolan Bai, Sidheswari Devi, and Vilayat Hussain Khan. Keeping in view the public interest in the recordings of such master musicians, AIR has liberally permitted the gramophone companies to release as many of these recordings as possible on L.P. discs/ cassettes. Some of the releases pertain to eminent artists like Faiyaz Khan, Bade Ghulam Ali Khan, Abdul Wahid Khan, Amir Khan,

Hafiz Ali Khan, Allauddin Khan, Onkar Nath Thakur, D.V. Paluskar, Ariyakudi Ramanuja Iyengar, Ustad Rahimmudin Khan Dagar, Pannalal Ghose, G.N. Balasubramanian & Begum Akhrar, etc.

The archival material is used by AIR for programme production, broadcasts, international programme exchange and for research and reference work. In addition, many AIR stations draw on the central archives as well as on the archives of their stations and broadcast regular programmes based on the recordings of old masters.

3. Limitation of present system and media

In view of the non-availability of adequate space, technical and other facilities, the growth of the archives has been quite restricted. A number of aural documents have degraded in quality because of the limitations of the media of storage. At present, the AIR archives does not have any system which can bring improvement in the quality of old and degraded archival materials. Also, no system is available for transferring the archival material on to a new medium which is suitable for long-term preservation.

4. Air plans for the proposed permanent setup for archives

In view of the above limitations, AIR has planned for a permanent sound archives setup. The site has been chosen in New Delhi, for various reasons. The proposed permanent building or AIR archives will provide extensive facilities for the storage of archival material, listening and dubbing facilities, tape and disc inspection facilities, facilities for improving the quality (de-noising) of old sound recordings and their transfer to digital medium (optical disc/digital audio tape), documentation library for old disc cartons, covers, clippings, photos and transcriptions of recordings, transcription booth, viewing and listening facilities for researchers and outsiders, broadcasting museum and other facilities.

The storage area will be absolutely dust free & fully air conditioned. The load on the air conditioning plants will be reduced by providing heat treatment to the roof. In addition, the building will be provided with adequate water proofing and antitermite treatment. It will have appropriate fire prevention, detection & control system. Special care will be taken in laying the electrical cables so as to avoid strong magnetic field in the vicinity of the storage areas. Adequate precautions will be taken to guard the precious tapes from getting damaged due to lightening surges by carefully locating/ running lightening conductor system.

The existing archives of All India Radio, located temporarily in Akashvani Bhavan, is being upgraded shortly with modern facilities for undertaking the work of de-noising of old and degraded sound recordings and transfer of audio material on to digital medium (tape/optical disc). This project of "upgradation of AIR archives" is being implemented by AIR with UNDP assistance. This modern state-of-the-art facility will enable us to 'clean' the old & degraded recordings, to the extent possible, by using computer-based digital audio signal processing techniques & then transfer these recordings, in digital format onto magnetic tapes or optical discs for long-term preservation.

5. Potential (of Archival Material) Available in the Country and Efforts Needed to Tap it

Special efforts are now being made to acquire for the archives, voice-recordings of eminent Indians and music recitals by prominent artists when they are in the top of their forms. Recordings of interviews/reminiscences of eminent persons, National Leaders, Freedom Fighters are also recorded and preserved in AIR Archives.

Apart from AIR, there are many music enthusiasts and organisations who, in their own way, have collected a large number of music recordings and who even possess rare musical instruments. No realistic estimate of this large private collection and its value is available. However, in due course of time, with more space and facilities, we would like to acquire such rare and valuable sound recordings as well as rare musical instruments from the private collectors and preserve them in the AIR archives for posterity. As mentioned earlier, folk music is an integral part of our ancient cultural heritage. Though our country still has a grat potential for folk music, the tribal areas which are rich in folk music and which are its important source, are slowly losing touch with their traditional culture. It will be in the fitness of things if more efforts could be made by individuals/voluntary organisations and others interested, in addition to the efforts by AIR, to search, identify, collect, record/ re-record this precious treasure of folk music and bring it to AIR Archives for proper preservation centrally. This could then be used in current programme production and programme exchange in AIR network and by bonafide users/ organisations inside and outside the country. In fact, tremendous efforts will be needed in this direction. This would enormously enrich the sound archival collection for posterity which would be preserved.

6. Conclusion

The present AIR archives is relatively a small setup. However, the facilities under the proposed permanent setup would provide considerable scope for its future growth and also equip it to discharge its responsibility fully and effectively as can be expected of a modern sound archives. We are fully aware of the tremendous challenge that lies before us, particularly in view of the importance of the precious archival treasure to the country and in view of the fact that if this material is lost damaged or destroyed on account of improper preservation, handling and use, and lack of safety, it cannot be regenerated and will be lost for ever. Therefore, preserving sound archival material for posterity entails very high degree of responsibility. Not only this, it is quite a difficult and costly affair too. This is more so when the technology related to the sound recording techniques and recording/storage medium is changing fast.

New techniques are being developed for recording of sound, its processing and storage on long lasting medium which require much less stringent environmental conditions and also pose relatively less problems in handling and use. Further, the Conventional medium and professional analogue audio recording/playback equipment are likely to fade away in another couple of decades or so. In view of this, selection of a new medium and technology for long-term digital storage of archival audio material is inescapable. While selecting, however, one has to carefully consider the pros and cons of each and adopt such technology and medium which are proven, durable, compatible and which can provide in-house record and reproduce capability and be able to retain the audio information safely and economically in original form for long time, with the assurance of efficient and accurate retrieval in future. Keeping the cost & efforts required in audio signal refurbishing & its storage, the change to the new format has to be gradual for any developing country. With these considerations we are going ahead and would like to interact with other organizations who are interested in the preservation of aural documents, especially for posterity.

Journal Publications in Africa : The Trouble with Authors and Readers

L.O. AINA

Introduction

The genesis and the current status of African library science journals have been well documented by Aina (1992). The picture painted in the paper is very disturbing as the study revealed that many African library science journals are faced with several difficulties, among which is the high mortality rate. Azubuike et. al. (1990) in their study of Nigerian science journals concluded that the average life span of an African journal is between two and five years. Yet it is an established fact that African authors in library science, disseminate their research findings mainly through journals. Only a negligible proportion of the literature of African librarianship appears in other formats such as textbooks, conference proceedings and technical reports. In a bibliometric analysis of the literature of librarianship in Nigeria from 1950 — 1973 by Afolabi (1976), it was found that 80% of the literature covered was journal literature. Journal literature in African librarianship is therefore very crucial to the development of the profession.

In the production of a journal, three major parameters are critical to its birth and sustenance. These are the publisher, the author and the reader. The role of each of these major players is well known. Thus it will not be repeated in this paper. The problems of the publisher of an African library science journal have been well covered by Aina (1992), therefore in this paper, attention will be focussed on the other two parameters, that is, authors and readers, with a view to finding out how each of these major players contribute to the high morality rate of library science journals in Africa.

Authors of Journal Literature in Africa

Studies have shown that authors of African library science journals are top flight professionals who are highly qualified. They are generally found in academic libraries and library schools (Nwafor, 1987 and Aina 1991). Thus one will least expect this high calibre of professional librarians in Africa to constitute a clog in journal publication in Africa. Unfortunately, this is the case. Most of the papers contributed by these professionals are generally descriptive without any sound theoretical basis. The papers are usually restricted to their immediate environment which has no general applicability. Even when empirical studies are carried out, the results are hardly valid.

In a recent study on the directions of the information professions in Africa, I found that 81.61% of the papers contributed by African authors to *International Library Review*, *Information Development* and *Libri*, between 1985 and 1989 were descriptive papers (Aina, 1991).

Third World Libraries, (TWL) a journal devoted to Third World Librarianship was so much concerned about the quality of manuscripts that come from the Third World that in its editorial comment in the Volume 2, Number 1 (1991) issue, it had this to say:

> "One realization that has come to me gradually is a troubling one. Library authors in developing countries write almost exclusively from a local point of view about a local situation. Nearly all the hundred articles that have come to TWL from Nigeria, for example, are about Nigerian problems, usually studied in a single library."

In the same editorial, the author also reported the same trend in Kenya. Another editor, this time, the editor of the *Nigerian Library and Information Science Review* was also disgusted with the lack of quality and scholarly manuscripts submitted to his journal. I quote again.

> "Most manuscripts we receive are not based on empirical research conducted by the authors. Surprisingly, it is still much more difficult to get well written theoretical papers making original contribution to knowledge or thought in the field." (Nzotta, 1992)

My experience as the editor-in-chief of *African Journal of Library, Archives and Information Science* is not very much different from the editors quoted above. Average, I receive five manuscripts per month making it an average of 60 manuscripts per year, I need only 16 manuscripts to constitute a volume of two numbers per year. In spite of this avalanche of manuscripts, I still find it difficult to get good enough manuscripts to make the volume. Sometimes, I have to solicit for high quality manuscripts from known authors just to maintain the high standard envisaged for the journal. It doesn't mean that known authors will give you their best papers, in most cases, they give you papers that have either been rejected by the so-called international journals or manuscripts that are very dated. When we started the *Nigerian Library and information Science Review* in 1982, we contacted many known authors — university professors, university librarians and other top professionals to give us manuscripts that will constitute the maiden issue. The editorial board was surprised at the quality of manuscripts submitted. Most of the manuscripts, were papers presented at conferences and workshops held several years back, most of them between five and ten years. This is the dilemma of the editor of an African library science journal. The trouble indeed, is with the author. It is therefore not surprising that because of the low quality of manuscripts submitted by African library science authors, most African library science journals are hardly indexed or abstracted by international indexing services. Of course, this indirectly contributes to the high mortality rate of journals, as the journals will be hardly known beyond their immediate environment.

Apart from the low standard of the manuscripts submitted by authors, it is a known fact that they hardly cite recent publications. In the same survey I carried out with African authors, I found out that only 25.82% of the publications cited by African authors were published within five years prior to research investigation. In such a situation, African authors will more or less be conducting their research in the dark, as they do not know the latest literature pertinent to the area of current investigation. Thus the African library science journal will not be in a position to serve as a medium for disseminating latest findings. This is also another trouble with African authors. Also some authors feel that the quality of a paper will be lowered if they cite local journals.

Readers and Journal Literature in Africa

Librarians and trainee librarians are expected to constitute the bulk of readers of journal literature. Unfortunately they hardly read local journals, even though majority of authors in African write mainly on their libraries and their immediate environment thus one will expect readers to consult local journals regularly. Unfortunately, this is not the case. In a survey carried out with 39 librarians employed in different types of libraries by Nwafor (1987), it was found that no Nigerian library science journal or indeed any African library science journal was listed among the top nine library science journals regularly read. The reason is not far fetched, African librarians hardly make personal subscription to journals published in Africa, rather, they read library Association journals of developed countries. The most popular journals subscribed to are *Library Association Record, Journal of Information Science, Journal of the American Society of Information Science, Quarterly Bulletin of the International Association of Agricultural Librarians and Documentalists.* They are able to obtain copies of these journals not necessarily because they are interested in the journals perse, but because they are supplied free to members, once one has paid membership fees. They therefore have access to these journals rather than local journals. Nzotta (1992) lamented the fact that no Nigerian subscribed personally to *Nigerian Library and Information Science Review*, and yet the journal has been appearing regularly for the last 10 years. Libraries are not better either. Some libraries in Africa do not even subscribe to library science journals. In a survey of library and information science collection by Nwafor (1985) in seven libraries in Jos, Nigeria, consisting of one university library, one polytechnic library, one college of education library, two special libraries, one public library, and a state branch of the National Library, it was found that two of the libraries had no library science journal in its collection, one library had only one which is a foreign based journal, another had six, five of which are foreign based journals. In the university library, only six out of the 40 journals subscribed to are published in Africa. This is the trend in most libraries in Africa. It is perhaps only at the University of Botswana Library, that there is a policy to acquire all African based library science journals. If readers do not personally subscribe to African based library science journals and libraries are also not subscribing to these journals, then there will be little or nothing for readers to read. The trouble with the readers, however, is that they do not impress it on their libraries to subscribe. Thus the onus is on the readers to make much recommendations, because if they do, libraries would subscribe as there is no foreign exchange involved in acquiring local journals.

When readers read local journals they rarely provide a feedback, thus it is uncommon to read letters to the editor in most of our local journals. Readers who are in a position to implement some of the recommendations contained in local journals hardly make use of such recommendations.

The Way Forward

The situation cannot be allowed to go on like this. The quality of research papers must be improved. The two way approach to this is for, libraries to budget for research, so that research grants can be made available to those who want to conduct research. Library Associations should also encourage members, by soliciting for research grants, on behalf of potential authors, from international bodies. Continuing education programmes in the form of regular workshops and seminars should be provided regularly for practising librarians on research methodology. This will enable them master the art of research. Even though all the library schools in Africa have research methodology courses in their curricula, there is no evidence that budding authors ever attended a research methodology course. In short, teachers of research methodology courses need to attend training of trainers courses to enable them teach their students effectively. It is hoped that IFLA/ALP (Advancement of Librarianship for the Third World Programme) will be very supportive in this area by organising such a training course.

Major libraries in Africa should adopt the policy of the University of Botswana Library by making it mandatory that they acquire all African library science journals. This will ensure that readers who otherwise could not subscribe because of financial difficulties will have access to such journals. Particising librarians and students should make it as a matter of professionals commitment to subscribe to journals published in their immediate environment.

REFERENCES

1. Afolabi, M.O. (1976) The Literature on Librarianship in Nigeria 1950—1973. *Nigrian Libraries* 12 (2 & 3) 179 - 192.

2. Aina, L.O. (1991) Directions of the Information Professions as Reflected in the Literature. *International Library Review* 23 (4) 365 - 380.

3. Aina, L.O. (1992) The Prospects of Reducing the High Mortality Rate of African Library Science Journals. *Paper Presented at African Library Science Journals Workshop,* Kano, Nigeria, 29-30 January, 14p.

4. Azubuike, A.A., Adeyomoye, F.I. and Okojie, V.O. (1990) High Mortality Rate and Some Related Characteristics of Nigerian Science Journals. *Paper Presented at the Fourth African Association of Science Editors.* IITA, Ibadan, Nigeria, 5-9 March, 13p.

5. Marcos, Guy A. (1991) Editorially Speaking : Does Research Have High Priorities. *Third World Libraries*, 2 (1) 4-6.

6. Nwafor, B.U. (1985) Nigerian Libraries Collection. *Nigerian Library and Information Science Review*, 3 (1 & 2) 71-74.

7. Nwafor, B.U. (1987) Nigerian Librarians and Publishing. *Nigerian Libraries*, 23 (1 & 2) 50—66.

8. Nzotta, B.C. (1992) Journal Publishing in Nigeria : An Editor's View. *Paper Presented at African Library Science Journals Workshop.* Kano, Nigeria, 29-30 January, p.2.

Library, Reference, Research, Documentation and Information Services to Members of Parliament in India

G.C. MALHOTRA

INTRODUCTION

Parliament is the single most important representative institution in any country which has opted for a parliamentary democratic polity. It is the symbol of the varied hopes and aspirations of the people. It is the supreme legislative and deliberative organ in such a political system. This, being so, it is only natural that the legislators raise here issues which have a vital bearing on the state of the nation political, economic and social. The international situation also comes up for discussion in the House from time to time.

With the rapid technological and scientific developments greatly influencing, nay revolutionising every sphere of human activity, the role and functions of the legislatures have also multiplied manifold. Apart from their conventional law-making function, today's legislatures, particularly those at the national level, have to grapple with newer problems and changing situations.

PARLIAMENTARIANS AND INFORMATION

Members of Legislatures, in their capacity as the elected representatives of the people, are invariably conscious of the onerous responsibility of living upto the expectations of their electors. It is perhaps no easy task to keep abreast of all developments taking place all around in order to meet the demands of a parliamentary life. If a member has to play an active and effective role in parliamentary proceedings - be it during question time, discussions on various issues or the legislative business - he has to be well-versed with the latest developments on a wide variety of subjects. In short, he is in constant need of information. Is it, that information as such as scarce ? Far from it. The problem rather is that there is too much of it from too many sources. There is proliferation of books, journals, newspapers and reports and the parliamentarians have an access to this vast material at a variety of sources. For example, Ministries and Departments of

Government, Public Sector Undertakings and other official agencies bring out regularly mass of literature highlighting their activities, achievements and future plans. Though all this literature is prepared by experts in their respective fields, some tilt or bias in their presentation cannot be avoided. Then of course there is the mass media - newspapers, radio, films, television etc. - which also contributes to the dissemination of information. Besides, various interest groups and lobbyists vie with each other to reach out to members through written word or in person with a view to stressing their own viewpoints on issues and problems concerning them. In this case too, a slant in presentation cannot be ruled out.

It might thus be seen that the problem with us, in the Parliamentary context, is not of the non-availability of information but its proper organisation and management followed by selective dissemination to parliamentarians who are hard pressed for time. As we all are aware, their parliamentary activities are not confined to attending Parliament sessions alone. They are simultaneously required to participate in committee meetings, attend to their constituency problems and as partymen to attend party deliberations as well. Whatever the nature of their engagement, they are always in need of one kind of information or other in order to develop an argument during a debate, ask a supplementary and even demolish an official claim. Such information may be required by them quite often in the House itself or in the Committee or sometimes even on their breakfast table for Party or Constituency work. They hardly have the time to spend hours in the Library or even cursorily glance through the mass of literature piling up on their desks to search and locate the right information required at a given point of time. They need carefully sifted and objectively analysed information, tailored to meet their specific requirements in the form of brief notes, statements, tables, statistical charts and the like. Time, of course, is of essence and if the required information is not made available to them within the stipulated time, the whole exercise may be infructuous.

ADVANCES IN INFORMATION SYSTEM AND CHANGING ROLES OF LIBRARIES

Let us now look at the information system from a different angle. The twentieth century has witnessed many significant developments in the field of science and technology. These revolutionary changes have had a considerable impact on the varied needs of human activity such as education, research, information etc., including the institution of Library which is the storehouse of wisdom.

The spectacular advancements in information and communication techniques have radically changed the conventional function of a Library. The new information demands of users have to be met by several activities based on documentation, information, analysis, consolidation and repackaging, computer based information system etc. The changes in the concept of the Information System are analogous to that of Solar System. The Greco-Egyptian astronomer Ptolemy had maintained that earth was at the centre of the universe with the Sun and other heavenly bodies revolving round it. Centuries later, the Polish astronomer, Copernicus established that the Sun was at the centre of the system with the earth revolving round it. In our context, it is the rapidly changing roles of the Library that has made the eminent Information Scientist Robert S. Taylor to remark that "In a metaphorical sense, we are moving from a Ptolemaic world with the Library at the Centre and information revolving round it to a Copernican one with information at the centre and Library as one of its planets". One may even venture to say that a modern day Library is verily a respository of the "intellectual technology" of a nation.

No man is an island by himself. Today more than ever before, he is inter-dependent on fellow beings. This symbiotic relationship is perhaps best exemplified in the interaction between the people and their elected representatives. Together, they endeavour towards achieving the cherished goal of a welfare society. For this venture, information is crucial. This being so, it is imperative that the elected representatives should receive on a continuous basis factual information on socio-economic problems, national and international political developments and scientific and technological advancement. Needless to say, this type of a specialised service can be provided only by a self-contained organisation or set-up within the Parliament itself.

PARLIAMENTARY LIBRARIES

The need for establishing and developing an independent and objective reservoir of information within the Legislature itself on which legislators, can freely bank upon, has, therefore, been long recognised the world over. Legislatures in many democratic countries - big or small - have developed their own library, reference and research services. Their range depends upon the available resources and the size of the legislature. Popularly known as the LRS (Legislative Reference Service) different Legislatures have adopted slightly varied nomenclatures to meet specific requirements.

An efficient LRS postulates a well-stocked and well-equipped Library manned by highly experienced and trained staff fully geared to meet multifarious information demands from legislators. LRS should also be in a position to identify, in advance, important issues and subjects likely to come up before the Legislatures and be ready with well-documented brochures, backgrounders, information bulletins, bibliographies on those subjects for free distribution to legislators even before they ask for them. Besides enabling the Members of Parliament to fulfil their parliamentary duties, these facilities offset at least partly the information advantage enjoyed by the executive power over the legislative power.

PARLIAMENT LIBRARY IN INDIA

Indian Parliament too has been conscious of this vital need of its members right from the beginning. The seeds of the present-day Parliament Library were sown well before our independence in 1947, as early as in 1921 during the Central Legislative Assembly days. It is thus just over seventy years old as compared to the US Congress Library which is almost 200 years old and the British House of Commons Library over 170 years. Though small in size initially, it was set-up with the express purpose of providing information to the members of the Central Legislative Assembly. Till independence there was a slow but steady increase in the collections of the Library. However, immediately after independence, with the Constituent Assembly involved in the drafting of the Constitution, there was a considerable growth in its collections.

The year 1950, saw the beginning of a systematic expansion of Parliament Library's collection. A humble beginning was also made by setting up a Members' Reference Service within the newly set-up Research and Reference Branch which initially functioned independent of the Parliament Library. Faced with the increasing demands of a nascent democracy, concerted efforts were made during the period 1950-

55 to further consolidate the Library by increasing purchase of books and entering into exchange arrangements with various institutions and organisations in India and abroad. Soon, Parliament Library became a repository Library for the publications of U.N. and its all allied agencies and also started receiving the Command Papers of U.K. and Government Publications from U.S.A and several other countries. Naturally, this expansion necessitated the reorganisation of the Library in the year 1956, then 1966 and again in December, 1977 with a view to further strengthening various services extended to members.

LARRDIS

Over the past four decades, the Library as well as Research and Reference Service have gradually developed into what is now known as the integrated Parliament Library and Reference, Research, Documentation and Information Service, more familiar by its acronym LARRDIS. The present set up and nomenclature is the result of major functional reorganisation of the Secretariats of the two Houses of Parliament brought about during 1974-75. LARRDIS though administratively under the Lok Sabha Secretariat, caters to all the information requirements of members of both Houses of Parliament - Lok Sabha and Rajya Sabha. With the strength of nearly 200 of researchers, professional and secretarial staff, the LARRDIS is housed in the Parliament building itself and is spread over all the four floors with the major collections in first floor.

As its name suggests, LARRDIS today functionally provides Library, Reference, Research, Documentation and Information services to the members of Parliament.

LIBRARY SERVICE

Parliament Library presently has holdings of about one million volumes of books, debates of Indian Parliament, State Legislatures of India and foreign Parliaments, reports of Central and State Governments and United Nations and its Agencies, Gazettes of Central and State Governments and other documents, including periodicals and publications brought out by the Lok Sabha Secretariat. With a budget of Rs. 1.7 million it is one of the richest repositories in the country. The total book collection of Parliament Library has also increased considerably over the years. The holdings of the Library which was approximately 6,75000 in 1985 had gone up to approximately 10,00,000 by 1992. Besides, the staff Library has holdings of 21,396. Presently, the Parliament Library receives 195 newspapers from different parts of the country and the world. Of these, 181 newspapers are from India itself. There are 35 English dailies, 40 in Hindi and 106 in different regional languages of India. The 14 foreign newspapers are received from U.K., U.S.A., Pakistan, China, Singapore, Sri Lanka, Indonesia, Afganistan, Malaysia and Nepal. Parliament Library also receives regularly 842 periodicals - 579 published in India and 263 from abroad. Of the 263 foreign periodicals, the UN and its Agencies account for 59 and the rest are from different countries. As for the 579 Indian periodicals, 403 are in English, 94 in Hindi and the rest 82 in various regional languages. The total number of books and other publications issued from the Library was 12,985 in 1985 whereas in 1992, the figure had gone up to 30,688. The total number of books and other publications issued from the Staff Library has also increased substantially, the figure being 10,024 in 1985 and 14,541 in 1992.

Acquisition

We lay utmost emphasis on the process of acquisition. Books and publications are selected from out of the entire field of human activity relating to almost all subjects, the only exception being books on advanced technical knowledge, pure sciences and light fiction. Actually, the legislative requirements of members are particularly kept in view while choosing the books.

Parliament Library acquires most of the books through purchase from approved booksellers who regularly supply the latest books on approval basis. The books are carefully examined at different stages with special reference to the needs of the Parliament Library and then selected for acquisition. In addition to this regular supply, the staff in the Acquisition Section consults the catalogues, publisher's announcements, book reviews appearing in various newspapers and periodicals, lists of additions received from various other Libraries and makes periodic visits to the local booksellers for the purpose of selection and acquisition of books for the Parliament Library. On another plane, under the Press and Registration of Books Act, 1867, all State Governments are expected to acquire and send a copy of all publications, printed in their State, free of cost to the Parliament

Library. Books are also received on complimentary basis from Members of Parliament and others. Books presented by foreign Parliaments are also added to the collections.

Parliament Library has extensive exchange arrangements with 124 governmental and non-governmental institutions in India and 73 institutions abroad which supply their publications in exchange for publications brought out by the Lok Sabha Secretariat. It is also a depository Library for all unrestricted publications of the United Nations and its allied agencies.

All Ministries and Departments of the Government of India including their attached and subordinate offices also supply copies of their publications, reports etc. free of cost of Parliament Library. Copies of the Gazettes, Budgets and reports published by State Governments are also received and added to the holdings of the Parliament Library.

Classification

Books and other publications are classified and catalogued according to the Deway Decimal Classification Scheme (20th Edition). The Library of Congress List of the Subject Headings (12th Edition) is adopted for assigning Key words to the publications.

Dissemination

How do we let members and others know of latest additions to the Parliament Library ? This function is primarily done through a monthly publication "Parliament Library Bulletin" which is brought out by the Library Division. Latest arrivals are also put on display at the 'New Arrivals' Counters. From time to time, book exhibitions are organised on various themes to mark specific occasions. The issue of books and other publications to members is regulated by the Parliament Library Rules framed on the recommendations of the Library Committee. Comfortable study rooms are provided in the Library for serious study of members.

Special Collections

Parliament Library possesses a rich collection of rare and art books. The earliest printed books available in the Library date back to 1671. Books on art, painting, sculpture and architecture cover a broad canvas of Indian history depicting different stages in its evolution. These include paintings of various schools of art such as the Mughal, Rajput, Kangra, Garhwal, etc. The foreign art collections comprise of the creations of celebrated artists like Michael Angelo, Leonardo da Vinci, Rapheal as also works of Chinese and Japanese Art, Russian, German, French, American and Arabian paintings. The Library also has two original calligraphed copies of the Constitution of India (in Hindi and English) as adopted by Constituent Assembly and signed by its Members. The copies were calligraphed by Shri Nand Lal Bose, the renowned artist from Shantiniketan. We are presently exploring ways and means for the long-term preservation of these documents for the benefit of posterity.

As a mark of respect to the memory of Mahatma Gandhi, the Father of the Nation, and to make available all the works by and on the Mahatma at one place, there is separate Section called *Gandhiana*. The Section contains about 1665 books in Hindi, English and several other Indian regional languages. Similarly, Parliament Library also have a separate section, exclusively devoted to the first Prime Minister and Architect of modern India, Jawaharlal Nehru, which contains books on and by Nehru, all located at one place.

Regional Languages Collection

The Parliament, in a way is the microcosm of the nation itself. Ours is a nation which abounds in diversity based on several factors, the most prominent among them being the languages. Each one of our major languages is rich in its own way with its distinctive literature. Together, these languages add to the richness of our literary heritage. Keeping this in mind, Parliament Library has also laid emphasis on developing its Indian Regional Languages Collections. A separate Wing containing 52,875 holdings in various Indian languages has been carved out in the Library.

Library Committee

A Library Committee is constituted every year by the Speaker, Lok Sabha, to advise him on all matters concerning the development of the Parliament Library. The Committee consist of six members from Lok Sabha and three from Rajya Sabha, nominated by the Presiding

Officers of the respective Houses. The Deputy Speaker of Lok Sabha is the *ex-offico* Chairman of the Library Committee.

COMPUTERISED INFORMATION SERVICE

Information handling has essentially three aspects : collection, storing and retrieval. As the quantum of knowledge grows, the number of information records also correspondingly increases. Handling of this vast magnitude of information with conventional manual methods, naturally, has proved problematic. In modern times, information scientists have embarked upon the development of a new information technology. Today, all around the world, computers are being used in library housekeeping functions like acquisition, cataloguing, circulation control, serials control, information storage, retrieval, content analysis and dissemination. Recently, under direction and dynamic leadership of present Speaker of Lok Sabha Shivraj V. Patil almost all important services of Lok Sabha Secretariat have been put on computerisation with the help of NIC and another leading Computer organisation, *viz.* Computer Maintenance Corporation (CMC).

For the purpose of introducing automation in the Parliament Library, the Computer-based information retrieval system named PARLIS (Parliament Library Information System) was started in December, 1985 with the help of the National Informatics Centre (NIC). Presently, the Computer Centre has 17 computers installed in the Parliament House and Parliament House Annexe—six 486, four PC-386, five PC-286 and two PC-XT with a number of terminals and printers being used for storage and retrieval of data. Two PCs located in the Computer Centre are connected with main Super Computer NEC S-1000 located at the premises of the NIC in Lodhi Complex, about six kms away from Parliament House.

PARLIS was designed within the Library for the benefit of Members of Parliament. It is a database of subject indexed references to parliamentary information. The database is created by the Library's Computer Centre. The data so far stored for on-line retrieval relates to subject index references of select questions and answers and various other kinds of business, including Government and Private Members' Bills in Lok Sabha and Rajya Sabha from 1985 onwards ; discussions in the Constituent Assembly on different articles and schedules of the Constitution of India; decisions and observations from the Chair from

1952; the reports of the Parliamentary Committees such as the Public Accounts Committee Estimates Committee, Public Undertakings Committee, etc.; the profiles of members of the Eighth, Ninth and Tenth Lok Sabhas and of Rajya Sabha from 1986 onwards; the socio-economic background of Members of First to Tenth Lok Sabhas ; details of Presidential and Vice-Presidential elections from 1952 onwards, discussions on Five-Year Plans in Lok Sabha and Rajya Sabha from 1951; Council of Ministers-Ministry-wise and name-wise from 1947; President's Rule in the States and Union territories since 1951; time taken on various kinds of business in Lok Sabha since 1977; etc. Also available for on-line retrieval are some of the statistical data on different areas of economy such as the country's Growth Rate, its foreign trade, Plan Outlays for public Sector, Per Capita Net Domestic Product, Per Capita Plan Outlay, Fertilizer Production, Imports and Consumption, Number of Job Seekers registered with Employment Exchanges, Power Generation, performance of Railways, etc. New Databases in respect of research and reference notes and lists of addresses of important dignitaries, etc. have also been created recently.

Over the years, considerable quantum of work has been undertaken by the Computer Centre. Thus, year-wise the number of records of parliamentary questions fed into the computer and available for on-line retrieval was 8,633 in 1987; 12,758 in 1988; 7,587 in 1987; 7416 in 1990 ; 10,687 in 1991; and 11,610 in 1992. The records of the number of Parliamentary bills for the year 1987, 1988, 1989, 1990, 1991 and 1992 were 249, 289, 160 220, 427 and 276, respectively. In the case of records of parliamentary debates, the figures were 282, 758, 670, 1371, 1,705 and 2,695 for the years 1987, 1988, 1989, 1990, 1991 and 1992, respectively.

It may thus be seen that during the last five years our Computer system has travelled a long way. The 37th Commonwealth Parliamentary Conference which was held in New Delhi in September 1991 and the 89th Inter-Parliamentary Conference in April 1993 provided an opportunity to PARLIS and NIC to extend a variety of information to the Delegates and others. For efficient storage and retrieval of information, a network was created by linking the Computer Centre at the Conference Venue (Ashok Hotel) to the Indira Gandhi International Airport, Parliament Library and the Satellite-based

NICNET. The computer stored information regarding the countries represented, bio-data of Delegates, their arrival and departure details, tour programmes, conference schedules, spouses' programmes and a vast array of information about Indian economy, and other tourist information.

Information Linkage

The NIC has already provided us the facilities of NICMAIL available on NICENT for efficient exchange of information. A protected mailbox with address *Lokmail* has already been given to the Computer Centre. Our Secretariat can now exchange messages between all the District Headquarters and sites operative under NICNET. The Computer Centre has already been linked with the Madhya Pradesh Vidhan Sabha, Bhopal, and the Karnataka Legislature through NICNET. The State Legislatures of Andhra Pradesh, Maharashtra and Uttar Pradesh have requested NIC for developing computer and communication facilities in their Secretariats. The State Legislatures of Bihar, Gujarat, Himachal Pradesh, Jammu and Kashmir, Kerala and Meghalaya have also initiated action in this regard.

The Parliament Library is at present in a position to have a direct access to international databases like DIALOG through NICNET. We are also in the process of establishing linkages with Parliaments of other countries having access to international networks like UUNET and INTERNET, Satellite-based foreign networks. This will facilitate exchange of information and resource-sharing with Parliament Libraries the world over. In response to our request, the US Congressional Research Service have already sent their INTERNET Electronic Mail Address for exchange of messages. The National assembly Library of Korea, the Library and Information Service of Yuan (Taiwan), the Consultative Council of Oman and the National Assembly of Quebec have expressed their interest in exploring the possibilities of exchanging information with our Library through international networks.

There are also proposals to develop our own national on-line network for inter-linkage of databases of PARLIS with databases of State Legislatures under the National Legislatures information System (NATLIS) and a multiple function/ service international network named as the International Parliamentary Information Network (IPINET) inter connecting databases of Parliament Libraries of other countries and databases the world over.

MICROFILMING UNIT

Parliament Library has a large collection of old databases, magazines, reports and other rare publications which are required to be preserved for reference over long periods. In order to preserve these resources and to effectively utilise the existing space, shortage of which is now being seriously felt, a Microfilming Unit was set up in 1988 in Parliament Library. The Unit is at present equipped with most modern Microfilm, Cameras, Processors, Duplicators and Microfilming Reader-cum-Printers. There are four Cameras (three for microfilming documents of smaller size on 16 mm rolls and one for microfilming documents bigger size on 35 mm rolls); one Processor; One Duplicator; and two Reader-cum-printers. There is Computerised Assisted Retrieval (CAR) system for retrieving of microfilmed documents. Over six lakh documents have already been microfilmed by the Unit since its inception. The records of historical importance microfilmed so far include parliamentary debates, *viz.* of Central Legislative Assembly, Council of States, Constituent Assembly, Lok Sabha and Rajya Sabha beginning from February 1921 to May 1990, all the Reports of the Indian Parliamentary Group and all issues of the quarterly publication, "The Journal of Parliamentary Information" from its first issue in 1955 onwards. The indexed data-entries pertaining to all the above debates have been fed into the Computer for facilitating quick retrieval. The Unit has begun microfilming of Papers laid on the Table of the House since 1980. About 800 'rare books' are also proposed to be microfilmed soon. Duplicate-copies of the microfilm rolls of all parliamentary debates are now kept in Library (Ground Floor) for viewing on the microfilm reader by members.

AUDIO-VISUAL UNIT

Computers, films, videos, etc. are increasingly becoming normal elements of our Library culture and their products contribute to our knowledge and general worldview. Video News Magazines covering important national and international events in different areas of politics, economics, law, etc. are brought out regularly by various organisations and agencies. Taking into consideration the information value of such audio-visual magazines, Parliament Library set up during the beginning of 1992, an Audio-Visual Unit for use and reference by members of Parliament. Language learning courses also form the integral part of the audio-visual collection.

Telecasting of parliamentary proceedings has also become a reality now in our country with the *Doordarshan* bringing various parliamentary activities to the millions of households through the small screen. Televising of select parliamentary proceedings in India commenced with the live telecast of the Address by the President to the members of both Houses of Parliament on 20 December 1989. After that, there has been regular video coverage of the Question Hour (since December 1991), Railway and General Budgets (since February 1992) and debates discussions on Motion of Thanks on the President's Address, Demands for Grants and Motion of no-confidence in the Council of Ministers (during 1992). Keeping in view the archival value of the these recordings, we are keeping a video copy of each of these proceedings in our Audio-Visual Unit. Important parliamentary functions and events like Conferences, Seminars, Lectures, Workshops and Tele-films on different aspects of Parliamentary Practice and Procedure are also being captured on video-cassettes. Video-cassettes of all the above-mentioned proceedings and parliamentary events, etc. are available in the Audio-Visual Library holdings. Various video magazines brought out by major agencies have also been procured.

Among the audio hardware, the Unit has one two-in-one radio-cum-cassette player/recorder and one Stereo double cassette deck with facility of high speed dubbing. The video hardware include one colour television with remote control along with a trolley-cum-cabinet and two VHS VCRs with remote control.

In view of the importance and utility of the electronic version of the official records of parliamentary proceedings and other parliamentary events, their current and archival reference and research value, a draft plan for a self-contained compact Parliamentary Audio-Video Division is on the anvil. The proposed project would have three Units within it : (i) Archival and Viewing Unit; (ii) Production Unit; and (iii) Post-Production Unit.

MEMBERS' REFERENCE SERVICE

This is perhaps one Service which is the most sought after by members, especially during Session days. It supplies on demand factual and objective information to members of Parliament, Presiding Officers and Committees on subjects of economic, political. Members who need the information, approach the Reference Desk in the Library (Ground Floor) and fill in the requisition slip indicating subject of the reference, date and time by which it is required. The Service is manned by Reference Officers who attend to Members' reference broadly on the subject areas allotted to them. In case where information is readily available in published documents it is given on the spot proverbially right from the tap. In other cases, the relevant information, bibliographical data or statistics is culled out from various authentic sources, arranged, compiled, edited and passed on the Members. The total number of Spot References attended to at the the Library (Ground Floor and First Floor) has gone up from 279 in 1985 to 3,550 in 1992. Sometimes, in response to Members' requests factual notes and write ups are also prepared and supplied. In all cases, information is tailored to the requirements of Members and given within the time stipulated by them which very often is quite challenging.

A comparative study undertaken by us shows that during the Eighth Lok Sabha (1984-89), 40 percent references were for the same day, 45 percent required within 2-3 days, 12 percent within 4-7 days and only 3 percent for more than seven days. The corresponding figures were 50 percent, 45 percent, 4 percent and 1 percent for the Ninth Lok Sabha (1989-91) and 46 percent, 42 percent, 10 percent and 2 percent for the first year of the Tenth Lok Sabha (July 1991 to 15 July, 1992).

The scope of material to be collected in response to members' references is normally limited to subjects connected with the immediate business before the two Houses of Parliament. But in actual practice, the Members demand information on a wide variety of topics, thus keeping the staff on their toes all the time.

It is a matter of satisfaction that the Members' Reference Service has become quite popular over the years. The popularity of this Service can be gauged from the marked increase in the number of references received and handled by the Service during the past several years. As against 700 references handled in 1970, 3,627 references were disposed of during the year 1980. Their figure was all time high at 5,167 in

1990. However, there was a slight decline in 1991 when their number was 4,683. But this number seems to be rising again in 1992 which can be attributable to the increased participating of Members in the debates of the two Houses because of telecasting of its proceedings which began on 2.12.91. An idea of this can be had from the following analysis based on the figures collected during the comparable period of 1991-1992. During the Sixth session of the Ninth Lok Sabha (27.12.90 — 11.1.91), in all 341 references were received with the average per day being 34. The corresponding figures were 355 and 29 for the Seventh Session of the Ninth Lok Sabha (21.2.91 — 12.3.91) and 2,203 and 43, respectively for the First Session of the Tenth Lok Sabha (9.7.91 — 18.9.91). With telecasting of parliamentary proceedings with effect from 2.12.91, there has been a perceptible increase in the number of references received from members. Thus, during the Second Session of the Tenth Lok Sabha (20.11.91 — 21.12.91), in all 1,037 references were received with the average per day being 47. The corresponding figures were 2,253 and 46 for the Third Session of Tenth Lok Sabha (20.2.92 — 12.5.92) and 294 and 49, respectively for the fourth Session of Tenth Lok Sabha (from 8.7. 92 — 15.7.92). By and large members have been appreciative of the quality of the material supplied in response to reference within the limited time but there is of course always scope for further improvement.

Anticipatory Reference Notes

While the Officers and Staff of the Reference Service are hard pressed for timely disposal of references especially when the Parliament is in Session, they get some breathing time during the inter-Session days. This time is devoted on the preparation of Background Notes, Information Bulletins and Fact-Sheets on subjects of contemporary interest and on topics which are likely to come up for legislation or discussion through other devices during the forthcoming session. This reference work is done in anticipation of the reference requirement of the Members of the two Houses and becomes very handy and useful for the Members. Some of the background Notes and Information Bulletins prepared recently include "Right to Information" ; "Reservations for Backward Classes"; "Statehood for Delhi"; "Technical Education in India"; "Role of Non-Resident Indians in Economic Development";

"Environment Protection"; "Central Plan Assistance to State"; "Child Labour and Status of Girl Child"; "Anatomy of Stock Market Scam"; "National Policy on Education : Evolution and Reconstruction"; "Earth Summit: An Overview"; "Banking in India"; "Independence of Soviet Republics and formation of Commonwealth of Independent State"; "English Schedule of Constitution : Inclusion of some more Languages"; "Public Distribution System"; "Current Price Situation"; "Tourism Promotion : Policy and Prospects"; "Indian Economy in 1991-92 : Performance and Prospects"; "Uruguay Round of Multilateral Trade Negotiations and Dunkel's Proposals"; "Eighth Five-Year Plan : Objectives, Thrust and Micro Dimensions"; "Railway Budget 92-93 — An Appraisal"; Union Budget 92-93 — An Appraisal"; "Indian Railways : An Overview"; "Indian Railways : Safety Performance"; "Railway Budget 1993-94 - An Appraisal"; "Union Budget : 1993-94 - An Appraisal".

Study Boxes

Besides preparation of anticipatory reference notes, there is system of making Study Boxes on subjects of topical interest. Each of these boxes contain the relevant literature such as books, reports and articles, etc. These boxes are placed in the Members' Reading Room in the Parliament Library for reference and consultation by members at their convenience.

DOCUMENTATION SERVICE

One of the principal adjuncts of a Library, is the Documentation Service. In Parliament Library, it was started in 1975. It indexes and prepares annotations of important books, reports and articles appearing in newspapers and periodicals received in the Parliament Library. The indexes and annotations prepared during a particular fortnight are classified and published in the form of an indexing periodical entitled *Parliamentary Documentation.* These are also fed into the Computer to facilitate searches. This data base, which is retrievable authorwise and subjectwise, serves as an invaluable aid for future research and reference activity. It also enables preparation of select documentation lists for use and reference of members.

PRESS CLIPPING SERVICE

The Press Clipping Service was started on a modest scale in the year 1956 with the limited objective of speedy disposal of references from members on current subject. The scope of the service has considerably increased over the years and accordingly it is now organised more methodically to serve as an essential and basic aid for Parliament research and reference work. All important news and views, which include editorial comments and articles from nine Hindi and nineteen English dailies are clipped and maintained in separate folders in accordance with a specially devised classification scheme. Press Information Bureau (PIB) releases, daily digest of news and views on matters of topical interest, etc., are also scrutinised for clipping purposes. Besides, the service maintains up-to-date sets of the releases of the Indian New and Feature Alliance (INFA). Weeding out operation is regularly carried out to release stacking space for more recent additions of news items. The total number of Press Clippings Folders has gone up from 8,640 in 1985 to 10,530 in 1992. The total number of newspapers added for Clippings was 7,986 in 1985 and 9,326 in 1992. Important Clippings of lasting value and interest, particularly, those having a bearing on constitutional, parliamentary and legal subjects are, however, retained permanently.

REPROGRAPHY SERVICE

The Reprography Unit which was set up in the year 1975, meets the urgent requirements of members for photocopying of important press clippings, parliamentary questions and answers, articles from periodicals and newspapers and extracts from books and other documents. The Unit, at present, is equipped with four xeroxing machines. Two separate photocopying machines have also been installed in a lounge of the Central Hall of Parliament House where members can get a photocopy of any document they want at a nominal rate.

RESEARCH AND INFORMATION SERVICE

The Research and Information Division regularly brings out books, monographs, brochures, backgrounders, etc. on matters of parliamentary interest, including prospective legislative measures which are likely to generate demands from members. The Division is organised into the following six functional Wings: (i) Parliamentary

Affairs Wing; (ii) Practice and Procedure Unit; (iii) Journal Section; (iv) Political Affairs Wing; (v) Economic and Financial Affairs Wing; (vii) Educational and Scientific Affairs Wing; and (viii) Social Affairs Wing.

A number of Brochures on various topics of parliamentary interest have been brought out by different Wings of this Division recently. These include "Legislative Councils in the States—their Creation and Abolition", "Broadcasting and Telecasting of Parliamentary Proceedings"; "Question Hour in Lok Sabha"; "Members of Lok Sabha—a Study in their Socio-Economic Background"; "Parliamentary Committees"; "Presidential Elections, Law, Practice and Procedure (1952-1987)' "Presidential Ordinances (1950-1989)"; "Legislators in India : Salaries and other Facilities"; "Electing the President", etc.

Research Notes are also prepared in the Research and Information Division for use at the Seminars held alongside the annual Conferences of Presiding Officers of Legislative Bodies in India and also other Conferences and Symposia organised by the Indian Parliamentary Group (IPG) and the Bureau of Parliamentary Studies and Training (BPST). Some Research Notes recently brought out included "Panchayati Raj Institutions in India; the Speaker and Party Politics"; "Union-State Relations : Recent Developments, "Erosion of Parliamentary System in India"; "Budget Committees in Parliament and State Legislatures" ; Evolution of the Office of Speaker"; "Uniform Civil Code"; "Anti-Defection Law—a Case for Review"; "Oil Crisis"; and "Constitution of India in Precept and Practice".

For the use of Indian Parliamentary Delegations going abroad on good-will visits and for participating in International Parliamentary Conferences held under the auspices of the Inter-Parliamentary Union and the Commonwealth Parliamentary Association, Briefs and Country Notes are also prepared in this Division.

Monographs

Monographs on subjects relating to Parliament and its functioning have also been published from time to time. With a view to reviving the memory of our eminent parliamentarians who played a distinguished role in the country's freedom struggle and who contributed so much to the building of modern India and its parliamentary system, a new Monograph series titled "Eminent Parliamentarians Monograph Series" was started in 1990. Fourteen such Monographs have been brought out in this series so far. They are on : Dr. Rammanohar Lohia, Dr. Lanka Sundaram, Dr. Syama Prasad Mookerjee, Pandit Nilakantha Das, Panampilli Govinda Menon, Bhupesh Gupta, Dr. Rajendra Prasad, Shiekh Mohammad Abdullah, Dr. B.R. Ambedkar, Dr. C.D. Deshmukh, Jaisukh Lal Hathi, V.K. Krishna Menon. M. Anantasayanam Ayyangar, S.M. Joshi and Raj Kumari Amrit Kaur. These Monographs generally contain the life-sketches of the eminent parliamentarians and select speeches made by them in the Lok Sabha and Rajya Sabha and in the Constituent Assembly in the case of members of the Constituent Assembly. In some case, articles on the dignitary by parliamentarians and other distinguished personalities from different walks of life are also included. Work on several other Monographs including those on Lal Bahadur Shastri, Y.B. Chavan, and other dignitaries are in progress. A new Monograph series called "Distinguished Parliamentarians Felicitation Series" has also been started recently. The first monograph in the series was on Shri R. Venkataraman, the Eighth President of India.

Recently in the Eminent Parliamentarian Series, on 20 August, 1992, the Prime Minister of India, Shri P.V. Narasimha Rao released a book "Rajiv Gandhi and Parliament" edited by Shri C.K. Jain, Secretary-General, Lok Sabha on the occasion of the 48th Birth Anniversary of the former Prime Minister. Besides a profile of Shri Gandhi, the book carries informative articles on various aspects of the life and times of the late leader. The book also contains texts of important speeches delivered by Shri Rajiv Gandhi in Parliament and also other speeches on significant occasions in our parliamentary history.

Periodicals

For the use of members, the Research and Information Division also publishes eight periodicals. *The Journal of Parliamentary Information* is a Quarterly which contains practice and problem-oriented articles on constitutional and parliamentary subjects from members of Parliament and other experts in the field. It also serves as an authentic recorder of developments in practice and procedure and parliamentary events and activities in Indian and foreign Legislatures.

The Digest of Central Acts is also a Quarterly containing synopsis of all Bills passed by Parliament and assented to by the President. *The Digest of Legislative and Constitutional Cases,* another Quarterly contains abstracts of judgements of Supreme Court and the High Courts involving interpretation of the provisions of the Constitution and certain statutes in important legislative and constitutional cases. *The Abstracts of Books Reports and Articles,* also a Quarterly, contains abstracts of important books received in Parliament Library and articles appearing in journals and leading newspapers, and synopsis of important official and foreign reports including those from the UN. The Diary of Political Events is a Monthly, containing a chronology of important news items and comments appearing in daily newspapers and replies to parliamentary questions about the performance of various public sector undertakings of the Union Government. *Science and Technology—News Digest,* a Monthly, contains abstracts of important news items, latest books, reports, articles, replies to parliamentary questions and other literature on science and technology. *I. P. G. Newsletter* is a quarterly publication which keeps members informed of the various parliamentary events and activities of the Indian Parliamentary Group, like exchange of Parliamentary Delegations, IPU and CPA Conferences, meetings, seminars, symposia, etc.

PRESS AND PUBLIC RELATIONS SERVICE

Parliament is essentially a people's institution and as such, its activities should get adequate coverage in the mass media so that the people are aware of the work of their elected representatives. The Press and Public Relations Wing attempts to bring the Parliament and the Press together. All matters connected with the media persons such as issue to them of passes for Press Gallery and Central Hall, car labels copies of all parliamentary papers such as bills, statements, reports, budget documents, etc. and provision of working facilities to media persons are dealt with in this Wing. Press releases on all important matters connected with the Sessions of Lok Sabha, meetings of the Parliamentary Committees and Conferences, visits of foreign Parliamentary Delegations to India and of Indian Delegations to foreign countries are also issued by this Wing. To facilitate publicity of parliamentary news, this Wing has the facility of a Fax machine to enable it to fax press releases to newspapers and other media offices.

TELEPRINTER SERVICE

In order to keep members posted with the latest happenings in the country and abroad, particularly during the Session in Parliament, teleprinter machines, fed by national news agencies, have been installed in Parliament House. Important News items received through those machines are collected, edited and displayed on news display boards located near the Ground Floor Library at regular intervals throughout the day.

CLOSED CIRCUIT TELEVISION SYSTEM

Vital information pertaining to the on-going business in both the Houses of Parliament is displayed on the Closed Circuit Television System (CCTV) at various places of the Parliament House and Parliament House Annexe. CCTV Monitors have also been installed for the benefit of members in the rooms of Presiding Officers, Ministers, political parties, senior officers of the two Secretariats and also at various common areas like the waiting Halls, Library Reading Hall and Refreshment Room. In the Central Hall, a large screen of the Hotline Projection Television has been installed to display prominently this information.

NEW PARLIAMENT LIBRARY BUILDING

From its humble beginning in 1921, the Parliament Library has grown into one of the best Libraries in the country, nay in the Asian region as a whole. The single most important problem that we are facing today is that of space. We have all been feeling for the past several years that the present accommodation allotted to Parliament Library is too limited to cope with the growing volume of literature received by it. We have worked out that a minimum space of 20,000 sq.m will be required for the proper stacking of about 3 million publications, which the Library is expected to have in the next forty years or so. The progress on a number of activities such as installation of Mainframe Computer, setting up of an enlarged video and audio Library, Microfilm Reading Room, Conservation Laboratory, etc., has been very slow for want of adequate space. This being the case, we have been working on the proposal for a new Parliament Library building which could accommodate not only the multi-dimensional expansion of the collection but also several other future modernisation programmes.

The proposed Parliament Library building shall have provision for all the facilities of a modern Library. It is expected to accommodate the needs of growth oriented collections, adequate space for reception and reference desks, self-contained conservation laboratory and for computerisation for library facilities and linkage of Parliament Library with the libraries of State Legislatures and those of Parliaments of Commonwealth and other countries of the world and other international data-bases. A closed circuit Television network is being planned for viewing the proceedings of the House. There would be sufficient, number of cubicles fully equipped with audio and video facilities and computer terminals. Conveyor belts would be provided for horizontal and vertical transportation of books and other materials.

The proposed building would also house an auditorium with the capacity of about 1100 seats with a permanent screen and well-equipped projection room; a VIP reception hall for ceremonial purpose; one Press briefing room; a Media Centre with facilities of STD telephone, FAX and Telex for the use of Accredited Press Correspondents on payment basis; one Library Committee/Conference room; and Archival room having temperature below freezing point to preserve audiovisual materials, computer tapes, microfilms etc. In short, it would be a functionally viable building which would not only take care of the Library's expansion but also provide for more advanced and sophisticated information storage and retrieval systems. Various Divisions and Wings of LARRDIS will also then function from the new building to provide more efficient and better coordinated services to members.

In the meanwhile, pending construction of the new library building, we are planning to construct temporary structures with all essential facilities for stacking Library publications. These temporary structures, located within the Parliament Estate, are likely to come up shortly.

Thus, we are on the threshold of a new era in information technology. We in Parliament Library are gearing up ourselves to face the challenges and opportunities posed by information explosion with a sense of purposefulness and commitment, in the larger cause of serving the Parliament and its members and through them the millions who make up this country. And under the benign guidance, blessings and inspiration given to us by our Speaker, Shri Shivraj V. Patil, the whole-hearted support of the Deputy Speaker, Lok Sabha, Shri S. Mallikarjunaiah who is also the Chairman of the Library Committee, and the co-operation of all members of Parliament and others, we are confident that we would usher in a new era in the service of our members of Parliament.

Origins and Status of Indian Manuscripts

M K PRAJAPATI

Introduction

The manuscripts are a part of our cultural heritage which enable us to peep into our history, literature, science and culture of the bygone days. India has one of the largest and finest collections of manuscripts in the world. This vast wealth of knowledge & information is distributed all over the country. According to a recent survey it is estimated that there are about three million manuscripts (mss.) of Indian origin in various libraries, institutions and private hands. Out of these nearly 0.15 million are available in Europe and north American libraries. Nearly 70% of these are in Sanskrit, Prakrit and Pali; 20% in modern Indian languages and the rest in Arabic, Persian and Urdu. Only a million of these are being indexed in some form or the other. Many different scripts were being used in producing these manuscripts, such as Grantha, Telugu, Malayalam, Kannada, Devanagari, Oriya, Bengali, Sharada, Arabic, Persian, Gurumukhi, Newari, etc., and the materials used in producing them are also of different types - e.g. palm-leaf, birch-bark, paper, cloth, woodboard, copper plates, stone etc. There are manuscripts on every subject - arts & crafts, astrology, astronomy, chemistry & medicine, language & literature, philosophy & religion, mathematics, ect. Some of these are artistically illuminated and illustrated which indicate that the art of calligraphy and miniature paintings of highest quality were common in India.

Writing was known to Indians for 5000 years as evident from the clay tablets and pottery works from Mohenjodaro and Harappa. The earliest known inscriptions are the Ashokan inscriptions of 327 B.C. There are also fragments of palm-leaf and birch-bark dated as far back as second century B.C. found in central Asia in Kharoshthi and other scripts. However, samples of complete works are available only from the 9th/10th century A.D. onwards. It is worth mentioning that thirteen plays of the famous sanskrit dramatist Bhas (200 B.C. to 200 A.D.) were discovered in a temple in 1912.

Ancient and Medieval Period

Ancient India was a great centre of learning. Students from nearby countries - China, Korea, Java etc. used to study here. Some famous libraries were well known to the scholarly world with established identities. Taxashila was the first known centre of learning in ancient India, which flourished from 600 B.C. to 300 A.D. Nalanda (400 to 1200 A.D.) was one of the most famous ancient universities of India. Its library was known as Dharmaganj and its three large buildings were known as Ratnasagara, Ratnadadhi and Ratnaranjaka. Two Chinese pilgrims Hiuen Tsang (629 - 645 A.D.) and I-Tsing (675 A.D.) visited the university and copied several Buddhist texts which were subsequently taken to China. A detailed description is available in their travelogues. Vallabhi is another centre famous for Buddhist and Jain culture (475-775 A.D) where it is said, all the Jain scriptures (Angas) were first scribed. Among other centres of learning Vikramshila, Vijayanagar, Dhara, Kalyani, Anahilawad, Patna, Thanjavur, etc., were prominent in their respective periods. Majority of these were destroyed during Muslim invasions and the rest due to other causes. Muslim invaders reached southern India at a much later period which partly helped in saving some of these centres in that region. Anand Tirtha, the great Hindu philosopher of South known as Madhvachrya, (1300 A.D) who travelled through northern India noted that "Utsana prayasa sarve kottyamsapi na vidhyate" (that all have been destroyed, nothing has survived)

Modern period

During the British rule India got exposed to European life and culture and with it came a new educational system. In the field of manuscriptology, British contribution is notable. Several surveys to locate mss., followed by catalogue preparation and preservation activities were started during 1850 onwards. Thousands of rare and valuable mss. found through these activities were taken away from India and deposited in several European libraries.

Those which remained in India are now stored in several institutions and private hands. There are hundreds of private collections and centres that have anything between 5 to 60,000 mss. whereas the figures for institutional collections may reach over 100,000. Among the institutional collections Sarasvati Bhandara Library (1791) of the

Sampurnananda Sanskrit University has 100,300, the largest Sanskrit manuscripts collection in the country. Out of all these only about 400 centres are familiar to the scholarly world.

Types of Manuscript Centres

1. Manuscript libraries
2. Oriental research institutions
3. National library
4. Academic institutions (universities, colleges and traditional Sanskrit pathasala, madrasas
5. Jaina Jnana Bhandaras
6. Religious institutions (Temple, Mosques)
7. Museums
8. Public libraries
9. Private collections

1. *Manuscript libraries :* There are only a few libraries with exclusive manuscript collections. Among these the Government Oriental Manuscripts Library, Madras (GOML), Tanjore Maharaja Serfoji's Saraswati Mahal Library (Thanjavur), and Andhra Pradesh Government Oriental Manuscripts Library and Research Institute (Hyderabad) are famous for their large and rich collections. The main activities of these libraries are to collect, preserve and publish mss. catalogues and critical edition of texts. GOML has so far published about 160 — the highest number of catalogue volumes.

2. *Oriental research institutions* are having the largest number of mss. The main purpose of these institutions are: Indological research; to collect and catalogue and preserve mss; to publish critical editions of scholarly works and journals. These research institutions have got a large research collection of printed materials on Indology. There are about 50 such major research centres now existing in the country. Each of these institutions is having an average of 10,000 to 65,000 manuscripts of Indic origin, of which the most well known

are : Bhandarkar Oriental Research Institute (Pune), Oriental Research Institute (Baroda), Asiatic Society (Calcutta), Adyar Library and Research Centre (Madras), Vishveshvaranand Vedic Research Institute (Hoshiarpur., Punjab), Trivandrum University Mss. Library and Oriental Research Institute (Thiruvananthapuram), L.D. Institute of Indology (Ahemedabad), G.N. Jha Research Institute (Allahabad), Rajasthan Oriental Research Institute (Jodhpur). These institutions are regularly bringing out critical editions of texts under well known Sanskrit and other Indological series; some also publish their own journals. All these mss collections are looked after by traditional pandits.

3. *National Library*, Calcutta does not have a large collection of manuscripts. There are about 3000 volumes and mostly part of some gifts belonging to some eminent personalities of India, donated by their heirs. The most famous Buhar collection comprises 952 volumes in Arabic, Persian and Urdu. Nearly half of the total Sanskrit mss (790) came also from a private donor (George Thibaut). The other significant collections of the library originally belonged to Jadunath Sarkar, Imambara, Vayapuri and Rewa. The library also records the availability of 182 microfilm rolls of Indian mss. through an UNESCO sponsored project. No catalogue has so far been published by the National Library for any of these collections.

4. *Academic libraries* (university, college and pathasala) : Several universities have manuscripts collected from the region either as gift or purchased. Generally mss. are kept in the libraries and in some cases, these are retained by the concerned language departments. College or pathasala collections are not well organised and rarely being used. They have no systematic collection development programme. Someone may have donated these as a gift to the library. There is a strong need to transfer such types of collections (average size: 500 mss.) to a larger academic / research centre having adequate facilities to prepare catalogues and preserve them. In some universities, manuscript collections are well maintained and some have published a few catalogue volumes also.

5. *Jaina Jnana Bhandaras* : In Rajasthan, Gujarat and Karnataka states there are a number of Jaina Jnana Bhandaras. In almost every village or township where some Jaina families live it has a manuscript Bhandara. At a rough estimate, a total of 800,000 mss. of Sanskrit, Prakrit and Apabhramasa languages are [reserved in these Bhandaras. Jainas have tendered a great service to the nation by preserving this cultural heritage for posterity and scholars. Bhandaras contain all types of mss. without discrimination of religion, race or subject. They are under the management of private Jaina trusts, temple or monastery. Majority of them are kept closed and sealed most of the time. Very little use is made of these collections. Muni Punyavijayaji and Muni Jinavijayaji visited several of these Bhandars and prepared catalogues, and it was due to their efforts that scholars came to know about these Bhandaras. Similarly Kashliwal and Johrmal Parakh published catalogues after surveying the Digamber and Svetamber Bhandaras respectively of Rajasthan. The Bhandaras are meant to be used by the Jaina monks only.

6. *Museum Collections* : Majority of museums contain manuscripts with illumination and miniature paintings or outstanding artistic calligraphy. However, some museums, such as, Orissa State Museum, Bhubaneswar (60,000), Municipal Museum, Allahabad and State Chandradhari Museum, Darabhanga each contain about 5500 mss. of all types. The Orissa State Museum is particularly famous for its beautifully illustrated Oriya palm-leaf mss. The museum has published several volumes of mss. catalogue.

7. *Religious Trust Collection* : This type of collections are found either in temple, mosques or dargahs. These are generally store house with very little use due to several types of restrictions usually imposed by the authorities.

8. *Public libraries* : Public libraries normally do not collect mss. except when a special gift is made to the library. They are preserved as a special collection without any definite objective, use or proper care.

9. *Private Collections* : There is no source to find out details of holdings of private collections in India. Generally traditional pandit families, ex-rulers of princely states, some scholars or interested persons, rare book and mss dealers may be having their personal collections of mss of their choice. Particularly those of the ex-rulers' collections are rich in terms of literary value or for their artistic qualities. In addition manuscripts on their own geneology and works written in praise of their dynasty by bards and court poets were available in these collections. Unfortunately it is difficult to make use of all such collections as they are meant for private use only.

Manuscript Surveys and Catalogues

After the British government's initiatives in survey and cataloguing of Indian mss there have been several major activities primarily due to the initiatives of a few individuals.

We may break these down into the following periods :

1. Early (1730 - 1867)
2. Renaissance (1868 - 1900)
3. National awakening (1901 - 1946)
4. Post independence (1947 onwards -)

During the first phase, some sporadic personal attempts were made to collect manuscripts mostly by some foreign scholars and civil servants; among them James Fraser, Sir Robert Chamber, Colin Mackenzie, Sir William Jones are notable. Fraser collected about 200 Arabic, Persian and Sanskrit mss. from Gujarat during 1730 - 40 and published a catalogue in 1742. Fraser's collection was the first set of Indian manuscripts ever taken away to Europe. Sir Robert Chamber (1774 - 79) Chief Justice of Bengal, collected 800 Sanskrit mss., which were subsequently purchased by the Konigliche Bibliothek, Berlin. Colin Mackenzie (1796 - 1806) while he was the surveyor of Madras Presidency had collected about 8000 mss., maps, inscriptions, local tracts etc. in several Indian languages. Later the collection was purchased by the East India Company, most of which was deposited in the India Office Library & Records and some in the University of Madras. These were catalogued by H.H. Wilson in 1828. Similarly

William Jones' collection was deposited in the Royal Asiatic Society, London. During this period the Asiatic Society, Calcutta (1784) and Sanskrit College, Benaras (1791) were established, and they also started collecting manuscripts.

The second phase covers only 33 years but it is the most important period in the history of locating manuscript collections. Radha Krisna, Chief Pandit of the Lahore Darbar put up a proposal to the Viceroy to conduct a survey of Sanskrit mss. This was accepted and actual survey work started in 1868. Well known Sanskrit scholars like Buehler, Kielhorn, Peter Peterson, Bhandarkar and others visited different areas of the presidency and collected several thousands of mss. for government collections. They also published several Notices of mss. after examining private and institutional collections. At a later stage, the manuscripts in government collections were transferred to Bhandarkar Oriental Research Institute, Pune in 1925. Bengal Presidency was surveyed by Rajendralal Mitra and Haraprasad Shastri. Mitra's "*Notices of Sanskrit Manuscripts*" were the first descriptive catalogue on European pattern, ever published in India. Similarly, Punjab by Kashinath Kunte, Oudh by Nesfield and Pt. Deviprasad, Southern India by Gustav Oppert and Mysore and Coorg by Hultzsch were surveyed and published Notices based on them. These surveys brought to light several lost or unknown works particularly in Sanskrit.

During the third phase several indological research institutions were established whose contribution in manuscript preservation and other allied activities were mentioned earlier. One notable feature of this period is that descriptive form of catalogues were prepared and published by Scholars like Gopinath Kaviraj, Kuppuswami Sastri, C.D. Dalal and others. Besides Sanskrit, modern Indian languages catalogues were also produced during this period.

After 1947 the Central and some State governments took some interest in the preservation of manuscripts. As a result some significant steps were taken :

1. Standard format to prepare a descriptive catalogue was designed.
2. Government Grants were made easily available for cataloguing and preservation of mss.

3. Several new institutions were established with the sole objective of collecting mss.
4. Special provisions were made under the Antiquity Act of 1972 that mss. should not be taken out of the country.
5. Another major outcome was the publication proramme of the Department of Sanskrit, University of Madras the "New Catalogus Catalogorum". Though the compilation was started in 1935, actual publications started only in 1949 and till date 13 volumes have come out. It is a national register of Sanskrit mss. containing notes on each work, author, and location of the mss. In this process several unknown and less known collections came to light as a byproduct of this programme.

Classification, Cataloguing and Storage

Modern classification schemes are not of much help for indological subjects. There is a need to develop a classification scheme in depth for Indology. During the medieval period manuscripts used to be classified under broad subject groups like, religion, philosophy, literature, astrology etc. The same method with some modification is still in practice. To catalogue Sanskrit and other Indian languages manuscripts some knowledge of the subject, language, script, writing method etc. are essential. Moreover, traditional Indian manuscripts do not have a title page. Cataloguer has to find out either from the beginning, end or colophon, where information about author, title, scribe, commentator or patrons are usually found. Authors sometimes do not provide any information about themselves. These manuscripts are old and several of them are incomplete. In such cases the cataloguer has to establish a co-relationship with the authors' other works. Since 1742 Sanskrit mss. catalogues are found in the following types - 1. Simple title list; 2. Title and author list; 3. General informative tabular catalogue; 4. Descriptive catalogue providing complete bibliographical data, besides beginning, and of text, colophon, extensive notes on authors and works, and various indices. Majority of the catalogues published in Europe are descriptive in nature. Presently in India catalogues are being prepared in tabular form with extracts and notes from selected mss. only. Generally the mss. are stored according to broad subjects or accession numbers. It is also found that in some places they are tied up in red cloth bundles by author or subject.

Writing Materials used for preparing manuscripts in India are - palm-leaf, birch-bark, paper, woodenboard, copper and other metal plates, clay tablets, leather, cloth, bamboo chips, stone etc. depending upon their availability in a particular region. For example, in South India and Orissa largely palm-leaf and in northern India paper were used.

1. *Palm-leaf* or *Tadapatra* in Sanskrit is the leaf of palm trees which grow along the sea coast. Its leaves are used for writing purposes after processing. Leaves are first dried and boiled and then again dried under sun. They are then cut into proper sizes and the surface rubbed with conch shell or stones. After these processes are complete the palm leaf is ready for use for writing. Actual writing is done by ink pen or metal stylus. The longest palm-leaf ms. 36" × 2" is available at the Jain Bhandara, Patan.

2. *Birch-bark* are known as *Bhurja-patra* and available in Kashmir valley only. The inside portion of the bark tree is taken out and after due process it can be used. The earliest specimen (of 2nd cent. B.C.) was found in central Asia.

3. *Wooden board* : Some specimens of woodenboard are found in Assam and Burma. The earliest Buddhist text *Vinayapitaka* refers to its use as writing material.

4. *Cloth and Leather* : Jaina Bhandaras of Patan and Jaisalmer contain some mss. written on cloth and leather. Buehler had also found a piece of silk cloth from Jaisalmer with Jaina sutras. The Sringeri matha also contains a large number of *kadita* written on cloth.

5. *Stone and Metal plates* (*silalekha / abhilekha* and *tamra patra/ tamrasasan*) : Generally, stone and metal plates as writing material were used by the kings and rulers for proclamation of donations, orders or religious teachings, though some literary works were also found on stone and metal plates. Among these, *Harikelinataka* of Chaahaman king Vigraharaj 4th and *Lalitavigraharajanataka* of his court poet Somadeva of 12th cent. are well known.

6. *Paper* : It has already been established that paper originated in China in 105 A.D. Nearchos, the Greek writer who visited

India in 327 B.C. mentioned in his travelogue that India used to make paper from cotton and other raw materials. But there is no evidence of any paper based manuscript fragments before 11th century A.D. The earliest known dated manuscript on paper is of 1089 A.D. which is preserved in Kashmir Bhandara. From 13th century onwards paper was used regularly in India for writing.

7. *Pen/Stylus* : To write on paper and palm-leaf with ink a pen made from bamboo was used. A stylus pen is used to engrave/ write on palm-leaf without ink.

8. *Ink* : In ancient and medieval period, several types of coloured ink especially gold, silver, red, black were used for writing. They were made from charcoal, burnt shells of almonds, cow's urine, gum, oil, gold, silver etc.

Preservation

There are very few libraries having proper storage facilities with airconditioning, fumigation chamber etc. for manuscript preservation. Traditionally, each ms. is tied up with cotton or silken thread, and then wrapped up with cloth and kept in wooden or steel cupboards/shelves. Sometimes each ms. is kept in specially designed separate wooden boxes or between two equal sized wooden boards. Generally these boxes or boards are decorated with colourful designs. In order to protect from direct heat, damp weather and some other harmful environmental factors mss. are kept in underground stores in some temples and institutions.

Islamic Manuscript centres

There are several centres in India where large number of Islamic mss. in Arabic, Persian and Urdu languages are preserved. The earliest ms. in this category belongs to 12th century A.D. During Muslim rule there was a tradition to appoint a known literary figure as the head of a royal library. For example, Amir Khusrau, well known Persian poet and scholar, was appointed by Sultan Jalaluddin Khilji (14th c.) as the royal librarian. It was also a tradition to appoint scribes with artistic approach to calligraphy in the royal libraries and madrasas, to copy manuscripts.

The most prominent libraries in India with rich Islamic mss. collections are : Khuda Baksh Oriental Public Library, Patna; Raza

Library, Rampur; Maulana Azad Library of Aligarh Muslim University, Aligarh, Darul'ulum, Deoband; Salarjung Museum, Hyderabad, Jamia Millia Islamia and Hamdard Institute, Delhi. Khuda Baksh Oriental Public Library is having a collection of 25,000 valuable manuscripts. It is one of the leading treasure houses of Islamic literary heritages in India. As compared to Sanskrit, Islamic manuscripts are in general, more artistic in nature with beautiful calligraphy, with illumination, miniature paintings and quality binding.

Indic Manuscripts in Overseas Libraries

At a rough estimate about 175,000 mss. of Indian origin (Sanskrit, Arabic, Persian and modern Indian languages) are available in institutions and private collections abroad. The largest number of mss. are in the United Kingdom - Oriental & India Office Collections of the British Library and the Bodleian Library, Oxford. Copies of some of the rare and valuable mss. are not available in India. Catalogues prepared by these European institutions are in descriptive form. Out of a total of 1400 volumes of catalogues, (including catalogues of some particular collections, published as journal articles) about 300 of them were published outside India, mostly in Europe. Works like, *Oriental manuscripts in Europe and north America* / by J.D. Pearson; *Census of Indic mss. in the U.S.A. and Canada* / by H.I. Poleman; *Census of exact sciences in Sanskrit* / by David E. Pingree and *Catalogus Catalogorum* / by Theodor Aufrecht give details of these collections and their catalogues. On the line of Aufrecht a *New Catalogus Catalogorum* project started in 1935 and by 1994 13 volumes were published (up to - 'Bahya') based on about 450 catalogues.

Epilogue :

1. Sanskrit mss. have been written in several different scripts. Hence it is difficult for a scholar to use all the manuscripts on a particular subject/ title.

2. Due to lack of plain paper copying facilities except in a few centres, distance users can not be served properly.

3. For effective use, there is a need to collect all scattered mss. from different places and preserve them in some zonal centres. Microfilm copies of all the manuscripts should be preserved in a more centralised place as a national repository of mss.

4. Similarly one microfilm copy of every Indian manuscript from overseas collections should be acquired on exchange/payment basis for this central repository.

5. There is an urgent need to prepare and publish mss. catalogues of all private and public manuscript collections in India which may help in discovering several source of lost or unknown knowledge.

6. Very few academic libraries or research institutions maintain a comprehensive collection of catalogues of mss. As a result research students / scholars are unable to check whether a particular ms. is available and where to look for it.

7. There is no such published directory or survey report similar in scope to Pearson's *Oriental manuscripts in Europe & north America* for the sub-continent. A directory containing information on Indian collections would be a very useful reference source in promoting effective use of manuscripts.

8. India possesses an enormously rich collection of manuscripts related to every branch of knowledge and creative work. But due to lack of systematic bibliographic control their use is very much restricted. Very few take up manuscriptology as a profession or feel interested in such a job due to low monetary benefits to a cataloguer.

Manuscript Collections in Indian Libraries with Special Emphasis on National Library

MD. SHAMIM AKHTAR

Introduction

It is significant that man's intellectual progress and the systematic recordings of his achievements are a very late development. In the primitive age, oral tradition i.e., the spoken word was the main medium of the transfer of human knowledge. Increasing needs and necessities caused mankind adopt or draw codes, signs and symbols based on ideologies which led to the origin of manuscripts (mss.) which means a drawing, a scratching or a writing of any kind, as distinguished from printed matter, is the most important source of information for a particular period of human civilization. Though it is difficult to ascertain its exact origin, it has been presumed that the first writing was done on soil by means of a human finger, followed by scratching upon trees and rocks. In order to reach the latest form of mss. i.e., a book, a document or the like written by hand in alphabets, a very large number of peculiar signs, symbols and scripts have been developed in the last five thousand years or so.

The importance of a manuscript is significant for sufficiently notable reasons. Before printing, manuscript was the main source of information. It is the basic historical evidence. It is the original source for the reconstruction of the past, and the most important documentation for the interpretation of parallel experience as well as for the clarification of false testimony or blurred reports. In this way every Mss. has its personality and reveals the personality of the scribe as well as the characteristics of his milieu. Ancient cultures, traditions and characters have deep impact on modern progress and they are authentically represented by related mss. Manuscripts have great research value which led to recognise their need and importance internationally. Consequently among other arts, Paleography came into existence which is the foundation of all history. Mss. even after its proper publishing cannot be declared useless and Librarians try to conserve an original sample of all mss. of significance. At present every country, every library in its capacity is serious to ensure proper collecting, proper use and proper preservation of manuscripts.

Manuscript Collections in India

India is a land of very ancient civilization and manuscripts form a precious part of its cultural heritage. Manuscripts have been greatly responsible for promoting education, training and development of the country since the ancient period. For understanding the history and culture of India the literary treasures that we have in the form of mss. cannot be ignored. The main credit goes to the Sanskrit mss. which have been continuously active for over 4,000 years. In Sanskrit and other Indian languages a book is called "Pustaka" or "Pusta". Pusta which means modelling, as with clay or metal, gives an obvious reference to the ancient writing materials in the forms of clay-tablets and metal seals. The discovery of inscribed seals, pottery and metal pieces among the Indus Valley shows not only the knowledge of writing in ancient India but also the media and form of their use. The Vedas do presuppose a written form of speech or language. Greek sources mention the use of cloth and inner bark of trees. In ancient India early 4th century B.C. Kalidasa refers to the birch bark as ancient writing material and till recently this was in use in Kashmir. Palm leaf was the most common material in which the bulk of old Indian literature has been presented all over India. The oldest palm-leaf manuscript, found in Nepal is about 700 years old. The other forms of material used for writing are cloth, cotton-silk, wooden boards, leather, metal plates etc.

As regards mss. collections in India it is difficult to make even a rough estimate of its as it is lying scattered in many known and unknown places of this vast country. A survey through secondary sources reveals that more than 22 lakhs of Indian mss. are deposited in libraries both public and private and 10 lakhs of different mss. have been listed in printed catalogues during the past 150 years. With reference to an all Indian survey on Sanskrit Mss., a report of some places may be given as : Kashi Sanskrit Vishwavidyalaya has perhaps got the single largest collection of manuscripts in the country.

There are nearly one lakhs manuscripts in Kerala University Library.

Research Societies and Institutions have more than 10 lakhs mss.

There will be over 2 lakhs Mss. in labraries and museums.

About one lakh manuscripts are available in Hindu temples and Maths. In Ahmedabad city alone the Jain Mandirs possess 75,000 volumes and about 2 lakhs manuscripts are in the palaces of old princely States.

Indian has several reputed centres dealing with large mss. collections in various regional languages such as Tamil, Telugu, Hindu, Bhojpuri, Oriya, Bengali, Gurmukhi etc., alongwith Arabic, Persian and Sanskrit languages. Some of these leading institutions are :

— (Mss.) Government Oriental Mss. Library, Madras

— (Mss.) Saraswati Mahal Library, Thanjavur

— (Mss.) Asiatic Society of Bengal, Calcutta

— (Mss.) Sanskrit College, Calcutta

— (Mss.) Khuda Baksh Oriental Public Library, Patna

— (Mss.) Raza Library, Rampur

— (Mss.) Salar Jung Museum Library, Hyderabad

— (Mss.) National Archives of India, New Delhi

— (Mss.) Rabindra Bhavan, Shantiniketan

— (Mss.) Theosophical Society, Adyar, Madras.

On the basis of surveys, important catalogues and other studies, it is estimated that the total number of mss. in all the languages lying in public and private collections all over the country is over 3 million of which only about one million have been listed in printed catalogues. In order to identify these mss., to catalogue and organise them and to make them available for proper use, some major projects are on, which include establishment of Central Manuscripts Library, undertaking a detailed survey of mss. collections and preparation of a Union Catalogue of Indian Languages Manuscripts Catalogues.

Manuscripts in the National Library, Calcutta

National Library, Calcutta, though the biggest library in India, does not have a very large mss. collection. It is the repository of the printed cultural heritage of the country. However, its small holding on mss. represents almost all basic and important branches of knowledge to a great extent. mss. mainly in book forms, personal archives, bound volumes of correspondence, loose letters and palm leaves include a major part which for their unique record and characteristics have proved their significance widely. Except the letters and correspondence in English the mss. are mostly in Arabic, Persian, Sanskrit, Bengali and Tamil languages. These mss. include authentic records, beautiful illustrations, fine calligraphy along with certain other qualities of interest. As regards the total number of mss. in the library, there are more than 3,000 vols. in different forms and a good number of valuable correspondence, diaries etc, which are broadly described below.

Manuscripts in libraries in different languages and forms may be represented as follows :

Arabic	681	Paper mss.	Arabic Script
Bengali	181	" "	Bengali "
English	255	" "	English "
Hindi	5	" "	Hindi "
Persian	955	" "	Persian "
Sanskrit	790	" "	Sanskrit "
Tamil	36	" "	Tamil "
Tamil	334	Palm Leaves	Tamil "
Urdu	21	Paper mss.	Urdu "

The National Library collection of manuscripts are mostly part of some gift collections belonging to eminent personalities of India which were donated by their heirs. Let us start with a few noted collections.

Buhar Collection

This is the oldest gifts collection presented to library in 1904. In 1775 A.D. it was founded by Sayyid Sadruddin of Buhar who was very eminent for his love of learning as well as for his performance as Munshi to Nawab Mir Jafer, Shah Alam and Warren Hastings. This precious collection comprises 1,515 vols. of rare books and 952 vols. of mss. in Arabic, Persian and Urdu languages. The collection is extremely rich on all important subjects which include Religion (mainly Islam), History, important branches of Art & Science including Medicine, Astronomy, Philosophy, Music and many volumes on poetry. The speciality of some of these volumes are, beautiful illustrations, styles of writing, authenticity of records etc. A few noted as most valuable are mentioned here.

Tarikhi-Harat

It is a unique history of Harat written in the beginning of the eighth century. A.H. by an author who was himself a witness to most of the events narrated them.

Ajaibul Makhluqat

A very valuable and rare cosmographical work composed in the beginning of the latter half of the sixth century A.H.

Khawar Namah

A rare narration in epic form relating to the warlike deeds of Ali (the 4th Caliph of Islam). Written in 17th century, this beautifully illustrated vol. represents the finest specimen of Indian miniature painting and calligraphy.

Sir Jadunath Sarkar Collection

This is one of the important personal collections which was gifted to the library in 1959. Among its 2,500 rare vols. in different languages it has 206 Persian mss. on the later Mughal period (1659 – 1837) and the early British regime in India. These manuscripts are generally transcripts of rare originals scattered in different libraries of India and abroad. They contain in valuable personal notes and comments by the historian representing useful references to the study of Mughal History. Most noteworthy in the collection are :

The Akhbarat-i-Darbar-i-mulla and the Araiz-o-Faramin

These are the Imperial Gazettes of the Mughal Government and are the most important sources of information on the administrative, social and economic policies of the great Mughals.

Haft Anjuman

A collection of rare letters representing the daily despatches of the pursuits of Dara, Jaisingh's Purandar Campaigns (1665) and his invasion of Bijapur in 1666. It is a very important collection of letters of Emperor Aurangzeb's time.

Ahval-i-Najeebuddaulah

A contemporary account of Nawab Najeebuddaulah who was raised to the office of Amirul Umara in 1756 and remained almost absolute master of Delhi until his death in 1771 A.D.

Thibaut collection

Belonging to the eminent lover of learning Dr. George Thibaut, the collection is one of the important collections presented to the Library. Having 410 mss. in Sanskrit languages the collection is rich in Indian philosophy, religion, literature, history, astrology etc.

A few noted volumes are as follows :

Brahmasutra Sankara-bhasyam, n.d.

on "Advaita Vedanta"

Cayanakarika, n.d., C. 17th century

on "Karmakanda"

Gargasamhita, n.d., C. 18th century

on "Jyotisam"

Sastradipikalokah, n.d., C. 17th century

on "Mimamsa"

Pancatantram, dated Samvat 1647, A.D. 1590

on "Pancatantra".

Vaiyapuri Palm-leaves collection

A very valuable collection on palm leaves donated to the library in 1960. It belonged to the great scholar and historian, Prof. V.P. Pillai.

The collection has 334 mss. in old Tamil, broadly dealing with literary classics, religious texts, linguistic work, such as dictionaries (in verse) grammatical works and collection of proverbs. Some important vols. are :

Mahabharatam,

Manual, 1682 (A grammatical work)

Divakaram, 1702 (A dictionary in verse)

A check-list is available in Tamil language noting all necessary particulars.

Manuscripts of Jibanananda Das

A Bengali collection of the eminent poet, Shri Jibanananda Das gifted to the library in 1979. Having 137 exercise books, 1 file and 14 loose items, the collection is rich in Bengali poems, novels, short stories and articles written by this well known litterateur. Several of these have been published, English translations of some poems made by the poet are also available in the collection. A few of many noted works are :

Rupasi

Shikar

Banalata Sen

There are several other collections and mss. of the eminent scholars & personalities which are briefed as follows :

Hidayat Husain collection	—	15 vols. (Arabic& Persian) mainly on religion (Islam) biography etc.
Imambara collection	—	140 vols. (Arabic & Persian) various subjects such as religion (mainly Islam), philosophy, history, literature etc.
Zakaria collection	—	43 vols. (Arabic, Persian & Urdu) mainly on literature & few others.

Harinath Dey collection	—	88 vols. (English) mainly on linguistics & literature, a few on Hinduism.
Mss. of Sarojini Naidu	—	4 vols. (English) mainly on poetry.
Mss. of Mani Burdhan	—	69 files (Bengali) on dance.
Ram Das Sen collection	—	103 vols. (Sanskrit) various topics, such as Alankara, Mimamsa, Vaisnavism etc.
Rewa collection	—	103 vols. (Sanskrit) various subjects such as Alankara, Dharmasastra, Jyotisam etc.
Mss. of Hari Das Nandy	—	60 vols. (Sanskrit) various subjects such as Advaita Vedanta, Samhita, Vaisnavism etc.
Mss. of Vishnu Dey	—	14 files (Bengali) on poetry.

In addition to the above manuscript collections the library has correspondence and diaries of prominent personalities. Let us describe a few of these.

Correspondence of Sir Tej Bahadur Sapru to and from elites of India and abroad. These letters mainly deal with the political situation of India during the early 20th century (covering a period of 45 years upto 1947).

The letters are available in 105 bound volumes and 32 files.

Correspondence of two eminent historians, Sir Jadunath Sarkar and Dr. Govind Sardesai. There are about 1260 letters written to and from eminent people during the period 1909 to 1953.

Correspondence of Ramananda Chatterjee to and from various persons of India and abroad written during late 19th and early 20th century (from 1895 to 1942). These 188 letters and 6 articles mainly deal with the social and political condition of India with special reference to Bengal.

Correspondence of Netaji Subhas Chandra Bose written during, 1926 — 1938 to his nephew Dr. Ashok Nath Bose with special instruction to contact eminent people mainly to create sympathetic awareness and support towards India's independence. These are 154 letters.

Correspondence of Sarat Chandra Bose to his son Dr. Ashok Nath Bose during, 1931 to 1945 including his election manifesto issued from Switzerland in 1945. There are also letters to his brother Subhas Chandra Bose which make a total of 216 letters.

After describing the above holdings of mss. and correspondence a statistical detail is furnished in Annexure I to give an idea of the total number of such documents available in the library.

Our effort is on to prepare catalogues of all above mentioned holdings and we have been able to publish the following vols.

Asutosh Collection : Sarat Corner ; Catalogue of Manuscripts, 1980. (Hand List)

Bishnu Dey : Catalogue of Manuscripts, 1980 (Hand List)

Catalogue of Persian mss. in Jadunath Sarkar Collection, 1972 (Mimeographed)

Catalogue Raisonne of Buhar Library, Vol. 1, 1921.

Catalogue Raisonne of Buhar Library, Vol. 2, 1923.

Harinath Dey : Centenary Volume, 1977

Sapru Correspondence : A check List (First Series), 1961

Vaiyapuri Pillai Collection : Palm leaf manuscripts in Tamil ; A check list, 1983 (Hand list)

Upkeeping & Preservation

The library in its capacity is alert towards preservation of its mss. Manuscripts, though kept in well-maintained air-conditioned area are given regular periodic checks. Necessary treatment is made available through different conservation skills and techniques which include binding, mending, deacidification, fumigation, lamination, encapsulation and micro-filming etc.

Many of the already described mss. collections and correspondence have been micro-filmed resulting in about 162 micro-film rolls. The library also records the availability of 182 micro-film rolls covering 1308 mss. with references to Unesco Government of India Project, 1966-67. These mss. which are mostly in Sanskrit, a few in Arabics & Persian etc. belong to 38 selected Mss. centres of 12 leading cities of the country.

List of centres enclosed in Annexure-II.

Readers Services

Serious readers and researchers are allowed access to mss. and other rare vols. Preferably on the basis of written evidence in support of their research work. We also take it as an essential part of our duty to maintain the agreement, if any, made regarding use of gifted documents. Reprographic services are available in the library and we allow reproduction of our holdings as per library rules. Reproduction of full text is permitted to institutions of repute under specific terms and conditions which often include reciprocal exchange in particular.

Future plan of action

There has been a need felt to appoint scholars/manuscriptologists to ensure proper editing and publishing of our manuscripts. Helpful checklists have been prepared for a good number of Tibetan Xylographs available in the library and we are in the process to print its catalogue soon. Proper indexing of personal diaries and letters have been given due importance and indexing of mss. in Bengali and English correspondence are under preparation at present. The National Library welcomes gifts of mss. and the library may also like to buy valuable mss., if available. The library will also try to get microfilms of copies of important manuscripts and ancient documents on India from different countries under the Cultural Exchange Programmes. It is proposed to adopt modern techniques such as computerisation, micro-processing etc. to facilitate all round mss. services. Considerable importance has been given to internationally approved measures regarding preservation and conservation of mss. which include improving awareness of preservation problem as the basic and vital factor. Alongwith response to advance training, national and international programmes there are efforts to establish channels for regular exchange of information with the countries within the region.

Conclusion

India is a vast country which has been laden with serious social problems. Consequently the heavy loss to its economy as well as to its culture as a whole did not exempt its library and information services. In spite of all these circumstances of concern we have been trying to promote among other responsibilities our all round library services as far as possible within the available infrastructure. Our future lies in sharing of what we have by exchanging our resources with similar institutions at the national and international levels.

REFERENCES

Kesavan, B.S. India's National Library, Calcutta, 1961.

Hasan, S.M.A. Catalogue of Persian Mss. of Sir Jadunath Sarkar Collection, Calcutta, 1972.

Diringer, David. The Hand-Produced Book, London, 1952.

Library Trends, Vol. 5, No. 3, January, 1957.

Biswas, S.C. papers on "Indian Manuscripts — Collection, Documentation and Preservation — A Summary Note" presented at the "National Seminar on Preservation of Cultural Heritage : Manuscripts and their future", organised by Raja Rammohun Roy Library foundation' in Calcutta in 1990.

Annexure-I

A statement of the Manuscript Collections Available in the National Library, Calcutta.

	Arabic	Persian	Urdu	Bengali	English	Hindi	Tamil	Sanskrit	Total
Buhar Collection	467	483	2	—	—	—	—	—	952
Jadunath Sarkar Collection	—	206	—	—	62	—	—	—	268
Thibaut Collection	—	—	—	—	—	—	—	410	410
Vaiyapuri Pillai Collection	—	—	—	—	—	—	370	—	370
Mss. of Jibaanananda Das	—	—	—	9	—	—	—	—	9
Hidayat Husain Collection	9	6	—	—	—	—	—	—	15
Imambara Collection	72	68	—	—	—	—	—	—	140
Zakaria Collection	9	29	5	—	—	—	—	—	43
Harinath Dey Collection	—	—	—	—	88	—	—	—	88
Mss. of Sarojini Naidu	—	—	—	—	4	—	—	—	4
Mss. of Mani Bardhan	—	—	—	69	—	—	—	—	69
Ram Das Sen Collection	—	—	—	—	—	—	—	103	103
Mss. of Sarat Chandra Chattopadhay	—	—	—	21	—	—	—	—	21
Rewa Collection	—	—	—	—	—	—	—	103	103
Hari Das Nandy Collection	—	—	—	—	—	—	—	60	60
Mss. of Vishnu Dey	—	—	—	14	—	—	—	—	14
National Library and other Collections	124	163	14	68	101	5	—	114	589
TOTAL	681	955	21	181	255	5	370	790	3258

Eminent Personalities and their Archives

Tej Bahadur Sapru		
Balkrishna Sheoram Moonje		On
Ramananda Chatterjee		social and political
Rabindranath Tagore		condition of India.
Satish Chandra Mukherjeee	several thousand	A few on literary

Womesh Chunder Bonnerjee	letters, diaries etc.	comments, spiritual
Jadunath Sarkar	Written During	evidence, potential
Govind Sardesai	1902-1947	biographies of
Florence Nightingale	(Pre-independent India)	eminent elites,
Sarat Chandra Bose		personal matters etc.
Subhas Chandra Bose		
Satyendra Prasanna Sinha		
Lalmohan Ghosh		

Figure at a glance

Paper Manuscripts	=	2,924 vols
Correspondence & Diaries	=	250 vols
Palm Leaves Manuscripts	=	334 vols
Tibetan Xylographs	=	878 items
Microfilms of Mss. & Archives	=	344 rolls

Annexure-II

National Library, Calcutta

List of selected centres regarding microfilming of Mss. under the Unesco-Govt. of India Project, 1966-67.

1. Andhra University Library, Waltair, Hyderabad
2. Asiatic Society of Bengal, Calcutta
3. Asiatic Society of Bombay, Poona
4. Assam State Museum (Kamrup Anusandhan Samiti), Gauhati
5. Bangiya Sahitya Parisad, Calcutta
6. Bhandarkar Oriental Research Institute, Poona
7. Bombay University Library, Poona
8. Bhuri Singh Museum, Jammu
9. Burdwan University Library, Burdwan
10. Bureau of Tamil Publications, Madras
11. Calcutta University Library, Calcutta
12. Dai-ra-tul Ma-arif-il-Osmania, Hyderabad
13. Deccan College, Poona
14. Govt. Oriental Mss. Library, Madras
15. Govt. Epigraphist for India, Delhi
16. H.P.T. College, Nasik
17. Historical & Antiquarian Studies, Assam
18. Indian Museum (Archaeological Survey), Calcutta
19. Khuda Baksh O.P. Library, Patna
20. (Shri) Mahavir Jain Public Library, Delhi
21. Nagpur University Library, Nagpur
22. National Library, Calcutta
23. National Museum, Delhi
24. Oriental Research Institute, Mysore
25. Oriental Research Institute & Mss. Library University of Kerala, Trivandrum

26. Osmania University Library, Hyderabad
27. Patna University Library, Patna
28. Raghunath Temple Library, Jammu
29. Salar Jung Museum, Hyderabad
30. Sanskrit College, Calcutta
31. Sayeedia Library, Hyderabad
32. State Archives, Hyderabad
33. State Archives, Srinagar
34. State Central Library, Hyderabad
35. State Chandradhari Museum, Dharbhanga
36. Venkateswar Oriental Research Institute, Tirupati, Madras
37. Victoria Memorial Hall, Calcutta
38. Tanjore Maharaj Sarfoji Saraswati Mahal Library, Thanjavur.

Serial Publications in India

PAWAN K. GUPTA

ABSTRACT

Serial publications in India

Newsletters served to communicate news before the origin of serial publications in India. In modern sense, the serials originated during the British rule in 1780. In the begining, the Europeans controlled the press. The Indian owned and the Indian language serials joined the scene much later. Since Indian mutiny in 1857, serials practised political journalism. Growth of education, scientific and industrial institutions, societies and associations, awareness among individuals, and political conditions, etc. were instrumental in the growth and diversification of serial publications.

The paper deals with history and present status of serial with examples and statistical data. It is an introduction to the provision of legal deposit, guides and union catalogues of serials, indexing and abstracting services, etc.

Serial Publication in India

India was under British rule till 1947. Since independence, India has made progress in all walks of life. With a population of 860 million India is a land of contrasts, a plural and a multi-lingual society, extending from inter-personal communication to satellite broadcasting, small newspapers printed on a treadle to multi-edition dailies printed using fascimile printing techniques, from an extensive broadcasting and television service to video newsmagzines, and with one of the largest film industry in the world.

The serial publication in India began much later than Europe. During the early period of British rule, however, the European newspapers were used by the Englishmen in India. This was perhaps one of the reasons for lack of interest on the part of East India Company, to create newspapers.

Although printing press was not known before the last quarter of 18th century in India, the journalism existed even in mediaeval India, in the form of news journalism. A number of private or official newsletters, called akhbars, were available towards the end of Mughal empire. There were news collectors stationed in various towns who transmitted newsletters to their masters. Colonel James Tod collected such news sheets and sent these to the Asiatic Society of Bengal in 1828. A large number of these news sheets of Mughal period are reported to be in the Royal Asiatic Society of London.

Genesis

The origin of serial publications in Modern sense in India can be attributed to enthusiasm and missionary zeal of individuals. William Bolt was probably the first person to think of initiating a newspaper, in the year 1768, but it was James Augustus Hicky who started the first Indian serial entitled Hicky's Bengal gazette or Calcutta general advertiser. Its first issue appeared on Saturday, January 29, 1780, announcing itself as "a weekly political and commercial paper open to all but influenced by none". Hicky was imprisoned in 1781 on the charges of disturbing peace. The second newspaper to begin soon was the India gazette or Calcutta public advertiser. It began on November 1, 1780. Thus the torch was lit and carried forward by others.

From those days upto the year 1857 (the year of Indian mutiny) the earliest newspapers were started by Englishmen, who came to India with East India Company. These catered mostly to the needs of Englishmen. This was followed by a period when missionaries started publishing newspapers in English as well as in Indian languages. For example **Dig-durshan** (or India's youth magazine) and **Samachar darpan** (a Bengali newspaper) commenced in 1818. This marked the beginning of the Indian language press. Upto 1820, but for the one Indian owned weekly in Calcutta, the **Bengal gazette** (1816) by Gangadhar Bhattacharjee, the Europeans controlled the press.

Later, to counteract missionary propaganda, some Indians started serials, *e.g.*, **Sambad Kaumudi** in Bengali and **Brahminical magazine** in English and Bengali came out in 1821. Some of the earliest serials in Indian languages were : **Mumbai samachar** (1819), Gujarati ; **Udant martund** (1826), Hindi ; **Madras Chronicle** (1833), Telugu. By 1830 there were 16 serials in Bengali. In this period serial publications in Bengali out numbered all other Indian languages. Even serials in Hindi language came later and were less in number. The Indian language serials and slow growth before 1857. Even the ones which existed were run by missionaries.

Upto 1867, Indian language serials mostly dealt with literary, social and religious issues. It was only after the mutiny that a substantial number of serials in Indian languages started. This trend continued till independence of India in 1947. In this period these serials actively took part in political journalism. In fact majority of newspapers, now in existence, are the ones that started after 1920.

Specialised Serials and the Growth of Institutions

The spread of education and the interest of the British Government, during colonial rule in India, to prepare Indian elite with western education, resulted into the creation of a large number of educational institutions. The first three universities were created in Bombay, Calcutta and Madras in 1857. Simultaneously the christian missionaries, to spread Christianity and the Indian natives to counteract their impact, started a number of serials. Also, before independence, organised scientific research started with the establishment of institutions, like the Botanical, Zoological, Anthropological, Archaeological and Geological Survey, etc. A few of the societies etc., that were established before independence are : Asiatic Society of Bengal, Calcutta (1784) ; Benares Mathematical Society (1908) ; Indian Institute of Science (1911) ; Baptist Missionary Society, Serampore (1813) ; Indian Institute of Experimental Medicine (1935), etc.

Such Institutions, many government departments, as well as individuals, were responsible for producing a large number of serials. This trend continued with much more vigour after 1947. For example the Council of Scientific and Industrial Research (CSIR), within a decade after independence, had created 20 research laboratories. By now there are more than 190 universities. A large number of R & D national laboratories are functioning under CSIR, Indian Council of Medical Research (ICMR), Indian Council of Agricultural Research (ICAR), Defence Research and Development Organisation (DRDO), etc. Indian Council of Social Science Research (ICSSR) and a large number of institutions in the area of commerce, business, industry, etc., have come into being leaving no conceivable area of human activity uncovered.

The growth of serial publications in India, as will be true of other countries, ran parallel to the growth of the institutions, and increase in the government's interest in the R & D, education, etc. The first specialised serial known to us, was a Asiatick Researches, started by the Asiatic Society, Calcutta in 1788. A few other serials of 19th century India are : Monthly circular letter relative to the mission in India (1907), Serampore ; Transactions of the Medical and physical Society of Calcutta (1823) ; Gleanings in science (1829), Calcutta ; Annals of Indian administration (1855), Serampore ; Indian economist (1869), Bombay, etc.

It is evident from the history of serials that a greater emphasis was on applied sciences and a few of the disciplines in social sciences, viz., economics, history, education, law, etc. This was due to more relevance of these disciplines to the society.

Present Position

According to the **Press in India** issued by the Registrar of Press, in 1985, there were 22,648 serials. In 1988, the number grew to 25,536. This excludes about 3000 miscellaneous serials. The annual growth rate of serials is decreasing continuously. It has come down from 7% in 1971 to 3.7% in 1988. Cessation of only 186 serials, as against 1050 registered for the first time in 1985, point out a low mortality rate.

The States publishing more than 1500 serials in 1988 were : Uttar Pradesh 3564 ; Delhi 3354 ; Maharashtra 2997 ; West Bengal 2612 ; and Rajasthan 1599. In 1988, there were 2281 dailies and 7948 with 1 to 3 issues per week. These were published in 93 languages and dialects. The languages with more than 1000 serials were : Hindi 8222; English 4458 ; Bengali 1828 ; Urdu 1728 ; Marathi 1273 ; and Tamil 1036.

In terms of ownership in 1985, out of 22,648 serials, 15,281 were published by individuals and 3593 by societies and associations. The Government produced 615 serials and 99 serials were published by foreign missions. USSR alone produced 45 serials. However, now after reorganisation of USSR, a number of serials have ceased publication.

In terms of content in 1985 (excluding 1913 serials published one to seven times a week) 8578 belonged to the news and current affairs ; followed by 3120 literary and cultural ; 1746 on religion and philosophy ; 800 on science, medicine and health ; 665 on commerce and industry ; 487 on social welfare ; 420 on films ; and 368 on labour. The estimates about number of serials in a subject varies in different sources, due to difference in estimates of total number of serials and differences in classification.

Press Laws and Legal Deposit

From the very beginning there have been regulations and laws pertaining to press. With restrictive laws and regulations the editors were even deported and penalty was imposed. The Press and Registration of Books Act was passed in 1867, providing for registration of all publications except governmental publications and preservation of copies. This continues, with amendments, to be in force even today. According to it, the printer of every newspaper was to deliver two copies of each issue to the government, as per the clause inserted in 1922; and one copy to the Press Registrar, as per the clause inserted in 1955. It is natural to believe that upto 1922 there was no legal deposit of serials. From 1947 to 1951, we are not sure about the acquisition through legal deposit by any library, due to confusion following independence of India. After 1951 one copy of each issue was required to be sent to the National Library, Calcutta.

In accordance with the Delivery of Books and Newspapers Act 1954 (newspapers added in 1956), a copy of each issue is required to be deposited with the National Library ; Connemara Public Library, Madras ; Delhi Public Library ; and Central Library (Asiatic Society), Bombay. Legal deposit is required under the acts, *i.e.*, of 1867 and 1954, amounting to 6 copies. Coupled with the effect of further amendments of the 1867 act by different states, one may have to deposit more copies of each issue of serials. It is believed that a large number of publishers/printers do not deliver the required copies, thus leading to incomplete legal deposit collections. Incidentally, the copyright act in India since inception does not have in its perview, the legal deposit.

Guides to Serials

The earliest attempt to compile a guide to serials in India has been traced back to 1955, when Rev James Long compiled **Returns relating to native printing press..... and a catalogue of Bengali newspapers and periodicals.... 1818 to 1855.** In the same year Tom Luke compiled **Indian press guide and eastern advertisers handbook,** Madras. In 1935, J.N. Gandhi's All India Press Annual, ed. 3 appeared from Lahore. A few guides to serials are : Current Indian periodicals in English : An annotated guide, 1978, ed. 2, compiled by N.N. Gidwani and K. Navlani, Jaipur ; Directory of Indian scientific periodicals, 1976, ed. 3 by INSDOC, New Delhi ; Directory of periodicals published in India, 1991 ed. 2, by Susheel Kaur and P. Sapra, New Delhi ; Press in India by Registrar of Newspapers, Government of India ; **Accession list of India : Annual serials volumes and Quinquennial serials cumulation** by Library of Congress Office, New Delhi.

The last three guides cover serials in Indian languages also. Where **Press in India** is extensive in coverage, the **Accession list in India** is extremely selective.

Union Catalogues of Serials

In addition to the National Library, Calcutta, serial collections of interest exist at National Science Library of INSDOC ; National Medical Library, Delhi ; Library of Indian Agricultural Research Institute, Delhi ; Laboratories of CSIR, ICAR, ICMR, DRDO, etc ; Bhabha Atomic Research Centre, Bombay ; National Social Science Documentation Centre (NASSDOC), Delhi ; Indian Institute of Science, Bengalore ; some large University libraries etc. A weak aspect of the serial collections in India is that there are gaps, specially of rare or near extinct serials.

The importance of up-to-date and comprehensive union catalogues does not need to be stressed here. A few early attempts to prepare union catalogues of serials are : **Catalogue of the Scientific serial publications in the principal libraries of Calcutta,** 1918, by Stanley Kemp, Asiatic Society of Bengal ; **List of scientific periodicals in the Bombay Presidency,** 1931, by M.B. Arte, Royal Institute of Science, Bombay ; Union catalogue of learned periodicals published in South Asia, Vol. 1, 1953, Indian Library Association. These were followed by a number of union catalogues covering a specific geographical area, viz., Baroda, 1928 ; Udaipur,

1962 ; Nagpur, 1963 ; Maharashtra, 1964 ; Rajasthan, 1968, etc., but all these were isolated efforts and have not been revised.

NASSDOC has done a commendable job by completing in 1976, the Union **catalogue of social science periodicals and serials** in 32 vols. It has 31,125 records. Its part for Delhi, last revised in 1982, has 5000 titles. Similarly, INSDOC has completed, in 4 vol., **National Union catalogue of scientific serials in India, in 1988,** with 36000 records. Before the **National union catalogue**, INSDOC had compiled separate volumes for different regions. The complete catalogue is also available as on line service.

National Medical Library has been bringing out the revised edition of the Consolidated catalogue of journals and other periodicals contained in the libraries of .... (nine libraries in Kasauli, Calcutta, Bombay, Madras, Coonoor, Rangoon and Shillong). Its first edition was brought out by the Indian Research Fund Association in 1933. The title was later changed to **Union catalogue of medical periodicals in Indian libraries.** Its fifth edition in 1962 has 2282 records, from 84 libraries.

Indexing and Abstracting Services

Surgeon Major D.B. Smith and J.M. Coates were instrumental in initiating the first abstracting service in India, the **Calcutta medical news** in 1880. Increased scientific and industrial research during and after World War II and publication of a large number of primary serials in India, acted as catalyst in initiating indexing and abstracting services in India. The National Institute of Sciences of India in 1935 started an abstracting services **Indian science abstracts, which ceased publication in 1939.** In 1949, UNESCO-SASCO (South Asia Science Cooperation Office) started the **Bibliography of scientific publications of South and South-east Asia,** which was continued by INSDOC till 1964, and later on replaced by the **Indian science abstracts (1965)**. INSDOC also published the **INSDOC list of current scientific literature,** from 1954-65. Now **Current Contents of Indian Journals** is an online service from INSDOC, which covers the contents pages of 1000 serials (available on diskette, hard copy, E-mail and Fax). There are a large number of indexing and abstracting services published by individual libraries, covering almost all disciplines, such as **Index to Indian medical periodicals, (1959), Delhi ; Irrigation and power abstracts (1943-). etc.**

In social sciences and humanities, too, there are a number of indexing and abstracting services. **Index India (1967 –) and the**

Guide to Indian periodical literature (1964 –) are good. The former is more comprehensive, covering about 1000 periodicals, whereas the later is very selective. A few other services, by way of examples, are : **Documentation bulletin for South-east Asia (1969–), Documentation in public administration (1973 –), Index to Indian legal periodicals (1963 –)** etc. ICSSR also brings out abstracting services in economics, geography, political science, and sociology & social anthropology.

A major lacuna in coverage is of Indian language periodicals, which deserves attention. **Hindi sandarbh** was published by Rajasthan University Library from 1969 to 1971. Similarly there is no service like Times index, London. However **Indian press index** (1968 –) and Index India (1967 –) index articles from selected dailies. **Index to the Times of India** (1973 to 1979) was a good attempt towards an index of a daily newspaper.

Recently the University Grants Commission (UGC) has developed information centres for science at Indian Institute of Science, Bangalore; and for social sciences at SNDT women't University, Bombay and M.S. University, Baroda. Information centre for humanities is yet to be created. These centres are to provide comprehensive information service to the researchers, throughout the country. Further the UGC has taken steps to create Information and Library Network Programme (INFLIBNET), for networking university libraries, R & D institutions and information centres. When fully established (between 1991 to 1995 it plans to have 60 to 80 nodes), it will provide a variety of services, including database search, union catalogues, document delivery, etc. This will go a long way to help utilise meagre resources effectively. Similarly a few other networks, like CALIBNET for Calcutta libraries, DELNET for Delhi libraries, SIRNET for CSIR laboratories, etc. are taking shape. All these developments, with the help of information technology, point towards a bright future, with easy, efficient and effective access to information in India.

BIBLIOGRAPHIC REFERENCES

1. Basu, Durga Das: Laws of the press in India. New Delhi, Prentice Hall, 1980. (0-87692-050-4).
2. Chitale, T.B.: Organization of documentation work in India. Indian Librarian. 25; 1970; 25-46.
3. Index India, 1967 - Jaipur, Rajasthan University Library. (Ed. by Pawan K. Gupta w.e.f. Vol. 22, 1988) (0019-3844).
4. Kumar, R.P. : Research periodicals of colonial India, 1780-1947. Delhi, Academic Publications, 1985.
5. Parthasarathy, Rangaswamy : Journalism in India; from the earliest times ..2nd ed. New Delhi, Sterling, 1991. (81-207-1116-5).

Library Information Services in Rural Areas : The Case of Indonesia

MASTINI HARDJOPRAKOSO

Introduction

Indonesia is an archipelago, consisting of thousands of big and small islands, scattered around the equator between the longitudes 95 and 141 degrees. About 40% of the territory or 2,027,087 square kilometers is land, while the other 60% is water. Most of the islands are mountainous and volcanic. It has a humid tropic climate.

Although most of the small islands are not inhabited, Indonesia with 182 million population by 1991, belongs to the most populated countries in the world after China, India, USA and Russia. The population is unevenly distributed and varies in density rate from 3 square km. in Irian Jaya to 13,365 square km. in Jakarta.

A little more than 20% of the Indonesians are living in urban areas, while the remaining 80% is characterized as rural.

Indonesia became independent in 1945. Administratively the Republic is divided into 27 autonomous provinces, including the Governorate of Jakarta. These 27 provinces are further divided into 350 autonome districts with 3500 subdistricts and around 65,000 villages. This large number of villages can be categorized into three groups, *i.e.*, the most advanced or selfsupporting villages, which are about 15%, developing or active villages, about 205 and the less advanced villages,which from the remaining bulk. The first 25 year National Development Plan, incepted in 1969 has brought a lot of significant changes in the living structure of the nation.

Although originally very diverse in social, cultural and economic backgrounds, the Indonesian today is evergrowing into one nation, who believes in the almighty God, humanism, national unity, democracy, and social justice.

Cultural and social welfare has been improved by the acceleration of education, health and social care and the implementation of the birth control and family planning programmes. Thousands of new schools have been established, enrolling more than 90% of elementary schools level children, and some other millions at secondary and tertiary level. Most of the subdistricts have their health centres with branches in potential villages. The annual birth rate is decreasing from about 3% in the sixties to around 2.1% in 1991. About 90% of the population can read and write and speak the Bahasa Indonesia as the national language.

Economically, Indonesia today is ready to leave the traditional agricultural economic structure and is growing fast to become a modern industrial power.

National System of Libraries in Brief

Libraries have been developed in Indonesia since early fifties, initially to support the educational sector. But because of lack of experience, qualified manpower and inadequate national social and political conditions, real and well planned library development has been carried out only since 1973. Together with the development of the national language and literature, library development has been considered since then as an independent item in the general development of the National Culture.

It has been established, that library services not only to accelerate education, but libraries prove also to be very efficient in achieving other national development purposes such as in the fields of research, culture, economy etc. The role of libraries as documentation and information centres became more and more dominant. It was this multipurpose scientific role of libraries that motivated the Minister of Education and Culture to issue a decree in 1980 to direct the establishment of a National Library and the National Library system, which should include the following components :

(*a*) A National Library in the capital of the Republic.

(*b*) 26 Regional or Provincial Libraries, in each of the capitals of the provinces outside Jakarta.

(*c*) Public libraries at district, sub-district and village level.

(*d*) Mobile libraries to serve specific defined groups (remote areas, hospitals, prisons, etc).

(*e*) School libraries.

(*d*) Academic/university libraries and

(*g*) Special libraries.

The decree also invited involvement of other departments, government and private institutions to participate in the development of libraries. Library development has become a real national concern.

All the departments for instance should take care of their own special libraries. The department of Home Affairs is responsible for the development and maintenance of public libraries, the department of Education and Culture for School and university libraries etc. According to the decree of the State Minister of Administrative Reform library work has been considered professional and accordingly the status of a librarian becomes functional.

The Increasing role of libraries for national development purposes resulted in the appearence of the Presidential decree number 11/1989 on the new status of the National Library of Indonesia. It is stated in the decree that the policy on library development at national level is in the hands of the Head of State, for which the National Library is assigned as the executive body to implement the national policy mentioned.

The status of the National Library, formerly as a library operational unit at the Department of Education and Culture has been improved and became a non-departmental government higher institution straight under the responsibility of the Head of State.

To accomplish its task the National Library has to fulfil a quadruple function. *i.e.*, as :

(*a*) National Centre for Deposit and Conservation.

(*b*) National Centre for Library Information.

(*c*) National Office for Library Cooperation, networking and manpower development.

(*d*) National Office for the development of library systems and standards, and accreditation.

Need for Information in Rural Areas

One of the motivations for the struggle for independence was the desire of the Indonesians to improve their material and intellectual standards. This desire was so strong that it has been included in the

Constitution as one of the objectives of the proclamation of the national independence, and accordingly always reflected in every national development programme.

For instance it is clearly stated in the national development general policy, that the core objective of the National Development Plan is to achieve the welfare of the Indonesian individual and the Indonesian society as a whole. This objective can only be achieved by the full participation of the whole nation. This means, that a large part of the population should be moulded in order to become an effective labour force, able to contribute to sustained economic and social development.

For such a big endeavour the population should be made literate and always interested in the acquisition of new information. The accessibility to information is a necessary condition for the development of economy, industry, social welfare, culture and other development purposes. The supply of information all over the country and especially to the rural areas, has become the concern of all departments, public and private information agencies. It is perhaps worth mentioning that since about ten years ago. Indonesia has introduced a satellite domestic information system more familiar by the local name of "PALAPA" to accelerate the distribution of information. By this PALAPA Indonesia becomes one information unit. Using PALAPA, information is distributed through networks of televisions, telephones and telegraphs, etc. Another channel for information distribution is through newspapers and other ephemeral reading materials. The so called "newspapers to the village" movement, launched in the last decade by the Department of Information is very creative and useful. Other departments are responsible for the provision of information on their specific assignment.

A lot of information is also supplied by the Department of Education and Culture in schools and by other outer school education. The departments of Health and Agriculture are also very active in the distribution of information in the form of booklets, brochures and pamphlets.

But for development purposes the quantity of information does not mean everything. On one hand information should be selected and deposed in location, readily accessible by the users. On the other hand people should be encouraged to use information accessible to them.

It is for these reasons, that both the ministerial and the Presidential decrees mentioned afore, that library services should be launched all over the country, from the centre to the villages.

Libraries in the Rural Areas

Library services in rural areas are carried out by :

(*a*) *City public libraries*

City libraries are located in the capital of a district, which administratively is a second level autonome region. The establishment of a city library is the responsibility of the local government, and supervised at central level by the Minister of Home Affairs. The National Library supports these libraries by providing technical assistance in the form of manuals. Some advanced city libraries have opened their branches in the subdistricts.

(*b*) *Village libraries*

A village library is designed to be established as an activity of the village reconciliation board chaired by the chief of the village. Because of local economic and social problems and lack of library personnel, only 5000 out of the 65,000 villages manage to set up their libraries.

(*c*) *Mobile Libraries*

In 1967 the Department of Education and Culture initiated the introduction of mobile libraries to accelerate library information services in the rural areas. Mobile library services are designed as public library extension services to remote areas, out of the reach of the existing public libraries. At present about 180 mobile libraries are operating in the country. The number is likely to be increased in the near future. In areas such as in Central Kalimantan, arrangements are being made to introduce floating library services.

Mobile libraries prove to be very effective for the development of reading (habits) and creation of book interest amongst people.

(*d*) *School Libraries*

The Director General of Elementary and Secondary Education has issued instructions to all schools to establish libraries in order to accelerate teaching and learning processes.

The progress is very slow because of lack of trained library personnel and limited financial resources. To lessen the problem, a bulkloan library system or popularly called a centralized system of school library services are now being introduced in some regions by the National Library.

(*e*) *Mosque Libraries*

To improve knowledge and skills of the Islam followers, who form the majority in Indonesia, about 3 years ago the Head of State encouraged the Moslem society to organize library services in the mosques. A mosque library is basically a public library with special reference to Islamic knowledge and literature. At the national level mosque libraries are under supervision of the Islamic Information Board in Jakarta. The National Library provides assistance in the form of manpower training and technical guidance.

Conclusion

Information plays a very important role in implementing national development endeavours. The accessibility of right and timely information is a necessary condition to development and modernise education, economy, industry, social and cultural welfare etc.

National development in Indonesia is aimed at improving the material and intellectual life of every Indonesian individual and the Indonesian society as a whole and to achieve a modern, just and prosperous nation, living peacefully as a member of the world society.

As 80% of the population are living in the rural areas development activities are concentrated in those areas. In line with this, the supply of information to the rural areas has gained a high priority in the national information system. With the introduction of sattelite domestic national information system, every part of the country has come within the reach of radio, television and telephone networks.

Although the people in the rural areas have already become acquainted with modern electronic mass media, at the social and economical condition there taking into consideration, the need of information in these areas will be best served by the use of libraries. Nevertheless library development in these areas still have to overcome problems such as, low reading habit, shortage of skilled library manpower, limited financial resources and the weakness of the national book production.

REFERENCES

1. Act number 2, 1989 on National Educational System, Balai Pustaka, Department of Education and Culture, Jakarta 1989.
2. Act Number 4/1990 on the deposit of printed and recorded matters, National Library, Jakarta, 1992.
3. Annual Reports, National Library, Jakarta.
4. Decrease of the Minister of Education and Culture No. 0101/1981 on national policy on library development. Department of Education and Cultural, Jakarta 1981.
5. 1945 Constitution, Department of Information, Jakarta.
6. Outline of the National Policy 1988 and 1993, Department of the Information Jakarta.
7. Presidential Decree Number 11/1989 on the Improvement of the National Library of Indonesia as a non departmental higher institution, Jakarta 1989.

Role of the Public Library in Combating Illiteracy

BARBRO THOMAS

The existence of a public library is in itself a monument against illiteracy. All efforts to eliminate illiteracy would be in vain unless reading material could be made available to those who have acquired the ability to enjoy reading.

UNESCO has in its educational work placed considerable emphasis on libraries. In order to put into practice the advice given, UNESCO set up pilot libraries to act as models and testing grounds. The first pilot library was established in Delhi. It was founded in 1950 by the government of India and UNESCO. The principal object was to provide reading materials for new literates in four languages; Hindi, Urdu, Punjabi and English.

In 1987 the United Nations decided to proclaim 1990 the International Literacy Year. UNESCO was invited to assume the role of lead organization for the preparation and observance of the year. The objectives for the International Literacy Year were among other things:

— to increase action by governments of Member States afflicted by illiteracy or functional illiteracy to elminate these problems.

— to increase public awareness of the scope, nature and implications of illiteracy as well as of the means and conditions for combating it.

— to increase popular participation, within and among countries, in efforts to combat illiteracy, particularly through activities of governmental and non-governmental organizations, voluntary associations and community groups.

Illiteracy has been considered a problem first and foremost for the third world, but in the preparatory work for this year UNESCO also focused on functional illiteracy. By doing so the Literacy Year became of global importance and a hidden problem was made visible.

IFLA's sections for Public Libraries and School Libraries actively supported UNESCO's goal. At the world Conference on "Education for

All" in Thailand (March 1990) the chairperson of the Section of School Libraries pointed out in a convincing way the role of the libraries as vital links in providing educational resources.

The subject of illiteracy has been dealt with for a long time within the Section of Public Libraries. In 1985, the Section formed a working group to review the involvement of libraries in literacy matters around the world and to plan a seminar to address this issue. The pre-conference seminar "Public Libraries Against Illiteracy" was held in Massy in connection to the 1989 IFLA General Conference in Paris. The base programme of the seminar was formulated and designed with four goals in mind:

— to bring together information on public library efforts against illiteracy around the world.

— to provide an opportunity for the participants to share experiences.

— to explore ways in which more public library activities could be planned to expand illiteracy project.

— to develop series of resolution for action by IFLA.

Linked to the IFLA Conference in Stockholm 1990 the Section organized a seminar devoted to the same topic. In connection with the 1990 General Conference a pre-conference seminar on "Public Library Policy" was also held where the question of illiteracy played an important role. Resolutions from the seminar included some very precise advice for the Section to add to the agenda.

In 1990 the Section received financial support from UNESCO in order to establish guidelines for public libraries working with illiteracy. In preparing these guidelines the discussions, papers, proposals and resolutions from the above mentioned seminars have been most valuable.

Is there a proper definition of illiteracy ?

The terms illiteracy and literacy have been used with various connotations. In 1958 UNESCO proposed that an illiterate person is one who "cannot with understanding both read and write a short simple statement on his everyday life." This definition of traditional illiteracy was adopted by UNESCO's General Conference in 1978. From another point of view "a person is literate who can with understanding both read and write a short simple statement on his everyday life".

The terms illiteracy/literacy are very often used in connection with certain conditions, for instance :

— basic illiteracy

— traditional mass illiteracy

— functional illiteracy

— instrumental illiteracy

— linguistic illiteracy

We are also familiar with the expressions "semi-literates" and "new literates". Recently in the library profession we have created the concept "information illiteracy" to define those unable to use the information offered in a technological society.

Basic illiteracy

According to UNESCO's estimate there were 948,1 million illiterates aged over 15 in the world in 1990. That is almost 30 per cent of the total population. 31 million were found in developed countries while the remaining part 916,6 million illiterates were in Third World countries. Those 916 million represent 35 per cent of the adult population.

Of course the illiteracy rates differ between Third World countries, between regions, between cities and rural areas, between groups of the population and between men and women.

In general the background factor is poverty. Very often there is a vicious circle: lack of primary education - illiteracy - poverty

In the first place, the serious problem of basic illiteracy, has to be fought with by investing more resources on primary education. On the other hand the role of public libraries should never be underestimated.

Functional illiteracy

The concept of functional illiteracy is rather new. It is not easy to draw a very clear line between basic illiteracy, as defined by UNESCO, and functional illiteracy which refers to the level of literacy which is needed in a complex industrialized society.

According to UNESCO's recommendation a person functionally illiterate is one who "cannot take part in all those activities in which literacy is required for effective functioning of his group and community and also for enabling him to continue to use reading, writing and calculation for his own and community's development".

The French language allows a distinction between the concepts "analphabets" and "illettres". The definition would be "Les illettres sont les analphabetes des temp modernes dans les societes industrielles". This is a way to express the fact that in spite of general primary education there are people who can not read and write properly.

The concept of functional illiteracy is not absolute. It depends on the level of society. A person can be considered functionally literate in one society but not in another depending on what skills are needed for "effective functioning". What is quite clear is that the rapid technical development of modern society will create an increasing number of functional illiterates. And that is a problem that indeed should concern libraries.

It is difficult to estimate the total number of functional illiterates. To a very large extent it is a hidden problem. Not being able to read is considered a shame in a reading society.

A number of investigations in the industrialized countries have proved that quite a high per cent of the population should be considered as functional illiterates. Some reports from highly industrialized countries have proved that up to 10 per cent of the population belong to this category.

There are men and women in highly industrialized countries who cannot understand a job advertisement, a train timetable etc. In documents reporting functional illiteracy from different aspects you very often find the example of somebody "reading" the newspapers upside-down pretending to read thus trying to hide their inability to read.

Functional illiteracy is not only a question of individual shame. It could also be a question of national embarrassment. A number of reports in Europe have revealed surprisingly high illiteracy rates. For instance that up to 25% of French children leaving school cannot read and write properly. Education Ministries do not want to talk too much about such figures.

Compared to basic illiteracy the problem of functional illiteracy might be considered marginal. It is not. If nothing is done now the total number of functional illiterates will increase concurrently with the technical progress. As it very often is with a hidden problem functional illiteracy is not easy to deal with. Everybody working in a public library should be aware of that.

New literates

Adults or children who have just obtained the reading skill could be included in the group of new literates. There are great risks that the new literates will very soon relapse into illiteracy if the obtained reading skill is not taken care of. The public library could play an important role by actively offering special reading material suitable for this group.

948 million basic illiterates, an uncertain but growing number of functional illiterates and the need of special care for the new literates - this is indeed a challenge for public libraries.

The role of the public library

It might be, or rather it is, wishful thinking to believe that illiteracy could be eradicated by the year 2,000. However we should keep that as a goal in mind. If we radically want to reduce the illiteracy rates no efforts should be spared. Every institution/organisation must participate actively. Even the public library. It is important that the public library defines the problem. Very clear objectives should also be established. It should be considered with which institutions/ organizations it might be possible or rather necessary to cooperate.

Public libraries operate on various conditions concerning resources, staff, premises, library materials or lack of materials. Reading traditions and the level of general education are also important factors.

To promote literacy is of course a very different task for example developing countries in Africa, Asia or Latin America and in the industrialized countries in Europe, USA, Canada or Australia.

In the developing countries the efforts to eradicate illiteracy has to be performed facing some or all of the following conditions :

— school age children not attending school due to limited educational facilities and resources.

— high drop out rates among school children and adults attending adult education programmes

— lack of expansion of formal and non-formal education activities

— new literates relapse into illiteracy due to irrelevant curricula, lack of trainers, lack of reading materials for follow up

— scarcity of affordable literature

— lack of adequate library service

— lack of reading habit

— inadequate funding to train enough personnel

— duplication of efforts due to the fact that the responsibility is scattered among several governmental and non-governmental bodies and not coordinated on a permanent basis by a suitable structure

— need for even young children required to work in order to meet basic economic needs

— a growing number of street children

And what about the fact that women represent the largest share of the illiterate population ? In 1990 the female illiteracy rate for the developing countries was 45% compared with 25% for men.

In the industrialized part of the world conditions are fundamentally different. In general, the compulsory school system has a long tradition. And generally speaking there is a high level of education. There is also a high level of industrialization. The standard of living is high but the society also demands a high standard of reading proficiency in order to meet basic everyday needs. Public libraries have a long tradition and have reached a comparatively high level of standard and service. Books are no longer scarce. Which in a way causes other problems. Illiteracy exists when it should not, as is true elsewhere illiteracy affects the most underprivileged groups. But as illiteracy tends to be regarded in practice as having been almost eradicated, the public libraries' degree of involvement (and indeed not only the public libraries) in this particular field in the past has been slight. The alarming reports received during the past few years that a number of young people are leaving school without being able to read and write, has however encouraged libraries to involve themselves in these problems.

Whatever the conditions, public libraries should not deny the problem of illiteracy, but try to identify the extent of the problem. The public library must actively promote themselves to avail cooperation with other institutions/organizations in the field. Library staff should also be aware that library service to illiterates and new literates is not a service that is in demand and the library has to play an active role in encouraging its use. And above all the public library should be made visible.

The book famine

A necessary but not sufficient condition in the combat of illiteracy is - books.

A consequence of Gutenbergs invention is that today in the Western World books are no longer scarce but are in surplus. While, in general, Third World countries suffer from acute book shortages. Gutenberg should be blamed for that.

In the industrialized world today reading skills might be threatened by the increasing entertainment, for example the surplus of television channels and the wide variety of electronic media. The reading habits of children might in the long run be affected in a negative way.

In a community with a surplus of books and an over - provision of light entertainment, public libraries can play an important role by providing books free of charge from a library structure that allows everybody, and especially the children, easy access to books. For public libraries in Third World countries the most urgent question is how to improve book provision. Which is not always a very easy task.

Books are not classed as priorities in competition with necessities such as food, clothing, medicine etc. Shortage of foreign currency and/or import taxation on books might effectively prevent acquisition. Sometimes an excessive bureaucracy might be the main obstacle. There might also be a lack of infrastructure in library buildings and supplies.

It will not be possible to solve all these problems all at once. It is a question of long term planning and gradual progress. Much has already been done but more remains to be done.

There are for instance a number of book donation programmes where the main stream goes from the industrialized part of the world to libraries in the Third World. Recently we have also experienced that new book donation programmes have been established to deliver surplus books to libraries and other institutions in the eastern part of Europe. It is important when book donation programmes are set up to weigh the pros and cons. In general they suffer from total lack of coordination. There is a risk that the stream of books too often will be arbitrary, that some countries will "fall between two stools" and that donation programmes will be dependent on "changing fashions." The cost of transportation should also be considered. By no means unwanted material should be sent.

Books donated are mainly n English or French which means that they are useful in anglophone and francophone countries. But it is of limited use if the urgent need is to build up a collection in the native language. It might also be the case that the content in the books published in the Western World is not at all appropriate for readers in the Third World.

Even if there are frustrating elements, book donations on the whole are ways of giving practical help to libraries suffering from a serious lack of material. It is important that close contact is established between donor organizations and the receiving institutions. The ideal situation for the receiving library is to have the opportunity to preselect the material. It is also of great importance that the donors should learn about circumstances in the receiving country.

It should be stressed that book donations can not replace acquisition. But donations could be the next best for a library in urgent need of reading material.

Book donation programmes and the establishment of twinning libraries could be further developed.

Among the planned activities within the framework of the UNESCO Programme to promote access to scientific literature is the establishment of a database on book and journal donation programmes.

It would supply a long-felt demand if a similar project could be set up based on the needs for public libraries to achieve used material. A Donation Programme Database for redistribution of books useful in literacy efforts.

The Florence Agreement

Another problem that ought to be focused is taxation. Taxation might in some countries be an effective obstacle for receiving printed material from abroad, whether donated or purchased.

In order to facilitate the exchange of publications, objects of artistic and scientific interest and other materials of information and to recommend international agreements which should promote the free flow of ideas, UNESCO sponsored the "Florence agreement and its Protocol".

The major purpose of the Florence Agreement is to make it easier to import educational, scientific and cultural materials. This document is of limited value if it is not actively used as a tool to reduce taxation obstacles. Public libraries could organize promotion of the Agreement to the Ministry in charge and to custom authorities.

Evidently the conclusion drawn is to eradicate illiteracy is a necessity. Sufficient books and other reading material are not available. One of the public library's most critical contribution to the literacy effort is the support it provides through its material in both print and non-print formats. Without access to books the reduction of the illiteracy rates will never succeed.

The necessity of cooperation

Since illiteracy is a very diversified problem public libraries can bot work in isolation but must seek cooperation with other actors in the field. Documentation from several literacy projects proves that cooperation is a prerequisite for success.

There are a number of projects that could be referred to but I will mention just one example: The Collaboration between the Jamaican Movement for the Advancement of Literacy (JAMAL) and the Jamaica Library Service, based on a report prepared by the JAMAL Foundation.

Jamaica has had a long history of a high illiteracy rates among adults. In 1970 it was estimated that up to 500 000 adults, representing

40 - 50 per cent of the population over 15 years of age were functionally illiterate.

In 1972 the National Literacy Programme was established. In 1974 the JAMAL Foundation was established to take over the activities. However there were hindrances experienced such as lack of ready access to books and reading materials written in simple English to meet the special needs of the new literates.

The Jamaica Library Service aimed to provide reading material free of charge to satisfy the various needs. The library structure with service points located island-wide made books accessible in every village. The Jamaica Library Service was considered to be the only institution to handle on a large scale the task of non-formal continuing education for so many new literates.

JAMAL and the Jamaica Library Service set up a programme of close cooperation. Senior staff of both organizations served on the national and local community committees, responsible for promoting their programmes. Special assistance was given by the Library Service in support of JAMAL programmes as:

— bookmobiles attended JAMAL graduation ceremonies to register the graduates as new library readers

— large print books were provided for new literates and special collections with easy material were built up

— booklists for new literates were distributed and tours for groups of students to visit libraries were arranged

— library buildings were used for teacher training and other JAMAL activities.

Efforts were also made on follow-up programmes. For instance to encourage local authors to produce material to meet the needs of the new literates. It was also agreed that the establishment of official links of cooperation between JAMAL and the Jamaica Library Service was beneficial to both organizations.

This is just one example, reported as successful. A number of other activities could be added. Generally speaking, cooperation has been established and that the librarians have stepped out of the ivory tower to meet the target groups in their every-day surroundings.

It would of course also be possible to identify a number of literacy projects that did partly succeed or did not succeed at all. Those cases might also be justified if we realise the mistakes to learn something.

I would like to mention just one case where lack of cooperation to some extent explains some failures. In the very interesting report "An Impact Evaluation of the Rural Press and Rural Library Projects in Tanzania" February 1992, made for UNESCO, a survey of the difficulties faced in a developing country is given.

As part of the Tanzania Adult Literacy Programme, rural newspaper and rural libraries were established in the early 1970's. The rural library programme was extended to the entire country and more than 3,000 rural libraries were set up. The rural library programme was not affiliated in any way with the National Library Service, which supervises other libraries in the country. It was also evident that there was no coordination between the adult education work and the Folk Development Colleges. Nor were there any linkage of the libraries in the Folk Development Colleges and the rural libraries under the Adult Education Department. What is evident from the report is a total lack of cooperation.

It is evident from the report that the libraries are not very heavily used. One example is a library with an average of five books borrowed each month. Books are supplied irregularly, and the collections are no longer attractive. Nevertheless the evaluation team emphasises that the rural library programme has had a positive feature. Most people in most wards now know what a library is and that you can read there. Most village people can now read and write. And this implies the need for a rich reading environment to encourage all of the literate villagers to use and develop their reading skills. With a better cooperation between the actors the result might no doubt have been more successful.

Towards the year 2,000

Between 1970 and 1985 the number of illiterates grew by approximately 59 million. Since 1985, the number has remained stable, and according to UNESCO's latest estimate there should only be a slight decrease by 2,000.

This stability in the number of illiterates means a decrease in the rate of illiteracy:

38.5% in 1970

26.5% in 1990

21.8% in 2000

The estimated 21.8% means 935.4 million adult individuals with lack of reading skills. With this perspective, only a miracle added with hard work could eradicate illiteracy and the goal could be achieved by the year 2,000.

To eradicate illiteracy is indeed a long term project. To achieve the goal, even if there will be delays it is necessary that all institutions and organizations join to participate. The public library should not be forgotten.

Even if the total number of illiterates is tremendous current development is still encouraging. It is easy to find a number of good examples in many countries where illiteracy rates have gradually been reduced.

Very often there is a connection between long term planning of efforts and success.

Final remarks

The International Literacy Year 1990 focused the problem of illiteracy. It was considered that illiteracy was not solely a problem for the Third World. The problem of functional illiteracy was also made visible. The value of a Literacy Year should not be underestimated. It is of vital importance to raise public opinion and general awareness. Besides, the eradication of illiteracy cannot be done without resources. Generous funding in combination with alternative priorities is a prerequisite. The success of the Literacy Year is not less. It encouraged funding for literacy campaigns and focused the need of primary education.

Public libraries can not by themselves solve the problem of illiteracy and the complexity of eradicating it. But the public library can play an important role in cooperation with other institutions and organizations working in the field. Public libraries must be aware of their potential internal force.

Every public library no matter where, should start to estimate the size and character of the problem and analyse how the library best could participate in the struggle against illiteracy. Public libraries, as we know, operate in a variety of conditions concerning resources or lack of resources. Whatever the conditions are, we must define the problem and then establish very clear objectives. The different target groups must be defined and priorities established. We must not and can not always do everything at once. If we want to succeed we must have clear strategies. If necessary, we must have the courage to decide what target group might be of most importance. Probably many libraries will find hat priority should be made to children. To concentrate on the children might be the best long term strategy.

The illiterate child will be the adult illiterate tomorrow.

It is desirable that the library staff is given the opportunity to become specialists. But it is also important that the whole staff is involved in the struggle against illiteracy. A few specialists might give the rest an excuse not to bother. To find the proper balance is a question of good management.

Collection development is of vital importance. The public library should analyse what material could be attractive to the population with reading difficulties, call attention to the problem and encourage publishing of suitable material.

Guidelines

To establish guidelines for public libraries working with illiteracy is a rather complicated task. Since needs and resources vary so widely it is almost impossible to formulate common standards or guidelines. Reservations must be made that some of the advice and examples given might not at all be applicable or relevant for some libraries but might be for others. Guidelines suggest what might be possible, but national/local conditions will dictate what is feasible. The gap between what is desirable and what is possible must always be kept in mind.

The International Literacy Year 1990 focused the problem of illiteracy. No public library should be unaware of the challenge. The public library must take an active role in continuing the work. Active support from UNESCO, not only financial, made it possible for the

Section of Public Libraries to outline guidelines for public libraries working with illiteracy. The guidelines have been prepared in close cooperation between IFLA and UNESCO. The Guidelines is one practical output of the Literacy Year and we hope they will encourage public-libraries to deal with the problem or at least not forget all about the problem as the Literacy Year 1990 fades away.

REFERENCES

Bekius, Rene, Current Western Book Donation Programmes in Africa. For how long ? Sustaining Western dominance or strengthening African cultural identity? Paper presented at meeting of the EADI working group on information and documentation, Paris 3 - 6 September 1991.

Compendium of statistics on illiteracy - 1990 Edition. Division of Statistics on Education Office of Statistics - Paris, 1990.

Dillsworth, Gloria, E.Basic Illiteracy and the Pubic Library - The Problem in Review. Paper presented at the IFLA Satellite Meeting "Public Libraries against Illiteracy", Massy. France, August 15 - 19, 1989.

Esperandieu, V. Lion, A. Benichou, J.P. Des illettres en France: rapport au Premier Ministre. Paris, La Documentation francaise, 1984.

Ferguson, Stepheney W. Acquisitions in the developing countries : problems and possible solutions: the Jamaican experience. Paper presented at the IFLA General Conference in Nairobi, 1984.

Final report, World Conference on Education for all: Meeting Basic Learning Needs. 5 - 9 March 1990. Jomtien, Thailand. New York, 1990.

Functional illiteracy: what public libraries can do to help people with reading and writing problems. An ideas pamphlet. Paper prepared with support from the Norwegian and Swedish directorates for pubic libraries and presented at IFLA Statellite Meeting "Public Libraries against Illiteracy", Massy, France, August 15 - 19, 1989.

Giggely. S. Rural community resource centres: a guide for developing countries. Commonwealth Secretariat. 1988.

Guide du bibliothecaire. Numero special. Janvier 1991.

Guidelines for public libraries. Prepared for the IFLA Section of Public Libraries IFLA Publications 36. 1986.

Harrity, Sara, Ranfurly Library Service: An example of Practical Work against Illiteracy. Paper presented at the IFLA General Conference, Stockholm, 1990.

Illiteracy in Latin America: facts, problems and prospects for the future. Prepared by Miguel Soler Roca or the Division of Statistics on Education Office of Statistics. UNESCO 1989.

An Impact Evaluation of the Rural Press and Rural Library Projects in Tanzania, 17 January - 5 February, 1992. With Recommendations and Possible Scenarios for the Future. Final Field Draft. Dar-es-Salaam, February 5, 1992. (Official version to be distributed from UNESCO, Paris.)

Importation of educational, scientific and cultural materials. A guide to the operation of the "Florence Agreement" and its Protocol. UNESCO, Paris, 1989.

Jessen, Karen, Collection development in public libraries in developing countries. Paper presented at the IFLA Presession Seminar on Public Library Policy, Harnosand, Sweden, August 13 - 17, 1990.

Kozol, J. Illiterate America. Garden City, NY, Anchor Press Doubleday, 1985.

Literacy programmes and the public library service in Jamaica. Prepared by the JAMAL Foundation. 1981. UNESCO journal of information science, librarianship and archives administration; III, 4, pp. 235-240.

Nagy, Attila. Illiteracy, seen form Eastern Europe. Paper presented at the IFLA General Conference, Sockholm, 1990.

Nothing to read ? The crisis of document provision in the Third World.Proceedings of the seventh Conference of the International and Comparative Librarianship Group of the Library Association. Westhill College, Birmingham, August 31st - September 2nd, 1989.

Parker, J. Stephen. UNESCO and library development planning. London, Library Association Publishing Ltd., 1985.

Partridge, W.G.M., Low budget librarianship: managing information in developing countries. Library Association, 1988.

Patte, Genevieve and Geradts, Alice. Home libraries in Zimbabwe. IFLA Journal 11 (1985) pp. 223-227.

Public Libraries against Illiteracy. Stockholm, Sweden, August 18th, 1990. Conference Proceedings compiled by the IFLA Section of Public Libraries. Stockholm, 1990.

Raseroka, H. Kay. Relevant library services in developing countries. IFLA Journal 12 (1986) pp. 288-291.

Rasmussen, Radha. Public library services to the rural areas of Southeast Asia. IFLA Journal 7 (1981) pp. 254-263.

Sagna, Remi. Bibliotheques a deux portes ou la bibliotheque scolaire et ses relations avec la bibliotheque publique. Paper given at the IFLA Presession Seminar on Pubic Library Policy, Harnosand, August 13 - 17, 1990.

Sousa Lanna, Rosa Maria de. Library extension: a surprise box. Paper presented at the IFLA Statellite Meeting "Public Libraries against Illiteracy", Massy, France, August 15 - 19, 1989.

Suckcharoen, Karmmanee. Literacy campaigns in Asia and Thailand. Paper presented at the IFLA Presession Seminar on Public Library Policy, Harnosand, August 13-17, 1990.

Tanguiane, Sema. Literacy and illiteracy in the world: situation, trends and prospects. International yearbook of education. Volume XLII - 1990. Prepared for the International Bureau of Education.

Thomsen, Pauli. The establishment off a library service to visually handicapped people in African developing countries. Paper presented at the IFLA General Conference in Nairobi 1984.

UNESCO office of statistics. Basic education and Literacy : World statistical indicators. Pairs, 1990.

UNESCO Statistical Yearbook, 1989. Paris, 1989.

Vélis, Jean-Pierre, Lettre d'illetrie. Nouvelles d'une contree recemment redecouverte dans es pays industrialises. Paris, 1990.

World Declaration on Education for All and Framework for Action to meet Basic Learning Needs. Adopted by the World Conference on Education for All. Jomtien, Thailand, 5-9 March, 1990.

PART III

Bibliographical Data Processing and Standardization

The Genesis and Development of ISBD (A)

R.A. CHRISTOPHERS

There were several strands of argument running through the cataloguing debates of the 1970s. As machine-readable catalogues and the possibility of access on different elements of the description became more common, the concept of main entry was called into question. Similar considerations governed the debate about the form of corporate headings, as to how far hierarchies should be preserved or direct headings made with suitable references. More pertinent to this paper was to debate on the description and collection of the entities libraries were now collecting as information came to be presented in forms other than that of the codex book. Was there a generalised description that could cover books, films, multi-media educational materialism, data-files and computer software ? It was unfortunate in some ways that the concept of the International Standard Bibliographic Description (ISBD) did not quite start at that point, and the initial stipulations were drawn up at a meeting of cataloguing experts organised by the International Federation of Library Associations (IFLA) at Copenhagen in 1969. The word "bibliographic" is a sign that the deliberations were restricted to the description of monographs in printed form, and this resulted in the publication of a provisional edition of ISBD (M) in 1971. This introduced the concept of meaningful "prescribed punctuation" into the description, along with a structured order of the bibliographic elements, linked closely with the development of machine-readability, and particularly influencing and influenced by the MARC format then being pioneered by the Library of Congress.[1]

By the time ISBD(M) was re-considered in Grenoble in 1973 and published as a first definitive edition in the following year, there were already signs of a need to extend the role of ISBDs to serials and then to material in other physical formats, and considerable debate raged between book-based traditionalists who saw ISBD(M) as a basis for the description of other media, and proponents of these new media who argued with passion that the book, if not exactly dead, was not the only inhabitant of the information world and there should be a fresh start on level terms to consider the best means of description. The response came from IFLA as the ISBD(G) — for general—which attempted a brief generalised format and was accepted as a starting point for development of specialised ISBDs by most protagonists, save a few who still felt it was too book based.

These debates were not very relevant to the initial thoughts of an ISBD for the description of older material, since there was no doubt that these were exclusively books, and the tensions over the compilation of ISBD(A) as it became known — A for antiquarian, ancient. alt-were of a different nature. These tensions arose from the realisation of rare book cataloguers that computers had appeared in the library scene and could affect the way they worked. There were negative and positive views on this : some could see no good in the new developments and contributed nothing to the debate, while others saw no need for or no chance of special treatment and would accept new rules and procedures in full, gaining something but losing much in the process. This was, a time of opportunity and this was taken up in the pioneering work of the late John Jolliffe, first in his proposals for the conversion of the British Museum General Catalogue and later, when Keeper of Catalogues at the Bodleian Library, with the LOC project (London, Oxford and Cambridge) which explored ways of making computers the servant rather than the master of the historical bibliographer, including the possibility of mechanised union catalogues, searching files by publisher, place or date, and the concept of the "fingerprint" as unique identifier, compiled from elements within the book itself.[3] One more somewhat negative concept in the ISBD(A) exercise and its implementation, and one with which I have not always dissociated myself is the sport of how to catalogue rare books in the way one would wish, without actually cheating while remaining consistent with the structure of a general catalogue and the format adopted. Without this give and take there would, however, be no place for any of the special characteristics of entries for older books in general catalogues. On the positive side, the computer offers an opportunity to rethink rare book cataloguing, and indeed all cataloguing, as more access is possible but structure may drive out exact transcription, as proposed in some of the schemes from the Institut de Rècherche d'Histoire des Textes in Paris. An accommodation with economics, theoreticians, systems staff and users has had to be sought, and while initial indications were that so much effort put into structuring a record paid very few dividends, the possibility of alternative sequences of output and then of on-line access began to allow rare book librarians to see the advantages of the new systems which had initially been forced upon them. These, and some of their applications, as well as more recent developments, which again question elaborate structures, will be discussed later.

The protagonists of ISBD (A) have been constantly questioned as to what they were trying to do and why did they think it was needed. When ISBD (M) was revised at Grenoble it was soon seen that a non-specialist group could not in two days of torrid heat cater for all that the then few interested rare book librarians were wanting. So there is a paragraph in ISBD (M) which states "The ISBD (M) is principally concerned with current publications. It therefore makes no provisions for the special problems of older books". At Grenoble I raised the question of such standards for older material, and by 1975 another part of IFLA, the Rare and Precious Books Section, had produced a *Project de norme ISBD pour les livres anciens*. This was very logical and had many attractive features, but did not quite fulfill the principles of the ISBD philosophy, which by this time was trying to work towards the generalised standard to apply to all materials. It allowed for most ISBD punctuation but also used angle brackets, contracted to a lozenge sign, <>, to indicate the place from which an author statement had been transposed. It was liberal in interpolations in square brackets, its collations included and indicated blank pages and the register of signatures, and a wide range of footnotes was allowed. This draft formed the basis for the eventual French national standard for the description of older material.[4] The examples assembled for it, and for subsequent work by Mme Dureau and her colleagues at the Ecole nationale superieure des bibliothéques at Villeurbanne, were extensively used in the eventual publication of ISBD (A), and it also started to give serious consideration to the "fingerprint" as a means of identifying editions. The draft was, however, not viewed as part of the main programme of ISBD development, partly on account of its origins from outside the Universal Bibliographic Control programme, and partly because it was felt to preserve title-page order at the cost of structure and of the use of angle brackets, which, although on most terminals are not on most typewriters. ISBD, being a system for both manual and computerized catalogues, and for transfer of records between the two, does not permit the use of characters not on typewriter keyboards.

It is worth observing at this point that it is the tension between the two forms of catalogues which was the genesis of most of the debates surrounding ISBD (A) in rare book circles. It is of general application, but particularly so in areas where the artefact rather than the content is described. In essence the argument is that for manual catalogues there is no need for prescribed punctuation as access points are limited and filing sequences are obvious, while in an automated catalogue the use of coded markers to produce prescribed punctuation is tautologous, for the coding can abbreviate or rearrange records as well as indicate filing order and there is no need to add punctuation which is not in the document. Meanwhile the protagonists of prescribed punctuation supported it as a means of exchanging records among libraries where languages, scripts, computer systems or developments of the catalogues themselves differed, and while eventual output might vary, original input could be made to serve all purposes and made once only.

The most important stimulus to the development of ISBD (A) was the initiation of the Eighteenth Century Short Title Catalogue (ESTC) at an international meeting in London in June 1976. This was seen from the start as an international venture in which records would be exchanged and updated in machine-readable form and new standards of cataloguing would be required. Given that one of its declared aims was also to be a contribution to the conversion of the British Library catalogue to machine-readable form and that the Library's current intake was by now being catalogued by the Anglo-American Cataloguing Rules (AACR), based on ISBD (M) and in MARC format, and that the British Library was taking the lead with the initial pilot project and as host to the data-base, it was natural that rules for compiling ESTC would be based on similar standards. Early on it was realised that at least initially and, as it has turned out, in the long term "Short Title" was a misnomer. The concept of the shortest possible title and annotations to distinguish editions had proved satisfactory for the pre-1640 period in the monumental revision of the *Short-title catalogue of books printed before 1640...,* by Katharine Pantzer.[5] Though rather less so for Donald Wing's single-handed work on the period from 1641 to 1700.[6] It could not be applied to eighteenth century material when it was obvious that typographical differences between editions and possible variations in the quantity, let alone the quality, of data given or omitted from reports from a variety of sources, would require full transcriptions. This was considered especially important for the manual card file in alphabetical order of title, and contributors were required not to omit any data in the early part of the title-page transcription. Once given, it seemed pointless to provide facilities for truncation, and thus ESTC made no use of subfields and prescribed punctuation in the titie area. It was therefore impossible to prune such records for publication, but equally it was considered that information once gathered should not be discarded, and that compared to print, the storage and output of longer records was not too costly either in microform or on a database, and that access could be improved, a policy which has been reinforced by the realisation of the power of keyword searching online and by adopting records derived through RLIN, which involved no effort in bringing long transcriptions from one edition of a work to another. Over the years ESTC has found it necessary to introduce a subfield to indicate the end of the significant title, supported by numerical filing fields to order records, but its original requirements considerably influenced the compilers of ISBD (A) and gave this the distinctiveness from ISBD (M) which has been both its strength and its weakness.

With ESTC under way and the assumption from the first of transatlantic participation in that project, it became essential for some agreement to be reached on description, since it was obvious that the ESTC project did not see ISBD (M) and the consequential MARC coding as acceptable. At one point there seemed to be agreement that for ESTC, full transcription and actual, not prescribed, punctuation would be allowed and written into AACR, second edition, as rules for all older material. However, this did not meet with American support, being dubbed "a silly scheme" by one cataloguing expert, and the Library of Congress did not feel it could go along with it. Thus AACR2 contains only minimal modifications for older material and ESTC continued with its own rules for description, along with headings based on AACR2.[7] Nevertheless, in the summer of 1977, IFLA had taken up the concept of an ISBD for older material and I was asked to chair a working group.

Our members were chosen by the Cataloguing and Rare and Precious Books sections, IFLA, and the membership comprised representatives from France, Hungary, Italy, Montenegro the former USSR (who communicated only by Telex, but have always been understanding and helpful), Bill Matheson from the Library of Congress, and Hugh Chaplin, retired Principal Keeper of Printed Books at the British Museum, to whom fell the role of seeing that our decisions did not stray too far from the ISBD norm. We concluded that a separate ISBD for older material was both necessary and desirable on grounds beyond the pragmatic requirements, or innate conservatism, of rare book cataloguers. The rationale for this decision and the areas where it was chiefly recognised are given in the introductions to the two editions of ISBD (A). In summary they were, the recognisation that to distinguish editions early title-pages needed transcription with the same detail and order as the original, as far as possible, that the inter-connection of printer, publisher and bookseller should be reflected in the imprint and that a complete collection of an ideal copy, in so far as one might exist, should be offered. The stipulations, as we are learning to call them, speak for themselves as a description of the ways in which we sought to balance structure and transcription.

The result was perhaps rather too full of options - the result of attempting consensus - and in practice it would be difficult in the context of a general catalogue to explain which options had been applied, e.g. when prescribed punctuation had been applied was it concealing actual punctuation, and if so, what? Had an author statement been transposed? How had the imprint been assembled? To the "full transcription" school, ISBD (A) was a "can of worms" which failed to give an exact transcription in spite of the effort applied. Any description short of this, unencumbered by prescribed punctuation, would be inadequate for special catalogues, and full collection and a comprehensive bibliographic apparatus were also seen as essential. Such feelings were strong in the French draft and in many specialised areas. To the "standardisers" the rules were a luxury, and access in a general catalogue could be served by ISBD (M) with, if required, exact transcription in notes. A further ingenious suggestion was the assignment of an International Standard Book Number for older books, an ISBN (A), which would identify the work and thus allow description to be contained within the bounds of ISBD (M). This could to some extent be met by reference to a published description for each item catalogued, and the "fingerprint" also came close to this requirement, but even that could not be guaranteed to be unique and the possibility of such a post hoc system of assigning reliable identifiers seemed remote.[8]

Thus the compilers of ISBD (A) might in the end be numbered among a third group, the pragmatists. Taking as a basis the policy that ISBDs are not standards or cataloguing rules, but guidelines for the cataloguing codes of individual national bibliographic agencies, the many options seemed to offer a way to each agency's being able to adapt ISBD (A) as a basis for its own rules. It is, however, arguable if this is fully logical, bearing in mind the aim that records should be internationally interchangeable. The compilers, however, would have stressed that their efforts should be seen in the context of general catalogues of various types of material and that whatever the rules used the serious bibliographer would need to see the original to determine full details, and certainly to discover points within the text which had not been distinguished as comparisons between copies had not been possible, nor in the context of a busy cataloguing department could be reasonably attempted. Some critics both at the initial and revision stage have urged ISBD (A) to become more of a manual of rare book cataloguing, but that is not its function, and it remains a rather stark and formalised set of rules. Furthermore, it is necessary to remind users that as titles are transcribed exactly, if a sequenced order is desired uniform titles have to be provided, and that is no concern of ISBD (A) as such. Thus ISBD (A) was issued in 1980 in the hope that it could bridge the divide by allowing some transpositions, omissions and structuring and by allowing prescribed punctuation either to override or stand beside actual punctuation. There were several rough edges on imprints—their sources, combining sources and structure - and on collation, especially for works with complex or no pagination.

By this time rare book cataloguers, having now awoken to the advantages the computer could give them, were not always well placed to exploit them as resources for both their acquisitions and special functions became almost universally scarcer. However, ESTC published revised rules[9] which if not based on ISBD (A) directly had originally, as we have seen been a formative influence on it.

Within the British Library's General Catalogue ISBD (A) was adopted for the description of earlier works, with the important variation that while prescribed punctuation was input to allow for correct filing and any exchange of records, it was not output into the fiche catalogues. National rules were published, based on the standard, and often with useful guidelines on cataloguing practice in Belgium, France, Hungary and Russia,[10] and work is still in progress in Spain. Most significant was the Library of Congress's publication *Bibliographic description of rare books* (Washington, 1981) which forms a basis for work in the USA and beyond. Essentially it was ISBD (A) veering towards the more structured base of AACR in its choice of options.

A review programme for ISBDs was set up in 1977 by the IFLA Office for Universal Bibliographic Control at the same IFLA World Congress where the first informal meeting of the ISBD (A) group had been held. It was agreed that each ISBD should be reviewed after five years, so ISBD (A), having not even started then, was among the last to be due for revision : a happy situation, since by the time this was due, many of the stipulations and much of the wording and structure in the parent ISBD (M) had turned out to be much more acceptable to the concepts of ISBD (A). The new working group did not actually meet, but conducted all its business by correspondence, with notable contributions from John D Byrum, who also chaired the review committee, and the late Dr Izabella Galamb of the Orszagos Szechenyi Konyvtar, Budapest, who provided many new examples and raised several fundamental points of interpretation. Indeed, the targets for revision were to extend the number of examples and give the descriptions a more universal aspect, taking in non-Roman scripts and reconsidering the use of the equals sign in parallel language statements, as well as harmonising the text among all ISBDs as far as possible. The ISBD (A) revision process, commencing in 1985, took account of these and also proceeded by circulating interested parties with suggestions for clarifying any problems which had emerged with implementation and asking if any new points needed to be made. In general, the effect of the revision period was to open up all the initial questions once more and at greater length, and a flow of correspondence ensued in various attempts to bring more structure to some areas, more detail to others. The provisions for rendering capital I, J, U, or V into lower case caused particular concern, and no universally acceptable solution emerged. With some exceptions there were few new candidates for examples, and while the colophon is more openly admitted as source for books in non-Roman scripts, the revision must still be said to be western based. On the whole, however, proposals which brought the text more into line with ISBD (M), itself being revised, were accommodated except when they seemed to threaten the distinctive nature of rare book cataloguing. Probably most significant was yet a further option to allow prescribed punctuation to be omitted in output if it was present in machine-readable form - already the British Library practice. Much attention was given to the best way of reconciling structure, wording, consistent use of sources and completeness for imprints, and suggested solutions were offered on matters as diverse as succinct phrases like "London, printed in the year 1742" or complex statements spread over title-page, colophon and within printers' devices. The final revised text appeared in 1991, but the process of leapfrogging of standards continued with the publication by the Library of Congress of its revised guidelines *Descriptive cataloguing of rare books)* (Washington, 1991) which took in some, but not all, of the stipulations of ISBD (A).

Meanwhile, in Great Britain, the Rare Books Group of the Library Association had been prompted by a discussion at Cambridge in 1989 of the problems encountered by rare book cataloguers in applying new rules to an old game, especially as there was a feeling that they had never been widely consulted about those rules. The survey, by Ann Lennon and David Pearson,[11] showed a wide variety of practices, many of them enforced as part of general library automation policies, but also a considerably raised appreciation, if still tempered by some suspicion of what automation could achieve if properly handled. Of 125 libraries responding, 99 were using AACR, 26 the ESTC rules, 11 the Library of Congress guidelines, and only 9 had adopted ISBD (A).[12] AACR cannot be said to embody ISBD (A) concepts, and indeed advice from even some of its author bodies is usually to use the Library of Congress rules instead for older books, so even allowing for ESTC and Library of Congress rules being in the same family as ISBD (A), these figures point to the slow progress of distinctive practices emerging in rare book cataloguing in a machine environment.

Now, just as the complexities and multiple codings are becoming possible and accepted as bringing additional retrieval facilities to the bibliographer's aid, a further shift in the scene can be detected. Given the lack of resources which had meant that most libraries have been unable to meet the exacting demands of detailed machine-based cataloguing, this may well bring relief from the quest for an ever-receding ideal. The generalised coding of records in ESTC and in the converted General Catalogue of Printed Books of the British Library have nevertheless made data more accessible than before and have made both conversion and loading onto databases quicker and more practicable, so that both are available in CD-ROM and BLAISE (the British Library's on-line bibliographic information service) and in October 1993 the latter will be available as on on-line public access catalogue. These methods of access to records may well not need such sophisticated input as did traditional linear outputs in printed, card or fiche form; the major caveat is that some form of structured arrangement needs to be preserved in order to give scholars the necessary sequences by title, language or date of publication. This should not prove too difficult to organise and thus actual transcription could continue unimpeded.

A further and practical development which will test the staying power and robustness of the principles underlying ISBD (A) is now underway in Europe, the proposal of the Consortium of European Research Libraries for a European database of hand-press period publications.[13] ISBD (A)'s many options were seen by some to be a stumbling block to its adoption as a standard, in that with its variations in capitalisation and in transcription, claims of uniformity would be specious if contributors followed different options. Meanwhile those not using ISBD (A) at all might be penalised even if their records were comprehensive and internally consistent, and conformed to the minimum level required by the database. As the convenor of the ISBD (A) working group, I attempted to justify the rules as fitting into a framework of similar descriptions for all materials, and that as such, given that cataloguers always beg to differ from each other, it bore signs of compromise in its stipulations both mandatory and optional. It seemed that just as ISBD (A) was not seeking to lay down a procrustean bed of rules, neither was the European database, and I urged that given firm decisions on the options

ISBD (A) could indeed still be a basis for cooperation. The Consortium did not see ISBD (A) as a stumbling block and proposed in spring 1992 that the highest standard of records would be according to ISBD (A). The proposed file structure is a 'members' file, consisting of discrete segments, but searchable in one search - with varying cataloguing standards - and on top of this a 'union file' with high level records (ISBD(A) standard) derived from the member file - also serving as its index. This view has been supported in a consultancy report by Tony Curwen, formerly of the Department of Information and Library Science, University of Wales, Aberystwyth. It now remains to be seen if ISBD (A), or a code based upon, is after so long actually capable of achieving in practice its aim of preventing the levelling down of standards for description of older material in the machine-readable age, as well as enabling the exchange of accurate, consistent and readily accessible records. To have done so would be a modest achievement in the advancement of bibliographical scholarship.

REFERENCES

1. R A Christophers is at present head of the Twentieth Century British Collections, Humanities and Social Sciences, British Library and was convenor of the ISBD (A) working group. The views expressed in this article are not necessarily those of the British Library or the working group. Many of the comments alluded to in the article are in private communications and working papers related to the compilation and revision of ISBD (A).

2. For an account of the development of the MARC format see, among other sources, *MARC: its history and implications/ by Henriette D Avram* (Washington: Library of Congress, 1976).

3. Published as *Computers and early books* (London: Mansell, 1974).

4. *Catalogue des monographies anciennes: redaction de la description bibliographique* (Paris La Defense : AFNOR, 1986) (Z 44-074).

5. *Short-title catalogue of books printed in England, Scotland & Ireland... 1475-1640 first complied by A.W. Pollard & G.R. Redgrave - 2nd ed... completed by Katharine F Pantzer*. (London: Bibliographical Society, 1976-91).

6. *Short-title catalogue of books printed... 1641-1700: 2nd ed.*, (New York: Modern Language Association of America, 1972-88).

7. For an account of ESTC see *Bibliography, machine-readable cataloguing and the ESTC/R.C. Alston and M. J. Jannetta* (London: British Library, 1978) : continuing developments are recorded in ESTC's "house-journal" *Factotum* (London: British Library, 1977-).

8. For a description of a method of fingerprint construction see *fingerprints = Empreintes = Impronte* (Paris: Institut de Recherche et d'Histoire des Textes, 1984). This brings very close the possibility of constructing a string of data unique to each publication, but at present there is no international agreement and the provision of data in the area of ISBD (A) equivalent to that for the unique ISBN has been left optional.

9. *The Eighteenth Century Short Title Catalogue: the cataloguing rules - New ed./ revised by J.C. Zeeman* (London: British Library, 1984).

0. *Példatát régi könyvek formai feltárásához* (Budapest: Országos Széchényi Könvytár, 1989).

Manuel de catalogage automatisé des livres anciens en format Intermarc (Paris: Bibliothéque Nationale, 1987) (Études, guides et inventaires, 6).

Pravila sostavlenia bibliograficheskogo opisania staropechatnykh izdanil. (Moskva: Bibliotéka SSSR imeni V.I. Lenina, 1989).

ISBD (A) : internationale standard voor de bibliografische beschrijving van oude monografieen (Brussel : Koninklijke Bibliotheek Albert I, 1985).

Regels voor titelbeschrijving von oude en bijzondere drukken. (Brussel: Koninklijke Bibliotheek Albert I, 1987).

Guide pour la description bibliographique des imprimés anciens et precieux/ traduction francaise. (Bruxelles : Bibliothéque Royale Albert I, 1991) (Archives et biliothèques de Belgique, no. special 43).

11. *Rare book cataloguing in the British Isles / Ann Lennon and David Pearson.* (London : British Library Research and Development Department, 1991) (British Library Research Paper, 94).

12. A Further 28 libraries used their own rules. The total exceeds 125 since some libraries used two or more systems.

13. *Retrospective cataloguing in Europe : 15th - 19th century printed materials / edited by J.M. Smethurst and F.G. Kaltwasser* (Munich : Saur, 1992).

Application of S.R. Ranganathan's Postulates and Principles of the General Theory of Knowledge Classification to Database Design and Information Retrieval

A. NEELAMEGHAN

S.R. Ranganathan's postulates and principles of the General Theory of Knowledge Classification, especially the analyticosynthetic methodology can be applied with advantage in structuring knowledge bases and object-oriented databases and organization of concepts in such information bases; designing schemes for classification and vocabulary control tools, such as, thesauri : generating various types of structured indexes; assisting user browsing in database/retrieved records, facet analysis of user's queries for better results in online retrieval; presenting retrieved records in a helpful sequence, etc. The paper briefly considers applications of the analytico-synthetic methodology and related postulates and principles to the design of specialized object-oriented database. Enhancement of user-friendliness of information retrieval by interfacing facet-analyzed query terms with thesaurus terms is demonstrated. Also, the usefulness of Ranganathan's generalized subject structure conforming to the analytico-synthetic freely faceted model is mentioned.

INTRODUCTION

Ranganathan's Holistic Integrative Approach

1. In any discussion of S.R. Ranganathan's approach to the design, development and use of information systems and services or a component thereof, it is necessary and helpful to bear in mind his holistic integrative approach. For the purpose of strengthening and achieving consistency in this regard, Ranganathan recommended use of a range of normative principles[13], proposed a typology among them establishing a hierarchy among the types or groups and suggested guidelines for their application. Briefly, the group of normative principles include:

Level 1: Basic Laws, (Law of Symmetry, Law of Impartiality, Law of Context/Local Variation, Laws of Interpretation and Law of

Parsimony) applicable to intellectual work in all areas of the universe of knowledge ;

Level 2: Fundamental Laws, (e.g. Laws of Physics, Laws of Biology, and the Five Laws of Library Science postulated by Ranganathan) applicable to a discipline as a whole;

Level 3: Canons, (e.g. Canons of Classification in Library Science) applicable to a branch of a discipline; and

Level 4: Principles, (e.g. Principles of Facet Sequence in Classification), applicable to a sub-branch or subdivision of a branch of a discipline.

Ranganathan provided also several postulates applicable at each of the above levels. His *Five Laws of Library Science* (11) which are information use and user-oriented, direct that any new principle, technique or strategy adopted should lead to users obtaining more pertinent information expeditiously when needed, presented in a form and format convenient to the target user group, saving of users' time and ensure a more efficient management of the information system and service, than was the case before the application of the new technique, etc.

Applications of Analytico-synthetic Methodology

2. Ranganathan's General Theory of Knowledge Classification, the postulates and principles and especially the analytico-synthetic freely-faceted methodology, which this paper will be discussing, have several applications, for example, in:

— structuring knowledge bases and object-oriented databases and organizing concepts therein in a helpful sequence;

— object-oriented analysis and design;

— preparing field definition table for database;

— designing schemes for classification;

— designing vocabulary control tools, such as, subject heading lists, thesaurus, classaurus, etc.;

— generating various types of structured indexes;

— assisting user browsing more conveniently in the database or retrieved records to zero-in on the specific subjects/objects of interest to him/her at the moment;

— facet-analysis of user's query and structuring search expressions for better results in online retrieval; and

— presenting retrieved records/ information in a sequence helpful to users.

Scope of the Paper

3. Some of the above applications have been discussed in other recent papers[8,9,10]. The present paper briefly considers the applications of Ranganathan's analytico-synthetic methodology and the related postulates and principles of his General Theory of Knowledge Classification to the design and development of databases, specialized and object-oriented databases in particular, and in information retrieval. Usefulness of Ranganathan's generalized subject structure conforming to the analytico-synthetic freely-faceted mode 1 is also mentioned. Enhancement of the user-friendliness of information systems by interfacing facet-analyzed query terms with thesaurus terms is demonstrated.

4. Databases mentioned in this paper are mostly object-oriented factual information bases. However, Ranganathan's subject structure model, analytico-synthetic approach and the related postulates and principles are applicable to the organization of subjects embodied in documents as in a bibliographic database.

WORKING DEFINITIONS

5. *Data entity* : A data entity is a set of objects that share one or more attributes in common among themselves and about which one may be interested in collecting descriptive data. The descriptive data collected about an entity is usually data about attributes of the entity of *attribute data*[8].

6. *Data model* : A data model is a scheme to represent the real world of data entities using information concepts and structure. For example, in databases to support decision making and planning by an aid agency relating to rural development in a country the real world 'target community' may be represented by information concepts, e.g. demographic pattern, economic indicators, social factors, ethnic factors, literacy levels, infrastructure, growth poles, etc[8].

7. *Subject* : A subject is an organized or systematized account of an entity or set of entities (an idea or group of ideas) whose extension and intension are likely to fall coherently within the field of interest and comfortably within the intellectual competence and the field of

inevitable specialization of a normal person[12]. For example, 'Coordination of Aid from the European Communities for Famine Relief in Bangladesh', 'Famines in Asia,' 'Disaster Relief Work', and 'Sociology' is each a subject; for, the intension and extension of the totality of ideas comprehended by each of the terms or term combinations can form a coherent, comfortable and convenient field of specialization of a normal person. On the other hand, not all of what is embodied in the 'Encyclopedia of Social Sciences' taken as a whole is a subject; for, the totality of all the ideas embodied therein cannot form a coherent, comfortable and convenient field of specialization of a normal person. It is a collection of description of a large number of subjects.

ORGANIZATION OF IDEAS IN SPECIALIZED DATABASES

8. Concept categorization and knowledge organization are used, in one form or another, in knowledge bases (e.g. specialized and object-oriented databases). Such organization of concepts also helps in recognizing the types of inter-relationship that may exist among concepts in the particular context of a subject, and in linking them accordingly with a view to assisting users browse and navigate more conveniently in the knowledge base; and in presenting the retrieved records or ideas in a sequence helpful to users. Ranganathan's analytico-synthetic method based on postulates and principles is helpful in deriving a more or less consistent concept categorization and knowledge organization in databases and their outputs. The resulting representation of subject/object has a higher heuristic value in browsing to zero-in on the specific entity/subject of interest to them at the moment. The facet syntax so arrived at is deemed to parallel more closely the way in which a majority of normal intellectuals arrange the component ideas of a subject when thinking, communicating, or seeking information about the subject[7]. Hence, users are likely to find the system more user-friendly than would be the case if the concept terms (descriptors) are placed any which way like 'peas in a bag', other aspects of the system remaining the same[5]. In a database consisting of case histories of hospital patients, developed by doctors who were also users of the system and who have not had any exposure to Ranganathan's postulates, principles and analytico-synthetic method, the grouping and organization of the database fields and their preferred sequence conformed to those that would have been arrived at by applying Ranganathan's analytico-synthetic methodology and the related postulates and principles[10]. A similar preference by specialists in forest management has been noted with the database on forests. Also, the analytico-synthetic methodology has been used in conceptualizing,

mapping and visualizing in convenient framework issues/concepts/ data entities of interest to specialized users (e.g. energy resource planners). The framework could be translated into fields of a database or schedule in a scheme for classification[8]. These and other examples of organization of concepts in databases of expert systems[15,16] indicate that the principles and postulates of the General Theory of Knowledge Classification make explicit the sequencing of ideas in the thinking process of specialists and thus provide general guidance for deriving consistent and helpful organization of ideas in specialized databases.

GENERALIZED SUBJECT STRUCTURE MODEL

9. Ranganathan's generalised model of subject structure[7, 9]:

(a) conforms to the definition of subject given in para 7;

(b) helps to minimize the range of search/browsing necessary in a set of records, to zero-in on the specific subject (s) of interest to the user at the moment;

(c) the power to discriminate/distinguish between specific subjects falling in different subject areas rests with the first component in the linear representation of subject, namely, the 'Object of Study' or Personality facet[9]; and

(d) is object or entity oriented (cf. Object-oriented Analysis and Design), implying that information seekers in general are interested in information about the attributes (Properties) of an object or entity (concrete or abstract) with a view to using, or manipulating, or changing the attributes ; or in finding out which object (s)/entity (ies) possess given property (ies), or particular values for the selected attributes. Examples :

(1) From a database on Syndromes, doctors may wish to know which *disease (s)* manifest of combination of the symptoms:

congenital; cyanosis; clubbling of fingers; clubbing of toes

(2) From a database of hospital patients records, doctors may wish to know which *patient (s)/ disease (s)* show a particular symptoms or a combination of given symptoms.

(3) From a database of socio-economic development indicators for the constituent states of a country, planners or researchers may wish to know which *constituent states* have particular values for a given set of indicators.

(4) From a database of profiles of small enterprises, users may wish to know alternative means of financing *small enterprises* in a particular country or state ? Or may want comparative data on *small enterprises* in a particular area (e.g. constituent state of India) receiving following types of funding and /or subsidies :

Term loan, State subsidy, Promoter's share, Soft loan, Seed capita, Development loan, Deferred payment loan, IFCI subsidy, IDBI subsidy, EDP subsidy, DIC subsidy etc.

DESIGNING SPECIALIZED DATABASES

10. It has been shown that there is much similarity in the steps for designing a scheme for classification and those of a specialized database. Therefore, the postulates, canons and principles of the General Theory of Knowledge Classification can be used in designing specialized databases with advantage. More specifically, application of Ranganathan's Canons of Characteristics in defining fields of Field Definition Table (FDT) of databases has been illustrated[8].

11. A database is made up of one or more files; a file is made up of one or more records; a record is made up of one or more fields and a field is composed of one or more data elements. A designer of an information storage and retrieval system starts with deciding on (defining) what data elements should make up which field on the basis of analysis of user needs, organizational analysis, the type of data model adopted and other parameters. Which set of fields should make up a record is another decision to be taken. Ranganathan's Canons for characteristics and postulate-based analytico-synthetic methodology are helpful in these decisions. In specialized databases, generally each record consists of fields each providing information on one or more attributes and methods of studying or manipulating them, relating to an object/entity of study (Personality facet) as illustrated in the following Object-oriented databases[8, 10]:

Database on/for	*Object of Study*	*Master Record Devoted To*	*Fields on Attributes*
Forest resources management	Forest (division)	Forest Division	Of Forest Division
Market for nonconventional energy	Nonconventional energy source	Energy source	Of Market for Energy Source

Biogas equipment	Biogas equipment	Biogas equipment	Of Biogas Equipment
Syndromes	Syndrome	Syndrome	Of Syndromes
Patients records	Patient	Patient	Of Patient
Toxicity of chemicals	Chemicals	Chemicals	Of Chemical Substance
Small industries	Small industries	Small industries	Of Small Industries

12. Users may also need comparative data on the attributes of the different objects of study which may be in different records. For example, from the Forest database, in which each record gives data on the attributes of a Forest Division, user may want to get comparative data on different forest products or acreage cultivated in the different Forest Divisions. The extraction of such date from the different records and presenting them to user in a helpful format can be time-consuming with manual files or records. On the other hand, with a computerised database such extraction and presentation is easier; it is a matter of designing suitable display format(s). An example from the Forest database is given in Annex 1.

INDEXES

13. Information storage and retrieval systems find it useful to provide alphabetical subject indexes as a means of fast access to the information contained in databases. The subject index may be a part of a single inverted file (author, title, subject, etc.) or a separate file. The helpfulness of the subject index entries to users depends in a large measure on how adequately the subject content (ideas) of each document (if a bibliographical database) or the information about the entity described (if an issue or object-oriented database) has been analyzed and represented precisely and comprehensively in the index structures or expressions. Such analysis and representation can be aided by Ranganathan's analytico-synthetic procedure. The Chain Procedure is one such methodology. In its first formulation in 1937, the subject index entries were derived from the corresponding Colon Class Number. As the latter was based on facet analysis of the subject of the document, each component idea and to some extent the nature of relationship among the ideas, could be represented in the class number and therefore the subject index entries represented near-precisely the specific subject(s) of the document. But when Chain Procedure is applied to

class numbers that did not represent all component ideas of a subject of a document, it results in subject index entries that are less precise and therefore less helpful in retrieval.

12. In a paper published in 1964[14], Ranganathan clarified that the work of facet analysis of subject of a document and expressing it precisely by synthesis of the component ideas using relevant postulates and principles so as to map the specific subject onto a data model for linear representation, must be done before a class number is assigned according to a scheme for classification, and that the expression of the specific subject can be used to derive subject index entries. Thus, the derivation of subject index entries was clearly separated from the class number. Using the precise expression(s) of the subject(s)[1] or information on the object or issue discussed, a computer can generate a variety of index entries (KWOC, PRECIS-type, POPSI, etc.[2-4]. The facet-analyzed expression of subject can be used in the database record in the place of or in addition to the descriptors. The usefulness of faceted expression of subjects in retrieval can be enhanced in a computerized system as discussed in the following section.

SEARCHING AND USER'S INTERACTION WITH SYSTEM

14. As the discriminatory power among different subjects rests with the Object of Study (Personality isolate) in Ranganathan's subject structure model, in searching for information in a database, it is advisable to start the search with the term(s) denoting this entity, if given. In the data format in a database, the leader/header/data directory for each record will register, among other things, the field tag and its attributes. If the search is started with the Object of Study term, which is relatively unique compared to other field values (e.g. attributes), the search will be faster and more economical. From the Syndromes database (see para 07) the combination of symptoms retrieves a few records. If the Object of Study (Personality facet) e.g. Heart is used as the first search term combined with the other attribute terms given, then a fewer number of records, only one record in fact, dealing with Tetralogy of Fallot, is retrieved.

15. Experience shows that user-intermediary-information system interaction or user-information system direct interaction helps in the more precise formulation of user's information need and in the searching process so as to improve the possibility of retrieving information/records pertinent to user's needs. Usually, terms representing concepts of interest to user are selected and combined using boolean and other operators to formulate search expressions. This

process of facet analysis and synthesis should preferably match user's perception of reality/problem/information gap. Ranganathan's analytico-synthetic methodology formalises the process leading to a more or less consistent search formulation. Experience also indicates that a properly facet-analyzed query can give better retrieval performance (6). Vocabulary control tools, such as, thesaurus, subject heading list, classification scheme etc., usually used in processing queries.

16. In a paper on Patients' Records database[10], a thesaurus-like tool was created using terms derived from the records of the database to facilitate user interaction with the system in information retrieval. User is helped to start from broad divisions of patient's case history through the hierarchy of subdivisions. At the same time, where appropriate the user can also view related terms. An example is given in Annex 2.

17. User interaction and search formulation can be facilitated, made more productive by linking the facet-analyzed query terms to appropriate thesaurus terms so as to provide for browsing and a wider choice of concept terms. This can be done manually by looking up relevant terms in a thesaurus or by automatically using a computerized thesaurus and database of queries. A record for a query can have fields for the Statement of Query (by user), for Facet Analyzed Terms, for Name and Address of User, for Dates (receipt of and response to), for Notes on Response, etc. Example of an on-line worksheet is given in Annex 3.

18. When the query is displayed, each of the facet terms can be linked to corresponding terms in the thesaurus as shown in the example in Annex 4. In the example, the OECD Macrothesaurus (computer readable) was used and Micro CDS/ISIS software (Unesco) for preparing the Query database. As the OECD Macrothesaurus is multi lingual (English, French, Spanish), each query term can be linked to terms in the different languages. Search using terms from one language will automatically search with the corresponding terms in the other languages.

19. What has been demonstrated does not preclude direct search in the database using query terms or facet-analyzed terms; or search in the thesaurus to select appropriate search terms followed by search in the database. Free text search is also possible.

20. A database of queries, recording facet-analyzed search terms, will have other uses as well, e.g. research on user needs, informetric analyses, updating thesaurus/classification scheme, search in the Query database first when a new query is received, preparing user profiles for SDI service, etc.

21. A similar facet analysis of the subject of a document (or information relating to an entity in a specialized database) can be done in inputting a record. The terms can be linked to corresponding terms in a thesaurus and displayed when the record is retrieved.

REFERENCES

1. Bhattacharyya, Ganesh. "Fundamentals of Subject Indexing". In *Ordering Systems for Global Information Networks: Proceedings of the Third International Study Conference on Classification Research,* Bombay, 1975. Edited by a. Neelameghan. Bangalore, Sarada Ranganathan Endowment for Library Science, 1978. pp. 83-93.

2. Devadason, F.J. "Computerization of Deep Structure Based Indexes". *International Classification,* 12 (1985) : pp. 87-94.

3. —. "*Computerized Deep Structure Indexing System.* Frankfurt : INDEKS Verlag, 1986. (FID/CR Report No. 21).

4. —. "Postulate-based Permuted Subject Indiexing Language as a Metalanguage for Computer-aided Generation of Information Retrieval Thesaurus". *International forum for Information and Documentation,* 8 (1983) : pp. 22-29.

5. Foskett. D. J. "Ranganathan and 'User-friendliness'" *Libri* (1992) [Special issue on Ranganathan].

6. Godert, Winfred. "Facet Classification in Online Retrieval". *International Classification,* 18 (1991) : pp. 98-103.

7. Neelameghan, A. "Absolute Syntax and Structure of an Indexing and Switching Language". In *Ordering Systems ... op cit,* pp. 165-176.

8. —. "Application of Ranganathan's General Theory of Knowledge Classification in Designing Specialized Databases". *libri* (1992) [Special issue on Ranganathan].

9. —. A Paper prepared for the Second ISKO Conference, Madras, 26-28 August 1992.

10. —. "Concept Categorization and Knowledge Organization in Specialized Databases: A Case Study". *International Classification,* 18 (1991) : pp. 92-97.

11. Ranganathan, S.R. *Five Laws of Library Science.* Bombay: Asia Publishing House; 1963.

12. —. *Prolegomena to Library Classification.* Ed 3. Assist. by M.A Gopinath. Bombay : Asia Publishing House, 1967. Chapter CR Section 2.

13. —, —, Chapter DC to DG.

14. —. "Subject Heading and Facet Analysis". *Journal of Documentation*, 20 (1964): pp. 109-119.

15. Vickery, A. and Brooks, H.M. "PLESUS - the Expert System Referral. " *Information Processing and Management*, 23 (1987) : pp. 99-117.

16. Vickery, B.C. "Knowledge Representation: A Brief Overivew." *Journal of Documentation*, 42 (1986): pp. 145-159.

ANNEXURE 1

FARM PRODUCTS: COMPARATIVE DATA

	Teak				Eucalyptus				Bamboo		
	1984	1985	1986	1987	1984	1985	1986	1987	1984	1985	1986
Palaghat	36	40	40	45	28	36	30	33	25	30	22
Trichur	26	46	42	35	38	45	32	23	27	29	32
Idukki	46	40	39	46	38	32	40	23	34	24	32
Trivandrum	43	45	23	35	38	23	51	42	35	32	21
Kottayam	45	40	40	32	38	36	29	42	35	30	21

ANNEXURE 2

ASSISTED SEARCH FACILITY

When you press any key, a screen will be displayed and you will be asked to key-in a search term. Type the term CASE, in lower or upper case. A list of the areas into which a case history has been divided will be displayed. Press <ENTER> key or the downward arrow key as many times as necessary to move cursor against the desired term e.g. SYMPTOMS. The press S key to select the term. Divisions of and concepts related to Symptoms will be displayed. As before move the cursor to the desired terms and press S key to select. Not options at the bottom of the screen for formulating search queries.

Press any key —

CASE

CASE

— SN Patient Case history is divided into following searchable areas

— NT Administrative information

— NT Complaints

— NT Symptoms/Signs

— NT Interrogation

— NT Investigation

— NT Pathology

— NT Treatment

— NT Postoperative

— NT Follow-up

— NT Recurrence

— NT Readmission

Y Next [B] Back [F] irst [P]age [S]elect [T]erm select [M]ake file add te[R]m (file) [C]reate term [A]dd relation [D]elete [Q]uery sa[V]e [?]display Query/save search [/]add e[x]it

INVESTIGATION

BT CASE
NT ANGIOGRAM

NT BLOOD

NT CARDIOVASCULAR SYSTEM

NT CT SCAN---CT SCAN

NT HORMONES

NT MYEOLOGRAM

NT NMR

NT X-RAY

  BT INVESTIGATION

  NT X-RAY CHEST

  NT X-RAY SPINE

  NT X-RAY SKULL

    BT X-RAY

    NT ABNORMAL

    NT SELLA GR. I

    NT SELLA GR. II

CT SCAN

BT INVESTIGATION

NT COMPRESSED

NT DILATED VENTRICLE

NT HEAD

NT HIGH ATTENUATION

NT II VENTRICLE

NT III VENTRICLE

NT INTRASELLAR

NT PARASELLAR

NT SPINE

NT SUPRASELLER

ANNEXURE 3

WORKSHEET FOR QUERY STATEMENT

Query Statement ....

....

....

....

Query in Facet Terms...

....

....

....

Name of User ....

Affiliation ....

Address ....

....

....

....

Date of Query ....

Date of Response ....

Remarks ....

....

....

....

....

ANNEXURE 4

EXAMPLE OF QUERY TERMS INTERFACED WITH THESAURUS

QUERY : Water resources planning and management in urban areas of Ethiopia

FACET TERMS : Regional planning> Urban planning> Ethiopia> Urban areas, water : Planning

THESAURUS TERMS

TERM : URBAN PLANNING

BT PLANNING

NT URBAN RENEWAL; ZONING

RT IFHP; LOCAL GOVERNMENT; LOCAL PLANNING; PHYSICAL PLANNING; TOWNS; URBAN DEVELOPMENT; URBAN PLANS; POLICY; URBANISM

TERM: ETHIOPIA

BT EAST AFRICA

RT ETHIOPIANS

TERM: WATER

BT RENEWABLE ENERGY SOURCES

RT HYDROLOGY; ICE; WATER CHEMISTRY; WATER CONSERVATION; WATER CONSUMPTION; WATER DISTRIBUTION; WATER LAW; WATER MANAGEMENT; WATER POLLUTANTS; WATER POLLUTION; WATER POWER; WATER QUALITY; WATER REQUIREMENTS; WATER RESOURCES; WATER STORAGE; WATER SUPPLY; WATER TREATMENT; WATER UTILIZATION

TERM : PLANNING

NT COMMUNICATION PLANNING; DEVELOPMENT PLANNING; ECONOMIC PLANNING; EDUCATIONAL PLANNING; ENVIRONMENTAL PLANNING; FOOD PLANNING; HEALTH PLANNING; HOUSING PLANNING; LOCAL PLANNING; NATIONAL PLANNING; PHYSICAL PLANNING; PROGRAMME PLANNING; REGIONAL PLANNING; RURAL PLANNING; SOCIAL PLANNING; TRANSPORT PLANNING; URBAN PLANNING

RT CARISPLAN; INFOPLAN; PLANNERS; PLANNING METHODS; PLANNING SYSTEMS

TERM : ETHIOPIA

BT EAST AFRICA

RT ETHIOPIANS

TERM : URBAN AREAS

BT HUMAN SETTLEMENTS

NT SUMURBAN AREAS; TOWNS

RT RURAL-URBAN MIGRATION; TURNAROUND MIGRATION; URBAN ATTRACTION; URBAN CONCENTRATION; URBAN LAND; POPULATION; URBAN SOCIOLOGY; URBAN-URBAN MIGRATION; URBANIZATION

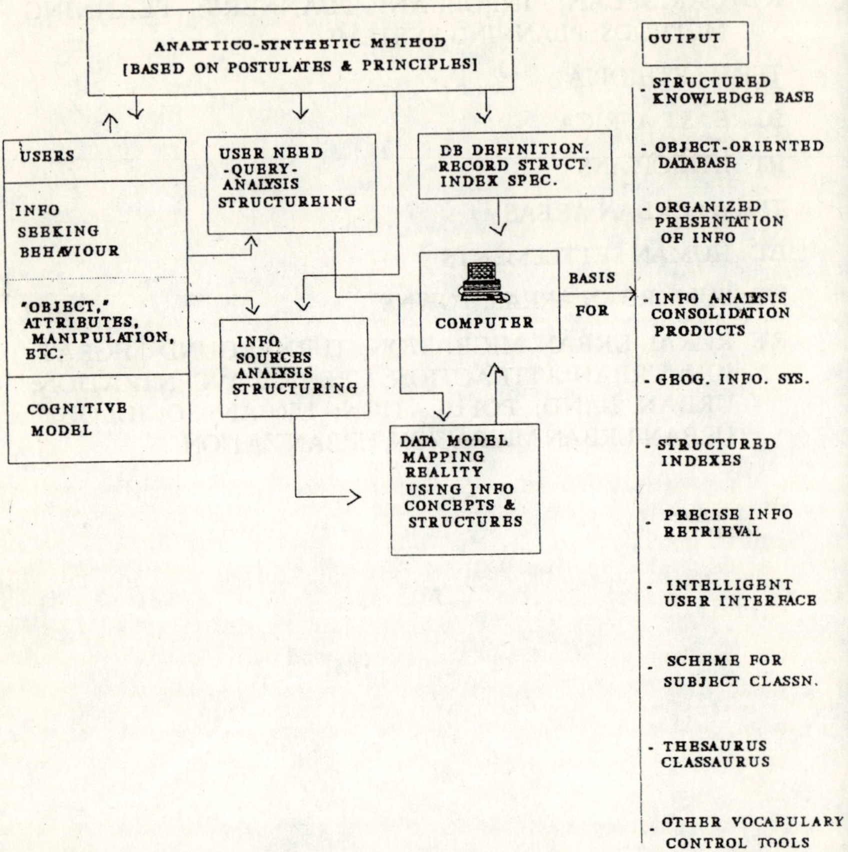
ANALYTICO-SYNTHETIC METHOD
[BASED ON POSTULATES & PRINCIPLES]
USERS
INFO SEEKING BEHAVIOUR
"OBJECT," ATTRIBUTES, MANIPULATION, ETC.
COGNITIVE MODEL
USER NEED -QUERY-ANALYSIS STRUCTURING
INFO SOURCES ANALYSIS STRUCTURING
DB DEFINITION. RECORD STRUCT. INDEX SPEC.
COMPUTER
BASIS FOR
DATA MODEL MAPPING REALITY USING INFO CONCEPTS & STRUCTURES
OUTPUT
- STRUCTURED KNOWLEDGE BASE
- OBJECT-ORIENTED DATABASE
- ORGANIZED PRESENTATION OF INFO
- INFO ANALYSIS CONSOLIDATION PRODUCTS
- GEOG. INFO. SYS.
- STRUCTURED INDEXES
- PRECISE INFO RETRIEVAL
- INTELLIGENT USER INTERFACE
- SCHEME FOR SUBJECT CLASSN.
- THESAURUS CLASSAURUS
- OTHER VOCABULARY CONTROL TOOLS

Interlibrary Loan (ILL) Protocol : Progress and Projects

LEIGH SWAIN and PAULA TALLIM

Abstract

The ILL protocol is a communications standard which permits the exchange of ILL messages between bibliographic institutions that use different computers, systems and communication services. Approved as an International Standard in 1991 (ISO 10160/10161), efforts are currently underway to develop and implement protocol-based software products and systems in order to realize the benefits of standardized ILL communications.

The focus of this paper is to provide a general non-technical description of the protocol and outline efforts underway to implement the ILL protocol in an ILL service environment. Projects underway which center on the use of the ILL protocol in an international lending environment will also be described.

In recent years, the number of books and periodicals exchanged through interlibrary loan has increased remarkably as libraries turn to resource sharing to help satisfy the needs of their clientele. The use of computers and telecommunications networks to support ILL services has also seen a marked increase. However, the proliferation of different computer systems and networks has made the automated exchange of ILL messages very complex such that a standard communications protocol to support the exchange and tracking of ILL message was required.

The National Library of Canada recognized the need for such a standard in the early 1980's and began working closely with libraries and technical experts to define a protocol for interlibrary loan (ILL protocol). After years of consultation and review, the ILL protocol was approved in 1991 as an International Standardized (ISO 10161/10161) by the International Organization for Standardization.[1]

The focus of this paper is to provide a general non-technical description of the protocol and outline efforts underway to implement the ILL protocol in an ILL service environment. Projects underway which center on the use of the ILL protocol in an international lending environment will also be described.

The ILL protocol is based on the Open System Interconnection (OSI) Reference Model[2]. Standard developed using this conceptual framework make it possible for computers and networks to operate with each other in a multivendor environment. The ILL protocol is one of several standards developed that will enable effective telecommunications among different computers and systems for library applications. The U.S. Library of Congress has developed an OSI-based protocol for information retrieval, termed Search and Retrieve which was also adopted as an International Standard in 1991 (ISO 10162/10163).[3] Libraries are also using a number of the OSI- based protocols developed for generic applications to support their operations. Examples include the X. 400 standard for message handling systems used to support the ILL services and the File Transfer and Access Management (FTAM) protocol used to transfer large files for the cataloguing function.

The ILL Protocol

By defining a standard for computer communications, the ILL protocol permits the exchange of ILL messages between bibliographic institutions that use different computers, systems and communication services. ILL systems that incorporate the ILL protocol can communicate with each other in a standard messaging format even when their ILL systems operate on different computer configurations. As the only common feature of these systems is the protocol module, libraries do not have to sacrifice local processing and operational requirements in order to exchange information.

The ILL protocol formally standardizes four aspects of ILL communications :

1. The number and type of messages exchanged in an ILL transaction.
2. The data elements contained within these messages.
3. The correct sequence for the communication of protocol messages.
4. The transfer syntax.[4]

The use of the ILL protocol enables an operator to record in a consistent and structured manner the various stages of an ILL transaction, for example, recording the fact that an item has been requested, received and then returned. The protocol does not introduce new processes but merely formalizes activities that were previously handled by manual means.

How the ILL Protocol Works

The activities supported by the ILL protocol are represented in the protocol as "services". These services represent actions that normally take place in ILL transactions. For example, the protocol services provided for the requesting library include: request to borrow (ILL-REQUEST), indications of receipt and return of the borrowed item (RECEIVED, RETURNED), request for renewal (RENEW), notification that the item is lost (LOST), cancellation of the request (CANCEL), etc. These activities are recorded in the local ILL system instead rather than by a manual process. Therefore, each step of the ILL request is stored in a computerised database.

An ILL request and all subsequent activities relating to it constitute an ILL transaction. Within a transaction each processing stage is identified by a transaction state. For example, when a request is sent, the state of the transaction for the requesting library is PENDING, when the request is received by the potential lending library the state of the transaction for that library is IN-PROCESS.

Standardization

The group within the International Organization for Standardization (ISO) responsible for the ILL protocol is ISO Technical Committee 46, Subcommittee 4, Working Group 4 (TC46/C4/WG4) which has overall responsibility for standards relating to the format and structure of bibliographic information interchanged in machine-readable format. The international standardization of the protocol was a lengthy process requiring consensus from a wide range of organizations representing numerous national standard bodies and interest groups. Additions and enhancements were added to the ILL protocol to meet numerous national lending requirements and service environments. The ILL protocol has evolved around one which is very flexible, rich in features and internationally applicable.

Protocol Support Activities

Libraries and vendors in both North America and Europe are proceeding with the development and implementation of systems that support the ILL protocol. While a great deal of effort was required to develop and standardize the ILL protocol further, organization and effort is underway to implement and use the protocol within the international library environment.

A variety of programs have been put in place to facilitate and coordinate the use of the protocol. These range from technical activities such as conformance testing to planning activities such as identifying resource sharing partners.

The real benefits of the ILL protocol will not materialize until protocol-based software products and systems are widely available and used. Libraries, however, are hesitant to spend scarce resources on unfamiliar technology. Similarly, software developers are hesitant to develop products for an uncertain market. The National Library of Canada, which carried out much of the work to develop and standardize the ILL protocol is actively engaged in a number of parallel support activities. In 1987, the ILL Protocol Implementation Program was launched to encourage software developers and the bibliographic community to adopt the protocol and incorporate it into ILL systems.[5]

The installation and use of these systems in libraries will significantly contribute to realizing the benefits of protocol-based messaging and improving access to library resources. As well, the National Library has developed a protocol-based ILL system for its own use. A preliminary version has been in operation since April 1987 and was recently upgraded to conform to the ISO version of the protocol. Canadian efforts to ensure the availability of products are primarily limited to the Canadian library environment. Other countries or national groups will have to determine the appropriate strategies for encouraging the implementation of the ILL protocol within their own countries.

Bridging Mechanisms

As with the introduction of any new standard or technology, it will be several years before the protocol is widely used and the critical mass of user libraries established to create a standardized protocol messaging environment. While some libraries will immediately acquire new ILL protocol systems, other libraries will choose to use their computers to partially automated ILL and/or merely to format messages off-line according to the format required by recipient libraries. This mixed environment can result in serious barriers to efficient ILL communications.

A number of bridging mechanisms based on the protocol were developed to allow ILL communications between the National Library of Canada and non-protocol based systems during the transition period before ILL protocol is widely used.

For example, a set of standard electronic mail messages (scripts) have been mounted on the public electronic mail system (ENVOY 100) used by many Canadian libraries. These scripts structure the ILL data to conform to the ILL protocol and allow libraries that do not have ILL protocol-based systems to communicate with libraries that do use such systems. Transparent to the user, the scripts also add the required encoding syntax to the message thus permitting libraries to send messages to ILL protocol systems in a machine processable format.[6]

In addition, the ILL systems developed through the ILL Protocol Implementation program are required to generate, along with the messages in machine-processable format, "eye-readable" messages which can be interpreted and processed by non-protocol sites.

Protocol Testing

An essential component in the successful promotion and adoption of the ILL protocol is protocol conformance testing. Each ILL system developed in Canada will be tested for conformance to the ILL protocol and its ability to interwork with other ILL protocol-based systems before it is released into the marketplace.

Conformance testing is the systematic test of a product's conformance to a particular OSI protocol and is essential in order to increase the probability that different implementations of the same protocol are able to interwork. There are two major areas of conformance testing activities : the development of test suites, and the testing of implementations.

A test suite is a collection of test cases or message exchanges covering nearly all possible implementations of a protocol. It is used with a conformance test system to evaluate how accurately an implementation of a protocol meets the requirements of that protocol.

The National Library of Canada has developed a test suite for the ILL protocol which will be submitted to ISO for standardization. The test suite and an ILL test system developed by the National Library is being used to test the implementations of the ISO ILL protocol developed by the contractors in the ILL Protocol Implementation Program. The National Library plans to make its test software available to the international bibliographic community to aid other institutions in developing their own test centres.[7]

Conformance testing, no matter how rigorous, does not provide fail-safe assurance that a given protocol implementation will interwork with other implementations, despite their both having successfully undergone testing. Conformance testing primarily determines the conformance of an implementation to a standard. Another type of testing - interoperability testing - determines the ability of implementations to interwork in an operational environment. Interoperability testing defines a set of tests which are executed between two or more implementations of the same protocol thereby ensuring that real systems interworking or interoperability will be attained in operational use.

The National Library is currently evaluating, in conjunction with protocol implementors, the requirements of interoperability testing and will conduct interoperability tests of the implementors' ILL products. With systems undergoing both conformance and interoperability testing, libraries can be confident that these systems will in fact be able to communicate and exchange messages successfully.

International ILL Protocol Activities

The ILL protocol has generated considerable support and interest in North America and Europe and is currently the focus of a number of projects.

The Interlibrary Loan Access Demonstration (ILLAD) Project

The Universal Dataflow and Telecommunications (UDT) Core Programme completed in May 1989, a study which indicated the feasibility of a joint pilot project between the National Library of

Canada and the British Library Document Supply Centre (BLDSC) to examine the use of the ILL protocol for the international exchange of ILL messages. The planning phase of a pilot project is now underway, with the U.S. Library of Congress added as a participant.

Project ION

A similar project involving the London and South Eastern Library Region in the United Kingdom (LASER), Pica Centrum voor bibliotheek automatisering in The Netherlands (Pica) and Minister de l'Education Nationale, Direction de la Programmation et du Development Universitaire, Sous-Direction Des Bibliotheques (SBD/SUNIST) in France has reached the implementation phase. Termed the "Project ION-the OSI pilot/demonstration project between library services in Europe for interlending services.", this three year project was initiated in early 1990 and is co-financed by the participants and the Commission of the European Communities (DG XII B).

The Project is being carried out in three phases, a specification phase to map out technical and service requirements, an implementation phase to establish operational protocol-based system in each of the three countries and the final phase which involves the use and evaluation of the system by forty-six libraries in the United Kingdom, The Netherlands and France. Phase 1 was completed in October 1990, implementation is well underway and Phase 3 has begun in the 4th quarter 1992.

The major objectives of the project are : (1) achieve interconnection between the three computerized library networks in each country in order to support and develop international interlending and messaging services, (2) improve the efficiency of international interlending services and (3) demonstrate the capabilities of OSI communication protocols in a message-oriented environment.

The operational systems being developed as part of this project involve the use of OSI-based protocols other than ILL LASER and Pica are using the Search and Retrieve protocol standard to support the search of the union catalogues to determine item locations, and the X.400 message handling standard to support ILL messaging.

International Forum on Open Bibliographic Systems

This growing international interest in the ILL protocol and the need to examine implementation issues pertinent to its use in an international context resulted in the creation of the International Forum on Open Bibliographic Systems (IFOBS). The group, composed of bibliographic institutions from Canada, the U.S. Great Britain and Europe, are examining a number of issues relating to the use of protocols for international bibliographic communication. A primary focus of IFOBS continues to be the development of draft International Standardized Profiles (ISPs) for bibliographic protocol standards, As protocols, by their nature, include a number of options, a profile specifies the options to be implemented from within a standard or group of standards. The establishment of an ISP for bibliographic protocols helps to insure that implementations conforming to the ISP support the same functions and can interwork.

As part of their ISP development effort, IFOBS has been collaborating with the European Workshop on Open Systems Expert Group on Libraries (EWOS/EGLIB). This group has been asked by the commission of European Communities (CEC) to develop European profiles for ILL and SR.

Conclusion

Following the standardization of the ISO ILL protocol in 1991, work is continuing to develop protocol-based ILL systems and to establish operational services within Canada and throughout the international library community.

However, future initiatives must also include a coordinated effort by libraries to develop local, regional and national interlending strategies and policies that exploit the potential of the ILL protocol to promote the sharing of resources and effective interlibrary loan services.

REFERENCES

1. Interlibrary Loan (ILL) Protocol ISO 10160/10161

ISO 10160: 1990 Information and Documentation - Open Systems Interconnection (OSI) - Interlibrary Loan Application Service Definition.

ISO 10161: 1990 Information and Documentation - Open Systems Interconnection (OSI) - Interlibrary Loan - Application Protocol Specification.

2. ISO 7498 Information Processing Systems-Open Systems Interconnection— Basic Reference Model.

3. Search and Retrieve (SR) Protocol ISO 10162/10163

ISO 10162: 1990 Information and Documentation - Open Systems Interconnection (OSI) - Search and Retrieve Application Service Definition.

ISO 10163: 1990 Information and Documentation - Open Systems Interconnection - Search and Retrieve Application Protocol Specification.

4. Turner, Fay The Interlibrary Loan Protocol: An OSI Solution to ILL Messaging. *Library Hi Tech* Issue 32 - (1990, No. 4) pp.73-82.

5. Turner, Fay. "Interlibrary Loan Protocol Implementation Issues. *Interlending and Document Supply*, vol 17 (3). 1989. pp. 77-83.

6. "ILL Generic Script Developed by the National Library." *National Library News*, Vol 21. June 1989. p.7.

7. Arbez, Giibert and Swain, Leigh. "OSI Conformance for Bibliographic Applications" *Library Hi Tech* Issue 32 (1990, No. 4) pp. 119-136.

8. IFLA International Office For UDT. *ILL Demonstration Project Feasibility Study Report*. Ottawa, National Library of Canada. 1989.

9. "OSI Pilot/ Demonstration project between library networks in Europe for interlending services." *Outlook on Research Libraries*. April 1990. pp. 8-9.

10. Plaister, Jean. "Project ION (OSI Pilot/Demonstration Project between Library Networks in Europe for Interlending Services)." *Libri*. Vol 41. No. 4 1991.pp. 289-305.

11. "Report on IFOBS Meeting Held September 23-34, 1991." *UDT Newsletter*. No. 17. Fall/Winter 1991. p. 2.

Role of National Library as a Bibliographic Centre in a Multi-lingual Situation : The Indian Context

KALPANA DASGUPTA

Introduction

The multi-lingual tradition in India is reflected in the diversity of its publishing and also has its imprint on the library system. The Library services in India can be called a multi-faceted activity which cannot be kept within the water-tight-compartment of the four types of library systems as are generally known. Therefore, the role of the National Library as a bibliographic centre has to deal with diversified facets. However, the major activities of the National Library naturally have to be within the spectrum of functions which are expected of a National Library; and India's National Library, therefore, cannot be an exception.

Background of the Present National Library

The National Library in India has a very rich heritage and the collection, historically, goes back to the Calcutta Public Library which was established in 1836. The same collection was then merged with the then Imperial Library and formally the Imperial Library was opened to the public in 1903. This Library became the National Library by an Act of Parliament in 1948. Though the Imperial Library had a good and rich segment of Indian language material, the colonial powers did not consider it right to make the Imperial Library a depository under the Press & Registration Act of 1867. The biggest lacunae of the Imperial Library collection regarding Indian language material started at that juncture. Therefore, the India Office Library & Records in the British Library has a much better collection of that period than the National Library.

Acquisition Policy for Collection Development

There have been many important committees to review the working of the National Library which laid down many important recommendations to activate the services of the Library. Some of the main recommendations of the Reviewing Committee (1969) in connection with the development of the collection on the subject 'India' are as follows :

1. Acquisition and conservation of all significant printed materials produced in the country to the exclusion of ephemera ;
2. Collection of printed material concerning the country wherever it is published and also acquisition of a photographic record of such material that is not available within the country ;
3. Acquisition and conservation of manuscripts of national importance ;
4. Planned acquisition of foreign materials required by the country.

One of the main recommendations of a more recent High Powered committee on National Policy on Library and Information System of 1986 reads as follows :

> "To collect and preserve the production of the nation in print and non-print form and all that is printed about the nation".

Enactment of the Delivery of Books and Newspapers (Public Libraries) Act, 1954

The Delivery of books Act which was passed in 1954 and later amended in 1956 has acted as the first milestone towards the aquisition of Indian language material in a systematic manner in independent India. The provisions of the said Act are as follows :

> *Delivery of Books to Public Libraries*—(1) Subject to any rules that may be made under this Act, but without prejudice to the provisions contained in Section 9 of the Press and Registration of Books Act, 1867 (XXV of 1867), the publisher of every book published in the territories to which this Act extends after the commencement of this Act shall, notwithstanding any agreement to the contrary, deliver at his own expense a copy of the book to the National Library at Calcutta and one such copy to each of the other three public libraries within thirty days from the date of its publications.

Delivery of newspapers to Public Libraries—Subject to any rules that may be made under this Act, but without prejudice to the provisions contained in the Press and Registration of Books Act, 1867, the publishers of every newspapers, published in the territories to which this Act extends, shall deliver at his own expense one copy of each issue of such newspaper as soon as it is published to each such public library as may be notified in this behalf by the Central Government in the Official Gazette.

Collection through Cultural Exchange Programme

The National Library also acts as the implementing agency under the Cultural Exchange Programmes of the Govt. of India and is, at present, maintaining exchange relationship with 205 institutions in 81 countries. These exchange programmes are of the great benefit for building the library collections by acquiring materials on Indology, translations of India classics, research reports etc. on South-Asia in general and India in particular from the signatory countries. Generally such publications cannot be acquired through the usual channels of book trade. To give some examples the Library has received very large percentage of books on India from exchange partners in France, Peoples Republic of China, Germany etc. During the year 1990-91, almost 61% of the receipts from France were on India.

The National Library also acquires through purchase material on India from different sources. In recent times the Library has procured full sets of xerox copies of these on India and other South-Asian countries from the UMI.

With such collection which can be used as a major source of information on 'India' as a subject, the National Library can play the role of the major Bibliographic Centre in the multi-lingual situation much more effectively.

Library of Microforms

The Reviewing Committee in its report recommended that the National Library's stock should be surveyed and lacunae mapped out. Since a large number of titles may not be available in the printed hard copy any more, efforts have to be made to identify them in libraries in India and abroad and acquire microfilm copies of the same. Therefore, the National Library has proposed to set up a Microfilm Library and acquire microfilm of materials from different libraries, specially from the former colonial powers.

Role of National Library as a Bibliographic Centre

The main functions of the National Library as a Bibliographic Centre have also been laid down in the recommendations of the reviewing Committee (1969) and the High powered Committee on National Policy on Library and Information System of 1986. According to these recommendations, the National Library is expected to act as follows :

1. Rendering of Bibliographical and documentation services on retrospective material, both general and specialised ;
2. Acting as a referal centre purveying full and accurate knowledge of all sources of bibliographic information and participation in international bibliographical activities ;
3. Provision of photo-copying and reprographic service ;
4. Acting as the centre for international book exchange and international loan ;
5. To render to the nation and to the world bibliographical and other services to meet the requirements of different user groups ;
6. To interface between the national systems and international systems wherever feasible ; and
7. To play a role of leadership in the country in the task of expanding and improving the library and information services.

The functions of a National Bibliographic Centre was discussed in detail at a National Seminar on Bibliographic Control in India held in the National Library in 1985. The main functions of the National Bibliographic Centre in the Indian context which emerged during the discussion are :

(*i*) To prepare current national bibliography and to develop automated system for publication of the Indian National Bibliography ;

(*ii*) To prepare retrospective bibliography ;

(*iii*) To prepare a national union catalogue of major libraries ;

(*iv*) To prepare general bibliographies and a special bibliographies ;

(*v*) To promote library cooperation for bibliographic activities ;

(*vi*) To render bibliographic information service ;

(*vii*) To undertake and sponsor bibliographic research ;

(*viii*) To adopt and promote adoption of international bibliographic standards ;

(*ix*) To exchange bibliographic records with other countries by agreements.

(*x*) To participate in international bibliographic projects and systems ;

(*xi*) To coordinate bibliographic activities of different institutions, organisations and individuals ;

(*xii*) To function as a central bibliographic referal centre ;

(*xiii*) To undertake user education programmes ; and

(*xiv*) To undertake any other activity conductive to the promotion of bibliographical services in the country.

Present Bibliographic Services

I. *Indian National Bibliography*

The Delivery of Books Act 1954 triggered off the possibility of the compilation of the Indian National Bibliography with the books supplied under the said act. Following the enforcement of the Delivery of Books Act, the publication of Indian National Bibliography started in 1958. It was started in the National Library by the staff of the Central Reference Library within the National Library campus. The Librarian of the National Library was the Chief Editor. But from 1970 the Central Reference Library has been publishing it independently on the basis of the deposits in the National Library under the D.B. Act. The entries in this bibliography give full bibliographical details in respect of the publications included in the Indian National Bibliography such as :

Classification number, feature headings, author, title, place of publication, publisher, year of publication, collation, size of the book, series, annotations wherever necessary. ISBN/ISSN, nature of binding, price, language-symbol and Colon Classification number.

The Indian National Bibliography was first published as a quarterly with annual comulations from 1958 to 1963 and its periodicity was changed to monthly in 1964 and continued upto 1977. 1978, 1979 volumes have been published as annuals due to unavoidable circumstances. It has been decided to publish 1980-81 & 1982-83 in two volumes of four parts. Since 1984, January the periodicity of this publication has been received to monthly.

Now, as per recent govt. decisions, the National Library will be made directly responsible again for the publication of Indian National Bibliography. The strength and the weakness of the coverage of Indian National Library is, therefore, the reflection of the National Library operation of the Delivery of Books Act.

At present, the Indian National Bibliography is in Romanised script with diacritics. The National Library used the Hunterian diacritics for transliteration. It was a major step towards standardisation of Indian language scripts for bibliographic purpose. With the advent of computers in library services, the National Library in collaboration with various institutions and libraries of India and with the representatives of Library of congress and the British Library developed a standardised list of diacritics for transliteration in an automated system.

India in its recent times has seen a very important development for automation of language scripts. This is known as 'GIST' (graphic and Indian Script Terminal) technology.

Since the correspondence between the Indian script alphabet is properly established in the GIST methodology, it is possible to transliterate automatically between the scripts. By transliteration we imply character by character transformation between the scripts. In this process the pronunciation of the original language is retained, although the script has changed. GIST allows any script to be transliterated to the Roman script with diacritic marks.

One of the important applications of transliteration indeed lies in the Library information systems. It is now possible for all the information about books to be entered accurately in the original script itself. This very information can be subsequently viewed in the script of one's choice. This will allow the foreign users to browse through the information in the Roman script, as has been the practice in most of the libraries. Through this transliteration facility, it is possible to publish bibliographies in multiple scripts, almost automatically.

Therefore, the future of Indian national Bibliography and any bibliographic services in India lies in a system which can produce bibliographic service in all the different scripts. In a multi-lingual situation, this plays a very important role because publishing in India is not restricted to the small group of large publishers. India's publishing is just as diverse as its language situation. There are giant publishers and there are small publishers, individual and family publishers etc. The Indian National Bibliography will mean very differently to small publishers if it can be brought out in the original languages. This is what the national bibliography in a multi-lingual situation should be. The National Library can no longer afford to remain in an ivory tower and produce romanised transliterated national bibliography for the intellectual research scholars alone. But it has to reach all corners of the country and should be used by all levels of users.

II. *General and Retrospective bibliographic services*

The main bibliographic services in the National Library are rendered through two specific divisions, set up for this purpose i.e. Bibliography (Special) and Bibliography (General) Divisions. The Bibliography (Special) Division is responsible for the publication of retrospective bibliography and indexing of important periodicals. The reviewing Committee of 1969 had recommended the publication of Bibliography on Indology series. The first volume of the series of bibliography on Indology is on Indian Anthropology, the second volume is on Indian Botany and the third volume has been published under the title "A Bibliography of Indology : Vol. III, Bengali Language and Literature. Under the same project, the said Division has taken up a separate project to bring out Modern Indian History which comprises three parts. Indexing of prestigeous journal 'Bengal Past and

Present' and 'Modern Review' have also been done by this Division. Indexing of the popular Bengali periodical, 'Pravasi' was also taken up earlier and this work has been done for the years 1900 to 1936.

Bibliography (General) Division is responsible for the preparation of select bibliographies and reading lists on different subjects on specific requests from research scholars, institutions, universities, government departments. Though these lists are selective, the Division makes all out efforts to include standard and basic documents from the National Library records and other secondary sources. This Division extends all possible help to the researchers in finding materials and also in compiling bibliographies.

The Division also caters to international commitments for bibliographical information. The Division has to compile and edit list of translations and list of bibliographies published in India. These materials are supplied to UNESCO for inclusion in the *Index Translationum* and *Bibliographical Services throughout the world* respectively.

This Division has now undertaken the responsibility of compilation of an important bibliography i.e. 'Tagore Bibliography'. This is an annotated and historical bibliography in four volumes. The volumes will be as follows:

Vol. I — Books by Tagore published during his lifetime-editionwise (Upto 1941)

Part-I - (Upto 1912)

Part-II - (1912 to 1941)

Vol. II (Part-I)

Tagore's books published posthumously till May, 1986 (Part-II)

Occasional Papers

addresses, monographs, pamphlets (English & Bengali)

Vol. III

Tagore in languages other than Bengali

(i) Original works of Tagore in languages other than Bengali.

(ii) Works translated by Tagore.

(iii) Translations of Tagore's works in languages other than Bengali by others.

Vol. IV

Books on Tagore

Part-I - Bengali

Part-II - Indian languages

(a) Other Asian languages.

(b) Languages of the rest of the world.

Such bibliographical projects emphasize the importance of the multi-lingual aspects of literary works. This historical bibliography of special nature will highlight through translations of the works, the gaps in such activity in different languages and the importance of translations in a multi-lingual situation. It will also help as a guide to future activities in translations so that there are no duplication of efforts.

Bibliographic Activities of the Indian Languages

The National Library is the depository of all materials published in India and on India in different foreign languages. Under these circumstances, the bibliographical services rendered by the National Library is very diverse. Starting from the supply of simple list of publications on given topics, statistical statements, bibliographies of retrospective materials, bibliographies of books translated from one Indian language to another Indian language or those of foreign languages into Indian languages are also part of the bibliographical services rendered by different divisions of the National Library. Bibliographic entries usually comprise author, title, subject, place of publication, publisher, year of publication, price and the annotated note etc., as the requirement necessitates. The bibliography on celebrities of India is a very major feature of bibliographical service, e.g. bibliographies by and on great personalities like Tagore, Nehru, C.V. Raman and litterateurs of international repute. Since the Library also functions very much as a public library in the Indian context, exhibitions are also part of awareness service through visuals and preparation of bibliographies on such topics are also part of the major activities of the National Library. Important exhibitions have been held in connection with life and works of famous statesmen and litterateurs as well as on important subjects in the Indian context.

Retrospective bibliographies with trend surveys of research will fulfil the major need of a National Bibliographic Centre which will act as a pointer towards future research. It will help in more systematic development of research in Indian languages and on subjects pertaining to India. Collaborative efforts with other national institutions such as the Sahitya Akademi, Indian Council of Social Science Research, Indian National Scientific Documentation Centre (INSDOC) etc. will strengthen the role of the National Library as an institution which will help in setting the future trend of research on India and not act only as a depository and repository of Indian reading materials.

Union Catalogue of Indian Resources

To actually act as the National Bibliographic Centre of India, it is necessary to be aware of two major areas i.e. what is available where and what is being published. For this purpose, the National Library has proposed two new schemes for fructifying these activities:— The compilation of National Union catalogue for books and setting up of a Monitoring Cell for National Book Production Statistics.

1. *National Union Catalogue*

An exhaustive National Union Catalogue will help in bringing about bibliographic control of reading materials available in different parts of India which is a long standing need for research. A comprehensive National Union Catalogue will also help in resource sharing and acquisition programme by (a) avoiding duplication of purchases (b) filling the lacunae on a national basis.

In compiling a Union Catalogue of Indian resource a number of problems immediately meet the eye. To start with the smaller, and sometimes not-so-small libraries with limited resources, have woefully imperfect card-indices or catalogues, which need modern revision by staff specially deputed to do this work in particular, which should include inspection on the shelf of all titles. Without such complete information at the local level, it is hardly possible to think in national terms.

In the Indian condition, the National Bibliographic agency will have to work in conjunction with the official agencies of National status and non-official agencies to act as the bibliographic centre and the major referral centre for Indian material. To clarify this point, it may be mentioned that the Union Catalogues of serials in the Social sciences and the scientific subjects are being compiled by the National Social Science Documentation Centre and Indian National Scientific Documentation centre respectively. Documentation activities for manuscripts are being taken up by the Indira Gandhi National Centre for the Arts. Proper linkages with all such agencies will have to be maintained to act as a National Bibliographic Centre.

2. *Monitoring Cell for National Book Production statistics*

One of the major problems of the National Library in particular and Indian libraries in general is that there is little idea about how many books are produced in India every year. It is widely acknowledged that the deliveries made under the Delivery of Books Act to the National Library and to the other recipient libraries fall much short of the number of books produced in India. But there is no means of discovering the dimension of this gap to form any accurate idea of the actual statistics.

The Library through resource persons and institutions in the different Indian states will collect reliable and representative statistics of books than is now available for the production of Indian National Bibliography. The Library will collate and compare the figure thus obtained with the Deliveries of books Act and supply the larger figures if reliable, to international and national agencies. This will also help in activising the Delivery of Books Act also.

Conclusion

The present Indian bibliographic scene is very scattered and is also plagued with the problem of institutions working in isolation. Each institution caters to its users in its own way and the scholars, therefore, are very confused about the bibliographic services rendered by different institutions. The scholars will very much appreciate if any central agency could render bibliographic service and information service both as a central nodal point or a referral centre for bibliography itself. The National Library must develop linkages with the other recipient libraries as well as with the major research institutions, national documentation centres and the academic libraries with large collections through the various networking systems which are being envisaged now. Within such linkages, the National Library of India can operate as a National Bibliographic Centre. The country as a whole will have to be divided into five zones and major regional/zonal nodal points will have to be set up for sch linkages.

The main thrust of bibliographic services in India should be the merger of concept of union catalogue and bibliographies. Retrospective bibliographic service should be able to also give the necessary information regarding the availability of the material. The preparation of union catalogue on a nation-wide basis is a large and continuous venture, but if bibliographic services which will be rendered through the various proposed and upcoming network systems in India, can prepare the databases with the information regarding availability of material involved, then the scholars in India will not have to look out for material which may be available within their own state or within their own zone and thereby will not have to undertake long distance journeys to reach the necessary information.

It is true that the National Library alone cannot play the role of the National Bibliographic Centre very effectively at present but with the modern technological developments, it is expected that India with all its diversities will still become an unified whole in the context of bibliographic services.

REFERENCES

1. Report of the Reviewing Committee on the National Library, Calcutta. - July 14, 1969.
2. Bibliographical Control in India: a seminar, 1985/ed.: Kalpana Dasguta. - 1988. - (National Library Conferences; No.2).
3. National policy on Library and Information system — a presentation/ Committee on National Policy on Library and information system, Department of Culture, Ministry of Human Resources Development, Government of India, New Delhi.-1986.

National Bibliography as National Memory : Is Popular Culture Forgotten ?

ROBERT P. HOLLEY

This presentation continues the theme, "National Bibliography as National Memory," of the Section on Bibliography's presentation at the 1991 Moscow IFLA Annual Conference. Marcelle Beaudiquez gave the keynote speech with responses from Alexandr A. Dzhigo, Russia; Barbara Bell. USA; and Zahia Fellah, Algeria. They all stressed the importance of national bibliography as part of the nation's cultural memory. While recognizing that the documents themselves are more significant than their bibliographic surrogates, all agreed that an accurate recording of publications is first step toward preserving intellectual culture. I came away from the program with the idea that a comprehensive national bibliography of all publications was the desired goal.

In thinking over this analysis of bibliographic remembering and forgetting, it struck me that this overriding principle of including every possible "memory" may not be true for all publications. Mr. Dzhigo for example speaks of the necessity for selectivity; but his criteria are more concerned with the format and availability of the documents. In fact, he stresses under the principle of universality the criterion of "value: inclusion of all documents of any social and cultural importance, regardless [of] the number of copies, type printing."[1] The speakers acknowledged that certain publications were difficult to record in national bibliographies because they are hard to obtain. Much "grey literature" often has intentional limited distribution; and its collection requires systematic effort, often at great expense of time and sometimes money. Other materials are ephemeral in nature without any desire by authors obtain copyright. In this class, I would place newsletters, handbills, brochures, and advertising matter. Inexpensive printing and photocopying has increased their number.

The type of material interested me the most was, however, those publications connected with "popular culture." My working hypothesis was that the published materials most likely to be seen by today's "common man," at least in the developed countries, would not be under effective bibliographic control. A judgment on their intrinsic worth or on their content would lessen their chances of appearing in the national system of bibliographic control. Thus, the scholarly journal with extremely limited circulation the volume of esoteric poems with a minuscule press run, and the dissertation to be read perhaps by only a handful of scholars would be more likely to be under bibliographic control than the inexpensive consumer-oriented publications seen by a high percentage of the country's population. Following this thought the scholar in the year 1992 with access to the few surviving national bibliographies of the the 20th century would have only a limited perspective on today's popular culture.

To test this hypothesis. I selected three classes of material: newspapers, mass market publications and erotic materials. For this paper. I considered only publications readily available in my own country, the United States. I would be interested to learn the results of similar surveys in other parts of the world. Since the United States does not have an official national bibliography as defined by the ICND. I used the OCLC database the largest bibliographic database available in the United States for my research. OCLC includes all records produced in machine readable form by the Library of Congress as well as millions of records contributed by other sources. In fact, as of 4 January 1992, the OCLC database contained 24,121,789 records and 423,783,047 locations for cataloged items.[2] It may not include a certain small number of records that appear in the *National Union Catalog*, but the OCLC database also has the advantage of giving the number of report in libraries. The finding in this paper came from my OCLC database searching during the period, 30 March to 3 April 1992.

NEWSPAPERS

I begin with a brief consideration of the success story in the recording of popular culture materials. Newspapers, seen by almost everyone on a daily basis for several centuries, have recently received increased attention in the United States and elsewhere. The United States Newspaper Program (USNP), funded by grants from the National Endowment for the Humanities (NEH), is a systematic effort to record and to preserve as many as possible of the estimated 300,000 newspaper titles published in the United States, while many lesser known newspapers, many with brief runs, are lost forever the USNP will go a long way toward recording and saving local news and local life as recorded in multiple sources each day.[3]

MASS MARKET PUBLICATIONS

The United States has a sophisticated distribution network for mass market publications. While book stores and magazine vendors also carry these publications. I chose the most popular American distribution point—the supermarket--for my study. Supermarket owners have discovered that many Americans, while waiting in line to pay for their purchases will make impulsive purchase of materials that are located at the check-out counters. Since these publications must appeal to a wide spectrum of American readers they represent popular culture in the broadest sense of the term. The selection normally includes both periodicals and popularly oriented inexpensive books. Many of the periodicals cover sensational topics and are not normally found in American libraries because they are of questionable taste and dubious reputation as well as being factually inaccurate. Nonetheless, they represent a wide-spread American cultural phenomenon.

On 29 March 1992, I visited a supermarket near my home. This Kroger store is located in Royal Oak, a suburb of Detroit, Michigan. Its customers are typical for a racially-mixed, middle-class American suburb. The store has 12 check out lanes, each with space for mass market publications. I recorded all the publications that I could easily find that day--55 periodicals and 16 books. I also included two special displays of books, both childern's literature, that appeared in the store. Each display included a series of titles under a unifying heading: *Young Indiana Jones and [eight separate tiles]* and *Walt Disney Fun-To-Read Library* with 6 titles available in a series of at least 12. Besides these publications, the supermarket had a separate section for books and magazines that more closely approximated the selection that would be found in a drug store, a magazine shop or a mass market bookstore. I did not attempt to list materials in this section because they were more likely to be held by libraries and under effective bibliographic control.

Searching the titles in the OCLC database partially confirmed my hypothesis for books but mostly disproved it for periodicals. Of the 16 books at the check-out counter, only two (12.5%) had bibliographic records in the OCLC database. In both cases the national cataloging agency the Library of Congress had not provided the cataloging; but they were cataloged instead by other libraries. Each book (*Count Your Calories* and *Eerie Tales of the Old West*) had two reporting libraries. The first series of children's books, *Young Indiana Jones and [eight separate titles]*, was under effective bibliographic control because the publisher participated in the Library of Congress Cataloging in Publication program. The cataloging record appeared in the publication and in the OCLC database with between 78 and 138 reporting libraries for each title. The situation for the *Walt Disney Fun-To-Read library* was more complicated. The record appears in the OCLC database as a set with four reporting libraries, but it was not cataloged by the Library of Congress. The individual titles in the set however do not have own bibliographic records.

The periodical titles included many mainstream publications such as *Elle, Good Housekeeping. McCalls,* and *Reader's Digest* with a large number of reporting libraries. At the other extreme, 10 periodicals (18.2%) had no record in the OCLC database -- *Archie Annual Digest Magazine. Classic Pillsbury Cookbooks, Easy-to-Do Crosswords Favorite Brand Name Recipes, Mystery Word Games TV Word Games, Your Body Your health,* and four publications in the specialized series of periodicals published by *Woman's Day Magazine*. To my surprise, however, many of the very popular periodicals were under bibliographic control because they had been recorded by the National Serial Data Program (NSDP) at the Library of Congress because publishers often wish to have an ISSN for their publications for reasons other than bibliographic control. At the same time that the NSDP assigns this number, it also provides a bibliographic record. I noted that seven such titles (12.7%) — *Archie's Story & Games Best of TV Guide Crosswords, Betty, Creative Recipes, News Extra Soap Opera Weekly Crocker Star* and *TV Crosswords* — have no other reporting library in the OCLC database besides the NSDP. For the future cultural anthropologist, the citation may be the only surviving reality because the issues themselves do not appear to be systematically collected by any library. Furthermore, "the bibliographic requirements of ISDS are not as full nor as detailed in their specifications as are those of the AACR, since the ISDS network intends to provide a basic bibliographic record which meets the general needs of an international community."[4] These popular culture periodicals have thus received only second-class entries in the national apparatus for bibliographic control.

To test my thesis that materials seen by large numbers of readers would not appear in the national bibliographic apparatus. I attempted to find circulation figures for all periodicals with fewer than 50 reporting libraries. As seen in Appendix A, I was able to find circulation statistics for 14 titles. Circulation ranged from 212.561 per issue for *TV Crosswords* to 3,758,964 per issue for the *National Enquire*. The average circulation for the five periodicals with no bibliographic record was 625,185. For the additional four periodicals with only one reporting library, usually the NSDP, the average circulation per issue was 1,250,586 including *Star* at 3,102,026. Since the NSDP does not collect the actual materials but only provides a brief bibliographic record, this means that no member of the largest library network in the United States is collecting a publication seen by over 3,000,000 readers each issue.

This conclusion does not consider one important variable that could account for the lack of bibliographic records--time. It is possible that these mass market publications do not appear in the national network of bibliographic control because they have been published too recently. I am more inclined to accept this possibility for the books in my sample. Most have 1991 or 1992 publication dates and may come under bibliographic control later. Yet I also have my doubts that this will be the case.

For the serial publications, I recorded any numbering information available on the current issue. For the six periodicals not recorded in the OCLC database, four had some such indication. None seemed to have recently appeared as can be seen from their listing in Appendix A. Two had issue numbers (#60 and #67); two gave volume numbers (Vol. 5 and Vol. 14). While these periodicals seem to have been published for some time, perhaps issues await cataloging somewhere in the United States.

EROTICA

My final class of material brings up the question of intellectual freedom, censorship, and suitability for library collections. Should national bibliography as national memory record for posterity those materials that some would consider the dark side of contemporary culture? Erotica and pornography have existed throughout history, but this genre has experienced explosive growth within the last 30 years. If pornography is an important late 20th century cultural phenomenon, should it not be recorded as part of national bibliography for future researchers?

If my research has any validity, libraries have collectively decided that the answer is no. For this presentation, I focused on two areas: men's magazines and X-rated videotapes. Unlike my research on mass market publications, I used two bibliographies that appeared in library publications. This decision also excluded time as a possible factor in explaining the lack of a bibliographic record since the most recent entry is from 1988.

For men's magazines, I used the bibliography that appeared in "A Brief Guide to Provocative Publications" by Richard Moritz.[5] His selection is especially relevant for my thesis because he states:

> The following is a selective guide to the current from-runners in the field of "nudie" magazines, chosen for their popularity and particularly for their availability at the news stand since they are regular *trade* publications not "porno books....." Trade magazines usually have articles on other topics as well, such as world affairs, fashion, movies literature, even if the main focus is sex.[6]

This inclusion of non-sexual materials, to my mind, gives these publications an important role in recording popular culture, albeit from a specialized perspective. My study on mass market publications showed effective bibliographic control for many popular culture magazines from a traditionally women's perspective. The same is apparently not true for popular culture from a traditionally men's perspective.

Of the 15 magazines fully listed or briefly mentioned in his articles, I could not successfully verify two titles (*Gallery* and *Game*) in the OCLC database because I lacked any information beyond the title, which had an extremely large number of entries in both cases. Only *Playboy* (6.6%) had a large number of reporting libraries. Four additional magazines (26.6%) had multiple reporting libraries that ranged from 4 (*Hustler*) to 37 (*Playgirl*). Five (33.3%) had a record from the National Serials Data Program for the same reasons as given above in the section on mass market publications. Four (26.6%) had no reporting libraries.

The final category that I reviewed is X-rated videotapes. For this type of materials, I used "A Connoisseur's Selection of X-Rated Videotapes for the Library"[7] by Robert H. Rimmer. This list appeared in a recent publication, *Libraries, Erotica, Pornography*, edited by Martha Cornog. Few of the films in the list combine sex and violence; none has child pornography. All can be legally purchased in most parts of the United States. In support of my theses that national bibliography often overlooks what is truly popular in contemporary culture, the article comments that "rentals of adult films at video stores in the 1980s exceeded 50 million rentals annually and hundred of millions of dollars."[8] The list, included as appendix C, gives 61 entries; a few have multiple titles for continuing series. Only 10 (16.4%) are available in the OCLC database in either movie or video format. Even these figures are deceptive. Two titles are considered mainstream movie releases (*Caligula* and *The Harrad Experiment*) and can be found in standard movie guides such as Leonard Maltin's *TV Movies and Video Guide*.[9] Five are documentaries on sexual topics including the anti-pornography study from the Candian Film Board. *Not a Love Story* that had the most reporting libraries 47. The others were *Guide to Making Love* (3 reporting libraries), *Reproduction of Life* (19 reporting libraries), *Secret World of Erotic Art* (2 reporting libraries) and *Shocking Asia* (2 reporting libraries). One video *Cafe Flesh* (2 reporting libraries) though intended for X-rated theatres, was redistributed as a cult film on the alternative cinema circuit because its theme of sex after a nuclear war was considered too negative for the traditional X-rated market. This leaves only two videos to fall solely into the X-rated class; but they are two of the most famous, *Behind the Green Door*, and *Deep Throat*. Each had two reporting libraries in the OCLC database. Perhaps the best know X-rated video *Debbie Does Dallas* does not appear on the list and is also missing from the OCLC database though it has sold an estimated 50,000 copies as the "most popular sex video."[10]

My research clearly shows that the two classes of erotica and pornography studied above are not well reported in national bibliography as represented by the OCLC database. Both are "forgotten" from this perspective. The very fact, however, that I could find lists of both materials shows that bibliography has not completely neglected them. Any future researcher will need to find specialized bibliographies beyond the national bibliography. Finding the materials themselves may pose additional problems. Rimmer does indicate that specialized collections are attempting to include these materials because "the Kinsey Institute at the University of Indiana, which has the largest collection of 'stag films' anywhere, is slowly building a tape library of adult films produced between 1970 and the present."[11]

CONCLUSION

To repeat my point is not so much to debate the intrinsic value of these materials, but the issue of national bibliograhy as national memory. The speakers last year spoke of the non-recording of materials as forgetting. Some of this forgetting is involuntary. The national bibliographic agency does not have the funds to acquire the materials or they are too difficult to locate. This is not true however, for many popular culture materials. They are readily available and inexpensive. I believe that the forgetting is voluntary and is a judgment on their intrinsic worth. I am willing to wager that all the materials in my sample have been copyrighted to protect their monetary value from copyright infringement. They have been received and rejected by the national bibliographic agency, the Library of Congress. Does this mean that we as librarians are in accord with universal Bibliographic Control only so long as we as gate keepers and possibly as censors approve of their content?

I also support the recording and the preservation of popular culture because citations to these materials appear in many other sources. Library users of the future will find references to *The National Enquirer* and to *Hustler* in "respectable" sources found in the national bibliography, but they may have trouble tracking down citations to the materials themselves in the cultural patrimony of the country's national bibliography. Actually finding examples to achieve first hand verification of our culture's reality may be yet more difficult. Do we mean what we say when we speak of the Universal Availability of Publications, or do we mean only acceptable publications?

I would also be interested in seeing this research extended to other formats and other countries. I have not considered comic books,[12] computer programs including games, handicraft materials, publications from local groups, video recordings of television productions, popular music, and other similar formats.

Perhaps it is inevitable that popular culture be bibliographically forgotten because its producers most often seek current economic gain and are not concerned with future preservation of their products. Perhaps some will even contend that it is better that future scholars do not find bibliographic listings in the national bibliography for the "trash" of contemporary culture. I, on the contrary, agree with Marcelle Beaudiquez that "la memoire est un constat du culturel sans judgement de valeur, celui-ci etant apporte par le temps."[13] Let us bibliographically list everything, and let the future decide about its worth. Today's "trash" may be tomorrow's treasure.

REFERENCES

1. Alexander A. Dzhigo, "National Bibliography of the USSR — Cultural Wealth of the Society," *57th IFLA General Conference Booklet 4. Division of Bibliographic Control,* p. 26.
2. *Independent Notes,* Vol 4 No. 2 (February 1992), p. 9.
3. The following provides a bibliography of publications on the U.S. Newspaper Program as reported in *Library Literature* though 1988: Robert P. Holley. "The Preservation Microfilming Aspects of the United States Newspaper program: A Preliminary Study," *Microform Review,* Vol. 19, No. 3 (Summer 1990), p. 130.
4. Mary Sauer, "National Serials Data Program," *Drexel Library Quarterly,* Vol. 11, No. 3 (July 1975), p.48.
5. Richard Moritz, "A Brief Guide to Provocative Publications. "*Serials Review* 9:4 (Winter 1983), pp. 7-10.
6. *Ibid.*, p.7.
7. Reobert H. Rimmer, "A Connoisseur's Selection of X-rated Videotapes for the Library," in *Libraries, Erotica, Pornography* ed. Martha Cornog (Phoenix, AZ: Oryx Press. 1991), pp. 240-249.
8. *Ibid.*, p. 241
9. Leonard Maltin ed.. *Leonard Maltin's TV Movies and Video Guide, 1990 Edition,* (New York: New American Library, 1989) pp. 153-154 & p. 462.
10. *Facts on File World News Digest,* March 16, 1984.
11. Rimmer, p. 242.
12. The following is a recent library publication on comic books: Randall W. Scott, *Comics Librarianship : A Handbook,* (Jefferson. N.C.: Mc Farland, 1990).
13. Marcelle Beaudiquez, "La bibliographie nationale comme temoin d'une memoire nationale, " *57th IFLA General Conference Boolet 4, Division of Bibliographic Control (14- BIVL-1-F)*, p. 21. (Memory is an affidavit of the cultural without value judgment, which time brings.)

APPENDIX A

PUBLICATIONS FOUND AT CHECK-OUT COUNTERS KROGER SUPERMARKET, ROYAL OAK, MICHIGAN, USA 29 MARCH 1992

Periodicals

Title	Holding Libraries	Volume Numbering	Circulation
Archie Annual Digest Magazine	0	No. 60	1,075,923
Archie's Story & Games	NSD		
Baseball Cards	40		
Best of TV Guide Crosswords	NSD		
Better Homes and Gradens	3,015	Vol. 70 No. 4	
Betty Crocker Creative Recipes	NSD	No. 67	
Classic Pillsbury Cookbooks (or Classic Cookbooks)	0	#134	
Cosmopolitan	60	Vol. 212 No. 4	
Countryside	135	Vol. 3 No. 2	
Easy-to-Do Crosswords	0		
Elle	226	No. 80	
Family Circle	61	Vol.. 105 No. 5	
Favorite brand Name Recipes Magazine	0	Vol. 5 No. 39	300,000
First for Women	31	Vol. 4 No. 13	
Glamour	1,911	Nothing	
Globe	1	Vol. 139 No. 13	1,201,299
Good Housekeeping	141	Vol. 214 No. 4	
Harper's Bazaar	1,602	Vol. 125 No. 3364	
Ladies Home Journal	2,736	Vol. CIX No. 7	
Mademoiselle	2265	Nothing	
McCalls	2,662	Vol. CXIX No. 7	
Mirabella	109	No. 34	
Muscle & Fintness	37	Vol. 53 No. 4	642,349
Mystery Word Games	0	#64 and #67	
National Enquirer	15	Vol. 3 No. 2	3,758,964
National Examiner	2	Vol. 29 No. 13	775,273
New Woman	496	Vol. 22 No. 4	
New Body	4	Vol. 11 No. 5	102,589
News Extra	NSD	Vol. X No. 29	
Newsweek	4,375	Vol. CXIX No. 13	
People	2,778	Vol. 37 No. 12	
prevention	20	Vol. 44 No. 3	
Reader's Digest	3,391	Vol. 140 No. 840	
Red Book	Not Verified	Vol. 178 No. 6	
Self	479	Nothing	
Seventeen	2,704	Nothing	
Shape	167	Vol. II No. 8	
Soap Opera Digest	92	Vol. 17 No. 7	

Periodicals Title	Holding Libraries	Volume Numbering	Circulation
Soap Opera Weekly	NSD	Vol. 3 No. 13	486,457
Star	NSD	Vol. 19 No 93	3,102,026
Success	523	Nothing	
Sun	Not Verfied	Vol. 10 No. 13	
TV Word Games	0	Vol. 14 No. 4	
TV Corssowrds	NSD	Vol. 13 No 16	212,561
TV Guide	637	Vol. 40 No. 13	
US: The Entertainment Magazine	310	Vol. 171	
Victoria	151	Vol. 6 No. 4	
Weekly World News	2	Nothing	
Woman's Day	1,124	Vol. 57 No. 7	
Woman's Day Favorite Home Plans	0		
Woman's Day Special: Kitchens and Baths	0	Nothing	450,000
Woman's Day Super Speial: Home Decorating Ideas	0	Vol. 11 No. 13	
Woman's Day Super Special : Family Celebrations	0	Nothing	500,000
Woman's World	26	Vol. XIII No. 13	1,279,280
Woman's Day Your Body Your Health	0	Nothing	800,000

Books Title	Holding Libraries	Publication Date
Best Baby Names	0	
Count Your Calories	2	
Eerie Tales of the Old West	2	
Get Organized	0	1991
Healthy Houseplant guide	0	
How to Talk to Your Cat by Lynn Allison	0	1991
How to Read Palms by Carlson Wade	0	1991
Miracle of Bible Healing Foods	0	1991
Miracle of Garlic & Vinegar	0	1991
Mystery Word Games	0	
Playtime for Kids	0	1992
Secret Word Games	0	
Social Security Manual	0	1992

Books Title	Holding Libraries	Publication Date
Uncanny Cats	0	1992
Unsolved Mysteries	0	1991
Your 1992 Oriental Horoscope	0	
Walt Disney Fun-To-Read Library:		4
3 Pinocchio's Promise 1986		0
4 Goofy's Big race 1986		0
5 Pooh's New Clothes 1986		0
10 Wise Grandma Duch 1986		0
11 Welcome Back, Snow white 1986		0
12 Scrooge and the Magic Fish 1986		0
Young Indiana Jones and the Circle of Dealth		81
Young Indiana Jones and the Curse of the Ruby Cross		81
Young Indiana Jones and the Ghostly Rider		81
Young Indiana Jones and the Gypsy revenge		78
Young Indiana Jones and the Plantation Treasure		138
Young Indiana Jones and the Princess of Peril		83
Young Indiana Jones and the Secret City		119
Young Indiana Jones and the Tomp of Terror		120

Sources for Periodical Circulation:

Standard Rate & Data Service. *Consumer Magazine and Agri-Media Rates and Data,* April 1992

Gale Directory of Publications and Broadcast Media, 12th ed. Detroit: Gale Researh, 1991.

APPENDIX B

MEN'S MAGAZINES

Title	Holding Libraries	Circulation
Best of Screw	0	
Celbrity Skin	0	
Cheri	NSD	
Gallery	Not Verified	
Game	Not Verified	
Harvey	0	
Hustler	4	1,066,537
Oui	9	
Penthouse	25	1,501,821
Penthouse Forum	13	
Playboy	571	
Playgirl	37	
Velvet	NSD	
Velvet Talks	NSD	
Viva	0	

Source: Richard Moritz, "A Briedf Guide to Provocative Publications", "*Serials Review*, 9:4 (Winter 1983), pp. 7-10.

Sources for Periodical Circulation:

Standard Rate & Data Service. *Consumer Magazine and Agri-Media Rates and Data.* April 1992.

Gale Directory of Publications and Broadcast Media. 12th ed. Detroit: Gale Research, 1991.

APPENDIX C

LIST OF X-RATED VIDEOTAPES

Title	Year	Number of Holding Libraries in the OCLC Database 3 April 1992
Alice in Wonderland	1975	0
American Babylon	1984	0
Angela, the fireworks Woman	1975	0
Autobiography of a Flea	1976	0
Behind the Gree Door	1975	2
Behind the Green Door, Sequel	1986	0
The Big Switch	1985	0
Blond Ambition	1981	0
Cafe Flesh	1982	2
Caligula	1980	13
The Dancers	1982	0
Deep Throat	1972	2
The Devil and Miss Jones	1972	0
Diversions	1979	0
Educating Julie	1984	0
Fallen Angels	1986	0
Famous Smokers	Various	0
Guide to Making Love	1973	3
The Harrad Experiment	1973	1
Hot Desires	1986	0
In all the Right Places	1986	0
In Love	1983	0
Le Sex Shop	1973	0
Love Theatre	1985	0
Love You	1980	0
Males in Motion	1985	0
Miss September	1973	0
Mondo Magic	1985	0
Not a Love Story	1980	47
Nothing to Hide	1982	0
Old, Borrowed, and Stag	1975	0

Title	Year	Number of Holding Libraries in the OCLC Database 3 April 1992
The Opening of Misty Beethoven	1975	0
Passages Through Pamela	1985	0
The Passion Within	1986	0
Pertty Peaches	1987	0
Punishment of Anne	1979	0
Raw Talent	1984	0
Raw Talent II	1986	0
Reel People, 1 & 2	1984	0
Reproduction of Life	1981	19
Ribald tales of Canterbury	1985	0
Rising Star	1986	0
Roommates	1982	0
Sailing into Ecstasy	1986	0
The seret Work of Erotic Art	1986	2
Sensational Janine	1979	0
Sexual Feedom in Denmark	1986	0
She Comes in Cclor	1986	0
Shocking Asia	1980	2
Skinny Dipping	n.d	0
Sodom and Gomorrah	1977	0
Sometime Sweet Susan	1975	0
Suzie Superstar	1983	0
Taboo 1-6	1983-1988	0
Taboo American Style, 1-4	1985	0
Talk Dirty to Me	1983	0
Three A.M	1975	0
Traci Lords' Fantasies	1986	0
Virginia	1983	0
Wet Rainbow	1974	0
Wickmerman	1973	0

Source: Robert H. Rimmer, "A Connoisseur's Selection of X-Rated Videotapes for the Library," in *Libraries, Erotica and Pornography*, edited by Martha Comong (Phoenix, AZ: Oryx Press, 1991).

PART IV

Liabraries and Information Systems

Strategic Planning for National Libraries in Developing Countries: An Optimist's View

STEPHENY FERGUSON

Various presentations on strategic planning for national libraries have been made in this IFLA forum but as far as I can ascertain, there have not been any which have treated the subject from the point of view of developing countries.

If we accept the definition by Steiner,[1] that "strategic planning is the process of determining the major objectives of an organization and the policies and strategies that will govern the acquisition, use and disposition of resources to achieve those objectives", then one can argue that this is not an activity that is likely to be affected by the location of the institution in which it is done. But there are other considerations. For strategic planning is affected by three basic influences, namely: the fundamental socio-economic characteristic and purpose of the organization, the values and philosophy of management, and the organization's strengths and weaknesses in the light of the external and internal environment.

Since these factors are likely to vary with different cultural, socio-economic and historical environments, then it is likely that the nature of strategic planning will be affected by the location of the organization.

In developing countries, the term "national library" can refer to widely differing organizations. They may include those libraries which display the basic characteristics identified by K.W. Humphreys[2] or they may also include organizations which are first and foremost public or academic libraries but which also perform some functions traditionally associated with national libraries.

In his paper "Strategic Planning in National Libraries" presented in Moscow in 1991, Maurice Line[3] considered the factors which make planning for national libraries different. He identified the following: "national libraries are usually much more directly subject to government than other libraries." Often resources may be suddenly reduced, drastically changing from year to year in an unpredictable manner and consequently they possess very little real autonomy.

The clientele of these libraries are less clearly defined than in other libraries. Consequently role determination is often done by governments rather than clients.

National Libraries have "international relationships and responsibilities in a way that few other libraries do". They must therefore adhere to international standards. Being a... "part of the nation's total library and information system", they cannot operate in isolation, and their choice of functions and the way they are performed may be influenced by what other libraries do as much as what they do not.

Mr Line concluded that "national libraries have therefore to plan under various pressures from government, often with reduced financial resources for an uncertain clientele with a wide range of possible functions, and in the context of the rest of the nation's library and information activities". He described the process of planning in national libraries as being "different", and pointed out that under such conditions of great uncertainty one obvious answer is that planning was done "with great difficulty".

Mr Line's assessment is very applicable to developing countries, but in these countries the situation is even more complex because of the characteristics of the basic influences on the process of strategic planning itemized above. Let us consider these and their effect on the planning process for national libraries in developing countries.

The Fundamental Socio-economic Characteristic and Purpose of the Organization

In developing countries, more so than others, there is a strong contradiction in the fundamental socio-economic purpose of the national library. Quite often the primary functions pertaining to the acquisition and preservation of the nation's cultural records are subordinated to, or are in conflict with other functions particularly when, as often happens, the national library doubles as an academic or public library.

Unless an organization can define its purpose precisely, it will lack a clear understanding of its basic mission and have great difficulty in constructing a strategic plan. Even in countries where the national library does not double as an academic or public library there is some difficulty in maintaining a consistent definition of its purpose to enable strategic planning.

Uncertainty and change occur in all societies, both developed and developing. However, in the latter the future is far less predictable. Changes in government policy as political changes occur can make mockery of a carefully worked out strategic plan. Changes in economic circumstances also have this effect as well, as under pressure of the International Monetary Fund or other such funding agencies, many small developing countries have no real say in shaping their economic policies and are forced to adopt a policy of privatization, or institute drastic budget cuts in public sector entities particularly where income earning capabilities are limited. In some countries the daily deterioration of the value of the local currency against other international currencies makes the situation even more unpredictable and unstable.

Even more perplexing and difficult, however, is the environment in which there is no clearly enunciated definition of the basic purpose of the library as happens in some countries. The library exists because it is established by the former colonial power and continues to exist as a symbol of modern society. However, no attempt has been made to redefine its role and function within the context of an independent nation seeking to achieve socio-economic growth. It therefore continues without direction in the absence of a clear mission statement. Where there is no clarity regarding the purpose, role and function of a national library, it will be unlikely to be able to attract the resources required to perform effectively.

Management Values

Management values here refer not only to the attitudes and values of those who have direct responsibility for the library services, but also to those government policies which impact on the organization. The absence or presence of enabling legislation may hinder or promote effective planning. Additionally, the perception of value of the library by government policy-makers, as reflected by the resources allocated for its operation, will also have an impact.

Where the philosophy of government as reflected by its policies, convey little recognition of the value of information resources in the society or little recognition of the role of the national library in facilitating access to information, then the strategic planning process may not be encouraged.

On the part of the managers of the library and information system, attitudes can also be of great significance. It may appear easier and far simpler for managers to practice "crisis management", reacting to problems as they arise in an environment where human, physical and financial resources are limited and there is a perception that planning will only lead to frustration.

Limited human resources may also influence management philosophy, because in situations where there are very few professionals, the manager may believe that the rank and file staff can contribute very little to strategic planning within the organization. The likely result is that plans when developed will originate from the top with little or no participation by the staff, and of course this will influence a lack of widespread commitment to the implementation of the plan on the part of such staff.

Strengths and Weaknesses in the Light of the External and Internal Environment

External Environment. Developing countries are characterized by a poorly developed infrastructure for libraries and information work. There is little appreciation of the value of information as a resource and the economy is weak and struggling. In addition, basic needs for housing, food, water, roads and educational facilities always take priority over libraries, both on the part of educational facilities always take priority over libraries, both on the part of governments and policy makers as well as the population itself. In this kind of environment, therefore, strategic planning for national libraries is not encouraged, nor is it perceived as being important, both by policy-makers in government and the population at large.

Internal Environment. The internal environment is equally discouraging. I have already mentioned the lack of trained staff, the poor infrastructure and limited financial resources. These, together with inadequate data and information support for the planning process, all make it difficult for any meaningful strategic planning to take place. However, as the title of my paper suggests, I am an optimist and in spite of the difficulties and problems inherent in the situation in developing countries, I believe that there are benefits to be derived from strategic planning for national libraries in developing countries.

Strategic planning can create a vision of how the library can contribute to the advancement of the society and can influence the decisions and actions which will shape the future of the library while prioritizing the allocation of limited resources in a manner which will enable it to meet the information needs of the community as effectively as possible.

The process of strategic planning, although difficult, time consuming and frustrating can secure far reaching benefits for developing countries.

Benefits

What then are these benefits?

Identification of Mission. First would be the benefit to be derived from clearly enunciating the mission of the organization. Such a mission statement will provide a clear vision of the library's role in the society. Associated with the mission statement would be the goals identified which will provide clear directions as to future activities and identify priorities.

Identification of the national library's mission and goals could also serve to educate policy-makers on the potential role of the library and the activities which it can perform in facilitating access to information, which is a valuable resource in the transformation process in which these societies are involved.

Creating Awareness. Bearing in mind that any plan developed for the national library would have to be submitted to government for its approval and adoption, then an added benefit can be immediately seen, as the opportunity could be used as a public education exercise. The draft plan, when distributed to government policy-makers, the advisory boards and to the community at large, can be used to motivate persons to become involved by providing feedback and suggestions which could help to shape and define the role of the national library.

Such discussions may result in modification of the mission statement, goals and plans, but it would certainly ensure that the objectives of the library are in keeping with the overall objectives of government and that the needs of the society are identified so that the plans are developed to meet these needs.

Achieving Consensus within the Information Community. Another benefit for developing countries is the effect which this could have in bringing the information community together. The national library should function as the chief focal point of the National Information System, providing leadership, while serving libraries as well as individuals. Plans when developed should be distributed widely throughout the library and information community to obtain input as to the functions which the national library should best perform in support of other libraries.

Strategic planning could therefore serve to mobilize the library community into taking a global look at the library and information services provision within the country and help them to redefine the objectives of their library systems, and to identify gaps, assign functions, and put in place the institutions which are required to strengthen the infrastructure.

Management Philosophy and Attitudes. Strategic planning if it is to be effective must involve widespread participation of the staff of the organization. This is necessary if there is to be commitment to the implementation of the plans which have been developed.

Management philosophy is therefore another area which could benefit from the introduction of this process as management attitudes would have to change to become more accommodating in seeking the participation of staff in the development of plans.

Staff Training and Development. Participation in the planning process will have spinoff benefits for the staff because it will result in staff becoming more knowledgeable about the strengths and weaknesses of the organization and increase their awareness about organizational matters. The process thus becomes a staff training and development activity, facilitating a better understanding of the role of the library, while helping individuals to clarify their position within the organization and to identify the contribution which they can make towards achieving the objectives which they have helped to develop.

Integration of Plans. The strategic planning process requires the formulation of measurable objectives, all directed towards achievement of the goals which have been identified. This demands integration of the plans for each division or department. All plans must be defined by a hierarchy of objectives which are geared towards the achievement of the broad goal. The process therefore ensures unity of direction as each department defines the strategies, programmes and activities which will realize divisional or departmental goals as well as that of the organization.

Evaluation and Performance Measures. Definition of measurable objectives provides the outcome indicators or criteria which are essential in the evaluation process. These outcome indicators provide the performance measures for assessing how effectively plans developed have been implemented and the degree of success or failure achieved in realizing the organization's goals. For the manager, performance measures therefore become a valuable tool for monitoring and controlling the implementation of the plan.

Improved Management Information System. A valuable by-product of the strategic planning process is the improvement which it encourages in the collection, organization and use of data for decision making. Information and data originating within the organization as well as from outside must be collected, organized, analysed and used, to identify trends and issues which will affect the organization. Such data will facilitate improved decision making, enabling more precise identification of priorities and better allocation of resources. An effective management information system will thus influence greater responsiveness to the local environment. In effect therefore strategic planning for national libraries in developing countries requires a great deal of effort, patience and commitment, not only because of the difficulties associated with such planning for national libraries in general, but also due to the peculiar problems associated with developing countries.

The benefits can, however, be rewarding and should by far outweigh the difficulties encountered in the process. It can create an awareness and consensus on the role and function of the library at all levels of the society. It forces the organization to consciously design and shape its future and to identify priorities in the context of its resources capabilities. It ensures data collection and analysis for better decision making, defines the strategies, activities and tasks which are required to ensure the implementation of plans, assigns responsibility for these and provides the mechanism by which results can be monitored and evaluated. In fact, effective strategic planning is one certain way of minimizing the effects of uncertainty and change on the fortunes of national libraries in developing countries.

REFERENCES

1. Steiner, George. *Top Management Planning*. New York: Macmillan, 1969.
2. Humphreys, K.W. "National Library Functions". *Unesco Bulletin for Libraries, 20(4):" 158-169 (1966).*
3. Line, Maurice B. "Strategic Planning in National Libraries": Paper presented at the 57th IFLA General Conference, 18-24 August, 1991 (IFLA Booklet 1: Document 94-NAT-2-E), pp. 1-4 until 1-6.

BIBLIOGRAPHY

Jacob, M.E.L.*Strategic Planning : A How-to-do-it Manual for Librarians*. New York: Neal Schuman, 1990.

Riggs, Donald E. *Strategic Planning for Library Managers*. Phoenix : Oryx Press, 1984.

Libraries and Library Science in India

SUSEELA KUMAR

The IFLA Conference is being held in September '92 for the first time in India. A country with an ancient and highly evolved civilisation, its strong oral tradition enabled the transmission of knowledge from guru to sishya in a paperless society and its religious scriptures, the rich and varied folklore, the fine arts and crafts survived from generation to generation. Centres of learning—Nalanda and Taxila were renowned centuries ago. The royal courts and religious centres had also built up vast collections of manuscripts, but the reading and writing of manuscripts were sacred tasks and access to them was limited to the chosen few. The advent of printing, democratised knowledge, which until then, had largely been locked up in racial memory, carved on stone, copper or crafted in manuscripts.

Librarians from other parts of the world attending the IFLA conference may have heard of Maharajahs and Monsoons. They will now perhaps see something of how this vast country with a polyglot, multi-cultural population of 860 million, scattered over 27 states and nine union territories is coping with the problem of providing 'Information of All'. 70% of the population lives in more than 5000 villages and is largely agrarian. But there is a growing industrial and post-industrial society. A country of contrasts—of the bullock cart and the jet plane, traditional methods of communication of knowledge and wisdom continue to hold sway even as the country is poised on the threshold of the Information Age and a new Paperless Society, spawned by the electronic age is threatening to take over.

After Independence in 1947 the need to develop libraries and information centres and educate personnel for library service was felt. Progress in education, increase in the number of institutions-academic, research, industrial and government, rapid socio-economic development and successive plans for reconstruction, which started in 1951, had brought about a proliferation in the types of libraries, and types of services required. In the last Five Year Plan period 1985-90, the entire library and information scene in the country was reviewed, discussed and a National Policy for Library and Information system formulated.

Coincidentally, in the same year 1986, a New Education Policy and Books Policy were defined.

GROWTH OF LIBRARIES

Public libraries

The concept of the public library emerged towards the end of the last century alongwith nationalism created by the activities of the Indian National Congress, but it was only by the middle of this century that most States accepted the need for library services as a vital tool for social reconstruction. Public library development is a state subject and with more pressing claims, they found it difficult to mobilise additional resources for this purpose. However most States and Union Territories have established State Central libraries and libraries at the district, block and village levels. Such public libraries belong to various categories - government administered, autonomous, semi-autonomous or in the form of local library authority, library board, or entirely private managed.

The earliest efforts to set up public libraries had been made in Baroda, Punjab and Andhra Pradesh. It was however only in 1948 that public library legislation enabling a library system to be planned came into being. It took Dr. S.R. Ranganathan, who drafted a Model Library Bill in 1930, almost two decades of perseverance and effort for the Madras Public Library Act (1948), the first of its kind in India to be passed. The Act came into force in Tamil Nadu, formerly known as Madras State, in 1950. The Connemara Public Library established in 1896, functions as the State Central Library and the system comprises 18 District Central Libraries, 1530 Branch Libraries, nine Mobile Libraries, 826 Part time libraries, making up a total of 2883 libraries. Special provision for home delivery service, research scholars, children, hospitals, prisoners in jail, estate workers and others have been included. The entire system is under a separate Department of Public Libraries headed by a Director of Public Libraries.

This model is not however replicated in its entirety in other states. Dr. Ranganathan also drafted the acts for Andhra Pradesh (1960), Karnataka (1965) and Maharashtra (1967). In 1972, almost the last major activity he organised was a National Seminar on Public Libraries, the aim of which was to encourage all those states which had not passed acts to do so. But since then, only four more States have adopted legislation - West Bengal (1979), Manipur (1988), Kerala (1989) and Haryana (1989).

Even among the States which have Library Acts, some provide for the levy of a library cess on property, as in Tamil Nadu with a matching grant by the government and in others the government meets the entire expenditure from its general revenue. The types and quality of service offered also vary from state to state and in general most public libraries offer only lending services.

The Delhi Public Library, was established in 1951, by the Union Ministry of Education, with technical assistance from Unesco as a pilot public library project. It has since developed into a metropolitan public library system, consisting of a Central Library, Zonal, Branch and Community libraries. It has a net work of mobile libraries serving Braille institutions, hospitals, and prisons and covers the whole of the Union Territory of Delhi.

The Central Government can play only a promotional role. Its efforts are channelled through the Raja Rammohun Roy Library Foundation which was established in 1972 to promote and support the public Library movement and develop the reading habit among the people.

ACADEMIC LIBRARIES

School Libraries

In state capitals sch as Bombay, Calcutta, Delhi or Madras there are a few schools with good libraries, but their number is insignificant in relation to the total number of schools. Most of these 'good' schools are also private owned or 'special' schools such as the 'Kendriya Vidyalayas' primarily for the children of defence personnel and Central Schools which are meant for the children of central government staff who are transferable. Such schools have better libraries than most of the state schools which are struggling to cope with the burgeoning student population and are more concerned with basic amenities such as enough classrooms, furniture and so on.

College Libraries

At the college level which students reach at the age of 16 or 17, every institution has a library. Here again standards vary a great deal according to whether they are government, private or missionary institutions. Most colleges provide at least the basic textbooks. Many of them have 'book banks' - multiple copies of standard textbooks, meant essentially for lending to those who cannot afford to buy them. These libraries provide an adequate lending service and some of them also offer reference service, and other extension activities.

University Libraries

The picture brightens as we go higher up the academic ladder. Many university libraries and particularly those in institutions which are 'deemed' universities provide efficient service. Institutions such as Central Universities, the Indian Institutes of Technology and Indian Institute of Science have well designed buildings, good collections and adequate trained staff. Besides lending services, these institutions offer reference and reprographic services. Some of them also provide CAS and SDI services and have on-going programmes of user education. The UGC provides grants for the purchase of books and equipment and for buildings. It also gives assistance for continuing education programmes for the professional staff of the institutions and colleges affiliated to it.

Research and Special Libraries

After Independence there was tremendous growth in the establishment of research institutions. Programmes of scientific research were greatly encouraged by India's first Prime Minister Jawaharlal Nehru, who believed that science and technology had the answers at least to some of India's problems. Several programmes of socio-economic development were launched and information as a vital input was beginning to be recognised. With the commencement of the first Five Year Plan in 1951, provision was made for national development on all fronts and in the intervening four decades, by the end of the Seventh Plan in 1990, a sea change has taken place. There are at present more than 2500 special libraries in the country in different categories—Science and Technology, Medicine, Agriculture, Social Sciences, Humanities and Arts.

Science and Technology

The institutional infrastructure in Science and Technology had to be strengthened a great deal to support national development. As part of this process library and information facilities for supporting R&D were created and central government is responsible for nearly 90% of the scientific and industrial research in the country. Under the central government there are two types of institutions engaged in scientific research—those engaged in research such as the Council of Scientific and Industrial Research (CSIR), Indian Council of Agricultural Research (ICAR) and Indian Council of Medical Research (ICMR), and those sponsoring research such as the Departments of Science and Technology, Defence, Environment and so on. There are also many scientific research institutions in the states and all these institutions have well-serviced library and information facilities.

In general, science and technology libraries are better developed than those in other fields. The managements of these libraries are aware of the pivotal role they have to play and there is considerable emphasis on information work rather than conventional lending library functions. Databases relevant to the work of the parent body are built up and CAS and SDI services provided. Most of the libraries are switching over to computerisation and more suitably qualified staff with a scientific background are being recruited. The status and conditions of service of staff in these libraries are on par with the scientists of the institutions.

Medicine

Although there are over 630 medical libraries attached to medical, dental, nursing colleges and hospitals, research institutions and government departments, except for the major libraries such as the National Medical Library and All India Institute of Medical Science, the services offered by the others vary a great deal and need to be strengthened and streamlined.

Agriculture

In this area, libraries are more evenly developed, and cover agricultural sciences, animal husbandry, fisheries and forestry. In addition to 23 state Agricultural University libraries and college libraries, there are, under the ICAR, research stations, national bureaus, and a national academy. In addition to the library of the Indian Agricultural Research Institute, which ranks as one of the national libraries, other important libraries are those of the Indian Veterinary Research Institute and the National Dairy Research Institute. Most of the agricultural libraries maintain comprehensive bibliographical databases and produce current awareness lists.

Social Sciences

Many of the libraries in the social sciences though part of the teaching and research institutions which were established in the 19th Century, developed at a phenomenal rate only in this century. Some of the well-known ones are those of the Asiatic Society of Bengal (1784), National Archives of India (1891), Gokhale Institute of Politics and Economics (1930), Indian Statistical Institute (1932), Tata Institute of Social Sciences (1936) and Indian Council of World Affairs (1944).

In addition to books and journals, their collections include reports, newspaper clippings, theses, records, annual reports and government publications. It is estimated that there are more than 550 social science libraries in the country.

Humanities and Arts

Libraries in the area of humanities are scattered all over the country. A few of these are Sahitya Academy, Sangeet Natak academy, Lalit Kala Academy, Asiatic Societies at Calcutta, Bombay, Indian Council of Phiolosophical Research, National School of Drama, National Museum, National Gallery of Modern Art and the rich collections of manuscripts in the Adyar Library and Research Centre, Bhandarkar Oriental Research Institute and Saraswati Mahal Library. Various religions institutions such as the Ramakrishna Mission have also set up libraries and there are quite a few research and teaching institutions devoted to particular languages—Sanskrit and Hindi. The Indira Gandhi National Centre for Arts established in 1986, has as one of its divisions a National Information System and Data Bank for Humanities and Arts called the Indira Gandhi Kala Nidhi, based on a reference library built up on modern lines. The data will cover verbal, visual, and aural material in all arts covering architecture, sculpture, painting, literature and music.

Government Libraries

There are a number of libraries attached to central and state governments ministries, departments and directorates. These libraries are equipped with adequate literature, statistical and other data to support planning, policy and decision making processes. Many of them are devoted to specific subject areas and can therefore be considered special libraries. The Central Secretariat Library and the Parliament Library are the largest in this category.

National Libraries

The National Library Calcutta, the National Science Library, the National Medical Library and the Library of the Indian Agricultural Research Institute at Delhi — are the four national libraries.

The National Library, Calcutta

It was established in 1903 as the Imperial Library. The library with a collection of more than 2 million comprising 18 lakhs of books in English and other foreign languages, nearly 4 lakh books in Indian languages, more than 3000 manuscripts, 76000 maps and other items also has several special collections donated by scholars. It receives Indian publications under the Delivery of Books Act 1954. These are covered in the Indian National Bibliography which the Central Reference Library has been producing since 1956. The National Library also receives the official documents of some foreign countries.

The National Science Library

Set up in 1964 as a project of the INSDOC, now housed along with its parent body in a modern building with all amenities, contains more than 1 lakh books, 4600 periodicals, and a good reference collection. It provides bibliographical, reprographic services and on-line access to international data bases in the field of science.

The National Medical Library

It has a collection of over 2.5 lakhs comprising books, reports, and bound volumes of periodicals. It receives 2000 periodicals and provides bibliographical and reprographic services. It also undertakes on-line search of POPLINE, MEDLINE and produces the Indian Index to Medical Periodicals and other publications.

Indian Agricultural Research Institute

The Library is one of the oldest and biggest of agricultural libraries in Asia. It provides adequate service for its own scientists and offers national level service.

National Deposit Libraries

Under the Delivery of Books Act 1954, the National Library Calcutta, the Asiatic Society Library, Bombay, the Connemara Public Library, Madras and the Delhi Public Library are expected to receive copies of all books produced in the country.

The Asiatic Society Library (1804), one of the oldest libraries has a collection of over 7 lakh books, 12000 periodicals, 2000 manuscripts and 600 microfilms. The building and other resources are inadequate and there has recently been a big drive to collect funds for improving the library and developing it as the State Central Library.

The Connemara Public Library (1896) is the State Central Library of Tamil Nadu. It has a collection of over 4 lakh books and 3700 periodicals. It offers lending, reference and reprographic services. The books published before 1930 are housed in a beautiful building of Anglo Italian architecture and the later ones is a new building within the same specious grounds.

Other libraries of national importance are the Parliament Library, the Central Secretariat Library and the Asiatic Society Library, Calcutta. The Khudha Baksh Oriental Public Library, Patna and the Thanjavur Saraswathi Mahal Library are noted for their rich collections of manuscripts.

Library Science Education

Education for librarianship had its beginnings in the school set up by the Maharaja of Baroda in 1891 with the help of William A Borden and later in Lahore in 1916 by Asa Dickinson, both Americans. The first full time certificate course however was started in Madras by Dr. S.R. Ranganathan under the auspices of the Madras Library Association in 1929. This was later handed over to the Madras University and became a full-fledged post graduate degree course in 1960. In 1957, the Centenary year of the Madras University, Dr. Ranganathan gave his life's earnings of Rs. 1 lakh for the endowment of the Sarada Ranganathan chair in Library Science, the first of its kind in the Commonwealth.

With the advancement and intensification of research activities in various fields, the need for supporting documentation and information services was felt and suitable training for library personnel became urgent. Library and Information Science (LISc) is now a recognised discipline of study and largely a post-graduate qualification. At the time of Independence there were only five universities offering courses but now there are more than 75 universities offering various levels of courses. Emphasis continues to be on the first professional degree-B Lib Sc and B Lib I Sc. About 2000 graduates qualify each year. The Master's programme which was of a year's duration after B Lib Sc is now increasingly becoming a two year course after the first general degree. Most universities admit eight to ten students and the annual out-put from the 50 or so library schools offering the Master's degree is about 300.

Library and Information Science is also offered as a subject at the undergraduate degree level leading to a three year bachelor's degree. So far only one college offers such a course and in general it is felt that it would be more useful for entrants to the profession to have a wider academic background and that a Bachelor's or preferably a Master's degree in a particular discipline would be a desirable minimum qualification for entry to professional education. About 30 universities enrol students for the Ph.D. degree and since 1977, one university, Delhi, conducts a one year post Master's M. Phil. degree course.

In addition Documentation Research and Training Centre (DRTC) Bangalore and the Indian National Scientific Documentation Centre (INSDOC) Delhi offer specialised post-graduate courses in Documentation and Information Science leading to Associateship of the respective institutions.

One or two universities still offer certificate courses for para-professional staff although they are generally run by professional associations.

There are now an increasing number of correspondence courses for B Lib Sc and even M. Lib Sc in several universities, Madras, Madurai, Mysore, Hyderabad, Rajasthan etc. The most recent is the Indira Gandhi National Open University (IGNOU). These courses attract much larger numbers of students and developments over the next few years have to be watched to guard against over production of qualified personnel.

Professional Associations

There are more than 60 professional associations, the largest of these being the Indian Library Association, (ILA) 1933, with over 2500 members and the Indian Association of Special Libraries and Information Centres, (IASLIC) 1955, with over 1500 members. Other national level associations are the Government of India Librarians Association, (GILA) 1933, the Society for Information Science, (SIS) 1975, Indian Association of Teachers of Library and Information Science, (IATLIS) 1967, and the Medical Librarians Association of India, (MLAI). Most of these associations organize annual conferences, seminars and continuing education programmes regularly, and produce newsletters, bulletins and other publications. The states also have associations of their own.

Recognising the usefulness of having a joint organisation to tackle the problems of the library profession as a whole, the (JOCLAI) Joint Council of Library Associations in India formed in 1982, with the ILA acting as the co-ordinator.

Areas of Development

Inevitably in to-day's 'global village', the electronic revolution which has succeeded the agrarian and industrial revolutions is also taking place in India, though slowly and unobtruvisely. But, whereas the sophistications of computer networking, computer output microfilming, computer aided reprography, facsimile transmission, opto-electronic video discs and other such have an important role to play in the modernisation of library services, conventional requirements like expanding the collection in existing libraries, starting new libraries within easy reach or the public, providing adequate documentation services, and efficient management of libraries are equally important. In all future plans therefore, there has necessarily to be a balancing of modernisation of conventional imperatives.

National Policy for Library and Information System

Though adhoc committees had been set up from time to time to review and recommend the lines along which libraries and library service should be developed and co-ordinated, in view of the rapidly changing information needs of society and the expectations of users of libraries, it was felt that a comprehensive country wide review should be carried out and a national policy defined. This was done in 1986 and a Report on the National Policy and Information System submitted to the government in May of that year. Based on this report an Empowered Committee drew up an Action Plan in May 1988.

Some of the main recommendations of this Committee are

— the setting up of a National Commission for Libraries and information Systems to oversee the implementation of the National Policy with responsibility for monitoring the progress and reporting periodically to the Government of India.

— Promotion of public library legislation in all the states and union territories and development of a system accessible to all rural and remote areas with suitable reading and A.V. material of local and cultural relevance in regional languages.

— Public libraries to be stocked adequately to support the various distance education programmes.

— All schools to have libraries with qualified librarians.

— Resource sharing to be promoted among all academic, special and research libraries.

— Library and information science curriculum to be updated, a suitable accreditation agency to be set up, a National Centre for Higher Education and Research to be established.

— An All India Library Service cadre to be established.

— The government of India to make adequate funds available for all such purposes.

Information Centres and Systems

The process of modernisation which had already begun in the 70's was considerably reinforced during the last decade. Existing information centres and systems were strengthened and new ones set up.

The Indian national Scientific and Documentation Centre (INSDOC) established in 1952 by the CSIR with technical assistance from UNESCO, is a national level information centre devoted to all branches of science and technology. Over the years it has built up a document supply service especially for reports, patents, standards, compiles bibliographies on well defined scientific subjects and has facilities for technical translation from about 18 foreign languages with an annual turn over about 15000 typed pages of translation. It also supplies micro-film and micro-fiche copies and the publishing programme covers the Indian Science Abstracts, National Index of Translations, Annals of Library Science and Documentation and Accession lists of Russian Scientific Publications.

Defence Science Information and Documentation Centre (DESIDOC) 1958 caters to the information requirements of Defence Research and Development Organisation (DRDO) Scientists and a computerised SDI service is being built up. It publishes a bi-monthly Patents information Alert, Defence Science Journal, News Letters and a bulletin.

National Informatics Centre (NIC) set up in 1975 by the Electronics Commission, Government of India is not a bibliographic information centre but a catalyst for increasing government productivity through appropriate applications of computer networks, data base methods, decision optimisation techniques and other information methodologies. It has developed a number of management information services on behalf of user ministries, some of which are related to finance, economic development, mines and minerals, forestry, tourism, energy, health, demography, education and manpower.

The Indian Council of Medical Research, (ICMR-NIC) Centre has been actively promoting awareness of medical information sources among medical practitioners and librarians. Interactive searches are carried on-line and information provided from Medline and Popline databases. The Centre is also building up bibliographic data bases of Indian material on tropical diseases, nutrition and other areas. The information is available to all parts of the country through NICNET.

A National Centre for Science Information was set up by the UGC in 1983 at the Indian Institute of Science, Bangalore to provide computer produced indexing and abstracting services to the faculty members and research scholars in universities and colleges. For this purpose it subscribes to several international bibliographic data bases. CAS and SDI services are provided.

A similar centre, National Social Science Documentation Centre (NASSDOC) at the Indian Council for Social Science Research, provides information support to Social science research activities.

Other well known information centres are the Bhabha Atomic Research Centre Library and Information Division, Bombay, National Institute for Health and Family Welfare (NIHFW) Delhi, Small Enterprises Documentation Centre (SENDOC) and the Centre on Rural Documentation (CORD) both at HYDERABAD.

Collaboration with global information systems and programmes such as UNISIST and MEDLARS has been developed, Commercial data bases such as CA Search, INSPEC, COMPENDEX are subscribed to and centres such as BARC and ICAR are Indian input centres to global information systems such as INIS and AGRIS respectively.

Nissat

The National Information System for Science and Technology was established in 1977 by the DST, Government of India, with the broad objective of inter-linking and co-ordinating a large number of information sources, systems and services into an effective network under an over all co-ordinating agency. The National Focal point (NFP) of NISSAT is located in the Department of Scientific and Industrial Research (DSIR) and already existing centres with potential for growth are brought into the NISSAT programme. Under the first phase Sectoral information Centres (SIC) were established.

—Leather Technology, at (CLRI Madras) Food Technology at (CFTRI Mysore) Machine Tools at (CMTI Bangalore) and Drugs at (CDRI Lucknow) Regional centres were also planned but for lack of finance and space have not been started. Centres for Chemistry, Textiles, and Bibliometrics were later, set up at NCL, Pune, ATIRA, Ahmedabad and INSDOC, Delhi respectively.

A specialised data analysis centre in Crystallography was set up in the Department of Crystallography and Biophysics, Madras University (NICRYS). The Centre receives global information on crystal data of organic and organo-metallic compounds on magnetic tape from Cambridge University and services specialist requests. Such information analysis centres are staffed by qualified scientists unlike the bibliographic centres which are staffed by librarians. Two other such hard data centres are on advanced ceramics (NICAC) at the Central Glass and Ceramics Research Institute, Calcutta and the Resource Centre on

Software for Bibliographic Applications at Andhra University, Vishakapatnam.

Through some of its sectoral centres at CLRI, NAL, NCL, IACS and INSDOC, NISSAT also functions as National Access Centres to International Data (NACID).

Environmental Information System (ENVIS), set up by the Department of Environment, Government of India in 1982, with the broad objective of developing national capability in collection, handling and dissemination of environmental information there are ENVIS centres devoted to special areas such as Pollution control, Toxic Chemicals, Coastal and Off-shore Ecology, Appropriate Technologies and Eco Toxicology, Renewable Energy and Environment. Bio-technology Information System (BTIS) and Patent Information System (PIS) are two more such systems.

Application of Information Technology

Many libraries are now introducing computer applications to library housekeeping operations and a few are attempting information retrieval. Data bases are being converted to machine readable form and NISSAT and other organisations such as INSDOC, DRTC, ILA and IASLIC are running special courses to train library personnel in computer application work.

Nicnet; The National Informatic Centre (NIC) has set up a satellite based government informatics network called NICNET with its centre in Delhi, regional centres at Pune, Bhubaneshwar and Hyderabad, and about 400 centres in state capitals and district headquarters. It is primarily intended to help accelerate government decision making process by providing better management information support, but libraries and information centres can also use its facilities by establishing linkages for carrying bibliographical information access across the country. It is hoped that eventually the public library system which is spread over all the 534 districts in the country will be able to use NICNET for providing speedy information even to remote rural areas. For the average citizen the network would provide information of day to day relevance through a system called General Information Services Terminal (GIST).

Indonet: is an integrated information management and distributed data processing facility spread over the country. INDONET covers computer centres in five cities—Delhi, Bombay, Calcutta, Madras and Hyderabad, with three other cities—Bangalore, Pune and Ahmedabad having access points. The computers are connected by means of P&T channels. It expects to cover 35 cities by linking via satellite and radio communications. INDONET will provide service as distributor to the data bases installed in the networks abroad TELENET and TYMNET through the International Gateway. National bibliographical databases will also be installed on INDONET.

Inflibnet: A major plan recommended by the UGC is INFLIBNET under which all university libraries and major research and special libraries would be linked by a computer network to facilitate transfer of information between most centres of national importance and create a common pool of information. Steps are being taken for implementing this network.

Ernet: The Education and Research Network set up in 1986 by the department of Electronics (DOE) with initial participation by leading academic and research institutions, the scientific and industrial research network SIRNET connecting all the CSIR laboratories have started functioning. SIRNET provides access to international databases through the ERNET. Yet another network is TIFACLINE, the technology information system set up by the Technology Information and Forecasting Council (TIFAC) under the Department of Science and Technology.

Major city networks : It was felt desirable that Metropolitan centres such as Calcutta, Delhi and Madras should have such computerised networking of libraries in the respective cities. With the initiative of and support from NISSAT two such schemes have been planned by the Computer Maintenance Corporation (CMC), CALIBNET in Calcutta and DELNET in Delhi. The CALIBNET is about to be launched. A similar scheme for Madras, the MALIBNET is under discussion.

Preservation of Cultural Heritage

India has a rich treasure of manuscripts, a major historical source of information on art, science, history and culture. It is estimated that there are about 30 million manuscripts—many of which have migrated to distant shores, some have perished and many others in private collections - their value not quite realised by the owners! About one million are said to be in organisations, a majority of which are facing critical preservation problems due to shortage of resources, technical facilities and trained manpower. The Indian National Trust for Art and Cultural Heritage (INTACH) and the Department of Culture, Government of India, have a project to collect data on Indian manuscripts both in the country and abroad. INTACH also helps Indian Institutions to obtain micro-film copies of Indian manuscripts from overseas. It is hoped eventually to transfer data on manuscripts and their texts on to CD-Rom.

Many national institutions are collecting material on visual arts and artefacts for preservation and research purposes - photographic collections of the Archaeological Survey of India, music and audio material of the All India Radio, material on all performing arts including folk and tribal arts and so on. The Indira Gandhi National Centre for Arts, (IGNCA) has as one of its main proposals the National Data Bank and Library of Arts and Culture.

International Linkages

India is associated with most of the UN Agencies and international non-governmental organisations. Dr. S.R. Ranganathan, was Chairman of the classification group of the FID for several years. India has designated INSDOC as the national member of FID since 1952. The country has good working relations with the Division of General Information Programme (PGI) of UNESCO.

Conclusion

Despite worldwide recession priority is being given to rapid development of social communication—whether through modernisation of libraries, extension of networks, E-Mail or tele-conferencing facilities. India which has had to leapfrog the Industrial Revolution now finds itself in the midst of the Information Revolution. The challenge to the information professional is to integrate the use of information into the fabric of society, in step with the realisation that information flow is the lifeline of modern democracies. 'Library and Information Policy and Perspective', a subject which the IFLA conference will be discussing is therefore timely.

University Libraries in India

K.A. ISAAC

History and Structure of University Education

A brief account of the history and structure of University education in India is necessary for a proper understanding of the set up of library facilities meant for supporting it. The year 1857 marks the beginning of modern university education in India, for it was in that year that the first three universities were started. Thy were (1) the University of Bombay, (2) the University of Calcutta and (3) the University of Madras. They were intended as affiliating universities with the responsibility of prescribing the syllabi for the courses offered by the then existing colleges located in their respective jurisdictions and for conducting examinations for the students enrolled in them. They had no teaching or research functions of their own. The total number of universities existing before 1947, the year of independence, was only 18. This has now swelled to 189 which include, apart from the conventional universities, institutions deemed as universities (Hereafter referred to as Deemed universities), institutions of national importance and universities specialising in subjects such as Agriculture, Medical Science, Science Engineering and Technology, etc. In this paper the term 'University' includes all these.

Table showing number of universities

Before 1990	1991-47	1948-49	1950-59	1960-69	1970-79
5	26	8	24	45	31

1980-89	1990-91	
46	4	Total : 189

The universities can be divided into three types on the basis of their structure and functions. The large majority of them are of the affiliating type. They affiliate to themselves the colleges within their specified area, lay down syllabi for the various courses and conduct examinations. They exercise general academic supervision over the colleges. They also offer post-graduate teaching and research programmes in their own departments. The second type comprises unitary universities which are solely concerned with teaching and research and have no colleges under them. In the third type are universities which, in addition to teaching and research responsibilities, have constituent colleges over which they have both academic and administrative control. They may be called federal universities.

There are four universities exclusively meant for women.

Distance education facilities are becoming increasingly popular in India. Several of the conventional universities offer correspondence courses. There are also four open universities specially established for this purpose.

Colleges

It can be seen from the account given above that students of university education in India include those enrolled in the affiliated/constituent colleges of the universities as well as in the departments of the universities. Of these the former forms the dominant group constituting more than 95% of the total students of higher education. There are as many as 7121 affiliated and constituent colleges which together enrol 44,25000 students for graduate, postgraduate and research degrees and diplomas and employ ,62,000 teachers. Therefore the standard of higher education is largely that set by the colleges and hence, libraries as important in the colleges as in the universities.

University Grants Commission (UGC)

The UGC was set up in 1953 by the Central Government and was given statutory status in 1956. Its name is suggestive of its role as a body disbursing grants to the universities. While this continues to be its chief function it is empowered to take all necessary steps for the promotion and coordination of university education and for the determination and maintenance of standards of teaching, examination and research in universities. Thus the policies and programmes of higher education in India have been largely directed by the UGC since its inception. While it is made responsible for the entire financing of the central universities, i.e., universities directly run by the central government, its financial support to the state universities is by way of supplementing the grants made available to them by the respective state governments.

Education Commissions

Th Universities Commission of 1902, the University Education Commission of 1948 Radhakrishnan Commission) and the Education Commission of 1966 (Kothari Commiossion) studied various aspects of university education in India and made appropriate recommendations for strengthening its base with a view to improving standards. The role of libraries in this respect and the need for developing them suitably have been stressed in the reports of all these commissions.

University Libraries

In the case of the early universities, libraries were started long after the starting of the universities themselves. This is because they had no teaching and research functions that needed library support. But after the enactment of the Indian University Act of 1904 which wanted the universities to assume direct teaching and research functions, it became necessary for libraries to be established in the universities. Even so, few libraries can claim to have been started simultaneously with their universities and there was always an interval between the origin of a university and of its library. Any instance of a University library being planned and developed before the establishment of the University and the starting of its academic and research programmes can hardly be found. This is indicative of a general lack of appreciation of the importance of the library in University education. Also the departments which were established had their own small book collections to depend on.

Budget

The sources of income for a state university library are (1) the grants received from its parent university and (2) developmental grants received from the central government through the UGC under each Five-Year Plan. As far as Central universities are concerned, the entire financial support is provided by the UGC. The Central university libraries are financially in a better position than the state university libraries. The annual budget of the libraries of the existing 189 universities shows wide variation. It ranges from as low as Rs. 56000 in the case of Gujarat Agricultural University to as high as Rs. 115,00000 in the case of the Indian Institute of Technology, Kanpur. But this comparison is not quite rational as the universities widely vary in respect of their age, size, subject, student enrolment and other relevant factors which have implications for the library.

There are certain norms for library expenditure recommended by different bodies. According to the University Education Commission, 1948, it should be worked out on the basis of Rs. 40 per student. The library committee of the UGC, 1959 (Ranganathan Committee) has recommended Rs. 15 per student and Rs. 200 per teacher. The norm according to the Kothari Commission, 1966 is Rs. 25 per student and Rs. 300 per teacher or 6.5 to 10% of the total university budget depending on the state of development of the library. Given the steep rise in the cost of books and journals the per capita rate ought to be much higher now, but library expenditure even now is much less than the rates suggested almost three decades ago in the large majority of universities. It is better to work out library budget as a percentage of the total university budget because, corresponding to the natural enhancement of the latter from year to year, the library budget is also bound to go up as it should. The Kothari commission norm of 6.5. to 10% of the total university budget is still an elusive target for most universities.

Book Stock

The size of the book stock ranges from less than 10000 in the case of new and small universities to 600000 or more in the case of old and big universities. The Delhi University started in 1922 stands first in this regard with a book stock of 11,49000. The book stocks of different universities include conventional books, bound periodicals, reports, patents, standards, theses, microfilms, micro fiche, micro cards manuscripts, etc., in varying numbers.

The number of books added per year ranges from 200 to 12000.

All the universities subscribe for periodicals, both Indian and foreign. Some also receive them gratis and in exchange of their own publications. There is wide variation in the number of journals received by different libraries.

A comparative resources position of different libraries on a reasonably comparable category basis shown in the following table. The figures relate to the year 1988-89, 1989-90 or 1990-91 as given in universities Handbook 1992.

Category	No. of Univer-sities	Budget range in Rs.	Collection range	Range of Annual Additions	Range of No. of journals
Started before 1900	5	1250000-2378000	150000-648000	5193-11425	500-2025
1990-1947	26	100000-4338000	40000-1149000	1500-13969	100-2145
1948-49	8	1400000-3100000	209217-400000	2923-3253	500-1200
1950-59	24	260000-11500000	4800-549329	640-7502	225-2400
1960-69	45	60000-4800000	31000-280000	584-9790	202-1340
1970-79	31	150000-6550000	52000-170527	3051-12075	155-1451
1980-89	46	100000-1950000	2000-155000	200-2154	48-800
1990-92	4	Details not available			
Agriculture/ Veterinary Science/ Fisheries/ Forestry Universities	31	250000-2941000	20892-600000	1977-6403	180-1948
Medical Sciences	7	1000000-3000000	12000-110389	640-1000	200-380
Engineering/ Science/ Technology	12	500000-11500000	500000-284861	2000-4558	305-2300
Others	19	56000-240000	23186-150000	445-5511	100-1700

The wide disparity in budget allotment in respect of comparable university libraries shows that there is no rational policy followed in funding of the libraries with the result that the growth of libraries is not uniform. Also, except in a few cases the budget does not take into account the steep rise in the cost of books and journals, increased and diversified needs of universities, increased enrolment of students and other such relevant factors. The funding is haphazard in that if it is enhanced in one year, it may be static in another year and may even go down in a subsequent year. No rational development policy for the libraries is possible in such a situation. The libraries of the subject universities especially those of the Indian Institutes of Technology are more advantageously placed in this respect. Many libraries are forced to cut down the number of periodicals subscribed for, from year to year.

Organisation of the Book Collection

The book collection has been classified and catalogued in all the libraries although in some there is considerable backlog. The classification schemes adopted are the Dewey Decimal classification, Colon Classification and the universal decimal classification. The Classified catalogue code of Ranganathan and AACR 2 are the catalogue codes generally followed.

Services

Loan of books and consultation of books within the library premises are services provided by all libraries. Almost all libraries also provide reprographic services of which xeroxing facilities are the most common. There are a few libraries which provide documentation services in the form of CAS, SDI and the compilation of ad-hoc bibliographies. These documentation services are oriented to the requirements of the research scholars of the universities concerned.

The use of a university library is generally restricted to the teachers and students of the university departments and of the affiliated/constituent colleges. But there are a few libraries which extend their services to the public also on certain conditions. This is particularly helpful to those who seek to improve their qualification by taking advantage of distance education facilities.

Departmental Libraries

The libraries set up in each university can be broadly divided into three categories. One is, a central library for the whole university with provision for the long-term loan of a specified number of constantly required books to each department. In the second category there is a central library and there are also departmental libraries with all the libraries and the entire library staff under the administrative control of the university librarian. A third set up is of extreme decentralisation in that the central library and the departmental libraries are independent parallel units with no coordination of any kind. This pattern, apart from being uneconomical because of the duplication of costly materials that it entails, also acts as a disincentive for the students to visit the central library and get exposed to wide variety of books. What is desirable and feasible for a country like India with severe financial constraints is to have a well stocked central library with provision for long-term loan of books to the departments. The justification for independent departmental libraries is also highly weakened by their ill-organised condition wherever they exist.

Library Personnel

The Calcutta University Commission (1917-19) was the first to make the recommendation that the University should have the services of a librarian who should have the salary and status of a Professor and should be a member of the Academic Council. The University education Commission observed that the library should have adequate and well qualified staff in different grades headed by a librarian of the calibre of a University Professor who has specialised in Library Science. Very detailed recommendation regarding library staff are available in the report of the Library Committee of the UGC. The Committee recommended that the professional staff of libraries should have parity with the academic staff in respect of salary and status. It also prescribed a staff formula for working out the staff strength of various categories in a library.

The present position is that while some libraries are headed by librarians of professorial status, some are headed by persons in lower grades. The obsolete tradition of honorary librarians holding charge of libraries is still surviving in a few universities.

Library Committee

Most of the university libraries have library committees. Some have a statutory basis and some are constituted through executive orders, there are advisory as well as executive committees. The Vice-Chancellor is usually the Chairman and the librarian the member secretary. The committee usually concerns itself with policy and developmental matters.

The Physical Plant

Almost all the university libraries except the very new ones have their own buildings thanks to the grants made available for the purpose by the UGC from its very inception. Although spacious, some of them suffer from functional defects due to lack of adequate consultation with librarians in the planning and designing of library buildings. There is increasing realisation of the fact that the physical atmosphere of the library made up of the building, furniture, lighting and other accessories should be attractive and conducive to quiet and serious study.

College Libraries

As already mentioned the students of the colleges affiliated to the universities constitute the large majority of the students of higher education in India and therefore should have the benefit of adequate library facilities. Each college has its own library, but there are various factors adversely effecting its effectiveness and usefulness. Some of these are inadequate financial support, inadequate staffing, lack of scientific organisation, poor physical facilities and a general apathy to the library.

The college libraries are also eligible for financial assistance from the UGC for buildings, staff and collection development.

Modernisation of Library Operations and Services

The idea of computerisation of library operations and services, although much talked about, is yet to become a reality. There are only a very few libraries which have gone in for computerisation. The main bottleneck is lack of trained staff. But efforts are now afoot for imparting training through refresher courses and other programmes and there is increasing realisation that this is something that cannot be put off indefinitely.

UGC Library Committee

The appointment of a library committee by the UGC in 1957 under the chairmanship of Dr. S.R. Ranganathan is an important landmark in the history of university libraries in India. The Committee studied in depth all aspects of university and college libraries and formulated comprehensive recommendations relating to each aspect. These recommendations have largely directed the UGC's policy towards library development. They have also influenced in some measure the policy of individual universities to their libraries.

Library Cooperation

Library cooperation and resource sharing as practised in the developed countries is practically non-existent in India. Inter-library loan, wherever practised, is more on the basis of bilateral understanding and contacts between individual libraries than as part of a formal framework. One serious hurdle to inter-library loan is the absence of a Union Catalogue of books. There are union catalogues of scientific serials and also of social science periodicals and serials, but they are not up-to-date. Now that xerox facilities are available in most libraries, it is not difficult to obtain copies of required materials.

A recent development is the starting of computerised Information Centres by the UGC. The one for science is located at the Indian Institute of Science, Bangalore. It is called the National Information Science Centre and maintains user profiles of scientists and provides current awareness and SDI services. A second centre for Library sciences, Education and Women's Studies and a third one for social sciences have been set up in the S.N.D.T Women's University, Bombay and M.S. University of Baroda, respectively. These services generate extensive demands for the original documents and for this purpose the periodicals collections of the universities concerned are substantially augmented with UGC aid.

Information and Library Net Work (INFLIBNET)

INFLIBNET is a major project which is under the active consideration of the UGC for being implemented during the Eighth plan period. This will be a computer-communication network linking libraries and information centres in universities, deemed universities, institutions of national importance, UGC information centres, R&D

institutions and colleges with the primary objective of modernising the operations of these libraries and making their resources known and accessible to each other. This will, not doubt, facilitate the sharing of the available national library resources for common benefit.

Conclusion

University libraries in India have undoubtedly made vast strides of progress since independence. But the progress has not been uniform and according to a rational plan. The growth has been somewhat jerky because of the vagaries of financial support from year to year. Appropriate university and college library standards in respect of all the basic ingredients of a sound library programme to suit the modern context should be evolved and adhered to. Above all, the importance of the library in university education should be recognised and all academic programmes should be so conceived and implemented as to make library use indispensable.

REFERENCES

1. Indian Universities Commission (1902). Report, Government Central Printing Office, Simla.
2. Calcutta Universities Commission (1917-18) Chairman, Michael Sadler, Report V. 4 1920-Author-Calcutta.
3. India, University Education Commission (1948), Chairman, S. Radhakrishnan. Report. V. 1 1952 Manager of Publications, Delhi.
4. University Grants Commission (India) - University and College Libraries - Report - 1965 UGC, New Delhi.
5. India, Ministry of Education Commission (1964-66), Chairman, D.S. Kothari. Report, Ministry of Education - New Delhi - 1966.
6. Association of Indian Universities. Universities Handbook Association of Indian Universities - New Delhi - 1992.

National Information Policy and the Third World Countries

KISHNI NAVALANI

Introduction

Neo-classical economic theory gained popularity in the post war period, which identified one of the factors of economic growth in men and the latter in education. "A positive correlation was found to exist between the level of development and literacy".[1] Economic and fiscal opinion continued to build models of economic growth which took into consideration, role of capital investment in human beings, human skills and trained imagination. Events further gave support to the view of education. Now, aim of "development is the constant improvement of the entire population on the basis of its full participation in the process of development and a fair distribution of benefits therefrom".[2] Information plays too important a role in society and its development. Therefore, information policy is indispensable as never before in order to set out basic directions, to establish and maintain a consistent framework to meet the developmental, educational and cultural needs, to adapt to the increasing uncertainty accelerated by change and complexity, to promote better use of resources so as to ensure equalisation of opportunities. "The fundamental premise of an overall national information policy is that any economic, social and political system will perform more efficiently if a mechanism is provided which ensures that government officers, decision makers, managers and researchers have timely access to up-to-date, relevant and reliable data and information".[3]

Policy is the main instrument of directing, planning, managing and development of library and information services in a country. The concept of library and information policy is a new and recent one, though in other areas it has had many innings and keeps being revised and adapted according to changing needs and trends. In 1967 Unesco published a booklet *Planning library services,* prepared by Carlos V. Penna. It pleaded that "the provision of effective library and documentation services to promote education and research at different levels and economic and social endeavour of various kinds requires that they be organised within an integrated system".[4] The over-riding influence of Carlos Penna, and his enthusiasm for national planning provided the impetus for the inauguration of the series and his ideas on the subject struck a responsive chord[5]. The new approach found adoption in the form of over-all national library development planning in conjunction with over-all national plans. The Intergovernmental Conference on the Planning of National Documentation Library and Archives Infrastructures (NATIS Conference) was held in Paris in 1974. One of the requirements of NATIS was identification of a national information policy. "Unesco had two studies made with a view to formulating a general policy of national planning of infrastructures for documentation, libraries and archives".[6] Among the five main themes of General Information Programme (PGI) identified, the first and foremost was "Promotion of the formulation of information policies and plans (National, regional and international)".[7] UNISIST meetings of experts on information policy and planning and UNISIST II Intergovernmental Conference, 1979 also recommended that all countries should elaborate national information policies and plans and organise and co-ordinate information resources in order to serve national development needs more effectively.[8] Many documents were since then issued in this regard.

In recent times a number of developments have evolved to stimulate interest in national library and information policy. Many Third World countries are formulating/have formulated National Policy on Libraries and Information Services (NPLIS) e.g. India, Zambia,[9] Egypt.[10]

NATIONAL POLICY ON LIBRARIES AND INFORMATION SYSTEM IN INDIA

Historical perspective

"The need for an integrated library system for India can be traced in the writings of Dr. S.R. Ranganathan as early as 1944".[11] His book entitled *Post War Reconstruction of Libraries* pleads for public libraries both urban and rural.[12] He suggested that "The library edifice of post-war India should be so planned that primary libraries are attached to regional centres, regional centres to provincial central libraries, these again to the national central libraries and this finally to the national central libraries of other countries and international library centres".[13] Because of his efforts, three states—Tamil Nadu (1948), Andhra Pradesh (1960) and Karnataka (1965) - had Public Libraries Acts.

After Independence, Government of India made various attempts to improve library service in the country. National Library of India Act, 1948 changed the name of the Imperial Library, Calcutta as National Library, India, Delhi Public Library was established in 1951, thanks to the Unesco sponsorship as a model public library. 1952 saw establishment of Indian National Scientific Documentation Centre (INSDOC). The Delivery of Books (Public Libraries) Act (1954) was amended in 1956. Five Year Plans included funds for improvement of libraries and the Community Development Programme gave impetus to rural libraries. Advisory Committee for Libraries[14] was set up in 1957, which recommended library service 'free to every citizen of India" and a pattern of library service in the country. Committee on Plan Projects (Study Team for Subjects Educational Schemes)[15] and the Working Group on Libraries (1964)[16] followed. Raja Rammohun Roy Library Foundation, an autonomous organisation was established in 1972 to promote and support library movement in the country, to provide funds to public libraries, and "to enunciate a national library policy".[17]

The fate of academic libraries is tied up with education policy and efforts in the country. University Education Commission (1948) and Secondary Education Commission (1952) recommended for providing academic libraries. The University Grants Commission (UGC) was set up in 1953 and is devoting attention towards the development of academic libraries at college and university level. The UGC appointed a library committee under the chairmanship of S.R. Ranganathan. Education Committee (1964) and subsequent National Policy on Education, 1968 recommended that library should be an important centre of education. Draft National Policy on Education, 1979 under post literacy programme stipulated that "the development of a rural library system is necessary to support the programme of continuing education".[18] Education Policy, 1986 also reiterates provision "in all educational institutions for library facilities".[19] The association of Indian Universities took initiative in 1986 to formulate a National Policy on University Libraries. The University Grants Commission has suggested the setting up of Information and Library Network

(INFLIBNET) to interconnect the people and resources of all universities, institutions of higher education and research laboratories.[20]

Under UNISIST Programme 1971, India created focal points. Unesco subsequently promoted NATIS concept. India adopted National Information System for Science and Technology (NISSAT) in 1977, a multi-tier system at present having national focal points, eight sectoral information centres, three information analysis centres, etc. Besides many databases and some networks have been created in various fields. India is also participating in development of international databases, such as INIS, AGRIS, APINESS. Planning Commission appointed Working Group on Modernisation of Library Services and Informatics for the Seventh Five Year Plan 1985-90, (1983). It attempted "to present an integrated plan balancing the modernisation and the conventional imperatives".[21]

Mention may be made here of National Information Centre, Planning Commission, Government of India, which was initiated in 1980 and is so far the largest computer system. It is developing a network - NICNET - to provide computing and communication infrastructure to aid planning and monitoring of schemes and decision making activities in the country. The system is presently connected with all the states and union territories, through interactive terminals in 437 district headquarters and intends to connect 51,000 block units.[22-23]

National Policy on Library and Information System was formulated by the Raja Rammohun Roy Library Foundation and also by Indian Library Association. It was a theme of discussion of conferences in 1977 and 1979 of Indian Association of Special Libraries and Information Centres and of All India Library Conferences in 1984 and 1991 of the Indian Library Association. Public opinion was also sought.

The Department of Culture, Government of India set up a Committee on National Policy on Library and Information System in 1985. The final report was submitted to the Government in 1986.[24]

Aims

Its main aims are :—

1. To foster, promote and sustain, by all appropriate means the

organisation, availability and use of information, in all sectors of national activity;

2. To take steps for mobilising and upgrading the existing library and information systems and services and initiating new programmes relevant to our national needs, taking advantage of the latest advances in information technology, etc.

Salient features

The most important task according to the policy "is to establish, maintain and strengthen the free public libraries". The thrust area should go to rural public library. The district library will be the apex library in a district, with public libraries at city, town and village levels as components. All the libraries in a state will form part of a network and the state network should eventually connect with the national level. Each state should enact its own library legislation.

The policy lays emphasis that libraries are central to education, hence no school or college should be established without a library and a qualified librarian. Primary schools, where such facilities cannot be provided, should share the resources of the community library and vice versa where community library does not exist, the primary school library be developed as to serve as the base of the village library. There must be a state level agency for proper development of school libraries of the state and a national agency for co-ordination at the national level.

For college and university libraries the policy invests authority in the University Grants Commission and suggests that all these institutes should share resources and establish linkages among themselves.

The policy recommends that the National Information System for Science and Technology (NISSAT) scheme of providing for different levels such as national, regional, sectoral and local should be further strengthened and expanded. Special libraries in Social Sciences and Humanities and in Language areas should be organised in similar systems. Information systems and data banks in various fields be developed. Parent institutions should have a strong commitment to provide support and infrastructure for libraries.

The policy stipulates functions of the National Library of India, Calcutta and recommends for a system of National Libraries consisting of the National Library, Calcutta, National Depository Libraries, National Subject Libraries and National Documentation/ Information Centres, Dormitory Libraries, National Databases of Manuscripts, etc. The National Library of India should establish effective linkages with all other National Libraries through a National Library Board and also between libraries, archives and museums.

Other areas, the policy touches are : manpower, modernisation of library operations and services and use of technology, union catalogues, standards, removal of barriers in communication, such as high postal tarrifs, etc.

The principal recommendation of the Committee is a national network of libraries within which will be accommodated libraries of different kinds and at different levels from the rural society to the modern city, from the school to the research organisation. And the implementing agency for it, as it is in the USA, would be National Commission for Libraries and Information Systems. It is to be constituted by the Government. There is a proposal for establishment of separate division in relevant ministries of states and Union Government for promoting the development of library and information systems. The policy states that the necessary financial support 6-10% of the education budgets for systems will be made available by the Government of India and the state governments.

PROBLEMS IN THIRD WORLD COUNTRIES

The Third World countries including India are mostly at a crucial and complex juncture. They are living through several centuries at the same time. Some people are living lives below poverty line, women suffer silently lives of drudgery. There are people in between trying to come up e.g. craftsmen and artists who excel in their sphere without literacy. At the other extreme are scientists, technologists, researchers, managers who can compete with the best in the world. The target groups or population segments have inequalities for whom the NPLIS is designed. And the organisation of the system has to take into consideration this complexity. Considering all these facts the National Policy in India rightly gives emphasis to public libraries and thereto rural areas which are most neglected.

Tradition is the tallest hurdle in making use of a library system. In the developed countries, library and information system is integrated with the education, work, culture and society. It has taken more than a century to develop. On the other hand, indigenous traditions are formidably rich, mostly in Asian countries. They go back to thousand years. For example, India had a very advanced civilisation more tham thousand years ago. Higher education and scholarship were encouraged. There were world renowned centres of learning having libraries, where even foreigners used to come in those days. They developed art and architecture of unsurpassed excellence. There was for masses and which is still true in many places, an informal kind of family education by which skills, sometimes a modicum of literacy and attitudes towards life, community and its institutions, the historical past, the cosmos and spiritual life were handed down from one generation to the next. "Education of this type will tend, however, to be conservative, neutral, if not inimical to economic development"[25] and change in such type of education and society is to take into consideration oral culture. Barring the elite class, there is hardly place for literacy and libraries. Mostly, library culture is conspicuous by its absence in rural areas in mos of the Third World. And wherever it exists, only a very small percentage of population is making use of it. The masses, due to ignorance, do not perceive literacy and library services important to them, because their ancestors have survived for centuries without them. Therefore, as it is rightly remarked, "An important choice is to be made : do we want to create a written culture and break with oral culture ? Do we want to create synthesis"?[26]

Since 1950, most of the Third World countries have seen expansion in education and literacy. Bu in this process, library services provided to the educated community grew not from bottom to up, but the other way round. Elementry schools have hardly any libraries. This has adverse effect on habit forming of reading and using a library. With examination - oriented education system, in these countries, most of the young persons have minimal interface with the library, they usually stop using it as soon as they complete their education or are out of it because of dropout. The NPLIS of India, focuses attention on children and school libraries and proposes that in every village either there should be primary school library or a community library, as aforesaid.

Africa, Latin America and Asia have 60.3%, 37.4% and 20.2% illiteracy, respectively. The condition in every country, and within each varies widely. Public authorities are unable to provide enough places to ensure effective access to schooling for all. Moreover, the development and the customs are still such that young children often contribute to productive activities and hence there is an opportunity cost.[27] The Third World countries have launched massive literacy campaigns and made policies for eradicating literacy, expanding school, adult and functional education, their goals being universal education. But their targets are more quantitative than qualitative, which is obvious because of population explosion, paucity of funds and time limits. The most serious deficiency hampering educational efforts is the scarcity of reading material and libraries because people have nothing to read and nothing to get from. Eventually, the persons acquiring ability to read and write relapse into illiteracy as fast as they acquire this skill for want of libraries and literature.

Literacy is not an end, but a means, "a contribution to the liberation of man and to his full development".[28] Some of the measures taken by the Third World countries or sustaining literacy, as surveyed by the Unesco Institute for Application were : newspapers, wall papers, magazines, texts/literature prepared for post literate supplementary readings,[29] etc. All this and extension literature produced by agencies like agriculture, health, banks and media people, etc. require an agency which can be none other than the library. Therefore, in these countries, literacy programmes are developing literacy centres. As reported by J.N. Newa, many countries in Africa have such rural libraries as part and parcel of literacy section.[30] In India, the National Literacy Mission also makes provision of libraries for post literacy period under Jan Shikshan Niloyam Scheme.[31] These libraries, though fully integrated with literacy programme, are isolated efforts and not components of national library and information structure of these countries. They may be duplicating efforts. They cannot cope with the even increasing volume of information and ever changing needs of the users. Besides, a library needs a perennial financial source to remain alive and be able to draw from the national system to provide information to one and all.

Any national policy, whether defacto or dejure, is inherently political will of a country. It has been rightly observed that "policy makers can have intelligent articulate economists to support with research and argument any particular policy or programme they wish to support".[32] H.K. Mchombu in his paper: Which way African Librarianship, sums up the situation, "Governments and decision makers do not fully support libraries. In particular, they have failed to institute and legislate national information policy".[33] Political will, which is essential for accepting and implementing NPLIS does not, in most of these countries, perceive it important. It is not on their priority list. In India also it has yet to be accepted by the Government of India, and after that at various state and local levels.

For implementing policy, finance is the driving force. Many Third World countries were witnessing economic growth and expansion till recently. Unfortunately, the economic crisis and stagflation have put these countries in tight financial position.The debt of these developing nations has risen sharply. Each country now finds itself with much more limited resources than were available a few years earlier on the one hand, and increase in population on the other hand which means more mouths to eat, more to be educated and provided other amenities. Financial situation of education surveyed by Eicher indicates that "Only a small minority of countries are increasing their effort, while a strong majority are reducing it".[34] Library and information services require besides manpower, reading materials, prices of which are sky rocketing. In such a situation, providing obligatory schooling or education to all, or a network of library and information system reaching everywhere in these countries, is more a wish than a reality.

Science and technology information is given top priority, thanks to UNISIST, UNISIST II and Unesco and information technology. Most of the Third World countries have infrastructure for this sector of information system though not as advanced as that of the advanced countries. They are participating in international information systems. Networks and systems are being formed to avoid duplication and wastage. Technology requires enormous initial investment and a lot of funds to maintain it, which is in short supply. Consequently, what should be the proportion of expenditure on high-tech network infrastructure and the grass root libraries is a moot point ?

Thus, the society may be categorised into four segments : the science and technology group the more advanced of the the all, the academic system, the public educated and the public neoliterate or illiterate mostly rural and poor to whom NPLIS has to cater to. They are the target groups. On the one end of spectrum is a group highly conscious of information, very dynamic, wielding power and influence which wants to have access to global information and a lion's share of library and information system expenditure; and on the other extreme end of spectrum is a group, ignorant of power of information, passive and poor, in large numbers and whose number is ever swelling, hardly having either infrastructure for getting information or the information sources of their level in the language which they understand and reaching for them requires a colossal initial investment, and continuous maintenance cost and manpower with missionary zeal to awaken and motivate them to use library and information service. National library and information policies proclaim to be all to all but do they honestly give proper priorities to these weaker segments ?

SUGGESTIONS

Awareness is the first prerequisite for use of any service or product. It is the starting point of any movement. The Third world countries attempt to build their library and information system on the model of developed countries. People swear by the services provided by the American libraries. It was shocking to learn that in such an information society. *Alliance for excellence : a nation at risk* omits reference both to the library and information resources and services.[35] Library service is not only to be provided but it must be thought/perceived as an integral part of education, information, development and recreation scene. We have to convince the population that a library is important in their lives. Awareness is essential for preparing public to use the services; to build pressure to provide a service and to educate the prominent citizens, the community leaders, legislators, the bureaucrats and the government, the importance of library and information services in the country. Evidently, it is compellingly necessary that the Third World countries make a drive in this direction and launch vigorously a campaign at international, national, regional and local levels through various media and marketing strategies.

Many programmes such as quiz are held/shown/viewed, which ask for information or provide information. To give information means to satisfy this urge at one time but to tell the source for getting information is to train people to get their information, throughout their lives. Therefore, such programme organisers should be encouraged to cover books and libraries to make people aware of them and how to find their information through them.

In my opinion, unfortunately, in the Third World countries, as in everything, so also in library and information services, the minority of elite are getting more attention than the majority. This has created further stratification on educational basis. The services are not accessible universally. Obviously, this lacuna needs to be corrected by providing high priority in the NPLIS to the grass root village and school libraries. This will incidently build the model from bottom to top. It will not only make prospects for higher achievements,[36-37] but will also provide motivation to use information and libraries, that there is more in this world "that could be exciting to know that there are ways of finding out and that there may be both pleasure and profit in such knowledge".[38] Once the habit is inculcated and interest stimulated, there is more likelihood of its being integrated in the lives of masses.

As a corollary to it, it is necessary to train manpower in rural librarianship. So, special courses should be offered in this area in library and information education in the Third World countries. The thrust of the courses should be to study information seeking behaviours and needs of these people, how to motivate them to make use of library and information services, and how to integrate these services in their lives/work/communities.

New technologies present images and sounds, which make them more rich in communication than the printed media. Research indicates that this media permits user experience of social presence, so its "sociability, warmth and personalness and sensitivity is next to face to face communication".[39] Hence, it seems congruent with the oral and traditional culture of the Third World countries. There is a need for producing documents in the media for libraries : conducting research on how to make them effective as also produce them economically. This requires innovation, imagination and experiments. Cooperation is required of authors, publishers, illustraters and librarians in production of materials for newly literates in the local languages. Therefore, universities, media centres, other such organisations and international agencies may be persuaded to take up this challenging work. Possibly, later on, there may be a need for an international agency for development of rural library and information sources and services, to give a lead in this direction, and to assist in exchange of information among the Third World countries.

Illiteracy and poverty go together. "Alleviation of poverty and eradication of illiteracy are integral parts of the development".[40] Therefore, the General Assembly of the United Nations declared 1990 as International Year of Literacy. Many international bodies such as Unesco, Unicef, UNDP, World Bank have recognised the vital role of libraries as partners in promoting and supporting literacy,[41] to remedy the costly social and intellectual waste in relapse in illiteracy. As a logical consequence of it, it is suggested that the United Nations declare International Year of Library to make public organisations and governments conscious of need for library and information services for individual advancement and national growth and thereby assist in creating political will in favour of library and information policy so essential for information have-nots to join the fraternity of information society.

REFERENCES

1. Myrdal, Gunnar. Asian drama : An inquiry into the poverty of nations. London : Allen Lane the Penguin press, 1968. 3v pp. 1541.
2. United Nations General Assembly. Thirty-fifth Session (1980). Agenda item 61(a). Development and international cooperation : International development strategy for the Third United Nations Development Decade, 23rd October, 1980, pp. 3.
3. Neelamegham, A. and Tocatlian, J. Establishment of a national information policy and strategy for its implementation. Paris; Unesco, 1987. (RP/1986-87/vii. 2.1)
4. Penna, C.V. The planning of library and documentation services, 2nd ed. revised by P.H. Sewell and Herman Liebaers. Paris: Unesco, 1970. Preface.
5. Parker, J. Stephen. Unesco and library development planning. London : Library Association, 1985. pp. 237.
6. d 'Olier, J.H. and Delmas, B. Planning national infrastructures for documentation, libraries and archives. Paris: Unesco. 1975. Preface.
7. Parker. *op. cit.* pp. 269.
8. Intergovernental Conference on Scientific and Technological Information Development, UNISIST II, Paris, May 28 June 1, 1979. Final report. Unesco, 1979, pp. 18 & 20.
9. Ferguson, Stepheny. Library associations and the advancement of librarianship in developing countries. IFLA, General Conference. 1990. Section RI, pp. 14.

10. Adams, S., Madkour, M.A.K. and Slameeka, V.A Proposed national policy of Egypt. Atlanta, G.A.: Georgia Institute of Technology, 1981.

11. Barua, B.P. "Towards a national policy on library and information systems." In National information policies and programmes : seminar papers. XXXVII All India Library Conference. III, Madras, December 4-7, 1991, Delhi : Indian Library Association, 1991. pp. 5.

12. Ranganathan. S.R. Postwar reconstruction of libraries in India. Madras, 1944.

13. *Ibid*. p. 15.

14. India. Advisory Committee for Libraries, 1957, Report. New Delhi : Ministry of Education, 1959.

15. India. Committee on Plan Projects (Study Team for Selected Educational Schemes). Report. New Delhi, 1963.

16. India. Planning Commission. Working Group on Libraries. Report. New Delhi, 1966.

17. India. Raja Rammohun Roy Library Foundation Memorandum of Association and rules. 2nd ed. 1987.

18. Aggarwal, J.C. and Aggarwal, S.P. National policy on education : Agenda for India 2001. New Delhi: Concept, 1989, pp. 20.

19. *Ibid* , pp. 59.

20. University Grants Commission, Inter-Agency Group. Development of an Information and Library Network (INFLIBNET): Report New Delhi, 1989.

21. India. Planning Commission. Working Group on Modernisation of Library Services and Informatics for the Seventh Five Year Plan 1985-90. Report. 1984, Preamble.

22. India. Ministry of Information and Broad-casting India, a reference annual. 1990. New Delhi : Publications Division, 1989.

23. *Nissat Newsletter,* 9, 3 (July-Sep. 1990), pp. 24.

24. "National policy on library and information system : A presentation" *Herald of Library Science,* 26 (1987), pp. 249-263.

25. Myrdal. *op. cit.* p. 1652.

26. Ndiaye, Raphael "Oral culture and libraries". *IFLA Journal* 14 (1988). pp. 45.

27. Eicher, Jean Claude. "The financial crisis in educational system." In: The prospects for educational planning. A Workshop organised by IIEP on the occasion of its XXVth anniversary edited by Francoise Caillods. Paris: Unesco, International Institute for Educational Planning, 1989, pp. 89.

28. Carron, G., and Bordia, A., ed. Issues in planning and implementing national literacy programmes. Paris: Unesco, 1985. pp. 5.

29. Dave, Ravindra H. "Designing a system of evaluation and monitoring for literacy and post-literacy programmes." In: Carron and Bordia. *op. cit.* pp. 287.

30. Newa, John M. "Libraries in national literacy education programmes in Africa South of the Sahara : The state-of-the art *International Library Review,* 22(1990), pp. 73-94.

31. India. Ministry of Human Resources Development. National Literacy Mission on Jana Shikshan Niloyam. New Delhi: The Ministry, 1988.

32. Klees, Steven J. "The economics of education: a more than sligthly jaundiced view of where we are now" In: The prospects for educational planning: *op. cit*. pp. 244.

33. Mchombu, Kingo. "Which way African librarianship". 56th IFLA Conference, Stackholm, 18-24 August, 1990. Booklet 8, pp. 4.

34. Eicher. *op. cit*. pp. 75.

35. National Commission on Libraries and Information Science (USA). Library and information services in a learning society: Annual report 1983-84. Washington, 1985, pp.14.

36. Fuller, Bruce. Raising school quality in developing countries Washington, D.C. : The World Bank, 1986. World Bank discussion paper 2.

37. IEA. Science achievement in seventeen countries : A preliminary report. Oxford: Pergamon. 1988.

38. Short, J., Williams, E. and Christie, A. The social psychology of telecommunications. London. John Wiley, 1976.

39. Judge, Peter J. National information policy. Cannberra : Department of Parliamentary Library, 1985. pp. 25.

40. Malhotra, D. L. "Literacy programmes in India. "*Bulleting of the Unesco Principal Regional Office for the Asia and the Pacific 30*. (Dec. 1989), pp. 127.

41. World Declaration on Education for All and Framework for action to meet basic learning needs. Documents adopted at the World Conference on Education for All: meeting basic learning needs. Jomtien, Thailand, March 1990. (Paris, Unesco, 1990). 134 Ex/29 Annex. pp. 33.

"Library History in India : Historiographical Assessment and Current Trends"

DONALD G. DAVIS, JR. and MOHAMED TAHER

The status and role of library history in Indian librarianship has a proud, if uneven, past. In 1988 a major survey sought describe and assess the current environment of this subfield in India with a view toward strengthening its position. Since that time efforts have continued to focus on the problems and issues of library history scholarship. The present overview deals with the historiography of libraries and librarianship in India, present-day considerations, and some modest projections. A clearer view of library history in India is the result.

Few would dispute the fact that the history of libraries, for a long time the province of antiquarians, has grown into a distinct field with distinguished authors, especially in the past quarter century or so. The founding of groups for those interested in the history of libraries within national professional associations was crowned by the establishment within IFLA of the Round Table on Library History in the late 1970s. By that time, several journals had begun to assume significance for the field and since 1973 the *Annual Bibliography of the History of the Printed Book and Libraries* has appeared.

The proceedings of the international symposium, "Library History Research in the International Context," held in Wolfenbüttel, Germany in April 1988, marked yet another benchmark on the road toward sophistication in the study of library history.[1] Survey reports on the status of library history research were presented by scholars from thirteen nations representing four continents. Though not all the news was uniformly encouraging, in general, the participants and the readers of the printed text felt that there was hope for the future.

One of the conspicuous omissions from the 1988 Symposium was a report on the status of library history in India—a nation known for its ancient, and medieval, as well as more modern, library establishment. Although the history and tradition of literacy and books among certain classes in what is now India is long-standing, the modern library movement has roots in the later eighteenth century with real growth appearing a century or more later. Programs for professionals library education developed in the principal centers of Bombay, Calcutta, Delhi in the 1940s, with others following during the 1960s. A number of relatively short surveys and monographic works dealing with Indian library history have treated various chronological periods, types of libraries, geographical areas, or a mix of these. Since the tradition is so rich, the library education programmes relatively strong, and the interest in pursuing national cultural history keen, questions that recur to the student of library history are: what is the status of library history in India? How can this be explained? and what might the future hold?

This curious situation caused one American library historianDonald G. Davis, Jr. of the University of Texas at Austin. to undertake a systematic overview of the scene in India during a five-week research tour in the summer of 1988 sponsored by the American Institute of Indian Studies. The project "aimed to study the current status of library history in India by cursorily reviewing the existing (English - language) bibliography, by surveying present activities, and by describing and evaluating the findings from an international and sympathetic point of view."[2] With longer stays in Calcutta at the National Library of India and in Delhi, the tour encompassed visits and interviews at eight library schools and nine other institutional libraries in cities along the route of 8,400 km. or 5,200 miles. The report that resulted has been widely distributed in the following two years.

The findings of the survey included description of the literature, the historians, the organization structure, and the general attitude towards library history within the profession.

The literature survey enumerated works written primarily as history, rather than description, and accounted for less than one hundred significant monographs, dissertations, scholarly articles, chapters in collected works, and whole volumes of collected papers can be identified as constituting a core bibliography for the field. Strengths include the public library movement, Muslim influence, the national library, and library associations; weaknesses include academic libraries, private libraries, library education, and comparative studies.

As for library history scholars, about a dozen (12) were identified as productive researchers and writers. Unfortunately, about half this number are in retirement or are continuing their research after leaving professional employment; as these cease their labors, the profession will sustain a great loss. On the other hand, there is a good group of widely scattered, younger historians who are just beginning to assume the responsibility of continuing the work of interpreting the profession to its society in historical terms; some of these live outside India.

The organization structure of library history is diffused with the best collection of printed materials in one place located at the National Library of India. Programs in library and information science have not given much attention to library history and even on the doctoral level, most of the dissertations have appeared have been done in other departments or overseas. There are no identifiable groups that bring persons interested in library history together and few conferences on the subject. The few historically-oriented articles that are produced appear in the general professional journals, or, more likely, in professional scholarly journals published abroad.

The general attitute of the profession and its historians seems to be discouragement. The elder scholars as well as their junior colleagues usually work alone and in isolation, sometimes with more affinity with their academic colleagues in historical or literary studies. They see little professional reward or recognition for such study from their fellow librarians, despite the rich sources for explicating the role of libraries and information in complex culture of a developing nation.

The survey concluded that despite the pessimism regarding the future of historical studies in librarianship, a situation resulting from at least four possible causes, the outlook for the future is not without hope. The challenge of coming years will be whether or not their can be agreement about the nature of the unfinished agenda. Two questions are critical.

> First, is library history a luxury for a few aberrant and possibly elderly members of the profession, or is it a topic that the whole profession, or a significant portion of it, can embrace with pride and enthusiasm? Second, is library history only the province of nations heavily influenced by the West, or is it a mark of maturing profession in any nation that is

coming to grips with its role in the cultural life of the country and contributing its part to that cultural record?[3]

Some possible steps envisioned for the future included formation of regional interest groups or one under the aegis of the Indian Library Association, regular programme meetings, an informal newsletter, occasional publications, and development of a model syllabus for library education programmes. Mention was even made of the forthcoming IFLA conference in 1992.

Today, that time has come and with it the opportunity to look again at India as a case study of the library and information profession of a great nation, trying to grapple with its glorious past, challenging present, and uncertain future. Historians, along with other social scientists, study human behavior over periods of time, hoping that analysis will shed light on situations and problems so that informed decisions for the future can be made with as much knowledge as possible.

Essentially, little has changed since 1988. Yet, there is evidence for hope. Some of the younger library historians are completing their doctoral degrees and have published their results. They need to be encouraged and to communicate more regularly with one another. Another major achievement is the splendid, two-volume compilation, *Humanities Information Systems and Centres* (1991),[4] that presents capsule descriptions of sixty-six specialized institutions in the fields of cultural studies, many of them being archival and rare book repositories. Most of these entries, many prepared by scholars who might form a nucleus of a library history network, contain substantial historical notes on the founding and development of the institutions and their libraries.

The identification of potential research topics and subjects for investigation is another specific role that library historians can play in their profession. For scholarship and the construction of the whole story of national cultural development there are a number of significant topics that suggest themselves. Many of these relate to what social and cultural historians and researchers are already doing; library historians can join them in their endeavours.

When contemporary problems manifest themselves, historians can examine the evidence and help to explain their context, offering some insight into possible solutions and alternative courses of action. In the case of India, it is not enough to wring one's hands and state that supported by more than two millennia of cultures that enjoyed literacy and book making, the nation's diverse libraries represent all of the various types known to the human race, including those of the most advanced countries. One must acknowledge that some outstanding examples may serve only as exceptions to the prevailing status of libraries and that fine looking organization charts and statistical tables do not always provide a clear picture of what the real situation is at the grassroots level.

Among the many potential contemporary topics that might invite the attention of Indian library historians are : (1) the underdeveloped status of public libraries, (2) the lack of genuine library consciousness in the library community, and (3) the appropriate role of the library profession.[5] These issues may, of course, be also relevant in other nations.

Firstly, on paper India appears to have a well-organized, functioning system of public libraries that attempt to supply the reading needs of all its citizens. In reality, in contrast with frequent public relations statements, the condition of most public libraries, large or small, urban or rural, city or village, is exceedingly poor. In fact, a case could be easily made that genuine public libraries, worthy of the name and with few exceptions, are, in fact, yet to be established. Modern public libraries that are user-centered, service-oriented, and collection-balanced centers for graphic records are still in the future. The reasons for this extremely slow development, despite early efforts in the early twentieth century to approximate the kind of service available in Europe and North America, are surely worth exploring. While one can rail against the effects of domination by colonial powers, primarily the British, and the lack of concern for the vernacular-speaking and reading populace, local and more recent decisions about priorities are certainly involved as well. Comparative treatment by state has only begun.

Secondly, the issue of library and information consciousness is relevant here. One could receive the impression that a commitment to the value of reading, information, and libraries is not high among library users and potential users, professional librarians, and sponsoring agencies. Some in the library establishment are convinced that even the government is interested in libraries and literacy on a marginal level. When more than sixty percent of the population is illiterate and when basic literacy elementary education is lacking, the whole society is held back and the notion of school libraries is unknown. Despite the noteworthy large cities in this country, eighty percent of the population are rural dwellers. Though individual states differ greatly in their provision of library service, a prevalent idea seems to be that passing library legislation by itself will result in great advances, whereas funding and implementation have frequently suffered. Studies examining the comparative affect of library legislation in various states could yield some fruitful insights that might provide guidance to future efforts.

Thirdly, a final issue for investigation is the role of the Indian library profession. Judged on its past, the Indian library establishment has been unable to mount an effective effort to achieve some short-term and medium-term goals with respect to library development. The tension between the specialized libraries connected with government agencies and the commercial sector and public libraries and libraries associated with educational institutions requires resolution for the benefit of all progress in library and information services. The profession, as well as the nation, require that personnel to staff all kinds of agencies be adequately prepared to support nationwide information issues. Professionalization means the leaving behind of many tasks, formerly thought to be appropriate for librarians; it also means that specialized information officers understand the vital necessity of the work that their colleagues undertake to promote books and reading among the masses of popular users.

In his 1987 presidential address to the Indian Library Association, T.S. Rajgopalan rightly remarked: "It is generally acknowledged that our libraries are underutilized in relation to investments being made on them. Non-use and low-use of libraries amount to wastage of facilities being made available. May be literacy rate, lack of reading habits, etc. are the causes for low use from the side of patrons.... User education programmes must be organized by libraries in a way that libraries are fully utilized."[6]

If library historians would address just these three contemporary issues on behalf of their colleagues, they would provide a valuable service to their profession and society. They could provide documentary evidence and support for the following proposition that point toward universal library service in India.

(1) The Society should be made conscious of the need for information.

(2) The people should make the government feel that the emerging information society needs—apart from food, clothing, and shelter—information for survival, information for development, and information for progress.

(3) The library profession, collectively and through its individual members, should assert its role positively in society, create user-friendly environments, and be more user-based than collection—and classification-based librarians.[7]

While library historians may not be prominent in the halls of government or in political campaigns, they can provide the background necessary for understanding issues.

This year that commemorates the centenary of S.R. Ranganathan's birth may be an appropriate occasion to reconsider the expression of opinion that he offered in a radio talk in April 1956:

> An account of the libraries in the first three periods (the Vedic, the Buddhist, and the Muslim) must necessarily depend upon the historical research. This has not yet been done. The library profession is too small in India to spare a person to fill up this antiquarian gap. Those trained in the scientific method of tracing history are too preoccupied with dynastic and political history to spare sufficient time for cultural history in general and library history in particular.[8]

This statement no doubt reflects the past feeling of many colleagues from India, as well as other developing nations, not to speak of the industrialized countries. However, if we as a profession do not seem to value our rich heritage, how do we expect others to do so?

REFERENCES

1. Paul Kaegbein and Paul Sturges, eds., "Library History Research in the International Context: Proceedings of an International Symposium, 14-15 April 1988, Herzog August Bibliothek, Wolfenbuttel, Germany," *Libraries & Culture* 25 (1990) : 1-152.

2. Donald G. Davis, Jr., "The Status of Library History in India: A Report of an Informal Survey and a Selective Bibliographic Essay," *Journal of Library and Information Science (Delhi)* 14 (1989) : 98-114. The report also appeared in *South Asia Library Notes & Queries* 26 (1989/1990) : 5-23, and *Libraries & Culture* 25 (1990) : 575-589.

3. Davis, "Status of Library History in India," JLIS, 106.

4. *Handbook of Libraries, Archives and Information Centres in India,* B.M. Gupta, coord. ed., vol. 9 in 2 parts, *Humanities Information Systems and Centres* (Delhi: Aditya Prakashan, 1991).

5. These Points derive from an unpublished manuscript by Mohamed Taher and Donald G. Davis, Jr., "Librarianship and Library Science in India: An Outline of Historical Perspectives" (Hyderabad, 1991) 187 pp. A comprehensive bibliography of nearly 350 items in English appears on pp. 122-142.

6. T.S. Rajgopalan, "Trends and Perspectives in Indian Librarianship," *Presidential Address, Indian Library Association Conference, 1987.*

7. Taher and Davis, "Librarianship... in India," 88 (slightly modified).

8. S.R. Ranganathan, Radio Talk of April 1956. Quoted in Taher and Davis, "Librarianship... in India," 3.

Information Services in a University Library—Will the 21st Century Bring Us Anything Different or Will It Be More of the Same?

A.J. EVANS

Almost exactly 20 years ago an FID seminar was held in Budapest alongside the 38th IFLA conference on the theme "Organization of Information Services in Less Industrialized Countries", Dorothy Anderson (at that time Director of the UBC office) and I presented a paper[1] the summary of which included the following:

> In a less industrialized country, internally, information services must be integrated as a part of the total library, bibliographical and documentation system, and will contribute as part of the national bibliographic service; externally information services will be the country's link with the international communications network; will draw upon that network to help fulfil the country's total needs in a particular field, or research area and will contribute to that network with items from its country's own scientific or technical specialist literature which will be recorded in the form acceptable to the international world.

The year before that, 1971, had seen the first UNISIST Conference in Paris and the Synopsis of the full report[2] prepared especially for that meeting included two interesting paragraphs (and indeed in retrospect *very* interesting paragraphs!).

> However, most experienced observers would agree that computer technology cannot provide a solution for all the problems of scientific communication. The traditional institutions of scientific journals, of abstracting and indexing publications, of textbooks and libraries have strong survival values, and will not be superceded tomorrow by console displays of retrieved text, or programmed instruction. The technologically advanced countries will be operating conventional and computer-based scientific information systems in parallel for a long time to come.

I think you might agree that statement is still, at the very least, some 95% valid.

The second paragraph I wanted to refer to was of a slightly different nature and was in fact

> *Recommendation 7. Library infrastructure*
>
> A strong library system should be recognized as an essential component of scientific information transfer in modern times. In collaboration with the international and national organizations concerned (IFLA, IATUL, etc.), UNISIST should direct its efforts to a statement of the minimum set of functions and levels of performance that scientific libraries, and eventually special depositories, ought to maintain for their optimum performance.

I said earlier that we are still only providing "information about information". That is only a half-truth in this age of full-text database services, but there is inevitably a price to pay. Even in a country such as India, which can hardly be called a developing country in library terms, the two inevitable problems of document supply and finance rear their ugly heads. Indeed the latter is not getting any easier anywhere, but it is a relative one. There is little doubt that one of the major problems that must be overcome, if at all possible, is that of frustration, frustration of knowing that all his marvellous information is available and then not being able to get hold of it for weeks or months or perhaps ever! If I may be allowed to parody Hamlet:

> To have or not to have, that is the question;
>
> Whether 't's nobler to use the human brain
>
> Or to take arms against a sea of troubles
>
> And install a tele-link to that far distant place
>
> Who hath no soul yet answers back incessantly.

You may remember earlier in the same play when Polonius was advising Laertes, he said "neither a borrower or a lender be". He was talking about money rather than books, however!

For the latter half of this paper let us try and move away from theory and philosophy and look in detail at a project we are carrying out at the University of Loughborough. It could be that it in a country such as India where, with its five Institutes of Technology and an enviable history of engineering education, there is a particular relevance. Also I noticed only recently that S.K. Joshi, the Director of the Council for Scientific and Industrial Research in India, commented that in the future funding from the Council would concentrate on industry-oriented research and give much less to "basic" research. An engineering-oriented retrieval system might, therefore, be of some significant interest.

We have been given the opportunity at Loughborough to investigate in depth a particular development by Engineering Information Inc. in the USA called "Ei Reference Desk". It is financially supported by the British Library Research and Development Department and also involves collaboration with their Document Supply Centre. Ei themselves have freely provided hardware and software as well as CD-ROM and access to online databases.

An integrated database and software package has been developed by them with the following features:

— Online information retrieval of Compendex files

— Offline CD-ROM searching

— Access to Table of contents service for current awareness

— A document delivery service (Ei DDS) which will use any of a variety of means such as post, fax, direct transmission, etc.

The particular feature of the development is the creation of a personal information workstation for engineers. The intention as such is *not* the consideration of information provision in the engineering area, but the workstation reference desk aspects using the Ei system as an example. The very positive bonus to the test group of engineers is that they are getting completely free high quality information provision to meet their actual and precise needs (even more so since the library has just started charging users for interloans!).

The objectives of the research project are as follows:

— The principal objective as already indicated is to investigate and evaluate the use of "Ei Reference Desk" in a technological university environment where there is an already established information service for engineers across the campus.

— To investigate the problems of document delivery in cooperation with BLDSC.

— To consider the use of such a "tool" on the context of user education.

It had also been hoped to investigate the possible linking of the Ei system with the University network (parallel with our OPAC) either through the library's own Data General machine or alternatively the University's mainframe. It now seems, however, that our hands will be full on the first three objectives and any further work will necessitate more time and more importantly more financial support.

We are however looking at such questions as:

— What is the best way of delivering Ei Reference Desk data and software?

— How can it be interfaced with other sources?

— What range of clients are best served by it and are there significant differences in the needs of various client groups?

— What value, perceived and real, does it have for clients?

— What documentation (guidance, etc.) is needed to supplement that which is provided by the system?

— Is there an impact on browsing/serendipity by providing a client/researcher with (apparently) all that is needed in one package?

— Is there an impact on client productivity through its use?

— What impact on document demand does it have?

— What impact on document use does it have?

A more explicit description was given by one of my colleagues at the UK Serials group conference earlier this year[3] with the title, "The Information Cornucopia: Experiments with an Integrated Workstation".

A test group has now been established of 37 members of academic staff and researchers evenly distributed between six engineering departments. Preliminary results suggest that most people prefer to do the searching themselves, after a basic training session rather than use an intermediary (in contrast o the King Research Inc. findings referred to earlier). However some of the results indicate, as we might expect, that the search would have had more relevance and been more comprehensive if somebody more familiar with the system had conducted the search. In many cases inappropriate search options and strategies had been used. Comparative studies are also being carried out throughout the trials between Ei Reference, online, and printed abstract sources.

We don't seem to have got very far with this in the last 20 years do we? I would indeed recommend that the full Study Report[4] of that UNISIST meeting well worth reading—it is a salutary experience!

In my own University we established our indepth information service in 1969, over 23 years ago, as distinct from the traditional readers services. At that time it was inevitably entirely manual although it was not that long after in 1975 when we carried out our first online search. At such times we thought that we had solved all our information problems, much like the situation 20 years before that when microfilm was said to be the answer to all our storage problems.

Only recently two of my colleagues wrote an internal report[5] with the aim of showing the University how information provision had, and indeed is, continuing to change and develop, not only as a result of information technology but also as a result of changes in teaching methods. These phenomena accompanied by rapid increase in student numbers are resulting in what can only be called "controlled chaos" where "firefighting" is the order of the day rather than "controlled development", albeit at a rather faster pace than or predecessors were used to in a traditional academic environment.

They commented on the fact that 'Increasingly sophisticated online searching techniques, the proliferation and scope of the number of online databases, CD-ROM databases, and the current and potential developments relating to distributed databases on networks have all had a considerable impact upon both information services and library users". Later in the report they went on to say, "Until relatively recently the vast majority of undergraduates used a limited range of library resources... mostly recommended on reading lists. In this way they became sufficiently familiar with the relevant library resources to be able to locate a good proportion of material for themselves (particularly with a good user education programme). In this context undergraduate enquiry work was reasonably straight forward. Information staff normally expected the more complex enquiries to arise from research and academic staff."

We are now, however, in an entirely different age. The introduction of online catalogues and even more the effect of CD-ROM has created a quite different learning environment for students. There is, however, also a word of warning that must be introduced here. Whilst electronic sources might be seen to resolve the problems of bibliographic access they do in fact also raise many new problems. Not only do students require guidance in making judgments about relevance and selectivity but the material they require is often no longer "automatically" available within the four walls of the library, thus placing additional strain upon budgets and services.

A more recent development is the availability of the ISI databases on the national academic network (JANET). We now have more than 500 registered users across the campus who, in the first year of operation, had almost 3000 access sessions. It should also be mentioned that this service is available from their own offices and thus the "drag" up to the library is avoided. At least that part of their information provision is!

But, we are still only providing information about information!

What are we actually trying to do to help this transfer of information? In general, and in the university world in particular, of course we are trying to provide the means for a scholar to add in some way or other to the sum total of human knowledge. It sounds a little pretentious but I would submit that is what it is. At the moment what happens in very simplistic terms is that a scientist thinks, reads around the subject, carries out some research, — writes down the results to tell the world how creative he's been, publishes it in the highest quality journal he can persuade to accept it, and then sits back in the hope that another scientist when he is reading around his subject will come across it. It may be of course that he "comes across it" by the thorough search of an electronic database or more likely (the cynics would say) by serendipity.

We are therefore dealing essentially with the mechanics of that bit of the whole communication process from the time the researcher actually writes his results down, to the time the next researcher picks it up from one source or another. Merely converting the quill pen to the electronic signal!

Traditionally it was essential to teach future reference librarians how to deal with enquiry work, how to interpret the user's needs and of course find the answers "on the library's shelves." In those far off days there was seemingly an acceptance that this was essentially as far as one could go. Now of course there is a growing lack of acceptance that unless the total world's output of research literature is searched then we are not providing an adequate service. "As the number of major databases available on our 'Joint academic network' increases, it is unlikely, given current funding levels, that the Library could make even a small proportion of them available to the campus community, however, desirable that might be. Although it is difficult to predict the precise nature of the impact on the Library of networked databases and end-user searching, recent experience with CD-ROM indicates dramatic and far-reaching consequences"[6]

On the matter of end-user searching it was interesting to see a view expressed by King research Incorporated.[7]

> Admittedly, end users of information do tend to perform some of their own information searches, particularly when they have become comfortable with available systems. However, as they do more searching they recognize that more of their time is being taken up with information searching and retrieval activities. They learn that there are numerous sources of information to choose from and that sources change over time, in terms of coverage, procedures for use, etc. Once they recognize the complexity of information searching and retrieval they begin to return to the intermediary.

This is, however, by no means everybody's view. In an excellent paper given by Michael Malinconico[8] at the Portuguese Library Association Conference in Braga earlier this year he posed an interesting conundrum when he said

> It is ironic that the new information services which will substantially increase users' need for the assistance of information specialists, will at the same time reduce their contact with those

individuals. Nor, can we expect that many users will seek assistance even though they need it.

In a rather different context such statements were of course made some 25 years ago when user education in university libraries was just beginning to blossom. It has if anything, however, improved and accelerated our professional activity rather than reduced it.

The first "published" information regarding Ei Reference Desk was given By John Regazzi, the President of Engineering Information Inc. in 1989[9] when he said, "It's unlikely the founders of Information Engineering Inc., or Engineering Index, as it was called 105 years ago, envisioned that some day the media of delivery would become almost as important as the scope of its index". One might argue that in our project we don't really care how and where the information comes from as long as it makes the customer happy!

The future grandiose plans of Ei are to establish an international network (EiNet) in partnership with the major technical information centres around the world in order that engineers and scientists can

- Access all engineering database (initially bibliographic)
- Capture bibliographic citations in a fast and convenient way.
- Order the full text of documents electronically.
- Receive delivery of full-text documents on request by mail, fax or over Internet or equivalent systems.
- Receive electronic newsletters.
- Communicate electronically between readers, writers and researchers through electronic mail, bulletin boards, etc.

All that by just sitting at one workstation! It is in effect the exact opposite of the chained library and much more likely to cause indigestion. Oh for the good old days! Whether I have answered the question I posed in the title of this paper is, however, now for you to decide.

REFERENCES

1. Anderson, Dorothy and A.J. Evans. "The Role of Information Services in a National Library and Bibliographic System" in *Organization of Information Services in Less Industrialized Countries*. FILD Seminar held in Budapest, 31 August—12 September 1972.

2. *UNISIST Synopsis of the feasibility Study on a World Science Information System.* Paris: Unesco, 1971, pp. 25 and 49.

3. *UNISIST Study Report on the Feasibility of a World Science Information System,* Paris : Unesco, 1971.

4. Woodward, H. and M. Hodgkinson. *Information Services in the Pilkington Library.* Loughborough University Library: Unpublished report, 1991

5. *Ibid.*

6. Griffiths, J.M. and D.W. King. "Evaluating the Performance of Information Centre Staff" in *Evaluating the effectiveness of Information Centres and Services.* AGARD Lecture Series, No. 160-4-1. Paris: AGARD, 1988.

7. Malinconico, S.M. "Technology and the Changing Role of Librarians and Information Specialists" Paper delivered at the Portuguese Library Association Conference, Braga, March 1992.

8. Price, S. and J.E. Davies. "The Information Cornucopia: Experiments with an Integrated Workstation". *Serials, 1992* (in press).

9. Regazzi, J.J. "Ei Reference Desk—The Electronic Library". *Newsidic 97* (October 1989).

ACKNOWLEDGEMENTS

I wish to record my very sincere thanks to my colleagues Eric Davies, Sandra Price, Hazel Woodward and Mary Hodgkinson for permission to reproduce portions of their unpublished writings.

PART V
Management and Training

The Management of Library Staff: Trends and Reflections

MAURICE B. LINE

This paper deals with some trends in the management of library staff, and comments on them critically. It is particularly concerned with motivation. It reflects my experience as a member of staff in four academic libraries under several bosses of mixed quality over 18 years, as a boss in four different libraries over 20 years, and as a consultant specializing in the management of change for the last five years. Of these three periods, the last has probably taught me most; it is much easier to see what is going wrong from the outside than when actually working in a library, especially when one is the boss.

Management has come to occupy a more and more prominent place in the literature of librarianship in the last ten years or so. There are no prizes for guessing why this should be so. The fact that libraries have become bigger and more complex is reason enough in itself; but to this have been added ever increasing pressures on public expenditure, which has reduced the money in real terms available to most libraries at the same time as the cost and volume of publications have continued to grow and as demand has tended to be heavier. All these factors have forced librarians to look at the way they manage their libraries. Cuts in public expenditure have led to demands from library authorities for greater productivity, cost-effectiveness and value for money. Staff reductions have made it necessary to seek economies in service provision. There have been crises before, but these were no more than temporary; there is no sign that the pressures of the last decade or so will go away, though they may get less intense. It is the good times that will be temporary in future, not the bad.

As if this were not enough, many governments decided as a matter of principle, and not merely in response to economic problems, to move as much of the public sector as possible into the private sector, on the grounds that this subjects everything to the "real" market, erodes the "dependency culture", removes waste, and leads to a great release of entrepreneurial energy. The net result will, according to the theory, be lasting progress and permanent profitability, albeit at the cost of temporary pain to many. The observation that wealth was commonly associated with success apparently persuaded governments to conclude that it was the urge to create wealth that led to success, and that therefore the desire for wealth - greed - should be encouraged; other motivators could be ignored. The poor were not forgotten; there need, we were told, be no conflict between greed of a few and the welfare of many, as previous generations had supposed; the wealth accumulated by the few would "trickle down" in due course.

So far it is the pain that appears likely to be permanent - it is certainly increasing, while the progress and profitability seem to be confined to a smaller and smaller number of people. There are moreover few signs that any relief will be long-lived. Meanwhile, while the argument rages, publicly funded bodies, including libraries, suffer.

This paper is not a political tract, but economics is inseparable from politics, and both profoundly influence libraries funded from the public purse. Nor is suffering confined to libraries in the public sector; for industries and business, struggling to keep afloat during the recession, are all too apt to sacrifice their libraries and information services. There is a further pressure that affects all libraries : this is from information technology (IT), which makes it possible to bypass libraries for many information services, including access to the documents whose collection and supply have always been the main function of libraries. IT's influence is fundamental, since it affects both the form and nature of the basic material with which libraries deal and the means of conveying it. Libraries of all kinds are having to determine exactly what they are there for. You can't manage anything unless you first know what business it is in; and the business of libraries is changing.

This all means that libraries have to take a radical look at themselves : what they are doing, why they are doing it, how they are doing it, and how to do it better. Strategic planning has become popular as a means of determining objectives and working out a strategy for attaining them. More recently, total quality management - TQM - has begun to be used in libraries; it is at the same time a way of life, a search for continuous improvement, and a set of techniques for the analysis and revision of procedures.

No measure taken to improve effectiveness will succeed beyond a certain point unless the commitment of staff is obtained. If staff have more demands placed on them they have to work harder; but they often do so unwillingly, and not well, and users suffer. Who wants to run, or use, a library with over-worked and surly staff ? Moreover, after a while stress can take its toll in sickness and poor performance. A poorer service carries the serious risk of losing institutional support and hence of suffering yet further cuts.

Reductions can be fought, and perhaps alleviated, but they cannot be avoided. The only solution is to scrutinize all activities to see which are really needed, and to examine if and how they can be improved; and to involve staff in all planning and implementation. The temptation to direct change from above must be resisted. Unless staff are involved they will not understand why changes are needed, and they will resent changes that are imposed on them. Moreover, either they will find imposed changes impossible to implement, because those ordering them have not understood all the implications, or they will implement them with a bad grace. After all, the staff who carry out processes are usually in much the best position to find out what is wrong and to identify means of putting it right.

Reductions in staff numbers have led to other problems. In former times individuals could expect to make some progress up the ladder of promotion as staff numbers increased at all levels. Also, because there was a greater general feeling of security, staff were prepared to take risks, and were more ready to move to other libraries, to jobs at a higher level or to more agreeable jobs at the same level. Now many libraries have a lot of staff who have been there for many years, who have no realistic prospect of promotion, and who for one reason or another cannot or will not move. They are not incompetent, so cannot be sacked. They are stuck. The problems of motivating such staff at the best of times can easily be imagined; and these are by no means the best of times. Somehow means must be found of harnessing the abilities and energies of these staff.

The problems of staffing do not end here. Although librarianship has been for many a second or third choice of career, most of those who have come into it have found it rewarding, professionally if not always financially. With the large increase in unemployment, more people are likely to go into librarianship with no real interest; it is simply a job, and a job is better than no job. It is therefore not only the tired and stale older member of staff who has to be encouraged to perform; the new and reluctant recruit also has to be motivated.

One "solution" that is being increasingly mooted to deal with the lack of mobility and staff staleness that is being increasingly adopted is to employ staff on limited term contracts. Some writers on management - e.g. Handy[1] - confidently forecast that peripatetic staff will become the norm; we can look forward to what have been called "corporate mercenaries"[2]. Short term contracts make it relatively easy to remove poor performers (although they would not apply to staff at present in post), but they bring their own problems : it is not much easier to motivate staff who are in danger of removal after a few years than staff who are in post for ever, and it is very much harder to build up a corporate spirit with such staff.

One is tempted to lament the official ideologies that have added to unavoidable pressures entirely avoidable ones; or to wait and hope that there will be a change of ideology. These temptations need to be resisted; there is no point in fighting against facts, which in effect means sacrificing our libraries to our own beliefs. At the same time we need to recognize the terms that governments and authorities commonly use for what they are : euphemisms for something unpleasant. "Rationalizing", for example, means simply "cutting"; I have never yet seen anything that has been rationalized and increased. "Delayering", the removal of one or more layers of staff in the hierarchy, has its virtues, but it is nearly always done to cut staff numbers and/or costs. "Downsizing" sounds a decent enough procedure, but it means no more nor less than shedding numbers of staff. If we have to cut back, let us call it cutting back.

As if the above were not enough, librarianship is being "deskilled". Some of us were always suspicious of the so-called "professional" skills of librarianship, which wrapped what were or should have been fairly simple and easily learnt skills in a cloak of obscurity and arcane mystique, which mystified some of library practitioners almost as much as it clearly did many users. Automation, in particular the ability to take catalogue records off remote databases, has changed all that, and the skills that many of us painstakingly learned are no longer of much use. What we do all need is managerial skills, which were not taught at all in library schools until very recently. So libraries are replete with skills they do not need, and lacking those they do.

How can staff be motivated ? This question has exercised managers and consultants for many years, and there is a large literature on it. One particularly influential writer is Herzberg[3], who distinguished between what he called "hygiene" factors - factors like work conditions and relationship with supervisors and subordinates, the absence of which leads to dis-satisfaction - and "motivators" - factors which have a positive influence on motivation. Money is a hygiene factor; it is important if staff do not have enough to live on, but cannot motivate for long because the search for more money has no end. Motivators include achievement, recognition, the work itself, responsibility, and (some way behind) advancement and growth. Herzberg also points out that "the psychology of motivation is tremendously complex, and what has been unraveled with any degree of assurance is very small indeed". There are no quick fixes.

The validity of Herzberg's concept has been shown repeatedly, both in research carried out in various environments and in practical experience. It is, however, one thing to know what motivates people, and another to use this knowledge in practice. There have been many failures, most of them due to following the letter of Herzberg without following the spirit. This has rarely been because of any malevolence on the part of managers; it is simply that they have not known how to handle people. A cold uncaring manager who goes through the motions of delegation will achieve nothing except to bring himself (or herself) and the theory into disrepute. Truly cold uncaring managers are probably rare; what are much more common are managers who are shy or introverted or just awkward with people. In libraries such people are unfortunately not uncommon. They cannot be blamed for this; many of them became librarians when the job was very different, when technical skills or scholarship in applicants were more highly rated.

A more recent concept is that of "empowerment"[4]. This is entirely consistent with Herzberg's theories. It means simply delegating responsibility (not merely work) to staff, giving them "ownership" of their jobs. Manz & Sims[5] advocate the "superleader", one who leads by leading others to lead themselves.

At this point it is necessary to make it clear that when the motivation of staff is discussed, it should mean ALL staff, from the most senior to the humblest attendant. Motivation knows no class or grade distinctions; you can't have a successful library where only the most senior third of the staff is motivated. Indeed, the breaking down of barriers of all kinds, whether of grade or department or sex, is an essential element in making a library work.

A starting point in motivating staff must be the presence of hygiene factors and the absence of demotivators[6]. It is astonishing that managers cannot see how they demotivate their staff in all sorts of ways. Many of these are seemingly trivial, like omitting to greet staff on meeting them in the morning - trivial to the manager, that is; but being treated as an inferior being, which is what such behaviour implies, is far from trivial to the member of staff concerned.

A next necessary step is to give staff positive as well as negative signals. Most supervisors criticize staff when they make errors - and even this can be done positively and supportively, with a view to ensuring that the same error is not made again - but rarely praise them when they do a good job. Praise cannot be given too extravagantly, otherwise it is devalued; but it is possible, and desirable, both to single out for praise an outstanding job and to show appreciation for continuous good performance. We all know from personal experience how even a little appreciation boosts our morale and encourages us to do better; the odd thing is that so few of us apply this knowledge to the work situation.

These are the elementary necessities and courtesies of dealing with people. They should not need to be stated, but they do. They can be, and must be, applied by everyone, whatever the management style or structure; and they do much to provide the human foundation that is necessary if organizational change is to be successful.

It is often assumed that human beings are naturally lazy, that few of them can really be trusted, and that very few have any ideas of their own. Motivation is therefore something that has to be injected into them, like a drug. Libraries that operate on such assumptions are unlikely to achieve much success in motivating staff. A far better starting point is to assume that most human beings have a resource of natural energy and initiative, which has been largely suppressed over the years by parental and social influences and the education system. This is not pie-in-the-sky idealism: the energies and initiative that most people show in their private lives is often astonishing. Nor do staff want to do little at work; this leads to boredom, and boredom is a very unpleasant feeling. Motivation consists largely of releasing the energies of people, of allowing them to express themselves at work as they do at home. It is not so much a positive set of actions as a series of removal processes - although positive action is usually needed to achieve the removal. The question to be asked is not "What can I do to motivate staff ?" as "How can I remove the obstacles that stop them being motivated ?"

Once this fact is appreciated, it becomes clearer how to motivate staff. It will always be pointed out that there are exceptions; there are a few staff who are genuinely lazy, and some who are willing enough but genuinely lacking in energy. To this I would (and do) respond that it is impossible to know what people are made of until they have been tested under a different system; I know of several staff who have been written off, only to prove themselves once managers take a different approach. And even if there are such people, this is no reason for applying the same assumption to all staff. Just as people respond to praise and encouragement, so do most of them respond to faith placed in them. Equally, they do not respond to distrust - or rather, they respond by a lack of interest and commitment.

Trust cannot be communicated easily through a long chain of people. This means both that senior managers - especially the boss - must meet their staff in person from time to time, and that the chain of command should be as short as possible. Industry has discovered that some links in the chain can be dispensed with; that is, the structure can be "flattened" to the benefit of all - except the individuals who comprise the redundant links. These can be "released from office" (another euphemism), or, more humanely, redeployed; there are ways of flattening structures without flattening the people involved. (I prefer "flattening" to "delayering", not just because it is less objectionable as a word but because it does not carry the same destructive connotations). A word of caution here : flattening the structure, or any other major change to the structure, can cause great damage if it is not handled well - which means explaining to staff why change is needed and giving them a full opportunity to discuss it[7].

Shorter reporting lines and more direct contact between managers and staff will be useful only if the managers in question are humane, sensible, listening and responsive people; and they will show none of these qualities unless they are both confident, humble and above all personally secure. Many of the problems of management arise because managers unconsciously work out their own insecurities on their staff. For example, they may see every suggestion from someone else as a personal threat, to their authority and themselves. A manager who feels secure, on the other hand, can mix freely with his or her staff without any self-consciousness, can listen to them attentively, and can delegate work to them readily.

The boss's role is crucial in setting the tone and style of management. If he or she does not set an example by listening, mixing, delegating and involving, there is very little chance that his or her managers will do any of these things. Few bosses seem to appreciate how conspicuous they are; they seem to think they can order their managers to be participative and so on while making no attempt to be the same. It is all too easy to dominate without realizing it. One or two mild put-downs are all that is needed to prevent staff from having ideas or expressing them. Simply putting one's own view before staff have had time to put theirs can stifle them. Why bother to speak if the boss knows what he wants to do already ?

There are several mechanisms that can be used to prevent staleness among staff. There is little chance that someone who has been doing the same job for ten or twenty years will be able to look at its purpose or nature clearly. It is desirable to have a regular programme of moving staff; it has to be regular if staff are not to feel singled out for special treatment. If there is an expectation on the part of staff that they will be moved - after consultation as to where they should move to - there should be little fear or resentment. A new challenge can call forth new inspiration in the most surprising people. It is not easy to introduce a programme of movement if there has never been one, and it may need to be done gradually. Some will resist, but these can usually be handled by suggesting that they try the new job and come back and talk about it if it does not work out. It is my experience, they rarely did; they had simply been fearful of change and wanted a safety net.

The introduction of team working can help a great deal[8]. The stronger tend to help the weaker along, and the interchange of ideas among staff at the same level can be very productive, since the atmosphere contains no threat. If the teams are given real responsibility for their work - if, for example, they design their procedures and work out improvements - a good deal of enthusiasm can be generated, and at the same time productivity is increased.

Most libraries are faced with a succession of new challenges. Too often the boss or one or two senior staff tackle these. It is usually more productive to give them as projects to selected staff or teams of staff, with instructions to deliver a report by a prescribed time. The first efforts may not be ideal, but they will improve; and the effect on the morale and motivation of staff will be surprising (but not of course if the report is casually dismissed).

There are smaller stimuli that can be given to staff. Even trivial exercises can motivates staff; we all like having our views sought.

Libraries are there to serve people, but in many a high proportion of staff work in isolation from users. This is both very unhealthy, as their work may not take users sufficiently into account, and unmotivating, since they get no feedback on their work from users. Dealing with the public can be very stressful, but it can also be very stimulating. No member of library staff should be without it, from time to time at least.

Major ways of motivating and involving staff are strategic planning[9, 10] and total quality management (TQM)[11, 12]. If strategic planning is to help in this direction, it must be carried out as a cooperative exercise, not done by the boss or a small senior team. A collaborative effort takes longer, but the extra time is more than justified, for then all staff understand what the library's problems and prospects are, have some say on the way the library should go and the strategy for getting there. They will also see where their job fits into the total scheme, and be able to comment on other areas of the library (as well as hearing the comments of other staff on their area).

TQM was developed in Japan after the war (by Deming, an American who could not find an audience for his ideas in the USA), and much of Japan's economic success has been attributed to its use. By its nature it involves staff, since it requires a meticulous analysis of every operation and process by the staff concerned. It is also a way of life : a search for continuous improvement, and a continuous concern with serving the needs of the customer. It is, however, immensely time-consuming if applied wholeheartedly, and it requires total commitment at all levels. Many TQM exercises in industry have failed or been abandoned, for one reason or another[13]. If used in a supportive atmosphere, TQM can help solve many of the problems of motivation. However, it can also be used manipulatively; staff may be required to spend a great deal of time on detail rather than purpose, and constant supervision of their progress and monitoring of their results can be utterly demotivating, as some Japanese workers have found.

If staff are to be asked to do projects, adapt to new challenges, carry out TQM exercises, and so on, they need to learn the requisite skills. Otherwise they will fail not only because of lack of skills but because they do not have the confidence. However, hard pressed a library may be, it MUST allow time for staff training and development; no library can afford not to do so. Important though initial courses in library and information studies may be, they are less important than continuing education, for the skills needed keep changing.

When all steps have been taken, their effect will be limited if the attitudes to work and people are not right. It has often struck me that people behave to others quite differently at work and outside work, as if the workplace somehow dehumanized them and turned them into machines that could be switched on, watched from time to time to make sure they were behaving properly, and taken to pieces and mended if they went wrong. Ordinary human courtesies and decencies are forgotten, and there seems to be no personal concern with the welfare of staff. But there is no inconsistency between a humane organization and an efficient one. Far from it : a library is unlikely to be productive and enterprising unless staff are happy, and staff are unlikely to be happy if their library is inefficient.

In conclusion, let us return to the political pressures with which this paper began. I have suggested that it is useless merely to lament them; we have to live with them, and extract as much good as we can from them. The concern with customers and markets - who are nothing more nor less than users and potential users - is entirely welcome, indeed long overdue in some libraries. The concept that everything can be subjected to market values is, however, both false and dangerous. The move towards greater efficiency is also admirable; the belief that libraries can go on increasing their efficiency indefinitely is untrue and can only lead to irretrievable harm. Likewise, pressures on staff numbers are not harmful up to a point, but beyond that they lead to exhaustion and a steady decline in services, at a time when demands are increasing in number and sophistication. In any case, it makes no sense to have seriously understaffed libraries at the same time as huge numbers of people are paid to be unemployed. And while we should use all the sensible management techniques that we can, we must take care that in doing so we do not deceive and exploit staff. We need to manage our libraries efficiently and humanely, but we also need to fight the larger battle for libraries as an essential force in society and culture, education and the economy. If library staff could feel that governments regarded libraries in this way, it might do as much to motivate them as any internal technique[14].

REFERENCES

1. HANDY, Charles. The age of unreason. 2nd ed. London : Business Books, 1991.
2. GOLZEN, Godfrey. "The return of Select." The Director, 46(9), April 1993, pp. 68-72.
3. HERZBERG, Frederick. "One more time: how do you motivate employees" Harvard Business Review, September-October 1987, pp. 109-102. (First published 1968; reprinted with "Retrospective commentary").
4. SULLIVAN, Maureen. "A new leadership paradigm : empowering staff and improving performance." Journal of Library Administration, 14(2), 1991, pp. 73-85.
5. MANZ, Charles C., & SIMS, Henry P., Jr. "Superleadership : beyond the myth of heroic leadership." Organizational Dynamics, 19(4), Spring 1991, pp. 18-35.
6. LINE, Maurice B. "How to demotivate staff : a brief guide." Library Management, 13(1), 1992, pp. 4-7.
7. LINE, Maurice B. "Library management styles and structures : a need to rethink ?" Journal of Librarianship and Information Science, 23 (2), June 1991, 37-44.
8. BOHANNAN, April. "Self-managing groups : the role of the external leader". Library Administration and Management, 7(1), Winter 1993, pp. 17-22.
9. JACOB, M.E.L. Strategic planning: a how-to-do it manual for Librarians. New York: Neal-Schuman, 1990.

10. HAYES, Robert. "Long-range strategic planning for libraries and information resources in the research university". Advances in Library Administration and Organization, 10, 1992, pp. 1-50.

11. MACKEY, Terry & MACKEY, Terry. "Think quality! The Deming approach does work in libraries." Library Journal, 117 (9), May 12, 1992, pp. 57-61.

12. RIGGS, Donald E. "Strategic quality management." Library Advances in Librarianship, 16, 1992, pp. 93-105.

13. HARARI, Oren. "Ten reasons why TQM doesn't work". Management Review, January 1993, pp. 33-38.

14. LINE, Maurice B. "Why isn't work fun ?" Library Management, 11 (5), 1990, pp. 15-17.

Probability, Statistics and Library Management

SUJIT K. BASU

Abstract

Use of statistical methods in analysing situations for understanding the role of underlying uncertainties cannot be over-emphasized. Extraction of relevant information from observations by exploiting such tools introduces elements of rationality in the decision making process pertaining to phenomena which are influenced by chance factors. Accordingly, the dicipline of statistics assumes an important role in the management of organisations including libraries. In this paper, we have tried to illustrate a few areas of applications of probability modelling and statistical methodology in analysing and planning library services. Some necessary probabilistic and statistical notions have been discussed for the sake of completeness.

I. Introduction

The scope of applications of statistical methodology is very wide and covers a varied spectrum of phenomena that demand a rational analysis of data pertaining to the phenomenon concerned so as to be able to grasp a rational understanding about the same. Naturally then one can hardly afford to remain indifferent to possibilities of such applications whenever, in particular, one is engaged in a managerial activity that concerns an entire system or a sub-system of an entire system. The basic appeal of the discipline of statistics lies in the powerful methodology that it encompasses for analysing the past to plan for the future.

Statistical techniques play an important role in decision making in many real life situations where uncertainties occur primarily as effects of unexplained laws of Nature. Statistics as a discipline provides sound methods, based on scientific logic, for collection, analysis and interpretation of data, quantitative or qualitative, pertaining to phenomenon under study. These in turn, guide us in making an optimum (in an appropriate sense) choice of one amongst several alternative decisions in the face of uncertainty.

In the following examples which arise often in the process of offering library services, we try to raise some relevant issues which can be adequately handled by various statistical tools which we will touch upon in this article. Though no claim is being made in respect of the exhaustivity of the issues in the following examples, these are expected to provide a general idea about situations where statistics can play a significant role in helping the decision maker.

Example 1.1. A library is planning to keep an appropriate number of copies of a book on reserve for over-night issue only. These copies can be issued on *first come first served* basis for over-night use only. Explicitly, these copies can be issued out each day between 4 p.m. and 5 p.m. and are to be positively returned by 12 noon next day. How does the library decide about the number of copies to be requisitioned for this purpose ? The difficulty lies in the fact that the demand on any given day is **uncertain**. To stock a copy for each prospective user may be the safest play, but it is certainly not the most optimal way of utilizing the available resources ; on the other hand, stocking too few copies of the book may be grossly inadequate to meet the objective of this service. It is, therefore, imperative that we build up a profile of daily demand of the prospective users and use the same to determine the number of copies to be stocked to meet a certain specified criteria. The methodology necessary for this purpose can be developed using statistical techniques. Obviously, one has to keep track of actual demands occurring over days. Do we really have to undertake this seemingly additional exercise every day ? If not, then for which days ? How will an estimate of the demand profile based on a sample of days compare with the actual profile that is based on all days in the past, present and future, specially because the future is unobservable ? The daily demand observed over a large number of days will basically give rise to a series of numerical figures ; how do we summarise the data then so as to make some sense out of this series of figures ? There may be a number of ways in which the same may be done which method do we employ ? These are just some of the issues that require to be looked into in developing an appropriate decision rule in this case.

Example 1.2. The management of a large library would like to know how much money should be kept aside in a certain financial year for overhauling damaged books. If we assume that each damaged book would cost the same amount for overhauling, then the issue basically boils down to assessing the number of books, presumably out of a huge collection of books, that would require overhauling.

How does the management tacle the problem ? Well, one way would certainly be to check through each and every book accessed in the library to decide whether it is damaged or not. What are the difficulties one is likely to confront in this method ? In fact, there are quite a few. Firstly, does the library have adequate resources, *viz.* manpower, money, time etc. to be able to undertake the exercise of complete physical verification of each and every book it has on its stacks ? In most situations, this exercise will be hardly justified given that the amount that is required has to be perhaps only a small portion of the overall budget being planned. As such, let us think of an alternative approach : instead of a 100% verification, what happens if we check up only a sample of manageable size ? But then we must be in a position to handle the various problems associated with the issue of estimating the number of damaged books which would require overhauling on the basis of our knowledge about a sample of books. Uncertainty arises because the sample may not depict the reality and different samples may lead to different estimates ; it is possible that most of the books that will be sample-checked would come from the lot of books that are comparatively less frequently used so that the proportion of damaged books in the **sample** would be substantially less than its counterpart in the **population** so that we would tend to under-estimate our requirements. Similarly, we may end up with an over-estimate of our requirements and in either case our planning will be unsatisfactory.

The basic issues that are involved then are as follows :

(*a*) How do we draw a sample from the population ? (*designing the experiment*).

(*b*) How do we analyse the information contained in the sample and then use the same to make an inference about the population ? (*Statistical methodology*).

(*c*) How reliable is the inference (*reliability of inference*).

In fact, in a given situation, there may be more than one way of picking up a sample and then we must be in a position screen out the one which would suit us the best. Of course, there will be a related methodology for analysing the sample findings given a particular design of the experiment through which we obtain the data and we should be in a position to decide on a specific design and methodology to be used to ensure the quality of decision making.

All these aspects are matters that fall within the purview of the discipline of statistics.

Example 1.3. Think of a library which has a separate section which accommodates all the rare collections and as such users do not have free access into the same. The requisition for a book belonging to that section is handed over at the main circulation desk. On receipt of a requisition, the clerk at the desk forwards the same to the said section. The book is issued by the main circulation desk to the concerned user upon its receipt from the said section ; the requisition slip is returned to the user with a note of regret by the section in case the same is not available in the section. The users have recently complained that the process is taking too long. How should the management respond ? Obviously, the service time for each user cannot be the same so that as far as an individual user is concerned, the amount of time that would be required to complete his service is uncertain. How should the management go about in forming an idea about the representative amount of time required to serve a typical user of services of this section ? It may be a good idea to maintain a record of such time taken in respect of each individual user. But this may be an infeasible exercise, given the resources available to the library, especially if the number of users is too large. As such, and also because all such future requisitions are unobservable at any given point of time, one is essentially constrained to look at a few cases only. In any case, such a survey will generate a series of numerical figures each representing the time required to serve specific users. How should the data be made to be intelligible ? How should the data be summarised so as to make some sense out of these apparently drab sequence of numbers ? How should the sample information be made use of so as to make a guess about the actual state of affairs pertaining to the totality? How do we select our sample so that the sample observations can be generalised to hold true in respect of the entire population of users ? Even if we are in a position to make an assessment about the general state of affairs, how much reliability should be attached to it, since after all the assessment is based on our observations in a single sample which is perhaps comprised of a small portion of the totality and the same could be quite different if we had a different sample (this refers to the 'uncertainty' part of this solution). These are some illustrative issues which *statistics* attempts to resolve in this and similar situations.

A number of the above issues would perhaps also be relevant in a situations when, say, certain library participates in an arrangement by virtue of which the requisition for a book not possessed by the library can be met by loaning the book out of a sister library (system of inter-library loan). Thus, after such a requisition is received, the library sends a request to a sister library for making the book available to it on loan. The book is issued to the requisitioner on its receipt from the latter, provided, of course, the same is available with it ; otherwise, the library takes it up which another sister library and so on. How does the library verify on the general complaint of its users that, of late, the service time involved has become too long ? All the discussions that followed the example in the previous couple of paragraphs also become essentially relevant here too.

Example 1.4. In the above example, suppose specifically, the complain is that on the average one waits for at least 40 minutes. Or, even the complain may assert that the service time tend to be longer when clerk-A (sister library-A in the latter example) handles the requisition than when clerk-B (sister library-B in the latter example) handles the same. The management may like to pursue these complains objectively to verify if these are tenable or not. Statistical techniques can be very satisfactorily used to achieve this goal.

Example 1.5. Consider a library counter where 'customers' (users) arrive for 'service'. Our objective is to look for a policy so that congestions can be avoided. Congestions are likely to arise in view of irregularities in the system. In general, neither the number of arrivals is fixed on all occasions nor is the service time same for all customers—these are usually subject to chance factors. As such the rate at which the service is to be provided from the counter is usually unpredictable. In any case, whenever the rate at which the customers arrive is too high compared to the rate at which they can be served, the resultant waiting time will be high ; by the same token, when the opposite is true, the services available from the counter may remain largely unutilized. This consideration may motivate us to look for suitable changes in the organization of the service facility on grounds of economy (should we increase the staff size, or should we reduce the staff size, or do we distinguish amongst the nature of services demanded etc.). But this will entail evaluation of alternatives, and that too under 'uncertainty'. Statistical methodology can be quite useful in deciding about the changes that are desirable for the system. Relevant results of the **queueing theory** can be quite handy in our efforts to establish arrival patterns, profile of services demanded in terms of nature, required time etc., which should help us in analysing the situations appropriately.

Example 1.6. Suppose there is a need to plan for proper utilization of stack pace in a library. Naturally, one would perhaps think in terms of moving out volumes that are not all that frequently used. As such there may be a need to relate the *age* (time since its publication) of a book with, let us say, its annual circulation. We can make use of the available statistical methodology relating to *correlation and regression* in this regard.

Example 1.7. For a library, suppose, it is required to plan necessary reinforcements in its services for the future. In this context, it may then be necessary to explore if the length of membership of members has any role on the extent of demand on its services. Does the length of membership have got anything to do with the extent [say, High (H), Medium (M) and Low (L)] of demand for its services ? If yes, does the demand tend to increase or decrease with increase in the tenure of membership ? Is there any way of quantifying the extent of dependence of one criterion *viz.* length of membership on the level of services demanded ? Many such issues can be very satisfactorily handled through statistical methods.

Example 1.8. Consider a machine having a normal life (time to failure) of 10 years. However, it may be necessary to replace a particular component once or more, during this life span owing to failure (s). If some spares are carried in the inventory to be readily available at times of need then, in principle, it should be possible to cut down the idle time to a large extent. But, the life span of the component is not deterministic and is subject to uncertainties i.e. it cannot be predicted accurately. As such, how many spares should be carried in the inventory so as to minimize the loss expected to arise owing to loss of production and other related costs ? More specifically, there are two conflicting costs, namely the cost of overstocking and the cost of understocking (i.e. down time, idle time cost incurred with regard to labour and costs related to emergency purchase etc.) which have to be balanced. How do we balance ? Obviously, we need to know the failure profile of all such components — viz. the ones that have already been used, are currently in use and will be in use. But this population itself is not observable and is at best conceivable ; as such how do we propose to construct the stated profile ?

This problem becomes even more complicated if we want to compare between brands of this component. How do we compare ? Since the respective populations are not fully observable, obviously this has to be done on the basis of information to be obtained from samples. But then how do we draw our samples ? How do we propose to generalize the findings from the sample ? How reliable will be our inference, as different samples may lead us to different conclusions ?

II. Some Statistical & Probabilistic Concepts

The basic frame which upholds statistical reasonings is provided by **probability theory.** As such, it will be appropriate to introduce certain basic probability notions at this stage. There are so much of uncertainties all around us, yet we must make decisions even occasionally at the risk of unknowingly being led into catastrophe. In such situations, it is of course nice to have access to an appropriate scale which would help us to describe the extent of uncertainties associated with various outcomes of different decisions.

Suppose in a statistical study, we are interested in a particular characteristic like time required to get a particular book back in the library upon recall, performance of an individual employee, annual maintenance cost of an equipment, number of defective copies produced by a copier per 1000 pages processed, lead time required in processing an order etc. The measurement of a character may vary from one unit to another; the characters which can be measured quantitatively are called

variables while those which are measured qualitatively are known as **attributes.** For example time to failure of a machine measured in terms of the number of hours served from start till failure is a variable; the religion or caste of an employee or the type of binding (hard cover, paper back etc.) are attributes. The collection of measurements of the variable or attribute under study on **all** units that are relevant comprises the **population;** any part of a population s a **sample.** Thus, if the variable of interest is the annual number of books issued by library user, and there are altogether 1500 users, then the population would comprise of 1500 numbers each of which would represent the annual number of issuances to one or the other user. This is, however, a **finite** population. But a statistical population need not always be finite; the performance of an equipment of a certain variety is an observation from the virtually infinite population comprising of measurements of performances of all similar equipments that have already been in existence as well as those which will be in existence in the future.

Obviously, it is infeasible for a decision maker to be able to take a look at the entire population for the purpose of taking an appropriate decision in a given situation; he only has sample information at his disposal at any given point of time. Any attempt to make a decision or conclusion regarding the population on the basis of the available sample information surely introduces some elements of uncertainty in his knowledge about the population and accordingly, the quality of his decision or conclusion depends upon the extent to which information relating to the population can be extracted from the sample through scientific analyses. In a managerial situation, where a decision has to be made in the face of uncertainty, one appeals to probability theory which provides the appropriate framework for data analysis.

A random experiment is one which when performed results into one amongst few possible outcomes. Thus, observing the demand of a particular library service on a day is a random experiment the outcome of which can be one amongst a number of possible values. Generally speaking, in a random experiment, the conditions under which the same is performed cannot determine its outcome precisely. A coin when tossed twice under apparently identical conditions may lead to two different results. Thus, while the set of possible outcomes of a random experiment may be known, there is uncertainty about the exact outcome in a particular performance of the same. The outcome is uncertain because the factors leading to individual outcomes are either not entirely identifiable, or even if these are identifiable, these may not be achievable while performing the experiment. In other words, uncertainty in random experiments is construed as effects of a factor or group of factors about which we are ignorant or which are unobtainable.

In any case, while dealing with such experiments, one may wish to quantify the likelihood of its different possible outcomes. In this context, it is useful to know that although the outcome in a single performance of the experiment cannot be predicted beforehand, it has been analytically established that the proportion of times a particular outcome E shows up *i.e.* the relative frequency of E in, say, n repetitions of the experiment **under identical conditions** becomes more or less a constant for large values of n i.e. it does not vary appreciably *in the long run* with the number n of times the experiment is being repeated. This constant representing the *long run relative frequency of E* is referred to as the **probability of the outcome** E and is written as $P(E)$. Thus $P(E)$ is the proportion of times the outcome E is expected to be observed if the experiment is repeated a large number of times. Therefore, when we say that the probability of obtaining the head when a coin is tossed once only is 0.5, we mean that if the coin is tossed a large number of times, then 50% of these tosses are expected to yield heads. Of course, we hasten to add at this stage that, this in no way implies that in 100 tosses of this coin, there must be 50 heads and therefore 50 tails. Similarly, when we say that the probability for the daily demand of a particular book on reserve to be 5 is ·01, we mean that out of a large number of days, only on 1% of the days the demand is expected to be 5.

How does one determine the probability of a particular outcome in a given situation ? In some cases, probabilities of the different outcomes can be determined from theoretical considerations *e.g.* say, symmetry. Thus, for example, in the coin tossing experiment, if there is apparently no reason to expect the 'head' in preference to 'tail', then in a large number of tosses, by symmetry, one would expect 'head' to appear exactly half the time, so that p(Head) = 0.5 and hence p(Tail) = 0.5.

In fact, the above argument can be extended to conclude that in case of experiments having a finite number of, say κ, outcomes none of which can be expected in preference to the rest (i.e. the κ outcomes are **equally likely**), each outcome has probability $(\frac{1}{\kappa})$. Further, suppose, we are interested in computing the probability of a particular happening *i.e.* **event** which is accomplished if the experiment results into any one of, say, r outcomes; a little reflection (recall that the probability of *an* outcome is its 'long term' relative frequency) will confirm that the required probability is $(\frac{r}{\kappa})$. Thus, for example, the probability of obtaining a defective copy of a book from a lot of copies of which a proportion π are defective is π. However, theoretical deduction of probabilities of various events relating to a large number of experiments having innumerable outcomes is not always possible and in such cases, these have to be analytically suggested and then confirmed through statistical techniques.

The basic idea behind the concept of probabilities of events is not difficult to comprehend. Think of a finite **population or universe** (*i.e.* the totality of all conceivable measurements in a given context) like all the 100,000 bound volumes in a library. The experiment is to select a volume 'at random' at a time and classify the same as *damaged or not damaged*. If we keep on repeating this experiment, then ultimately, the population being finite, we will exhaust all the 100,000 volumes and hence the proportion of damaged volumes in n repetitions (i.e. n sample observations) eventually equals the proportion of damaged volumes possessed by the library. Even in the case where the population is so large that it cannot be exhausted through repeated experimentation, such a phenomenon should intuitively hold and this has been analytically verified to be so.

It should by now be clear that a sample observation is generated by repeating the relevant experimentation once and through repetitions under identical conditions, one actually approaches the population of all possible measurements on the variable under study. In this sense, therefore, $P(E)$ can be interpreted to be the 'relative frequency' of E in the population.

The reader may already be familiar with the concept of a **frequency distribution** which is a tabular arrangement for displaying the relative frequencies (or simply the frequencies) corresponding to different values or categories of values pertaining to the phenomenon under study. Similarly, a **probability distribution** is a description of probabilities of values or classes of values pertaining to the phenomenon under study.

Example 2.1. Containing on Example 1.1, suppose that the probability distribution of the daily demand for the particular book is as follows :

Daily demand :	0	1	2	3	4	5	6	7	8
Probability :	.05	.15	.22	23	.17	.10	.05	.02	0.1

As per the above table, the probability for the daily demand would be, say 2 is 0.22; this simply means that if the demand is observed over a large number of days, then on 22% days it is expected to be 2. Also note that the sum total of the above probabilities is 1.0 so that the probability for the demand to be 9 or more is **zero** i.e. the demand can never be number more than 8.

Example 2.2. (Binomial Distribution). Suppose that the authorities estimate that of all the requisitions, a fraction π relates to publications dated as far back as 25 years or more. Thus the probability that a requisition will concern such an old publication is π. What is the probability that out of a total number of n requisitions on a day, the number of requisitions for old books will be 0 or 1 or 2 or... or, n ?

To fix ideas, take the case $n = 2$. Think of a large number N such days each registering only two requisitions. Out of first (say, in order of arrival of the requisitions) N requisitions, $N\pi$ are expected to be concerning old books and $N(1 - \pi)$ are expected to be for newer books. Thus, on $N\pi$ days, the first requisition received involved old books; out of these $N\pi$ days, on $(N\pi)\pi$ days the second requisitions are again expected to be for the old books and on the remaining $(N\pi)(1-\pi)$ days, the same are expected to concern newer books. Again, out of the $N(1-\pi)$ days on each of which the first requisitions concerned newer books, on $N(1-\pi)\pi$ days, the second requisitions are expected to concern old books and hence on $N(1-\pi)(1-\pi)$ days, the second requisitions also are expected to involve newer books. Thus, out of N days each registering two requisitions only, on $N\pi^2$ days, both the requisitions are expected to involve old books, on $2N\pi(1-\pi)$ days exactly one requisition is expected to concern an old book and hence the remaining requisition is expected to concern a newer book and finally, on $N(1-\pi)^2$ days both requisitions received concerned newer books only. Hence, the proportion of days on which both the requisitions are expected to concern old books is $N\pi^2/N = \pi^2$; proceeding this way and recalling that the probability of an outcome is the proportion of times the outcome materializes in a large number of repetitions of the experiment, we have the following probability distribution :

No. of requisitions for old books	0	1	2
Probability	$(1-\pi)^2$	$2\pi(1-\pi)$	π^2

Note that the above probabilities are the successive terms of the expansion of $(\bar{\pi} + \pi)^2$, where $\bar{\pi} = 1 - \pi$.

Extending the above arguments, we find that if on a day, there are n requisitions, then the probability that the number of requisitions which involve old books is 0, 1, 2,..., n are as follows :

No. of requisitions for old books	0	1.................r......... .		n
Probability	$(1-\pi)^n$	$n(1-\pi)^{n-1}\pi$	${}^nC_r\,(1-\pi)^{n-r}\,\pi^r$	π^n,

$$\text{where } {}^nC_r = \frac{n(n-1)\,(n-2)\,\ldots\ldots\,(n-r+1)}{r\,(r-1)\,(r-2)\,\ldots\ldots\,3.2.1}.$$

Note that the above probabilities are the successive terms of the binomial expansion of $(\bar{\pi} + \pi)^n$ and hence such a distribution of probabilities is known as a **binomial** distribution. Observe that the situation described above resembles that of n tosses of a coin which falls head with probability π or of a single simultaneous toss of n such coins; in either of these cases, the variable in which one would be interested is the total number of heads (like total number of requisitions in favour of old books).

Example 2.3. (Poisson Distribution) Suppose, patrons arrive at a service counter in library in such a manner that the chance of an arrival in small intervals of time is proportional to respective lengths of such intervals, more than one arrival over such intervals are predicted beforehand, is a *random* variable whose probability distribution is given by the mathematical formula :

$$P(\text{No. of arrivals is } r) = \frac{e^{-\lambda}\lambda^r}{r\,!}, r = 0, 1, 2, \ldots$$

where e is a number which is approximately equal to 2.73 and λ is the average number of arrivals per unit time which is one hour in this particular instance.

It can be further provided that in such a situation, the successive arrivals take place with an average interval of $(\frac{1}{\lambda})$ hours between them and the probability that the time between two successive arrivals exceeds, say, x hours is $e^{-x/\lambda}$. This phenomenon is described by saying that the time between two successive arrivals is **exponentially** distributed.

The distributions that we have discussed in Example 2.1, 2.2 and 2.3 (excepting the one discussed in the last paragraph) are called **discrete** distributions since they correspond to measurements (like number of requisitions for old books, hourly number of arrivals etc.) which adopt one amongst a set of values that are discrete. On the other hand, measurements like height, weight, distance, time etc. are *continuous* in nature, i.e. theoretically, these can be measured on a continuous scale. It is only because of non-availability of proper measuring instruments that such measurements are reduced to be discrete. As is already known, a frequency distribution corresponding to any such measurement can be diagrammatically represented by a **histogram**; a histogram is a diagram which comprises of adjacent rectangular bars constructed over adjacent intervals of values of the variable under study such that the area of a particular rectangle is equal to the frequency of the interval on which it stands. However, if we have a large number of observations (through a large number of repetitions of the underlying random experiment) relating to such a measurement and the class intervals are made sufficiently small, then the outline of the corresponding histogram would look almost like a smooth curve. Also, since the experiment has been repeated a large number of times to produce this smooth curve, the area under the same over any interval can be interpreted to be the probability that an observation will fall between the two end points.

can be interpreted to be the probability that an observation will fall between the two end points.

We have already come across the exponential distribution which is one such distribution. The most important such distribution seems to be the **normal** distribution of measurements having average μ and variance (scatter around mean) σ^2 *[for the definitions of average and variance, see that last para of this section]* as described by the curve

$$f(x) = \frac{1}{\sigma\sqrt{(2\pi)}} e^{-\left(\frac{(x-\mu)}{\sigma}\right)^2}, -\infty < x < \infty. \qquad (2.1)$$

Note that the above function when graphed will lead to a diagram in which the portion lying to the left of the axis $x = \mu$ is the mirror image of the portion lying to the right of the same axis. The area under the above curve between any two points c and d for a given pair of values of μ and σ is the probability that an observation picked up randomly from an population having average μ and variance σ^2 will lie between c and d. Such probabilities for various combinations of values of μ and σ can be easily computed using statistical tables.

Under what circumstances, such a distribution is likely to be of use ? This question has been very comprehensively answered by what is known as the **Central Limited Theorem.** In fact, the probability distribution of a measurement which is subjected to influences of a large number of independent factors can be adequately modelled by a suitable normal distribution. As asserted in the Central Limit Theorem the probability that the sample mean, based on n independent observations drawn randomly from a population having mean μ and variance σ^2, exceeds any given number x is approximately equal to the area under the normal curve (2.1) above with, of course, σ replaces by $\sigma/\sqrt{n}$, between x and $+\infty$.

We conclude this section by formally defining the concepts of **mean** and **variance**. Consider a population consisting of N measurements. Suppose that the distinct measurements are known as $x_1, x_2, \ldots, x_k$; there are altogether $N_1\, x_1$'s, $N_2\, x_2$'s, ..., $N_k\, x_k$'s so that $N_1 + N_2 + \ldots + N_k = N$. The average μ and variance σ^2 of these values or alternatively, of the population consisting of these values are defined as

$$\mu = \frac{N_1x_1 + N_2x_2 + \ldots + N_kx_k}{N} = \rho_1x_1 + \rho_2x_2 + \ldots + \rho_kx_k\,;$$

$$\sigma^2 = \frac{(x_1 - \mu)^2N_1 + (x_2 - \mu)^2N_2 + \ldots + (x_k - \mu)^2}{N}$$

$$= \rho_1\,(x_1 - \mu)^2 + \rho_2\,(x_2 - \mu)^2 + \ldots + \rho_k\,(x_k - \mu)^2.$$

Notice that ρ_i is the probability that a randomly picked up measurement from the population equals x_i. As is well-known, the average μ represents the magnitude of the measurements while the variance σ^2 gives an idea of the extent of scatter of the measurements on either side of the average. A small value for σ would indicate that the measurements in the population are tightly scattered around μ while a relatively large value for σ would mean that the measurements are widely dispersed around μ. Both μ and σ thus present a summary of the measurements. These provide useful information regarding the behaviour of the random phenomenon under consideration in the absence of complete knowledge about the relevant probability distribution. For example, the **probability that a randomly chosen measurement lies between the limits $\mu - \varepsilon$ and $\mu + \varepsilon$ cannot be smaller than σ^2/ε^2**, where ε is any specified margin. This probability can be easily computed if the relevant probability distribution is completely known; otherwise, the above fact (which is known as the **Chebyshev's Inequality**) can be of guidance, given that μ and σ are known.

III. Illustrative Applications of Statistical and Probabilistic Concepts

In this section, we propose to illustratively discuss applications of statistical methods and probabilistic models in tackling some of the situations posed in the examples discussed in the previous sections.

Example 3.1. Let us refer to Example 1.1 and its continuation in Example 2.1. Suppose, it is decided that only two copies of the book will be kept in reserve. On a given day, the demand cannot be met in case the demand on that particular day exceeds 2, the probability for which is equal to 0.58 (0.23 + 0.17 + 0.10 + 0.05 + 0.02 + 0.01), so that with a stock of 2 copies on reserve, the demand cannot be met on 58% days. On the other hand, if 5 copies are stocked for this purpose, the demand cannot be met only on 8% of the days.

Supposing that only 5 copies of the book is available on reserve, the probability that on a given day, the demand cannot be met is 0·08. One can now use the binomial distribution with $\pi = 0{\cdot}08$ to calculate probabilities that out of n days, the stock out will occur on at most r days, for $r = 0, 1, 2, \ldots, n$. For example, if $n = 90$ (the length of a quarter in a school year), then the probability that the stock out will take place on at most, say, 4 days is 0.15 approximately. Similarly, the same probability can be computed for various combination of values of n, r for Policy-s of stocking s copies. These should help in deciding the actual policy that the library would like to pursue depending upon its requirements.

Using the formulae given at the end of the last section and appealing to the long term relative frequency concept of probability, we calculate that the average number of demands per day is 2.98 (≅ 3) and variance of the daily demand is 2.8596. If we did not know the detailed probability distribution excepting for these two summary measures, we could make use of the Chebyshev's inequality to claim that the probability that the demand would exceed 5 is at most 0.41 (in fact, this probability when computed from the given probability distribution is only 0.08). As in this particular example, this benchmark value for the required probability is way above the actual value of 0.08. An alternative approach would be to try to estimate the entire probability distribution. For this purpose, one may consider a **random** sample of say n days and obtain the frequency distribution of daily demand as follows :

Demand	0	1	2	3	4...
No. of days	n_0	n_1	n_2	n_3	n_4...

The probability of the daily demand being r is then estimated by $\frac{n_r}{n}$, $r = 0, 1, 2, \ldots$. It can be theoretically proved that these estimate the corresponding probabilities quite closely, provided the size of the sample is reasonably large, viz. 25 or more.

Example 3.2. When a patron is looking for a particular book, then one of the two things may happen : either he locates the book in the shelf ready to be borrowed or, the book may already be in circulation and he files a demand for the book. In the jargons of **queuing theory,** in the first instance, his service starts immediately while in the latter instance, he joins a queue and awaits his turn for the service to begin since his 'arrival' has taken place during the 'service time' of the previous 'customer'. As such, the relevant results of queuing theory can be made use of two analyse, for instance, the average number of patrons waiting in the queue, the average number of copies in circulation, expected demand rate, average duration of time a copy is retained by a borrower, average duration of waiting after putting in a demand for a copy, etc.

Example 3.3. Suppose, it is necessary to estimate the number of books that have been lost from a certain library. Let us assume that as per register, the library should have N number of books. Whenever, N is larger, the task of physically ascertaining the number that have been lost can be expensive both in terms of time and money. Hence, alternatively one would be interested in estimating the same. There are many modes of sampling; we consider the estimation process based on **random** sampling. Looking at the main accession register, we select n books through a process of lottery (random sampling) and physically verify how many of these are lost; let a proportion π_n of these belong to this category. This is taken as an estimate of the fraction π that have been lost out of the totality of N books; note that π can be interpreted as the probability that a randomly selected title has been lost. In any case, then a reasonable estimate for the number of books that have been lost is $N\pi_n$. The motivation for estimating π by π_n as defined above lies in the theoretical fact that repeated selection of books ultimately exhaust the entire set of N books in which eventuality $n = N$, so that then $\pi_n = \pi$. Obviously, the value of π_n depends on the particular sample of books that gets selected through the random mechanism that is followed. For example, suppose, the library has 10 books of which actually 3 have been lost; of course, the latter fact is not known *a priori*. Now, if decide to take $n = 2$, and $\pi_n = 0$ or 0.5 or 1.00 according as the two books selected at random are amongst the 7 that have not been lost, or exactly one of the two books chosen is amongst the three that have been lost, or both the books chosen are amongst the three books that have been lost. This observation helps us to visualize that π_n is basically values assumed by a random phenomenon. An application of the Central Limit Theorem establishes that the degree of consistency of the estimator π_n at any preassigned error margin $\varepsilon > 0$, i.e. the probability that the error of estimation does not exceed any given margin ε is approximately equal to the area under the normal curve (2.1) between the points $-\varepsilon_n$ and ε_n where $\varepsilon_n = -\varepsilon(\sqrt{n})(\sqrt{\pi(1-\pi)})^{-1}$, irrespective of the true value of π; naturally, then with increasing sample size n, this area under (2.1) over the interval $(-\varepsilon_n, \varepsilon_n)$ expands to 1. As such, whenever the sample size n is large, then π_n is expected to be close to the true value π.

It may be added here that like proportions, as an estimate of the population average, the sample mean based on a random sample drawn from the population is also quite reliable, provided, of course, the size n of the sample is reasonably large.

Example 3.4. Let us refer to Example 1.4; we intend to statistically verify whether the allegation (hypothesis) that clerk-A takes more time compared to clerk-B to serve a customer is tenable or not, before really proceeding to take action against clerk-A on the basis of the complain. Understandably, this comparison will have to be made on the basis of the **population** average handling times of the two clerks; however, precisely these are the quantities which are not known. As such, based on the data supplied by a random sample of n patrons, the (sample) average $\bar{x}$ of their handling times is computed; similarly, the (sample) average $\bar{y}$ of their handling times is also computed. Since, $\bar{x}$ and $\bar{y}$ are expected to be close estimates of their corresponding population counterparts which are **not** known, performances of the two clerks will have to be made on the basis of the magnitude of the difference $(\bar{y} - \bar{x})$. Given a level of reliability for the conclusion which has to be made on the basis of random findings described above, the criticality of the magnitude of the difference can be judged with help of statistical tables.

Example 3.5. Let us refer to Example 1.7; here, we wish to decide if the extent of demand [High (H), Medium (M) or Low (L)] is in anyway influenced by the length of membership; suppose that patrons are classified into three groups depending on the length of their membership as follows :

Group A : Length of membership $\leq$ 5 years ;

Group B : Length of membership between 5 and 10 ;

Group C : Length of membership > 10 years.

Let ρ_{AH} be the probability that a randomly chosen patron happens to be a Group-A member in terms of his tenure as a member in the library **and also**, he is amongst those who put high demands on the library services; ρ_{AM}' ρ_{AL}' ρ_{BH}' ρ_{BM}' ρ_{BL}' ρ_{CH}' ρ_{CM} and ρ_{CL} have similar probabilistic connotations. Suppose, that the total membership is N; naturally, then $N = N_H + N_M + N_L$ and, also $N = N_A + N_B + N_C$ where N along with the appropriate suffix would indicate the number of members belonging to the appropriate category either in terms of the length of membership or in terms of the extent of demand placed on the library services. Similarly, N with a double subscript will indicate the number of patrons with dual classification; thus, for example N_{CM} is the number of members who not only are members for more than the past 10 years, but also place medium demands on the library services. Thus, $\rho_{AH} = N_{AH}/N$. If the extent of use of library facilities is **independent** of the tenure of membership, then the N_A members of Group-A will be distributed in classes H, M and L in the **same** proportion as N members are distributed in these classes, i.e., $N_{AH} / N_A = N_H / N$. As such, whenever, the extent of services demanded is **independent** of the length of membership, then $\rho_{AH} = (N_{AH} / N) = N_A (N_H/N)/N = (N_A/N)(N_H/N) = \rho_A \rho_H$; similarly, under the assumption of independence of the two criteria, *viz. length of membership* and the *extent of services demanded,* $\rho_{AM} = \rho_A \rho_M$, $\rho_{AL} = \rho_A \rho_L$, $\rho_{BH} = \rho_B \rho_H$', etc. Thus, independence could be established if we could check out all 9 such equalities. But this is not feasible since these probabilities are typically not known. As such, we take a **random** sample of n patrons and classify them in terms of both the criterion. No, n_A, n_{AH}, etc. will have the same connotations as N_A, N_{AH}, respectively, excepting that the lower hand n's relate to the random sample and not the population. In fact, the data derived from the sample can be organized as in the following table :

		Extent of Services Demanded			Total
		H	M	L	
	A	n_{AH}	n_{AM}	n_{AL}	n_A
Length of Membership	B	n_{BH}	n_{BM}	n_{BL}	n_B
	C	n_{CH}	n_{CM}	n_{CL}	n_C
Total		n_H	n_M	n_L	n

Following the arguments as in Example 3.3, p's can be estimated by the corresponding sample proportions; thus, e.g. ρ_{AH} can be estimated by n_{AH}/n, ρ_A can be estimated by n_A/n, etc. and as such, under the hypothesis of independence of the two criteria, then the **expected number** of patrons who belong to group-A in terms of tenure of membership and also to the category-h in terms of the intensity of his use of library services should be $n(n_A/n)(n_H/n)$; the expected number of members belonging to the other 8 combinations of categories can be similarly computed. The correspondence of these **expected** members and the corresponding **observed** number of members falling in the different combinations of levels of the two criteria can be worked out in the form of what is known as a **(contingency) chi-square** which is a number that measures the **distance** between the expected and observed cell frequencies; this distance is computed by summing $(f_{eij} - f_{oi})^2/f_{eij}$ over all cells, where f_{eij} and f_{oij} are the expected and observed frequencies of the (i, j)-th cell in the above table. Obviously, if this distance is significantly large, then we would doubt the hypothesis of independence between the two criteria. Given a level of reliability for the conclusion which has to be made on the basis of random findings described above, the criticality of the magnitude of the above distance can be judged with help of statistical tables.

Example 3.6. (Regression). We refer to Example 1.6. One of the major objectives of many investigations is to make predictions. For instance, it may be necessary to predict the number of circulations of a publication based on its *age*. In order to be able to make such predictions, we try to establish an algebraic relationship connecting the two measurements *viz.* the number of circulations in a year (*dependent variable)* and the age (*independent variable*) of the publication. Consider the following data :

Age of book (x) :	3	7	2	1	8	10	2	5	13	9
Circulations (y) :	40	31	43	48	23	22	47	33	8	23
(*last year*)										

Plotting these 10 pairs of points viz. (3, 40), (7, 31)..., 9, 23) on a graph paper, we get a scatter diagram which gives us a fairly good idea of the nature of dependence of y on x. In fact, here we observe that all the points seem to be lying more or less on a **straight line**, so that the relationship between x and y can be taken to be approximately linear. However, as will be evident from the scatter diagram, many straight lines can be drawn which would approximate the exact relationship between x and y. The problem, therefore, is to decide which of these would provide the best results. This is resolved using what is known as the method of **least squares.** The least squares principle considers that line which minimizes the total (squared) error that would be committed as the one providing the best fit to the scatter. That is, we position the line so as to minimize the sum of squares of vertical distances of the given points in the scatter diagram from the line. The logic of the least squares principle should thus be geometrically clear.

When the above principle is made use of, we come up with the following prediction equation in the present situation :

$$y = 48.60 - 2.80x,$$

Thus, a book which was published 7 years ago, is expected to be circulated approximately 29 times, on the average. These computations can be carried out with help of standard packages.

Acknowledgement

I am indebted to Asok Mukhopadhyay, Librarian, Indian Institute of Management Calcutta for many helpful discussions we have had during the preparation of this article; these helped me to see issues from a librarian's perspective.

Information Systems : The Logic of Enquiry

PETER G. UNDERWOOD

The well-known writer on management, Robert Heller,[1] has identified three reasons for the failure of a business. The first reason, or major error, is a failure to react to competition; the second is the making of unsound decisions when the competition becomes so great as to force belated reactions and the third is a failure to recognise and act on opportunities. An important question for the profession must be, 'Are these errors also apparent in the information world and how should we cope with them ?' A particular problem in the management of library and information services is that, whilst it is acknowledged to be important that the design of information policies for library and information services should take account of developments in the political and social environment within which they exist, there is little to guide the process of policy analysis and eventual social engineering.

To take Heller's points in turn, it might seem easy to dismiss the first reason for failure, that of failing to react to competition, by suggesting that library and information services are unique: there is no one offering an alternative source for the kind of services which libraries and information centres supply. However, in the context of an increasingly complex commercial world, it is difficult to sustain this view for long. Whilst it may be true that some activities of library and information services, such as the storage of vast quantities of printed and other materials, are not offered by others it is evident that there are many sources for the main raw ingredient: information. Studies of information users have shown that libraries and information centres are low on many people's list when it comes to choosing a source. The profession has lived with this fact for many years arguing, perhaps, that the sources that people *do* use are not the best or that the assistance available from properly-qualified library and information service personnel would have increased the possibilities of success in finding *relevant* information. However, what the profession must now confront is a world where there are other high-quality sources for information which can be used, quite successfully and with little preparation, directly by information users.

The second error, that of making unsound decisions in the face of competition, arises out of a panic reaction. The manager becomes aware that something is badly wrong and seeks to put it right. Unfortunately, the speed of the reaction may be so great that little thought is given to *why* the problem has occurred: the manager has become a firefighter, seeking to stamp out the flames. The problem with fires is that they break out again in a different place unless the source of the fire is found and the blaze quenched. Firefighting may appear to solve problems quickly but, in the long term, it will ensure that a manager is kept busy and can pay little attention to anything else. In this way the third error arises almost automatically because few managers will be able to find time to consider opportunities when they are so busy trying to solve problems. To take a specific example, the development of direct searching of databases, either remotely through external data networks or locally through in-house databases or CD-ROM, could be perceived as a strong threat to the traditional expertise of the information worker. As such, the manager of a library or information service serving an organisation in which such developments are taking place might be tempted to react strongly against the spread of end-user searching. The argument might be advanced that searching by those unskilled in such matters is almost certain to be defective, inefficient and, thus, wasteful of resources. But, what evidence could one prove that searching by experts in information retrieval would, without doubt, produce better results ?

In an increasingly competitive environment the concern of managers of library and information services must be not only with the survival of our library and information services but also with their development within a clear and coherent framework of policy. Just as in any other sector of the economy, our services can only survive if they continue to develop, but there needs to be a clear view of the direction that development should take to best meet the developing needs of users. A confident expectation that the profession can continue to do tomorrow just what has been done today will lead to a gradual decline in the perceived value of library and information services because users are fast becoming aware that information is available from other sources.

An information system represent, in the broadest sense of the term, a mixture of people and technology working within an operating environment which is itself part of an overall, general, environment.[2] The culture of the organization maintaining the system, together with the values, beliefs and behavioural norms of the individuals involved with the system as client for information or as information worker prescribe and assign roles for the system and for the participants.

New roles, technologies and environments encourage practical responses to the problems of designing information systems. Responses must be guided by careful enquiry into the needs of potential users, identifying circumstances, existing knowledge and beliefs. Such *activity systems* vary between both individuals and groups, yet the goal of an information policy designer must be to encourage a unified approach or, at least, a limited number of approaches, to problems of information provision.

The choices facing managers in relation to the design of an information system may be summarised in a set of elements representing the organization :

Mission	—	the 'business' that the organization is in
Objectives	—	the desired future positions or roles for the organization
Strategies	—	the general directions in which the objectives are to be pursued
Goals	—	specific targets to be sought at specified points in time
Programs/projects	—	sets of activities which consume resources and through which strategies are implemented and goals pursued
Resource allocation	—	allocation of funds, personnel, etc., to various units, objectives, strategies programs and projects.

Together these represent the strategic choice elements which confront all managers. Most organizations will deal with some of them but may fail to deal explicitly with them all. It is only through a careful review of all elements that a balanced approach to the challenge of designing an information system can emerge. In doing this, some care is needed if the future rather than the past is to be reflected. The mission statement, for example, ought to address opportunities and strengths rather than describe the current 'products' and status quo of the organization. Strategies should be concerned with new, or improved, products and new, or extended, markets rather than concentrating on present outputs.

The most important condition for the effective implementation of a planned information system is that the relations between the strategic choice elements are clearly defined and carefully analysed. This is necessary in order to ensure that potential conflicts of interest are identified and remedies developed and to ensure that opportunities for synergistic approaches are not neglected.

Erich Jantsch,[3] in an important article about change, identified four dimensions of planning. One of these is called the 'Time and causality' dimension it provides a strong model for developing a coherent approach to the management of the future.

Jantsch is concerned with strategy : that is, the achievement of specific, chosen, goals. He recognises that one approach is to explore causality or, to put it another way, to consider the effect of present strategies on existing users. By recognising a causal link it is possible to adjust the provision of services to more nearly meet the present needs of users. Over a period of time it is possible to become so familiar with the needs of users and with the characteristics of the services offered that a manager can be fairly confident in predicting the effect of any change in strategy. The concern of the manager then becomes one of the efficient use of resources and seeking to improve the services currently provided to a set of users whose needs are known quite well. Jantsch calls this 'normative forecasting' and it could be summarised as 'the past is a good guide to the future'. The benefits associated with this familiarity also conceal a danger : it is easy to slip into a mode of management which concentrates only on normative forecasting and the adjustments to strategy which this dictates. To guard against this danger Jantsch also develop the idea of 'exploratory forecasting'. This type of forecasting attempts to consider the opportunities which the manager might seek to address : the new markets, potential user groups and new products which might be developed. This exploration concerns the future, of course, so this is where the element of 'time' as a dimension comes in.

Deciding to do something different by choosing to address one of these opportunities will result in the diversion of resources from one or more of the present range of activities offered by a library and information service unless the base of resources can be enlarged. Managers tend to think of resource management as being concerned with sharing out available resources according to need : economists regard all resources as being limited and try to establish the pattern of use which will lead to the greatest benefit for users. In doing this they consider the opportunity cost of a project as well as its direct, apparent, cost. This means that they seek to consider the effect of *not* supporting one project so that another *can* be supported. Jantsch reminds us of the need to think a little like the economists by linking the exploratory and the normative forecasting activities : in other words, he recommends that there be a healthy tension between them. By paying attention to both types of forecast the manager is prevented both from becoming a firefighter and from becoming a 'blue sky' visionary.

There can be little doubt that the future of library and information services is bound up closely with the development of Information Technology. Whilst the concept of the provision of an adequate level of service should never be confused with the mere existence of technology it is fairly clear that many of the activities performed by libraries and information centres, and the services they offer, can be enhanced and many new services can be developed, using suitable information technology in an appropriate way. Michael J. Earl' identifies information technology as the major developing strategic resource of the 1990's and he explores a series of frameworks which aim to encourage managers to think creatively about the application of information technology. The first of these framework types is called an 'awareness framework': its use is to raise awareness in an organisation of the value and potential of information technology. The second allows an exploration of opportunities through the use of analytical tools such as the techniques of systems analysis. The third framework, called a 'positioning framework' is concerned with assessing, developing and improving information technology applications in an organization. Clearly the framework types encourage discussion of issues which should be regarded as serious by any library or information service manager but I want to suggest that it is the second which has tended to be most used in our work. In part this is because so much of managerial energy has been expended in the specification and design of new systems that comparatively little attention has been given to the task of assessing the impact of these systems on users and their perceptions of the range of services offered by libraries and information centres. A search of the professional literature for studies of how the use of information technology has affected people in the information world quickly reveals that most of the studies are concerned with effects on staff. If managers do not also seek to consider the effect on customers, that is, the information users, then it is difficult to maintain that information technology is being managed in a strategic manner.

Why should this preoccupation with systems development at the expense of a consideration of system impact have arisen ? I suggest that it is in part, at least, due to the methods of systems analysis and system design that we have tended to use. The development plans and reports on the implementation of computer systems in libraries and information services reveal that, in most cases, the approach has been to use what have come to be called 'hard' methods : that is, they are methods which are highly-structured and rigorous but neglectful of the social and political context in which the system they are modelling will be used. A typical example would be the design of an acquisitions system. 'Hard' analysis would concentrate on determining the purpose of the system, the rules by which it operates, the inputs to it and outputs from it, their origin, form and destiny. The throughput of the system would be determined and any problem areas identified and investigated. The result would be an analysis of the system which revealed its logic and showed clearly the flow of data within it and how it was linked to other system. It would not, except as a passing comment, reveal anything about the people who operate it, their need for job satisfaction and their place in the political network of the organisation. The richness of the culture of the organisation would be lost because the method of 'hard' analysis pays no attention to such matters. This is not to suggest that the 'hard' approaches have not been successful in the past : there are many examples of apparently successful systems which have been implemented using 'hard' techniques but it must be remembered that many of these systems were first or second generation systems using computers, often lacking in sophistication and rarely integrated with other system. Such systems were, essentially, replacements for manual clerical routines which were, themselves, well-defined and unambiguous in their range of operations. The design of such replacements was considered to be largely a problem of choosing appropriate technical solutions. We are now designing systems which affect the way in which people work to a much greater degree, which may be directly accessible to our users and which may be much less easily defined.

What is the way forward ? An alternative is offered by the use of 'soft' systems methods. Such techniques, pioneered by Peter Checkland,[5] have begun to be used to analyse systems and problems which are less well-defined than clerical systems and which contain a strong social element as well as a technical element. Examples of use can be found in the design of health-care information systems[6], where the objectives of the various people and organizations involved may be unclear or in opposition, where values may be difficult to define and where there may be several apparently successful solutions to problems and multiple possible paths to their achievement.

'Soft' systems techniques provide powerful means of, or frameworks for, describing, analysing and designing information systems. The techniques are sensitive to the approaches, or views, that people have of their knowledge domain. By identifying the nature of the domain it is possible to define its boundary and, by a process of comparison, to identify the characteristics of common elements. A possible classification of the main elements usually found within a system includes Client, Actor, Transformation, Weltanschauung, Owner and Environment (to use Checkland's criteria[7]). These will be briefly examined later in this paper.

The process of identification of the main elements within the context of a 'soft' systems approach encourages a consideration of the 'socio-technical' aspects of the environment of an information system. Some environments, for example, are dominated by technology addressing a relatively well-defined domain of knowledge, some by political considerations in which the source of the information, as well as the means for its identification, may be value-laden. An information system designer cannot neglect such aspects if the design of an information system is truly to reflect the needs of users.

This 'soft' systems approach encourages a forward, strategic, view of information management and policy provision, which highlights the point at which technological change can offer opportunities and also identifies the points at which other, social, considerations assume importance. Successful strategies will also be adaptable to unexpected events, helping to balance the pro-active and reactive aspects of policy management.

The framework may also be viewed as a 'systems approach' to information-handling in organizations : one which emphasises components and relationships rather than tasks and procedures. The systems approach tries to integrate information about people, procedures, problems and performance rather than trying to deal with each as a separate notion.

Other components of a systems approach could be the organizational arrangements : aspects of formal and informal communication, delegation, negotiation, task assignment, rewards, leadership, all of which can affect the performance of an information system. The environment also influences the system in terms of the opportunities, demands and constraints within which the system must try to operate.

The 'soft' systems method depends on gathering a series of views, or 'cognitive maps' about a problem, opportunity, or existing task which identify the ideas, beliefs, values and attitudes of those having some interest in it. For each 'human activity system', thus recognised, some care is taken to establish 'root definitions' using criteria developed by Checkland[8] which serve to identify;

Customers	—	those who would be victims or beneficiaries of the system;
Actors	—	those who would carry out the activities of the system;
Transformation	—	what input is transformed into what output by the system ?

Weltanschauung — what view of the world, or assumption, makes this system have meaning ?

Owner — who could abolish this system ?

Environment — under what external constraints does this system operate ?

The root definition establishes what a system *is*. The next step is to build a conceptual model, based on the criteria just identified, which shows what the system *does*. The model is used to stimulate about changes which could be both desirable as improvements in the way in which the system operates and acceptable within the culture identified by the root definition.

Soft systems methods help the designer and managers of a system to identify conflicts of interest and seek out ways in which such conflicts may be resolved whilst also offering a means of exploring opportunities of improving existing systems and designing novel approaches. It is this dual approach which makes them a powerful tool for the design of information systems where the human component is still an essential part.

It must be acknowledged that the 'soft' methods are still in the course of development and that any project is likely to require a mixture of 'soft' and 'hard' methods to achieve a satisfactory answer. Little conscious use has been made of 'soft' techniques in investigating library and information centre design[9],[10] but if we are to move from problem-solving management to a creative style of management which seeks opportunities and tries to fit the technology to the human condition then the 'soft' approach must become the favoured tool of the library and information service manager for learning about the information environment and assisting in managing the future.

REFERENCES

1. HELLER, Robert. "Hard core reform", *Management today*, November 1990, p. 42.

2. UNDERWOOD, Peter G. *Managing change in libraries and information services: a systems approach* (Bingley, 1990), p.23.

3. JANTSCH, Erich, "Forecasting and systems approach: a frame of reference", *Management science* 19 (12), 1973.

4. EARL, Michael J. "IT and stragegic advantage: a framework of frameworks", *in Information management: the strategic dimension,* edited by Michael J. Earl (Oxford University Press, 1988), pp.33-53.

5. An excellent starting-point for the study of 'soft' methods is *Systems thinking, systems practice,* by Peter Checkland (Wiley, 1981).

6. CHECKLAND, Peter *and* SCHOLES, Jim. *Soft systems methodoloy in action* (Wiley, 1990), pp. 89-123.

7. CHECKLAND, Peter. *Systems thinking, systems practice* (Wiley, 1981), pp. 225-227.

8. CHECKLAND, Peter. "Techniques in soft systems practice part 2: building conceptual models', *Journal of applied systems analysis* 6, 1979, pp. 41-49.

9. An interesting exception is offered by Peter Checkland in "Achieving 'desirable and feasible' change: an application of soft systems methodology", *Journal of the Operational Research Society* 36 (9), 1985, pp. 821-831.

10. An extended study and critique of the approach can be found in *Soft systems methodology in action,* by Peter Checkland and Jim Scholes (Wiley, 1990), pp. 59-87 and 277-302 passim.

Educating Users About Catalogues and Cataloguing : The Impossible Dream

SHARON A. HOCAN

You are not the first librarians to ask questions about users' interactions with library catalogues. In fact, there is a sizeable body of library literature which explores this interaction from various perspectives. Questions which has been asked, range from "How do patrons use a library catalogue ?" to "What do users need to know about library catalogues ?" These variations reflect the bias of the questioner; the first was asked by the cataloguers who were interested in improving the catalogue for the user, the other asked by user education librarians who were designing handouts, lectures or computer-assisted aids which explain how to use the catalogue.

The American literature of users and catalogues was sparked by William M. Randall in a speech to the Catalogue Section of the American Library Association in 1931. He challenged the attendees to improve the catalogues, not by studying the catalogues or the rules, but through "an intelligent study of the patrons themselves ; their mental equipment, their background, and their needs."[1] Shortly thereafter, a catalogue use study was conducted which focused on how patrons used library catalogues. The number of such studies increased steadily from the 1930s to the 1970s. In his review article, "Catalog use Studies and Their Implications", James Krikelas identifies fifty-four catalogue use studies conducted in the United States.[2] They include all types of libraries and categories of users. However, a suitable shift in focus occurred in the studies conducted after 1960. While earlier studies analysed the interaction of the user and the catalogue with the objective of improving the catalogue, letter studies analysed the user/catalogue interaction with the objective of designing an automated catalogue.[3] A resurgence of catalogue use studies occurred in 1980s. Researchers continued to study the interaction of users with library catalogues, but the catalogues were automated catalogues, and the methodologies used were tailored to the new technology. (It was as if card catalogues had disappeared from all libraries and were miraculously replaced by online catalogues !) The focus of the studies also shifted from emphasis on the elements of the catalogue record interpretation of catalogues codes to the problems inherent in searching in an online environment.

User education in the United States began in the 1930s, but the vast quantity of library literature about user education dates from the mind 1970s. While user education librarians studied and learned from the catalogue use data, their interest was not in how to change the catalogue in order to facilitate use, but in how to help the user understand the catalogue that existed. Therefore the literature varies from very practical advice on what catalogue elements to teach in a one-hour lecture to conceptual approaches for instruction about the card catalogue. However, the user education community was blossoming at the cusp of change. Automated catalogues were close at hand ; the shift to users interacting with catalogues in an online environment became a fact in the early 1980s. Since that time, the literature of user education has been dominated by studies of users and online catalogues.

What have we learned about Manual Card Catalogues ?

What does the literature of catalogue use tell us ? Krikelas summarized the findings in the catalogue use studies conducted before 1970 :

(1) Students comprise the largest single group of catalogue users.

(2) The approaches taken to searching a card catalogue vary and are related to the patron's educational status ; the frequency of known-item (as opposed to subject) searches increases as the educational level of the patron increases.

(3) The majority of catalog inquiries are made to identify English language material, of relatively recent date, in order to complete classroom assignments.

(4) The most frequently used information on catalogue cards is author, title, subject headings, call number, and date of publication.

(5) Between 70 and 80 percent of all searchers are successful to the extent that a user is able to identify some relevant document ; of the failures, 5 to 10 percent are attributable to the fact that the document is not in the library's collection.[4]

While these generalized findings do not help the questioner whose purpose is to improve the card catalogue, they do have implications for user educations librarians. Statements 1 and 2 focus on the user. They harken back to William Randall's speech of 1931 when he urged the study of patrons, their mental equipment, their background and their needs. Statement 1 tells us that most users are students. While that is not terribly enlightening for the librarian in a college or university setting, it is a somewhat surprising finding for a public library. In both settings, the user education librarian can anticipate that the typical user is a student gathering material for a class assignment. Statement 2 provides some guidance as to what that typical student "brings" to the library.

Known-item searching increases with the educational level of the patron. Why ? Faculty or graduate students gather information from colleagues, from conferences, or from reading/browsing in the literature. They use their established network to gather citations. Students do not have personal networks. Having neither a network nor in Depth knowledge of a discipline, their approach to the card catalogue must be subject approach. It follows that need for instruction in the subject approach to a card catalogue becomes very important to the design of user education materials for the typical user—student.

Statement 4 is central to the cataloguer's question. "What elements in a catalogue record are useful ?" and to the user education librarian's question, "What elements in a card catalogue should be included in instruction ?" However, the most frequent use of those five elements does not exclude the need for other information to be present on the card. And, explaining those five elements in a written handour or a one-hour lecture is still a formidable task. It is only when statements 4 and 5 are linked that observations and conclusions can be drawn by both cataloguers and user education librarians. How does the user behave when a search fails ? What causes failure ? What can be improved in cataloguing codes or principles, or taught in user instruction in order to help the user achieve success ?

The studies of card catalogue use indicate that success in a known-item search is directly related to the amount of and accuracy of the information held by the user. For an author search, the more accurate the information, the more likely that success was achieved. That is, if the user had in hand a first and last name, correctly spelled, and a middle initial, then the success rate was very high. However, the relationship was not so evident between amount and accuracy of information and success rate of title searches.[5] Catalogue use studies also tell as us that "when the users possessed information about the author and the title, the majority preferred to look first under the author. Second tries were almost equally divided between title, author, and the subject approaches. The third trial is marked by a sharp increase in searches by subject."[6] These observations suggest that when failure occurs, more information on the catalogue card is utilized in succeeding attempts.

What causes failure ? Krikelas lists six difficulties that were identified by various studies :

> (1) filing rules used in catalogues ; (2) subject headings—the absence of certain terms or the use of terms too general for the user's needs; (3) the "see" and "see also" structure ; (4) the lack of title added entries ; (5) inaccurate bibliographic information possessed by the patrons ; and (6) call numbers.[7]

Several of those points of failure relate directly to the codes and principles of catalogues ; filing rules ; subject headings ; cross references; completeness of entry ; and call numbers. But the only statement that readily suggested an area for improvement for the cataloguers was the lack of title-added entries. In response to these findings, title-added entries were more often included in a card catalogue.

These findings are more useful for user education librarians. The need for instruction in subject searching already has been identified by a data relating to the typical user, the data on failure rate reinforces that need. In addition, the data suggests that instruction should cover filing rules, cross references, interpretation of bibliographic information in a citation and an explanation of the presence or absence of call numbers or the use of different call number systems (*i.e.*, Dewey and the Library of Congress).[8]

Let's apply what has been learned thus far to the design of an instruction module focusing on the most successful approach to the card catalogue—the author. The need to educate the user about cataloguing codes and local practices becomes immediately apparent.

* If the user has a complete author name and the name is rather unique, then the success rate should be very high ; little or no instruction is needed beyond the identification of the basic arrangement of the catalogue (dictionary, divided, etc.).

* If the user has incomplete author information, no title information, and the author name is common (Smith), then the user needs to be guided to directories, biographical dictionaries or to a reference desk. The goal is to teach the user how to enhance an incomplete citation.

* If the user has a citation in which the author is a corporate body, then the principles of choice of main entry become important. And, if the catalogue is very large and very old, multiple cataloguing codes may co-exist within the same catalogue.

* If the author's name is Shakespeare, then uniform entry and filing rules become critical to a user's success.

It is clear that even with a known-item, author approach to a card catalogue, the user education librarian must anticipate points of failure and include basic cataloguing codes and principles as part of user instruction. Therefore, the user education librarian must understand what the points of failure are likely to be and how to apply a cataloguer's philosophy in order to teach the user how to avoid failure?[9]

What have we learned about online Catalogues ?

The automation of library catalogues produced a plethora of new literature about users and online catalogues. In the United States a nation-wide study funded by the Council on Library. Resources in the early 1980s anticipated the flood of new search data both in methodology and results. It compared catalogue use and users of several online systems ; however, it utilized not only the traditional survey approach but also a new technique, "transaction analysis."[10]

Transaction analysis is the recording of all commands issued by a user, all system responses, and the elapsed time for each. It is a reliable technique for recording the use of a system by a user and for analysing user errors ; it does not tell you the users' intentions or if the user was satisfied. Transactions analysis became a popular methodology for catalogue use studies by cataloguers, online system designers and user education librarians. Although their goals were vastly different, the results were strikingly similar and surprisingly different from catalogue use studies in manual environment.

First of all, the most common search approach was a subject search not an author search. This was discovered in the initial Council for Library Resources study and is still true a decade later. And, in addition, subject searching causes the most user failures. Review articles by Nancy J. Williamson (1984) and Ray P. Larson (1991) summarize the various studies of subject searching in an online environment.[11]

A second difference lies in the errors which cause users failure. Spelling errors in citations are now compounded by user typing errors. No-hits for author names result because a first name is entered before a last name. No-hits for title searches result because an article is used (a, an, the).[12] Users now must not only understand the principles of cataloguing, but they must also understand the difference between using a manual card catalogue and an online catalogue. Anne Lipow, in an insightful article about online catalogues, lists major differences between the two. For example, "The online catalog screen offers no visual clues to indicate size of collection and database being searched ; no sense that the collection being searched was built over time by human beings. The card catalog—its size, its interfiling of crisp new cards and yellowing dog-eared cards, its varying type fronts and penciled notes—provides the searcher with that information."[13]

Third, differences in catalogue software produce different search results. Whereas in the past, standardization in catalogue code and classification allowed a school child to move with relative ease between a high school catalogue and a public library catalogue, the superimposition of nonstandardized software brought chaos. Search results in different catalogues are different and the difficulties for a remote user with dial-in equipment are compounded.[14] User education librarians must now teach procedural search techniques and database architecture as well as cataloguing concepts and principles.[15]

The Challenge

The advent of online catalogues, and with them, the ability to review user transactions, offers new opportunities to analyse the impact of cataloguing codes and practices on user behaviour. However, the same caveats exist for catalogue use studies in an automated environment as in the manual environment. While there may be a typical user, the variation and range of needs is still extraordinary. A novice in one discipline may well be an expert in another. A user in a small public library will utilize the catalogue much more efficiently than the same user would, the catalogue of a major research library. The completeness and accuracy of known information will affect the search pattern. The ability to "translate" citation information to catalogue code and filing rules will influence success. Then, there is the question of "What constitutes success" ? Is the search a failure if the item is not in the collection or it is successful if the original item is not found, but the user is led to other relevant items during a subject search ? In spite of these caveats, the potential for research about user behaviour in an outline environment is still vastly superior to studies conducted in a manual environment.

Research on user behaviour in an online catalogue environment needs to be continued, but the original goal of improving the success rate of the user by changing codes or practices is now only one part of the challenge to librarians. I belive that search should be broadended to include : 1) the impact of extending the scope and depth of the traditional card catalogue, 2) the impact of cataloguing codes and practices for users of multiple catalogues via state, national or international networks and 3) user interaction as influenced by multi media or hypercard or artificial intelligence.

The results of catalogue use studies in a manual environment did not contribute substantially to the cataloguer's quest to improve user success rate by improving cataloguing. The potential in an online environment for that outcome is greater. However user transactions must be tested against current cataloguing codes and practices. Analyses published to date are still at the identification stage ; researchers must move on to the application stage. For example, we know that most users will choose to use author information (if available) on the first or second foray into the catalogue ; only then do they use a wider range of catalogue information. Are those other elements different in an online environment ? Misspelling of an author's name results in no-hits ; should cross references to and from variations of names (even mistakes in typing) be expanded in an online environment or will the flexibility of key word and/or boolean searching on the second or third search attempt obviate the need for the extra work by cataloguers ? Those are only two of a myriad of questions which could be studied.

The online catalogue that we know today is virtually a replica of the paper card catalogue that dominated libraries for a hundred years. Automation offers alternatives at reasonable and affordable costs. However, there are many, many questions to be asked about potential impacts on users of extending the scope and depth of the traditional card catalogue. Lets look at a few of the possibilities: 1) Subject headings which are too general or out-dated have been identified as causes for user failure in traditional card catalogues. The technical capacity to instantly and automatically "change" subject headings has the potential to aid the user. But who will "authorize" the change ? Who referees the choice between the heading of cancer for lay people and carcinoma for health science professionals in a catalogue used by both ? Will multiple discipline oriented thesauri exist "alongside" or "behind" general subject headings ? How will users behave in that environment ? 2) Access to monographs in a manual environment was by author, title and a few chosen subject headings. Contents notes could be looked at if the user "found" a card. Automation has enhanced access to information on the "card" by allowing more fields to be indexed. Contents notes are searchable in some online systems. Should the concept of content notes be expanded by adding the table of contents for monographs to the catalogue record ? Should indexes of monographs be added to catalogues ? Users browse books on shelves using table of contents and/or indexes ; that need could now be fulfilled online. How would that best be done ? How would users behave in expended information environment ? Would the results be useful and cost effective ? 3) For most libraries the main card catalogue has provided access to books and journals. Audio-visual materials, newspapers, microforms, non-roman alphabet materials, maps, manuscripts and government documents often had separate catalogues. MARC standards for many of these formats have aided in expending the online catalogue to include more than books and journals. However, the fit is not comfortable for all formats. Archival and manuscript cataloguing records are distinctly different from the traditional monograph record. We must understand the problems encountered by a user in an online environment which presents distinctly different looking records. The phenomena will be repeated with art and architectural representations, museum pieces, and geographical information, to name a few. 4) Many libraries have mounted "card catalogues" and "indexes to journals" on a single mainframe. A library menu allows a user to select one or the other. Why not integrate them to allow the user to move seamlessly from article to journal title to call number/location ?

All of the above possibilities fall directly within the cataloguers goal of providing the link between the user and information. The other two areas that I suggested for research encompass a wider sphere, but nevertheless, will directly impact your work.

We know that the development and adoption of the UNIMARC format has standardized the layout of online catalogue records, but does this standardization aid the user in moving from one automated environment to another ? Evidence is to the contrary. The ability of users to "surf" the internet from one library catalogue to another has brought howls of confusion and consternation. The differences in search software have destroyed the consistency of expectations which you strive to create. The catalogue professionals, have been remarkably successful in creating international standards for catalogue content ; perhaps now is the time to begin to think about standards for catalogue access and presentation. And, finally, the third area of search involves the new online technologies. How could multi-media hypertalk or artificially intelligent front-ends be used to improve the success rate of the user ? I dream of the day when I can whistle a tune to a catalogue screen ; first the "card" and then the text of the music and then a video would appear on my screen. MTV via your catalogue ! Is that so far fetched ?

In summary, the literature of catalogue use studies extends over 50 years, yet there has been little progress toward the goal of increasing user success rates. In fact, we seem to have regressed. Recent studies show even lower user success rates in subject searching in online environment than in manual environment. For cataloguers, the greatest single contribution to user success was—and continues to be the standardization of cataloguing codes and classification both nationally and internationally. There is a predictability to library catalogues in spite of the multiplicity of cataloguing software in today's online environment. For user education librarians that predictability became the guidepost for instruction. Standardization is a key to future success. As librarians, we need to expand the scope of cataloguing beyond its current boundaries, experiment with screen forms and study variations for access. In all cases the effects on users must be studied, but in each case the ultimate goal should be standards predictability brought about by standards.

REFERENCES

1. James Krikelas, "Catalog Use Studies and Their Implications." *Advances in Librarianship 3* (October 1972) : 196
2. *Ibid.*, 217-220.
3. *Ibid.*, 197.
4. *Ibid.*, 210.
5. *Ibid.*, 206.
6. *Ibid.*
7. *Ibid.*, 202.
8. The following references are examples from user education literature ; Anne K. Beaubien, *Learning the Library*, (New York : R.R. Bowker Company, 1982), 168-169 ; Mary George and Sharon Hogan, "Teaching Tough Stuff : What's 3 × 5 and Full of Holes?, *Research Strategies* 1 (Summer 1983): 136-138; ...., "Teaching Tough Stuff: What's 3 × 5 and Full of Holes ? Part 2, "*Research Strategies* 2 (Winter 1984) : 50-55. In the United States, the clearing house for user education materials is project LOEX, Center of Educational Resources, Eastern Michigan University, Ypsilanti, MI 48197. Materials that were developed for instruction about the card catalogue are available for loan.
9. Two articles are particularly insightful for user education librarians are Elizabeth L. Tate, "A Guide for Searching in Anglo-American Main-Entry Catalogs," *Advances in Librarianship* 12 (February 1983) : 151 172 ; Martha M. Yee and Raymond Soto, "User Problems with Access to Fictional Characters and Personal Names in Online Public Access Catalogs," *Information Technology and Libraries* 10 (March 1991) : 3-13.
10. Joseph R. Methews, Gary S. Lawarance, and Douglas K. Ferguson, *Using Online Catalogs : A Natonwide Survey.* A Report of a Study Sponsored by the Council on Library Resources. (New York : Neal-Schuman Publishers, 1983).
11. Nancy J. Williamson, "Subject Access in the On-Line Environment", *Advances in Librarianship* 13 (September 1984) : 50-97 ; Ray R. Larson, "Between Scylla and Charybdis : Subject Searching in the Online Catalog," *Advances in Librarianship* 15 (September 1991) : 175-236.
12. A particularly detailed article describing patron errors is by Rhonda N. Hunter, "Successes and Failure of Patrons Searching the Online Catalog at a

Large Academic Library : A Transaction Long Analysis," *RQ* 30(3) (Spring 1991) ; 395-402.

13. Anne Grodzies Lipow, "The Online Catalog : Exceeding Our Grap," *American Libraries* 20 (October 1989) ; 863.

14. Problem of off-site patrons are described by Sally Wyman Kalin, "The Invisible Users of Outline Catalogues : A Public Services Perspective,"*Library Trends* 35 (Spring 1987) ; 587-595.

15. A useful compilation of user education literature about online catalogues is found in Frances C. Nowakowski, "Bibliographic Instruction for Online Public Access Catalogues : An annotated Bibliography," in *Subject Access and Bibliographic Instruction : Two Sides on the OPAC Problem.* (Halifax, Nova Scotia ; Dalhousie University School of Library and Information Studies, 1988), 73-93.

Training Non-Cataloguers about Cataloguing

BARBARA J. FORD

The card catalogue in dictionary form has been replaced or supplemented in a number of libraries by new forms of catalogues that are computerized and can be displayed on a screen or printed as needed. Providing a catalogue and an authoritative record of holdings is one of the important roles that libraries have played and will need to continue to play as technology changes. Although the purpose of cataloguing has not been essentially changed by advancements in technology and standardization, the methods of constructing catalogues and presenting them to the public are different. Such changes will probably continue as the capability for mass storage of data increases with the use of devices such as the optical disk.

These changes in library catalogues have made it more important than ever to be certain public services staff understand cataloguing practices. The public services staff need not only to assist catalogue users but should also be involved in shaping catalogues that will serve the needs of users in the electronic environment.

Library Environments

The Environments of libraries have changed as the resources and technologies available and the needs and characteristics of the people they serve have changed. Since the direction of change in libraries is generally from the simpler to the more complex, more staff expertise is needed. In the current library environment there needs to be more than dependence on work experience and increasing reliance on training. Training is needed to teach job skills, to upgrade skills, and to evaluate current library practices to see if they should be replaced with new ones. Training of non-cataloguers about cataloguing is a necessary response to change in the catalogue. Like other organizations, libraries are becoming more dependent on skilled employees and on the education and training through which these employees acquire skills. Success in automated libraries depends on teaching people what their work requires them to know.

The catalogue is the library's most valuable reference tool and without it the expenses of collection development and public services staff are not efficiently utilized. The capabilities of today's automated catalogues enable librarians to carry out activities in a variety of locations and can make the historical division of labor between cataloguers and reference librarians less necessary. Even when cataloguers create the bibliographic records the distribution of terminals throughout the library provides various staff with the potential means to enhance, amend, and delete records. While online catalogues are deceptively easy for the novice to use, they are definitely not yet self-service tools. Reference librarians and other staff will need help deciphering online records and retrieving materials for their own use and to assist users.

Most library staff and many library users are now comfortable with computers. That comfort and knowledge provides flexibility in staff assignments and in training activities. Some believe that it is too costly to extend the expertise of technical services departments to public services librarians. Most agree however that improvements in and enhancements to online catalogues are needed to better meet the needs of users. Because they hear what users are saying, public services librarians should be involved in the design, implementation, and improvement of online catalogues. Public services librarians need to work with technical services librarians and systems designers since all three groups have skills essential to the creation of the catalogue. To work with technical services librarians and systems designers, public services librarians must be well educated about the online catalogue.

Public Services Staff

Research and development in the 1980s focused on ways in which online catalogues could be more responsive than their earlier counterparts to the needs of library users. Yet in the March 1992 issue of *Information Technology and Libraries* a discussion of catalogue user interface design states that service-oriented librarians combined with a mediocre online catalogue will provide better real user service than a first-rate catalogue with no librarians in sight. If libraries accept this statement and follow this approach this means that training public services librarians about cataloguing is vital.

Once public services staff have a thorough understanding of the way the catalogue functions, they should also take part in identifying problems and correcting these problems to improve the catalogue. Public services staff, due to their high level of catalogue use and interaction with the public, are often the staff who hear about users problems with the catalogue. They need to be well informed to help users solve problems and to accurately report problems needing cataloguing attention to the cataloguing staff.

Public services librarians and cataloguers must work in collaboration to ensure that the best possible online catalogues are developed. Librarians with cataloguing responsibilities should be involved in the collection development and service programs of the library to be aware of user needs. Public services librarians need to be trained about cataloguing to meet user needs. Some authors propose the integration of public and technical functions but unless this happens public service librarians will need to be trained about cataloguing to provide the best service to library users.

In many graduate library school programmes cataloguing is no longer a required part of the academic programme. Often, it is only after someone begins work in public services that they realize how much they need to know about cataloguing. Sometimes public services librarians do not know enough to realize how much they do not know. It then becomes the responsibility of the library to help these non-cataloguers learn about cataloguing. Cataloguers need to work closely enough with public services librarians to be aware of what they may not realize they need to know.

Catalogue Issues

All library staff, not just those in the cataloguing department, need a basic knowledge of cataloguing. The ability to identify a publication and to determine its main entry is essential. In public services the staff must know how to use the catalogue, be able to show the patron how to use the catalouge, and know the kinds of information that can and cannot be found in the catalogue. This requires a basic knowledge of descriptive cataloguing and of the rules for main entries, filing rules, subject heading construction, and of the classification scheme.

The online catalogue can be used remotely by those not present in the library and often provides access to various in-process files not previously available to the library users. Catalogue maintenance becomes a public issue as all library staff and library users have access to files previously not widely available. With proper information and training, various staff can help with maintenance issues by identifying what needs to be changed or improved. The online catalogue can be a focus for change in the library as more information is available to be used in a wide range of settings and staff with various experiences and backgrounds work together.

With online catalogues it is important that libraries respond to the expressed and unexpressed needs of users. Often assistance is not requested and users make assumptions that may not be valid and do not locate needed information. We know from research studies that the preferred method of learning is trial and error, followed by online help. When users do a subject search, they are almost as likely to fail as to succeed in retrieving even a single relevant hit. We also know that most users change their intentions as they progress through information seeking tasks. Most users do not want to spend time learning how to use the catalogue - they just want to locate the information they need quickly and easily. Users are not always seeking to perform optimally. As access becomes a bigger issue and collections grow at a less rapid rate, the catalogue as a bibliographic surrogate is even more important for library users. Thus having a well presented and comprehensible catalogue is even more essential.

Catalogues that provide transaction logs offer opportunities to learn about what public services librarians and users may not know. Cataloguers may want to spend time observing how public services staff use the catalogue and how they respond to user requests. When one works with the catalogue in the intense way that cataloguers do they may not realize how different some aspects are to non-cataloguers.

Training in the Online Environment

In the online environment with new work patterns and library units dependent upon one another, quality training will be critical. New techniques and approaches will be required and it may often be most effective to do centralized training in the online environment. As library functions are automated training materials will need to be developed, staff may need to be trained as trainers, and time will need to be allocated for staff to learn. Librarians will need to learn how to handle the disruptions that can occur in an online environment. Training and retraining will have to occur frequently as changes in online systems are implemented. Staff will need to see the broad picture and understand the relationship of various library tasks. In an online environment more training will be needed and training will need to be continuous.

With these challenges many libraries will find it necessary to develop some training for public services librarians (and other non-cataloguers) on cataloguing issues. These staff need to know the standards that are used in creating the catalogue and be able to explain them to users. Training should be ongoing since automated systems users reach learning plateaus and need continuing encouragement to expand their knowledge and understanding. This is especially true with catalogues that have distinct staff and public catalogue functions. The public services staff will quickly forget the staff side of the online system if they do not use it often.

The first step in planning training is to identify job changes or problems that may require training and to assess the extent of the skills problems that could be encountered and consider options for addressing them. Involvement of those to be trained as partners during the planning process is essential. Staff to be targeted for training should be identified early in the process.

Carefully planning training sessions is essential and there are several prerequisites to a successful training session. The expected outcomes must be articulated. The trainee must see the need for the expected change and believe the session will be a beneficial step toward change. Follow-up should be planned for the training sessions.

Technology adaptation occurs in stages. Technology makes new and different approaches possible and ultimately transforms behaviours. Training can help to bring about this transformation. There may be a need to recognize various learning styles and varying levels of adaptation to technology. Library administrators need to be certain that training is a routine part of library activities and that time is allocated on a regular basis for training. Each library must take responsibility to be certain that appropriate training is available whether within the library or through other means.

Professional Organizations and Publications

Library organizations and library publications directed toward public services librarians can also be important venues for education about cataloguing issues. As library literature becomes more specialized and voluminous it becomes less likely that public services librarians will read publications directed to cataloguers. Cataloguers should direct some of their effort in writing for journals read by public services librarians. Offering workshops in collaboration with organizations of public services librarians could also be prove effective. As librarianship and the work performed in various specialities become more focused, training and publishing efforts must be directed toward nonspecialists.

Rather than each library developing its own training sessions, it may be more efficient and effective to focus general cataloguing training efforts on what can be provided by professional organisations and publications. However, each library will need to provide training specific to its catalogue and environment. On-the-job training cannot be effectively replaced by other types of education or training and each library should plan for appropriate internal and external training activities in its budgeting and allocation of staff resources.

Conclusion

The online catalogue provides opportunities for changes in libraries and the services we provide to library users. Cataloguers need to take an aggressive role in being certain that public services librarians get the training they need to help catalogue users make the best use of this valuable tool. Effective training increases efficiency, effectiveness, and productivity for public services librarians. By working with public services librarians, cataloguers may also get some ideas on how to make the online catalogue more responsive to user needs and expectations.

While the ultimate goal should be to develop a catalogue that can be used by public service librarians and library users without training, until such a point is reached training of public services librarians will be essential. Without such training public services librarians cannot help to develop a catalogue that will be more responsive to the needs of library users.

The online catalogue provides an impetus and opportunity to better meet user needs. Dialogues and partnerships are required to create the catalogues that will more effectively meet user expectations. The challenge for cataloguers and public services librarians is to work cooperatively to use technology to continue developing catalogues that respond to user needs.

REFERENCES

Trudi Bellardo. "User Interfaces for Online Public Access Catalogs: A Research Workshop," *Bulletin of the American Society for Information Science* 18 (4): 27, April/May 1992.

Marty Bloomberg and G. Edward Evans. *Introduction to Technical Services for Library Technicians*. Littleton, Co.: Libraries Unlimited, 1981.

Jennifer Cargill. "Integrating Public and Technical Services Staffs to Implement the New Mission of Libraries," *Journal of Library Administration*, 10(4): 21-31, 1989.

Anthony P. Carnevale, Leila J. Gainer, Ann S. Meltzer. *Workplace Basics: The Essential Skills Employers Want*. San Francisco : Jossey Bass, 1990.

Pauline Atherton Cochrane. *Redesign of Catalogs and Indexes for Improved Online Subject Access*. Phoenix, Az.: Oryx Press, 1985.

Walt Crawford. "Starting Over: Current Issues in Online Catalog User Interface Design," *Information Technology and Libraries* 11(1): 62-76, March 1992.

Sheila D. Creth. *Effective On-the-Job Training*. Chicago: American Library Association, 1986.

Maurice J. Freedman and S. Michael Malinconico, Editors. *The Nature and Future or the Catalog*. Phoenix, Az.: Oryx Press, 1979.

Eleanor Gossen, Frances Reynolds, Karina Ricker, and Helen Smirensky. "Forging New Communication Links in an Academic Library: A Cross-Training Experiment, "*Journal of Academic Librarianship* 16 (1): 18-21, March 1990.

Michael Gorman and Associates. *Technical Services Today and Tomorrow*. Englewood, Co.: Libraries Unlimited, 1990.

Sheila S. Intner and Janet Swan Hill. *Recruiting, Educating, and Training Cataloging Librarians*. New York: Greenwood Press, 1989.

Lois Kershner. "Training People for New Job Responsibilities: The Lesson Plan, "*Library Resources & Technical Services* 34 (2): 251-255, April 1990.

Anne Grodzins Lipow. "Training for Change: Staff Development in a New Age," *Journal of Library Administration* 10 (4): 87-97, 1989.

Jesse H. Shera. *The Foundations of Education for Librarianship*. New York: Becker and Hayes, 1972.

Information Needs of the Librarians of Developing Countries and the Palisades they Encounter in Obtaining these Information

WIJETUNGE PRADEEPA

We have been providing information for others since the origin of our profession and those who obtain information from us have been changing the society utilizing that information. How would this change affect us, can we face the change without redefining our profession, can we survive with the amount of professional information available for us at the moment, should we devote more time to develop an information system for ourselves. My paper is an attempt to answer some of these issues.

Emergence of librarianship as a recognized profession is a fairly modern development. In the later part of the 19th century, with the growth of the complexity of their functions, libraries found it necessary to develop new technical skills in classifying and organizing the large volume of information available. Librarian's main role during this period was to select, acquire and organize the material be they books, journals or non-book material and to make them available for those who come in search of information.

However, it becomes evident that this traditional role played by the librarian is not sufficient at all for the modern library, because the libraries and their role in the society are changing rapidly. And two factors are contributing to this change more than anything else.

The first and foremost can be said to be the developments in information technology. Later part of the 20th century is experiencing a brisk advancement of technology which has been felt by the librarians as well as the library users. With the development of micro computers most of the libraries have become ardent users of them. Computer technology goes further to link individual computers into Local Area and Wide Area Networks by which communication between distant libraries is made possible. In addition Laser technology is revolutionizing the information storage and retrieval aspect by means of CD-ROMs. Librarians of developing countries cannot circumvent the influences of these technological products. Library users become aware of these modern technologies when they interact with the libraries of developing countries which satisfy their information needs in a more sophisticated manner. As a result of this awareness they pressurize the local librarians for a more upto date and quality service than merely presenting them with books and periodicals on neat rows of shelves. In order to face this changing environment with forcefulness, we must be cognizant of these modern inventions.

Secondly the unstable economic conditions of the developing countries is making a colossal impact on the role of the library in a large scale. Library services are badly affected when it comes to cost reductions since very often they are chosen as the first item to be curtailed. The librarian in this instance has to keep on struggling to satisfy the ever increasing user demands with an ever decreasing or stagnant budget.

Hence the present day librarian is confronted with the task of fulfilling two inversely proportional objectives - namely to provide better and modern library facilities to users and to keep house with a limited budget without letting the quality drop at the same time. The modern librarians of developing countries have to step into a multifaceted role which embraces traditional as well as non-traditional areas of librarianship, to deal with these two contradictory objectives.

This multifaceted role can be viewed as having three major facets in addition to the professional facet - namely the management facet, social facet, and the technological facet. To play this new role successfully the librarian needs information. What sort of information is that ?

Information needs of management facet of the librarian

Management is concerned with accomplishing certain defined activities and it is people who accomplish the work. The balancing of activities and people become the task of the manager. Yet, the successful manager does not act purely on his intuition, but on a theoretical knowledge of decision making, planning and marketing concepts. The librarian can be described as a manager without doubt, since he or she is concerned with accomplishing certain activities, and balancing these activities and people who accomplish the work. Accordingly the librarian can benefit by applying the theoretical management concepts to attain his goals.

The modern day librarian obviously has to make crucial decisions on library procedures, and necessarily should employ long and short term planning. These two concepts become specially important when attempting to achieve the expected standards with ever decreasing resources. On the other hand the librarian requires to advertise his products in order to survive. Products of information technology like CD ROMs and commercial online databases, detracts the user away from the library by providing them with the facility of obtaining information, avoiding the library. Even if this situation is not yet visible in developing countries we may anticipate it with our rapidly developing commercial sector. It becomes the duty of the librarian to safeguard the position of the library.

To meet these challenges, present day librarians in the developing countries need a wealth of information relevant to the management concepts which can be employed in the library management.

Information needs of the social facet of the librarian

Modern libraries can be described as open systems - which interact on a large scale with external organizations like professional bodies, book publishers, manufactures and various other groups, in contrast to the traditional libraries which existed in isolation as closed systems - with less interaction with the external organizations. In the era of modern technology, while we appreciate and encourage technological developments to be adopted in the libraries, we should at the same time appreciate the human behaviour. No technology can perform its function independent of human beings. If this fact is not taken into consideration, human beings who will be affected by these technological innovations will always show a kind of hostility towards them and will consequently develop defence mechanisms like absenteeism, slow work rate, postponement of duties, avoidance and even resignation at the end. As a repercussion of pressing economic problems and changing work environments, staff depression might increase while motivation decrease. The librarian will have to play the role of a psychologist or psychoanalyst in overcoming these problems. To tackle this kind of human-centered problems the social facet in his role will be immensely beneficial.

With the introduction of new technological products, the role which the librarian has to play as an educator is intensified. It is not underestimated here the role of traditional librarian played as an educator but the modern librarian who introduces products of information technology especially the computers in their libraries will have to go to the user groups in a more personalised or individualistic manner.

In the effort of developing this social facet of our profession we need information related to human behaviour, psychology, psychoanalysis, methods of education and many other fields of social science.

Information needs of the technical facet of the librarian

As I mentioned earlier the change in the society is caused mainly by information technology. Librarians are compelled to use products of IT, especially computers. In order to achieve the full benefits of the technology, he must then posses a technological knowledge. Yet, this is not to say that the librarian should be an expert in the field, but at least a basic knowledge in Electronic Data processing will become useful.

The problem solving methodology used in computer technology consists of four stages namely the analysis of the problem (systems analysis), design of a solution (systems design), implementation of the system and review. These stages are commonly known as the system life cycle because this process works in a cyclical manner.

Introduction of modern information technology in our libraries can be contemplated in the light of the systems life cycle. Lets consider the purchase of a computer the library as an example. We may believe that the computer will solve our problem if we procure one, but at this stage we have to consider whether our problem can really be solved by using a computer or at the first instance whether we actually have a problem at all. The first stage of the system life cycle-the systems analysis stage can be employed in the endeavour of answering this question. Secondly if it is established that a computer can solve our problem we have to make decisions on the suitable hardware, software, and personnel. This is the stage of systems design. Thirdly the selected system have to be implemented. For this, things like electricity, air conditioning, installation of machines, user training and various other site preparation work has to be dealt with. Finally when the system is activated, we have to evaluate it against our expected standards.

In performing all these functions it is not denied that the librarian has to seek assistance of a multiplicity of professionals other than library staff, especially computer personnel. To obtain maximum service from these personnel, the librarian must be able to express his needs and requirements in a way in which the professionals understand and also the librarian must not let them confuse him by using their glossy trade vocabulary.

To acquire this kind of technological knowledge, the librarians must have access to information, related to all stages of systems life cycle.

Information needs of the professional facet of the librarian

With the impact of modern technology, the volume of information generated is increasing rapidly. The annual output of information is so large that we begin to wonder as users of information whether we are losing control. On the other hand, this wealth of information generated with the aid of technology has not been utilized in its maximum capacity. The librarian as a professional has an important role to play in this environment of information explosion.He should be acting as the agent of information transfer between the producer and the client.

In this process we have to expand the horizons of our traditional professional duties - the selection, acquisition, organization and the dissemination of information. To perform these functions efficiently we need current and advanced information relevant to the traditional role of librarianship.

Palisades we encounter in obtaining information

The aforementioned discourse revealed the number of fields in which we librarians need information for the advancement of our career. Yet there is a question we can pose. Are we capable of fulfilling these information needs within our countries. It is obvious that this is not viable. It is a sad fact that sometimes we come across information relevant to our neighbouring countries or even to our own countries in foreign libraries, mainly in developed countries. This information is not available for us. What are the palisades that prevent us from receiving the information which is essential for our professional survival. The main palisade can be said to be the distance between the information generators and its potential users in developing countries. As a result of this far too great distance, we are not aware of the existing information. The application of theories of other disciplines in librarianship cannot be assumed unless we are made aware of their relevance.

Once we realize the importance of such other disciplines, then we face the selection of suitable literature. The concept of information explosion is predominantly existing in the developed countries. Vast amount of literature is published on each specific subject. We are not in a position to obtain all the information or even to know of their existence. It is true that we receive publishers catalogues for books and non-book material, but the extensive amount of information published in journals is lost for us. One can argue that we can subscribe to reference tools like indices and abstracts which cover most of the published information. Yet obtaining hard copies which contain the actual information is not an easy task.

We have to go through abstracts and keywords to select what we require and then request the hard copies from the available sources. Because of the distance between the information and the potential user, a considerable period of time is lapsed before receiving the hard copies. By that time we may no longer need that information. Sometimes the abstracts and keywords may mislead us by giving the wrong interpretation and the final product may not be what we expected.

Employing the new technological developments, information can be produced in a multiplicity of media, in addition to the printed form i.e. magnetic form,micro form, audio visual form or electronic form. But in most of the developing countries the technology still available in our libraries is only the Gutenberg technology. Hence, however important a piece of information may be, if it is not produced in a format which we can make use of, it bars us from using the information.

Even the printed information can be in a plethora of languages which we donot comprehend. This too can be one of our barriers to access information. For instance most interesting applications of micro CDS/ISIS are published in Hungarian, Russian, Slovak and other non-English languages. But however much they are useful we cannot use them because of the language barrier. Even the vast amount published in English cannot be said to be useful since only a limited of our colleagues are literate in English. Common language of communication is one of the reasons which brought us all here to this IFLA conference, but the information produced here in the major languages will not be fully available for those who know only the vernacular.

The core of all our palisades in obtaining information can be said to be the cost of information. The information generated in the west is highly priced and the problem is further aggravated by our increasing exchange rates. In obtaining information from the generator, the high cost not only consists of the hard copy cost, but the postage, reprographic charges, telecommunication charges if used, are also included. If high cost reference tools like online searching or

CD/ROMs are used, their cost also will be added. It is obvious that the individual librarian cannot afford all these costs, not even the hard copy cost. And our employers are also not in a position of bearing them. On the other hand the employers do not realize that we librarians need so much of information to survive.

Last but not least, culture can also be a palisade for us in obtaining the information. A good example for this is my absence from the conference. Our cultural beliefs did not allow me to change my plans for tomorrow hence prevented me from attending the conference personally and I have been deprived of the opportunity of listening to the valuable presentations made today and sharing information with the colleagues from most of our neighbouring countries.

How could we then rectify this problem. We have to find answers to our main problems. We must get closer to information or information must get closer to us. Not only that, the information should be in a medium and language suitable for us and at a convenient price. In this endeavour, collective decisions of librarians becomes important since it is not much that they can do as isolated individuals.

What we have to do is to establish national and regional information systems for us, not for science & technology not for social science but purely for library & information science. The task of this information system must be collecting, organizing and dissemination information among the librarians at national and regional levels. During this process information should be translated into suitable media and languages enabling the librarians of the particular country and the region to utilize them. In order to reduce the costs, policies should be formulated in a way in which the high costs can be shared among the members.

In this endeavour too we will have to face the problem of financing such projects. We must convince the respective governments of the importance of our career development for the overall development of the society in order to obtain financial assistance from them. Foreign funding sources also could be approached in addition to the central governments.

"Librarianship: profession, semi-profession or mere occupation?: surveying the process of change and development in British librarianship today"

MIKE FREEMAN

The paper will not attempt to enter into the wider debate regarding the nature of professions and the arid 'traits' and 'characteristics' argument but will try to address some of the issues in librarianship (particularly British librarianship) centred around the concepts of 'profession' and the professionalization process. The author takes the view that Wilensky[1] advances: that all occupations are placed on a continuum of professionalization. Some progressing, others remaining static and yet others moving backward. This seems an eminently commonsensical and observable model carrying within it the central concept of *movement* along a spectrum, whilst responding or failing to respond to societal and occupational changes.

Wilensky writes of a "cycle of professionalization" using what he calls 'First Events' as significant cumulating markers or milestones on the occupation's voyage across this continuum of professionalization. This concept of 'first events' is echoed by Reader's[2] observation that an occupation's rise to professional standing can be pretty accurately charted by reference to the progress of the relevant professional association. Abbott[3] sees the professionalization process as a natural evolutionary force, leading eventually to the Utopia of *all* occupational groups becoming true professions. He introduces the idea of 'jurisdiction' as the link between a profession and its work and claims, reasonably enough, that every profession aims for a "heartland of work over which it has complete, legally established control". Identifying the "heartland" of librarianship has not been to easy and establishing complete and legally established control—and thus occupational closure - has proved elusive. All does not flow smoothly in this slow movement across a continuum from occupation through semi-profession to full professional status. Pressures bear down upon these evolving groups of workers: the professions as a whole now have to grapple with such concepts as 'privatisation' 'value for money' and 'deregulation'. The agencies of appeal against and control of the professions continue to multiply (e.g. the various Ombudsmen for Banking Local government and Insurance in the U.K.) and the traditional deference and acquiescence of the general public to the authority and mysteries of the professions steadily diminishes. A growing and serious threat on the horizon is that of 'deprofessionalization'. As the bulk of professionals now work within an organisational bureaucracy (whether a Hospital or a Public Library Service) where control is usually from above and where they are merely salaried employees then elements of deprofessionalization will creep in. This leads to two groupings for loyalties: one to the profession and one to the oganisation. This duality of allegiance often leads to role strain and role dissonance. Murphy[4] argues that three factors are weakening and destroying professional monopolies today. These are: (A) Information Technology providing management with powerful tools to control and standardise professionals and their work. (B) managers professionally trained as such, are managing and controlling professionals more and more, and (C) cutbacks in resources, combined with overproduction of professionals is weakening the power of professionals in general. These points apply increasingly to librarians and do not portray a comfortable secure future for professionals and their work. Goode[5] remarks that "an industrialising society is a professionalizing society" - an observation of some comfort and relevance to Third World societies undergoing industrialization. But what happens when that society moves into a Post-Industrial phase? Will the demand for professionals reduce? What will happen to the image and status of the professional in such a society?

Looking historically at the origins and development of librarianship and information services (LIS) in the UK there seem to have been several significant "First Events" (to use Wilensky's phrase): key stages in the movement along the professionalization continuum. A major stimulus was the 1850 Public Libraries Act, which fuelled the rapid growth of the urban Public Library sector (the largely rural Countries had to wait until 1919 for their own founding and funding Act), with the growth of publicly funded libraries came the need for appropriate staffing. The banding together of these scattered library personnel led to the formation of the Library Association in

1877 (the American Library Association having been founded the previous year). The LA embarked rapidly upon drawing up an education and training system for library workers complete with certification (1882), running examinations (1885), gaining a Royal Charter (i.e. State recognition) (1898) and setting up an Official Register of Librarians (1909). The Library Assistants' Association (LAA) was founded in 1895, merging with the LA in 1929 and renamed as the Association of Assistant Librarians (AAL) very much now the largest Group within the LA's internal array of Groups and Branches. Other significant players in the UK LIS arena are the Institute of Information Scientists (IIS) founded in 1958 and ASLIB (the Association of Special Libraries and Information Bureaux) founded in 1924. This latter is in many ways not a professional body: it is not a "qualifying association" certifying and overseeing practitioners but is more a loose grouping of special libraries and information units plus some personal members. The IIS, however, is more of a true professional body; validating course, awarding qualifications and having two grades of professional membership. One of the major initiatives of the last few years has been the Saunders proposal of 1989 whereby the unification of the LA, ASLIB and the IIS into one large, comprehensive and powerful body of LIS workers — probably under a new name — was analysed and discussed exhaustively. Interestingly, this proposal echoed Abbot's[6] remark on the possibility of a "unified information jurisdiction" being formed — although he was encompassing librarianship/information science/computing/ documentalism/ management information systems within his definition. Regrettably, the Saunders proposal was rejected in 1991 after many months of tortuous discussion. Perhaps Cronin's[7] provocative remark that "there is no information profession. There are information workers: a large and heterogeneous population... a dynamic sector is best served by a deregulated educational environment" is quite perceptive and prophetic.

Nevertheless as a generalization, the image and status of librarians has risen reasonably well over the years, the remorseless 'trading up' of entry qualifications to librarianship has led to a virtually all — graduate profession. It would not be surprising to see this spiralling upwards process extend towards embracing the American system of a first professional qualification being a Master's in Library Studies (MLS), such is the pressure of 'academic drift'. This would turn British librarianship into a postgraduate profession with all that implies in terms of salaries, status, curricula and length of professional training. There are still some lingering doubts about whether librarianship is a 'true' profession and is in fact more akin to a 'semi-profession' and is still in movement along the professionalization spectrum towards the goal of full professional status. Simpson and Simpson[8] reason that the prevalence of women in a body of workers leads to a more bureaucratic internal organisation and to a semi-professional status. Goode[9] famously stated that "school teaching will not achieve professionalism nor will librarianship". These observations seem dated, dogmatic and certainly anti-"Equal Opportunities", but nevertheless librarianship in the UK is still a female majority occupation (73%: 1989 LA Survey) and yet the top professional posts are predominately held by men. Encouragingly things are changing for the better, reflecting societal changes but it will be a slow and difficult process.

The major professional LIS body in the UK — The Library Association - now possesses most of the significant professional characteristics to be acquired during the professionalization process : full time occupation; university level professional education and training of some length; Royal Charter (i.e. official State recognition); code of conduct and an internal disciplinary mechanism; altruistic service to the community; general political and numerical dominance of the LIS sector of work. The glittering prize of State Licensing and consequent occupational closure and control continues to elude the profession however.

Librarianship can be perceived as essentially functionalist, serving the central values of society such as education, information and culture. Arguably, librarianship can also be seen to be exhibiting monopolist tendencies today; seeking to dominate and control its sector of work driving towards occupational closure and exclusivity. Perhaps it has always done this and only now do we fully recognise it. Major problems lie within the fact that most LIS professionals and support staff work within large and bureaucratic organisational settings and that the capacity and inclination by laymen to judge "professional competence" is increasing, thus weakening the mystique, power and exclusivity of the profession. Dundy and Wasserman[10] observe that "as the professional seeks institutional rewards, security and status he pays for them with compliance and conformity at the expense of his professional obligations". They see librarianship as marginalized and incompletely professionalized - in effect, a semi-profession.

A Further issue is that of the 'uniqueness' of LIS work and whether there exists a demonstrably irreducible core of professional work - Abbott's "heartland of work" idea again. He maintains that boundaries between professional jurisdiction tend to break down in work environments (particularly in overstressed, overloaded workplaces) and the process of 'workplace assimilation' takes place. Professional tasks become diluted or deprofessionalized as a result. If a good paraprofessional or library assistant can perform as well as a mediocre professional then what implications for professional status, high salaries and professional control and jurisdiction follow? There does seem to be a squeeze occurring to a certain extent on many professional librarians: they are under threat. At the top layer from non-librarian managers and IT experts and are being nibbled away at the bottom level by a growing number of non-professional LIS workers. Should the professional body therefore welcome these intruders and competitors into their membership? By extending 'hospitality of membership' to all involved in LIS work (however loosely defined) does this action then dilute and dissolve the central core of librarianship and threaten the purity and integrity of the profession? Should the LA have tightened up and restricted membership further if its role, function and aspirations as a true professional body are to be maintained and developed? Or is incorporation a clever and effective method of absorbing and controlling new threats? Arguably, by grasping and promulgating the concept of 'hospitality' to all the many and diverse LIS workers in the UK (and overseas) the major professional body — and thus the profession itself — has weakened irretrievably its claim to true professional status. Roberts[11] calls this "a highly significant step in that such a policy contradicts a century of professional striving to mark out a distinct and protected, area of technical differentiation now thought impossible to preserve". So perhaps the LA is being supremely pragmatic and realistic in its policy of 'hospitality' and indeed there may be considerable benefits of cross-fertilisation, new ideas and vigour which will accrue from such a policy. In the evolution of LIS professional bodies throughout the world this question of 'hospitality' is bound to arise, given the rate of change and the growing diversity of the information world we inhabit. Mac Donald and Ritzer[12] in similar vein comment that "in order to control the market the occupational body must include anyone with a reasonable claim to expertise but such inclusion brings in marginal practitioners who lower the standing of higher status members". There is an unresolved conundrum here: a conflict between exclusivity and expansibility.

Another problem arising during the professionalization process is whether the putative professional body actually reaches its goal intact, either in numbers or in its original role and function. There seems to be an interesting phenomenon linked in to the size of the body of workers itself and whether it is subject to 'limits of growth'. Drawing parallels from nuclear weapon design it becomes possible to form a model of a "fusion-fission" process operating upon the LIS profession. In the first stage, a group of disparate, scattered and numerically small workers in the LIS field are subject to external pressures or "initiators', which propel these workers into a coherent grouping with common aims and interests thus reaching a "critical mass" and forming a sustainable embryonic professional body. An "initiator" might well be a piece of legislation. e.g. the UK Public Libraries Act of 1850, or a threat from an unexpected sector, e.g. computing personnel. Whichever it is, the group of workers thus compressed into a tight common interest association invariably sets out along the professionalization route, acquiring the trappings and traits of a traditional professional body along the way. The fusion process continues to grow inexorably and dominance numerically and politically over the work sector is established. Then "systems disturbance" (as Abbott calls it) arises: the professional body has grown too large and unwieldy: special interest and regional groups of practitioners feel neglected and isolated: communications breakdown follows, culminating in the inevitable "fission" process. Groups of disaffected and alienated LIS workers split away and form their own miniature specialist associations and start up on the long process of professionalization again. The Irish poet, W.B.Yeats summed up the paradox neatly: "Things fall apart: the centre cannot hold". This model may seem too mechanistic and pessimistic; the life and death of a profession is perhaps not one long, sustained nuclear explosion but rather a series of stop/go manoeuvre, false trails, reverses and sudden spasmodic leaps forward. This returns us to

Wilensky's observation on the progress or otherwise along a continuum of professionalization.

In conclusion the profession of librarianship in the UK seems now to be approaching crisis point after many years of steady development and consolidation. The arrival of the "information society" with its far-reaching developments in information storage and retrieval is forcing reappraisal and radical change upon the profession in all its aspects, and particularly upon the education and training of professional librarians to meet the information challenges of the 21st Century. A quote from the influential BLRD&D Report "Information UK 2000"[13] illuminates the probable future environment within which the future LIS professional will operate:

> "More widespread use of technology more automation, more computer literacy amongst the population at large, greater commercial pressures to sell information products of various kinds to the public - all these factors will tend to weaken the position of the traditional librarian or information scientist."

The key word, of course, is "traditional". This plethora of information will have to be handled effectively whatever the "tools of the trade" might turn out to be in the future. Kendrick[14] sums it up neatly for all of us, and the author agrees with his essentially upbeat and optimistic view of "things to come" for the LIS profession:

> "The doomsayers who predict the dispersion and demise of the library are wrong. As knowledge continues to multiply the need for expertize - to collect, categorize sort, retrieve and advise and comfort bewildered users - will also multiply".

REFERENCES

1. WILENSKY, H.L. (1964) "The professionalization of everyone". *American Journal of Sociology,* Vol. LXX, No 2, Sep. 1964.
2. READER, W.J. (1966:163) "Professional Men" London: Routledge.
3. ABBOTT, A. (1988:71) "The system of profession", Chicago university of Chicago Press.
4. MURPHY, R. (1990:71) "Proletarianization and bureaucratisation: the fall of the professional" *in* TORSTENDAHL, R. and BURRAGE. M *eds* "The formation of the profession" London: Sage.
5. GOODE, W.J. (1960:902) "Encroachment, charlatanism and the emerging professions" *American Sociological Review. 25.* (6).
6. ABBOTT, A. (1988:65) *Op. cit.*

7. CRONIN, B (1988:39) "Bringing eduction for information workers into the 1980s". *ASLIB Information,* Part 16(2) Feb. 1988.

8. SIMPSON, R.L. and SIMPSON, I.H. (1969:197) "Women and bureaucracy in the semi-professions" *in* ETZIONI, A., *ed.* "The semi-professions and their organization" New York: Free Press.

9. GOODE, W.J. (1969:281) "The theoretical limits of professionalization *in* ETZIONI, A.. *op. cit.*

10. DUNDY, M.L. and WASSERMAN, P. (1968:16) "Professionalism reconsidered" *College and Research Libraries, 29 No 1, Jan 1968.*

11. ROBERTS, N. (1991:452) "A profession in crisis, *Library Association Record, 93.*(7) July 1991.

12. Mac DONALD, D. and RITZER, G. (1988:258) "The sociology of the professions" *Work and Occupations, 15* No.3, Aug 1988.

13. BRITISH LIBRARY RESEARCH AND DEVELOPMENT, DEPARTMENT. (1990). "Information UK 2000: a Report", London: BLRD&D.

14. KENDRICK, C. (1986:127) "The University Library in the 21st Century", *College and Research Libraries,* March 1986.

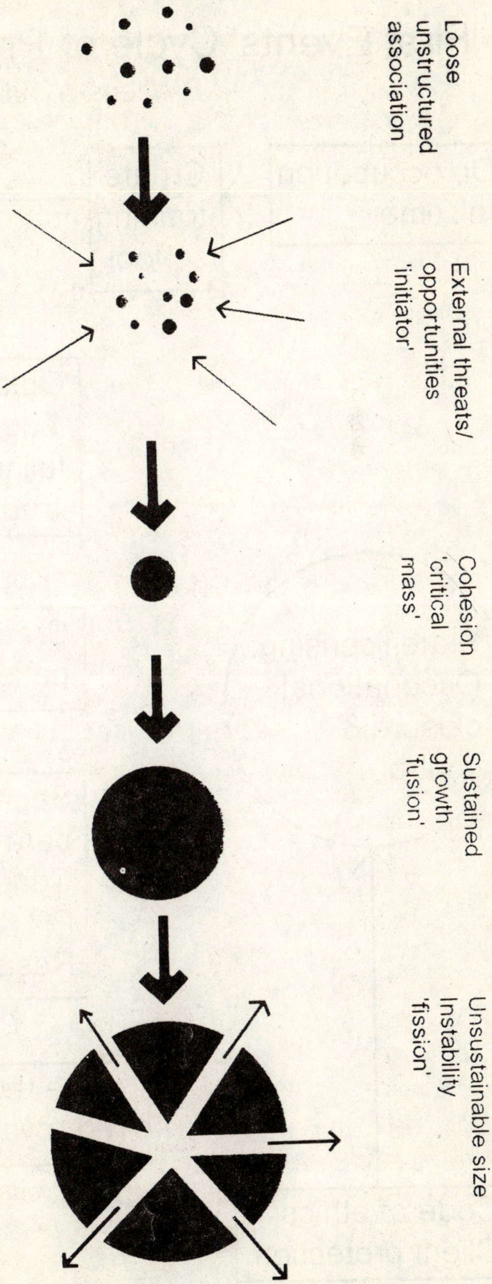
Loose
unstructured
association
External threats/
opportunities
'initiator'
Cohesion
'critical
mass'
Sustained
growth
'fusion'
Unsustainable size
Instability
'fission'

'First Events' Cycle of Professionalization

(Wilensky 1964)

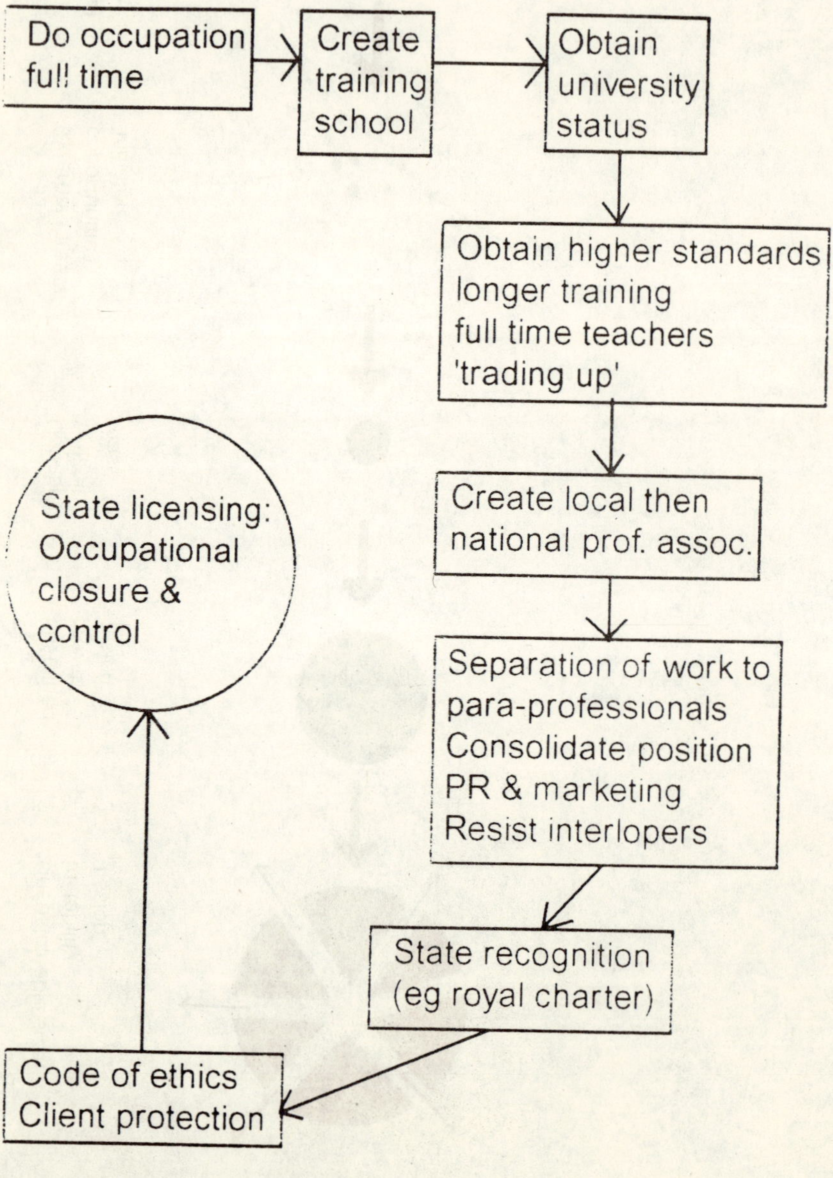

PART VI
Information, Technology and Databases

OSIRIS, A Microcomputer-based System "Online serials Information, Registration and Inquiry System"

SUZANNE SANTIAGO

The development of a microcomputer-based software called OSIRIS (Online Serials Information Registration and inquiry system) was a project supported by the past Medium-Term Programme (1986-1991) of the IFLA Section on Serial Publication. OSIRIS is designed for the registration of serials, local management of databases dealing with serials and retrieval of information, production of bibliographies and catalogues that could be derived from them. Being based on a microcomputer, it allows small and medium-size projects on serials to take advantage of automation at limited cost.

The purpose of this paper is to present the way the project was conducted and its result, the OSIRIS software, that is presently available for distribution.

Background and Developments

The idea of OSIRIS was first presented to the ISDS Directors' meeting in 1986 in Budapest by Mr Jacso and Mr Szucs, the creators of the software. The project was welcomed by the network and formally accepted by the ISDS Governing Board in 1987. The work started with the evaluation of needs, the finding of partners and the establishment of procedures.

The first draft User's Manual was delivered by the creators to the ISDS International Centre in 1989. The specifications of the software and the schedule of actions could be presented to the Standing Committee of the IFLA Section on Serial Publications in August 1989 at the Paris Conference.

The support and work of the following institutions and persons should be mentioned here:

— Unesco authorized ISDS to use Micro-CDS/ISIS, the Unesco developed PC software for management of databases, as the underlying software of OSIRIS, and granted ISDS a license to distribute it.

— IFLA, recognizing the international value of the project for the serial community, supported the idea and granted financial support for training and documentation.

— The creators of the software, Mr, Jacso and Mr Szucs, continued to work enthusiastically towards completion of the package, though time having elapsed since the idea was raised, they were involved in other professional ventures.

— The two test Centres, Hungary and Ireland, their Directors, Ms Szilvassy and Ms Fletcher, and staff dedicated much time and energy to a thorough scrutiny of the software and documentation, thus greatly facilitating the work of those who would use OSIRIS after them.

— Finally, the staff of the ISDS International Centre, Mr Rozenfeld, head of the computer section above all, set a high priority in the coordination work between users and creators, and put all their ISDS experience in the service of project.

This paper should be a collective paper because it draws much of its content from technical documents, reports on tests and working sessions, and from the User's Manual.

This paper will first sum up the steps taken in order to reach the final product, as they are explicit of the objective that was aimed at. The draft Manual presented to the Standing Committee in August 1989 was a basis for further discussion on the necessary developments, i.e., a thorough adaptation of a powerful underlying software to specific requirements. A first pilot version was available in spring 1990 for installation

The two ISDS National Centres that had volunteered and had been chosen to test the package (software and documentation) were Hungary and Ireland. In addition to their willingness to dedicate the necessary efforts to the experiment, they were representative of different types of users. The Hungarian Centre had been involved in the project from its very origin. It was a medium-size centre and the Hungarian language itself was an additional difficulty (a non-Indoeuropean language with diacritics). The Irish Centre, on the other hand, had a small size database to manage, was a complete beginner in OSIRIS, and, moreover, had never used a microcomputer before.

The two centres thus combined several of the difficulties different users would experience, and their valuable comments provided a better understanding of the user' needs. They helped find suitable solutions before there was a larger distribution of OSIRIS.

In order to create the conditions for successful tests, the OSIRIS system was installed in both centres and staff trained in local sessions, thanks to the financial support of IFLA-Hungary in May 1990 and Ireland in July 1990. The first period of tests raised a number of questions that had not been addressed previously, technical problems that required corrections and improvements that were felt necessary by regular users in their daily routines. Reports were submitted to the ISDS Directors' meeting in October 1990 and development work continued in order to answer the comments and proposals put forward by the testers.

A second version of the software was ready for delivery in 1991 and was reinstalled in Hungary in September, without external help.

Results of the test were presented at the ISDS directors' meeting in October 1991. Facing few technical problems with the second version, the Hungarian Centre proposed further developments that would be welcome in a future version of the software and focused on recommendations to users on how to include OSIRIS appropriately in their working procedures. In the meantime, the Irish Centre reviewed the User's Manual to make sure that a user with no experience in PC would be able to follow step-by-step instructions when left alone with the package.

During the whole process, the International Centre reported to the creators, organized priorities in the developments - those needed immediately and the desirable ones that had to be postponed for a future version. The creators took into account all requests, finally having to handle a larger project than anticipated at an earlier stage. The final stage took more time to reach than expected and announced in 1989 but the delay is largely counterbalanced by the quality of the result.

The Software

It is a difficult task to describe software. The alternative is either to repeat the technical specifications and User's Manual, which may prove a rather tiresome experience for the audience, or to outline the description, which is frustrating for the speaker who would like to present the many features and advantages the application offers.

The description below will be limited to the size and scope of a general presentation; those interested in more detailed information can request it from the ISDS International Centre. OSIRIS software uses as an underlying software Micro-CDS/ISIS developed by Unesco (Version 2.3). It is a powerful textual information and retrieval system.

In addition to its searching capabilities, the option for indexing, the sorting and output formatting it offers, Micro CDS/ISIS allows for customization of the basic software for specific applications.

In the OSIRIS application, some functions are simply tailored adaptations of existing Micro-ISIS functions (indexing, retrieval sorting of records), others have been developed specifically for OSIRIS purposes (ISSN verification, immediate data checking during data entry, record validation, import and export functions....). The functions developed on OSIRIS allow the user to:

— set up the OSIRIS environment
— load and invert the initial database
— create, modify and verify records
— update in inverted file
— search the database
— display, sort and print subsets of the database
— transfer records.

The users are provided with a package including both Micro-CDS/ISIS and its Manual and OSIRIS and its Manual. Once the installation is carried out, the use is in one single environment and users need not be specialists of Micro-CDS/ISIS. The license to use Micro-CDS/ISIS is provided with the OSIRIS package.

— a PC/XT, PC/AT, PS/2 or 1005 compatible with 640K RAM
— Minimum 2 Mbyte free hard disk capacity for the programme
— Minimum 2.5 Mbyte free hard disk capacity per 1,000 records.
— PC-DOS/MS DOS Version 3.3. or higher.

Before the installation of OSIRIS, attention is drawn as to the hard disk capacity requirements. User need to adjust their hardware equipment to the size of their local database. Lastly, some experience with microcomputers (or initial training) is necessary, in spite of the efforts made to tailor OSIRIS and make it as user-friendly as possible.

The operation related to the use of OSIRIS are first "one-off" activities when setting up the system, then recurring ones dealing with the current activities. OSIRIS users will first set up the OSIRIS environment: install ISIS, install OSIRIS, create the initial database. In the case of ISDS National Centres, the initial database is imported from the ISDS International Centre. Other types of users may also receive subsets of the international database on request, according to several criteria (ISSN, dates or language of publication, etc.)

Then OSIRIS will allow any of the following current activities : creation, amendment, validation of records, retrieval of information from the database, sorting and formatting of records in order to produce indexes, bibliographies and, when applicable, transfer of the records.

Records created and handled with OSIRIS are ISDS records. They consist of the same fields, subfields, mandatory elements with some few adjustments due to the underlying software. Differences were introduced in relation to local information and character sets.

Additional fields (9xx) were created for local needs. They can be used to make local notes about a records, can be displayed and searched.

The character set available with the IBM PC and compatible microcomputers had to be taken into account also. This was a serious challenge within the project.

There was a conflict between character coding in the ISDS database (ISDS character sets for the international database and exchanges within the network are ISO standards 646, 5426 and 2022) and the limited character representation of personal computers. The basic ASCII character set or the Extended ASCII Character Set (EXACS) are not sufficient to represent all characters present in ISDS records as a consequence of the universal scope of the database.

To quote Mr Jacso from the User's Manual : "A compromise had to be made among : (1) the need for sending to the International Centre records using the ISDS character set; (2) the limitations in displaying characters using EXACS; and (3) user convenience."

Gizmo notation (character triplets), nearest equivalent notation and conversion in the import and export programmes answered in the best possible way the three conditions. A detailed description of the solutions will not be given here but it is worth noting that great attention was given to this issue, which is one of the major difficulties in international bibliographical databases handled on the PC.

Local fields, character representations in connection with local equipments and keyboards, options offered in some functions make it necessary to customize individual versions of OSIRIS to stick as closely as possible to the user's requirements. A questionnaire is sent to all future users in order to provide answers to their specific local needs.

Applications

Originating from ISDS, OSIRIS's primary objective is to facilitate the registration of serial publications within the network. The facilities provided by OSIRIS make it a valuable working tool for a far larger part of the information community dealing with serials. Concerning ISDS, the advantages are twofold.

Before OSIRIS, National Centres sent their records to the International Centre on worksheets or tapes. Centres that have no access to a mainframe fill in worksheets. The worksheets method is a slow process : checking at the International Centre, external keyboarding, checking of the keyboarding, finally processing of the data. If, for any reason, a record is rejected and needs to be sent back to the National Centre, the whole process has to be repeated. The procedure delays the availability of the data in the ISDS Register.

In addition to the delays, with manual procedures by lack of automatic checking procedures at a local level, several types of errors can be introduced and the records will be rejected when processed by the International Centre. The advantage of maintaining the local ISDS database with OSIRIS are many in terms of correctness of data :

— the internal structure of the record is checked : errors on tags, fields, subfields, their repeatability or mandatory presence cannot occur. The correctness of the codes used in the record (frequençy, country code, language code, status, etc.) is immediately checked.

— the validation process checks the records within the local database; uniqueness of ISSN, uniqueness of key-title. With checking procedures at the local level, there is only one possible case of rejection of a record: a title that is unique in a national database may not be so when checked against the complete international database.

The export function can be used at any convenient time and data greatly gain by a timely introduction in the ISDS Register and early availability to all users. What could seem an internal ISDS improvement ends up being a better service to all those needing available ISSN and ISDS records.

The use of OSIRIS should not be seen as strictly limited to a few ISDS National Centres. The package is available for all who wish to maintain serial bibliographies and even Union Catalogues. Keeping in mind the physical limitations of the hardware, all institutions dealing with less than an average 30,000 record can use OSIRIS.

Bibliographies can easily be produced. The OSIRIS users can create and amend records that can be selected, sorted and printed. They can import ready-made records from the ISDS Register and amend them if necessary. Local fields are available which can contain legal deposit notices, address of publishers, inventory numbers, etc., and of course holding statements in the case of a Union Catalogue. Many countries with small and medium-size local production could thus create their national bibliography and print it. Small and medium-size cooperative systems and Union Catalogues could take advantage of a ready-to-use software requiring little hardware investment.

Conclusion

The present software will live on and be improved. Valuable comments on future developments have been received from users. The most recent version of Micro-CDS/ISIS that was not available when the programming started will provide additional facilities. There will be new ideas in the course of a larger current and regular use of OSIRIS.

In its present "final state", OSIRIS is welcome as a great improvement in working procedures. The objective is reached. OSIRIS is now in the installation phase. Following Hungary and Ireland, the ISDS National Centres of Poland and Italy were installed in early

1992. Delivery to Czechoslovakia Turkey, and Romania is under way. ACCIS (the United Nations Advisory Committee for the Co-ordination of Information Systems) was the first organization, outside ISDS National Centres, to be installed. Other external users and 10 National Centres expect to receive OSIRIS.

The International Centre organized a collective training workshop on the occasion of the ISDS Directors' meeting in October 1991, attended by 12 Centres. Since a lack of finances prevented local training in each case, the experience will be repeated next year.

The issue led to a great awareness of the importance of the documentation. Users are geographically scattered. Support is sought for the organization of local or regional training. ISDS wishes to thank here its first voluntary sponsor : the UK Cataloguing and Indexing Group, which, on the occasion of its Jubilee, presented ISDS with a cheque in support of the training of an OSIRIS user. The common satisfaction of those involved in the venture, and the positive reception by users, open up bright prospects. The IFLA Section will be kept informed of the future developments of a project to which it granted its active support from the very beginning.

About the author:

Suzanne Santiago is Chair of the Section of Serial Publications and Director, CIEPS, International Serials Data Systems, 20,rue Bachaument, Paris 75002, France.

[Ms. Santiago's paper was delivered during the 58th IFLA General Conference, Delhi, 30 August—5 September 1992.]

The Application of Information Technology (IT) in Public Libraries in Developing Countries

PETER BORCHARDT

Those who wish to get a better idea of the problems related to the application of computer technology in third world public libraries should look at the literature published on this topic in the last ten years. Then they get a rather pessimistic view which is not very encouraging. "Lack" and "constraints" are the words most used in these articles, and in fact it seems that people from industrialized countries have a lot of illusions of what could be possible. Everybody who has experience in third world libraries can share the experiences expressed.

Furthermore the term "developing countries" is not very precise. It comprises a whole bundle of countries which are not homogeneous at all. This is also reflected by the degree of development of libraries and library automation, there are so called "developing countries" in Southern America and Asia where library automation has advanced to a degree (not in all places, of course) which sometimes seems to be superior to the developments in some Southern European countries, and there are, on the other hand, countries, where we do find a very poor development, especially in Africa, even if we can state that on this continent there are enormous differences between the countries.[1] Unfortunately a world-wide survey on library automation and IT applications in developed or developing countries does not exist, so we do not really know what has already been achieved (and could serve as model), and it will be rather impossible to gather these data.

Nevertheless there seem to be problems connected to IT applications in (public) libraries which are common to a whole range of countries which will be described here, though this is not the place to state in detail the differences in librarianship between the so-called "developed" and "developing" countries, this has been done in other publications[2] :

One very serious problem is the role of libraries (and here especially public libraries) in society and the lack of appreciation by national decision makers. Generally, public library development is not a priority. This fact is known to northern countries too, but in the economic situation of developing countries this may be fatal. "A critical look at the current state of library and information services in Africa would ... sow that much of the optimism of the 1960s has given way to serious doubt, and the impressive growth of the earlier times has been replaced by stagnation and, in many cases, decay."[3] The idea that public libraries could have something to do with information handling and access to information also by means of IT is still rather unknown to decision makers, a fact that is often deplored by librarians.[4]

As long as one of the most serious problems in developing countries, the high rate of illiteracy, is not solved or on the way of being solved, and as long as public libraries in these countries are not prepared, staffed, and equipped to play a vital role in the struggle against illiteracy, it seems rather understandable that nobody seems to be inclined to put money to technical equipments in places were even the basic needs in the provision of literature cannot be satisfied adequately. "A large proportion of this potential clientele (of public libraries in Africa) lives in rural areas and is illiterate. The information and knowledge needs of this section of the population have been largely ignored by the prevailing book-centred philosophy of "public" libraries. Furthermore they have not been able to serve in the much needed and challenging role as agents for mass mobilization. This has led some critics to question the relevance of public libraries to the needs of the overwhelming proportion of the population for whom they exist to serve.... Public libraries are becoming volnerable and unless they can identify themselves with the new societal goals and objectives they are unlikely to be allocated a share of the nation's resources adequate for their needs. The result will be the continued underdevelopment of libraries as a whole, and public libraries in particular." [5]

Libraries, especially public libraries, in developing countries suffer from considerable lacks and constraints :

— Lack of funds,

— Lack of trained staff,

— Improper physical facilities for the library,

— Small number of users,

— Small collections,

— Inadequate equipment.

"As for the public libraries, it is fair to say that on the whole, they have been experiencing decay rather than development since they were first established."[6]

In this situation, some authors warn about negative and unwanted effects in introducing new technologies. Igwe states : "If ... the intricacies of the electronic age through which other societies are presently passing are introduced the traditional set up, the impact will be desastrous because no institution, be it library or such a related establishment, is ready for the change. The libraries have inadequate equipment and virtually no personnel to cope with a change of such complication and dimension"[7], and another point is stressed by Davies : "In developing countries where there is no sufficient employment opportunities and labour costs are low, it is feared that the use of computers will cause greater unemployment."[8]

Moreover, technical and related constraints should not be underestimated: "The assumption that technologies could be transplanted to other cultures without sufficient understanding of the needs of the users, and the lack of forethought regarding the support needs of the information systems themselves have been basic problems."

"The hardware required by advanced information technologies must have continued maintenance and support staff in order to function properly. The physical conditions required by many computer systems are often not available. Most developing countries are tropical with high temperatures, humidity or dust. Electrical problems are common with either blackouts or power surges that can damage both the hardware and software and makes it difficult to have an air-conditioned, dust-free environment. Many developing countries have areas without electrical power of any kind. The software used with computer systems cannot be developed in the country due to lack of training and experience. Thus, the software that is developed does not take into account the specific needs of the situation."

"Often there is a poor information infrastructure in developing countries. Telephone services are often poor, and the quality is poor for data transmission."[9]

These conditions make it difficult to think about the introduction of modern IT to developing countries or, at least, to the less developed countries. It is clear that any IT must be designed after the specific needs of those countries, i.e. it is important to think about the appropriate technologies : "These advances (of western countries in IT), however, have been geared to the needs of large organizations and developed countries. Their use presupposes a developed economic infrastructure, a high level of education and supporting technologies. Care must be taken then in presuming that these advances will solve the information problems of developing countries...it must be remembered that the communications technologies...which the developed countries often take for granted are also extremely important for a country's access to information."

"Developing countries have information needs that differ from those in developed countries.... The need for the appropriate information to meet the developing countries basic needs cannot be met using the large databases of the developed countries."... "The introduction of information technologies into developing countries has often led to disappointment and disillusionment on the part of the countries involved and the outside agencies. The systems have fallen into disuse. The information made available is inappropriate..."[10].

So it is not surprising that up to now IT is not very widespread in developing countries, especially in Africa—and where we find IT applications we can be sure that it will be in the first place an academic, research or special library, not a public library, and it is significant that even in "more advanced" developing countries like Kenya the introduction of information technology to public libraries is not even mentioned in a national development plan[11] (but it must be remembered that we have examples of public library computerization in South America, for example in Sao Paulo).

Even if a public library would be considered by decision makers to get a computer equipment, it would still face considerable problems, described by Were for Kenya (which can be supposed to be alike in other countries of the region, too) : "Libraries in developing countries are forced to turn to donations for high technology projects.... Recipient institutions tend to underestimate the financial implications of such aid :

— No provision is made for possible enhancements of the donated equipment which have to be financed locally. The donor will often give the minimum configuration.

— No provision is made for long term professional systems and programming staff required to maintain the system.

– There is a lack of awareness of the financial implications resulting from such running costs as maintenance, spare parts, stationery, additional storage facilities, etc."[12]

And even if the money would be granted to buy a system configuration and the software, the problem remains : "Distance from manufacturers of systems ... limits the scope of choice. Turnkey systems such as Geac, Plessey Pen, Automated Library Systems ... are still considered the best for libraries.... None of these firms is currently represented locally. Maintenance becomes a serious problem ..."[13]. "Computer science is a highly marketable profession and very well paying in private sectors. Librarianship on the other hand falls under the low-income professions in Kenya and it becomes impossible to retain library staff trained in this area"[14]. Everybody who uses automated systems and modern information technology knows that breakdowns can occur rather often, and without immediate support by manufacturers or specialized staff members these events can paralyse the whole library.

But as most of the public libraries in developing countries have small collections, a little number of users and circulation and only small funds, the question is whether the introduction of IT equipment in this situation is really justified. Would it not be better to spend the small funds on books and other library materials ? This question can only be decided within the countries.

But it must also be noted that "such societies cannot simply reject modern information technology either, since they have to participate in international networks, even if these are dominated by "Northern" technology. Therefore the major question is : Can the development of new hardware and software be geared to the needs of societies in the South ? There seems to be little hope that mainstream producers in the North will basically change their development efforts, since the market of industrialized countries will continue to be their main asset in the foreseeable future"[15,16]. And recently Banjo stated : "Finally since African libraries have been so closely linked, for good or ill, to the developments and products in Europe and America another potential source of crisis is the technological revolution ... which will result in the widening of the existing technological gap, unless necessary measures are taken. The sign now is that there is little evidence of computer literacy in Africa and worse still, there is little appreciation of the need for it. Yet these developments are bound to have crucial repercussions in the provision of library and information services in Africa, for whether we accept the need to maintain the present pattern of relationship with the developed world or not, the need to adopt the new technology will become imperative sooner or later, in order to ensure accessibility to the new formats in which the information of the future will be packaged."[17]

So, what can be done — and what can the IFLA Section on Public Libraries do ? It can point out the difficulties and try to show ways how to overcome these difficulties. Up to now, only little or no consideration has been given to the specific IT problems for Public Libraries in developing countries. If we look into the UNISIST Newsletter we can see that until today no pilot project (funded by international organizations) in IT use for Public Libraries has ever been started. This indicates that no developing country has ever felt the necessity of and priority for fund raising for such a project.

On the other hand technological developments of the last few years have led to a new situation : Hardware costs have decreased dramatically (and will continue to decrease), and the software problem is still a problem, but there might be a chance to overcome it. This could mean that it might be easier even for public libraries in developing countries to go the IT way, even if not all problems mentioned above are already solved.

The first question of a public library that wishes to introduce IT will always be : Do I really need it ? And for what purposes ? It is very important to define the fields of application in order to get the right answers and the right decisions. The classical fields of IT application in Public Libraries are :

— cataloguing and retrieval of catalogued data

— circulation control

— serials control

— automated acquisition

— bibliographic research

— internal applications (housekeeping, statistics, word processing etc.)

To these joint more sophisticated applications (data exchange, use of external databases, interlibrary loan, networking and online ordering etc.) which will surely not be necessary in all kinds of libraries. The more powerful a system is, the more it costs, and the hardware and maintenance needs are increasing. Moreover, online searching in external databases is rather expensive and needs good telecommunications infrastructure which is not always given in developing countries. But the use of CD-ROM might be an alternative, as it enables libraries to search in large databases without needing an online facility, a CD-ROM drive connected to a PC will do, and the development of CD-ROM production in the last years (parts of it distributed by international organizations for very attractive prices) is rather promising[18]. Nevertheless Public Libraries have to ask themselves what they really do need.

A very good, short introduction which resume the basic features and problems of IT application in developing countries is given by Jacinta Were in a training document of the German Foundation for International Development[19].

A basic equipment will consist of a PC (microcomputer) and the appropriate software to run the system. Today it is possible to get a PC (IBM-compatible), AT or 386-PC with 1-4 MB RAM and a 80-120 MB hard disk, VGA screen and printer for less tan 5,000 US $, and this equipment will do for smaller Public Libraries. CD-ROM devices can be linked for less than 1,000 US $. But it is strongly recommended to use hardware which can be supported and maintained locally ! To these costs must be added the current costs for running the system [storage and backup facilities (floppy discs), printer ribbons or cartridges for laser printers, paper, spare parts, cleaning material, etc.]

The real problem is the software : Professional software for libraries can easily cost more than 20,000 US $, and no Public Library in developing countries can afford it. Another problem linked to this has already been mentioned : Experience shows that sophisticated software needs a lot of maintenance which is expensive and which can only be given if the manufacturer is not too far away.

This problem is common to all kinds of libraries and was one of the reasons for UNESCO to develop a software for libraries and related institutions, a software originally designed for mainly smaller special libraries : CDS/ISIS, which is available in the latest version 2.3.

Up to now there seems to be no public library which uses CDS/ISIS (at least, UNESCO did not answer our respective questions), but for them, too, it would be worth looking at it closer. The first advantage is that CDS/ISIS is distributed free of charge to non-profit institutions in UNESCO-member-states. The second advantage is, that CDS/ISIS runs on PCs and can be used even on slow and old PCs. The third advantage is that CDS/ISIS is multilingual (English, French, Spanish, even a version for Arab characters is available).

A disadvantage seems to be that UNESCO does not offer any support to users of CDS/ISIS. But in reality that does not seem to be a problem. There are several thousands of installations all over the world, not only in developing countries, and there are hundreds of user groups world wide. This concept of user groups is not a bad one : One user can help the other in the same country or even city, the user groups formulate proposals and wishes for further development of CDS/ISIS, and up to now UNESCO has always considered these proposals to a certain extent in developing new versions. Reports of these user groups are published regularly in the UNISIST Newsletter, as well as informations on developments of further applications done by individual users. So the CDS/ISIS user community can profit of developments done in other places.

CDS/ISIS is destined for bibliographic and other textual applications and is capable of operating multiple applications under a single user surface, including library housekeeping (but up to now no circulation control), documentary activities, referral services, and administrative tasks, and a UNESCO supported pilot project, conducted by the Pan American Health Organization, has proved the capability of CDS/ISIS to operate a CD-ROM database distributed to hundreds of sites in Latin America.

One application (Spanish) developed in Lima, Peru, allows it even to use the system without computer skills and without familiarity with CDS/ISIS. "A routine for setting up the system is included and one only needs to introduce the diskettes to load the software automatically into the micro-computer"[20]. The German Foundation for International Developments offers regularly training courses in the use of CDS/ISIS, in Germany or on site.

The system can manage an unlimited number of databases with a maximum number of 16 million records in each database, which will be more than sufficient for most public libraries in developing countries.

A detailed test of CDS/ISIS version 2.3 has been published by P. Nieuwenhuysen[21], showing that it is a highly competitive software with still some features that could be better, but on the whole it is very attractive. Having a closer look to this software and testing it in different Public Libraries, reporting the experiences to UNESCO and urging UNESCO to consider, for further developments, the specific needs of public libraries, could be a promising and practical way to IT use in Public Libraries in developing countries.

REFERENCES

1. cf. Olugboyega Banjo, A. : Library and Information Services in a Changing World : an African Point of View, in : Int. Libr. Rev. (1991) 23, 103-110.

2. cf. R. Gassol de Horowitz : Librarianship. A Third World Perspective, New York 1988 (Contributions in Librarianship and Information Science, No. 59).

3. Olugboyega Banjo, op. cit. p. 105.

4. Igwe, P.O.E. : The Electronic Age and Libraries : Present Problems and Future prospects. In : Int. Libr. Rev. (1986) 18, 75-84.

Were, J. : Problems of Automating Libraries in a Developing Country : Kenya. In : L. Hüttemann/F. Inganji (eds.) : Use of Computers in Information Handling. Report on the DSE/PADIS Training Workshop held from 21 April to 2 May, 1986 in Nairboi, Kenya, Bonn/Addis Abbaba 1986, 97-103.

5. Olugboyega Banjo, op. cit. p. 106.

6. *Ibid.*, p. 107.

7. Igwe, P.O.E. : The Electronic Age and Libraries : Present Problems and Future Prospects. In : Int. Libr. Rev. (1986) 18, 79.

8. Davies, D.M. : Appropriate Information Technology. In : Int. Libr. Rev. (1985) 17, 251.

9. *Ibid.*, p. 250.

10. *Ibid.*, p. 248-249.

11. cf. James M. Ng'ang'a : A National Information Service. In : L. Hüttemann (ed.) : Management of Information Resources Sharing and Networking. Papers and Lecture Notes of a Training Course held in Mobasa/Kenya, 15-26 April 1991. Bonn : Deutsche Stiftung für Internationale Entwicklung, 1991, p. 5-15.

12. Were, op. ct. p. 98.

13. *ibid.*, p. 99.

14. *ibid.*, p. 100.

15. Baark, E. : Appropriate information technology : a cross-cultural perspective. In : Unesco J. Inf. Sci., Libr. and Arch. Adm. (1982) 4, 263-268.

16. cf. also : Eyitayo, A.O. : Status report on the attitude of automated library system vendors to investing in Nigeria. In : Program (1989), 23, 247-256: "The responses also revealed that Nigeria (and in general, less developed countries) is not considered to be an economically viable market to invest in for now." (p. 254).

17. Olugboyega Banjo, A. : Library and Information Services in a Changing world : an African Point of View, in : Int. Libr. Rev. (1991) 23, 108.

18. cf. Wright, S. : Application of CD-ROM technology to libraries in developing countries. In : Program (1990) 24, 129-140.

19. J. Were : Computer Applications in Libraries and Documentation Centres: What a Manager Needs to Know. In: L. Hüttemann (ed.) : Management of Information Resources Sharing and Networking. Papers and Lecture Notes of a Training Course held in Mombasa/Kenya, 15-26 April 1991. Bonn : Deustche Stiftung für Internationale Entwicklung, 1991, p. 84-89.

20. UNISIST Newsletter 18, No. 1, 1990, p. 14-15.

21. Nieuwenhuysen, P. : Computerized Storage and retrieval of structured text information : CDS/ISIS Version 2.3, In : Program (1991) 25, 1-18.

The Mahābhārata Database Project : A Note

SUBHAS C. BISWAS and SHEELA DAGA

1. Background

A new era has begun in the field of indological research and scholarship as a result of the emergence and application of information technology. While physical and social sciences have used the computer as a research tool for several decades, computer - assisted research in humanities is newer. To a large extent, this is due to the fact that till date, only a few humanistic disciplines have managed to create data banks sufficiently large to enable research and scholarship within computing environment. Today, scholars in the field of classical languages and literature, linguistics, ancient history and philosophy, religion etc. depend heavily upon and benefit from the access to the massive body of texts and documents available in such corpora as the *Thesaurus Linguiae Graceae (TLG)*[1] data bank.

Indologists and Sanskrit scholars all over the world are well aware of the advantageous position of their colleagues in Greek classics, because of the existence of *TLG* and other digital archives of classical literature. *TLG* helps them generate concordances and study metres and syntax efficiently. The benefit of creating machine readable corpus of Sanskrit texts would be enormous. The total volume of the Sanskrit literature is many times larger than Greek and Latin put together. This presents such problems of sheer magnitude that no one can write anything about it without knowing that what is said is only partial. Many Sanskritists in the west are computer-literate, and several successful computer-based research projects have been completed. On the other hand, there are only a handful of Indian Sanskritists and Pandits, who are familiar with computer application in research.

In 1988 (October 27-29), the Center for Asian Studies, University of Texas at Austin, USA, organised a seminar on the creation of Sanskrit database with the participation of eminent Sanskritists and computer experts. It was decided to undertake a pilot project, as a joint venture, of entering the *MAHĀBHĀRATA* into a machine-readable file. The Central Secretariat Library (CSL), New Delhi, shall be the other partner for the pilot project with prime responsibility of encoding the text (4 volumes) of the Pune edition of the *Mahābhārata (Mahābhārata Samhtā .)* The text will be put in machine-readable form in an appropriate format with standardized mark-ups, jointly agreed upon by both the institutions. CSL will input the text in original *Devanāgarī* script. A memorandum of understanding was signed between the UT at Austin, Center for Asian Studies, and the CSL to that effect in December 1990.

2. The Mahābhārata and Indian Literature

Of all the epics we have inherited from the distant past, from the civilisations of antiquity, the *Mahābhārata* is the greatest in terms of the humanistic significance of characters and episodes, and in the insight to man's destiny revealed in their interlocking. *Mahābhārata* is one of the largest epics in the world. It contains 1,00,000 *Ślokas* or verses. With its eighteen *parvans* (Books or Cantos), twelve hundred chapters and over two hundred thousand lines of verses, the *Mahābhārata* is eight times as long as the *'Iliad'* and the *'Odyssey'* put together, three and a half times the *'Bible'*.[2] It is an all inclusive literature and not a single homogeneous work. For centuries together, the *Mahābhārata* has been popular not only in India but also in several other parts of the world. Making reference to the characters and codes in this book is a mark of erudition. From the fifth century B.C. saints, scholars, poets and dramatists have quoted copiously from it. In the second century B.C. a Greek envoy referred to precepts culled from this epic. In the sixth century A.D. the whole poem was recited in temples at Cambodia.[3]

This book is a treasurehouse of the Indian culture, both secular and sacred. The epic provided the material and ideas for numerous narrative poems and dramas of classical Sanskrit literature. Its translations became the foundational classics for many of the Indian vernacular languages in the formative phases of their evolution, and generated once again a vast body of narrative poems and dramas in these languages too.[4]

Besides classical literature the *Mahābhārata* has had a great impact on the folk literature, creative works of arts - music, dance, sculpture, paintings etc. For example, in Kerala the *Nalopākhyāna* is presented in the form of music and dance. *Pandavānī*, a folk ballad is also very popular in central and northern India.

The bulk of tribal names found in the *Mahābhārata* may surprise even a modern surveyor of ethnography. It quotes many more names of tribes and tribals, than any other piece of literary work of Indian antiquity. The emergence of caste from tribes, is a basic fact of the Hindu social system. The great epic represents that crucial era of transition, when the decline of tribal culture had begun by ascendence of powerful monarchies in the political set up of the country.[5]

The *Smrtis* and even modern law are indebted to the *Mahābhārata* for the exposition of the intricacies of jurisprudence and Hindu law. The other major significance of the epic is that it contains the *Bhagavadgītā* and several other philosophical tracts. It also provides interesting study of India's vegetations, flora and fauna. It is most relevant for the study of geography and environment of India.[6] To the students of Sanskrit literature the *Mahābhārata* so far as it reflects the ancient life of India, will always remain an invaluable treasury. Some references are found, which are very significant for medicinal benefits.[7] The similes used in the *Mahābhārata*[8] provide useful hints for the study of metals and gems. Oldenberg authoritatively proclaimed that 'in *Mahābhārata* breath the united soul of India and the individual souls of her people'.

3. Project Infrastructure

A Technical Review Committee was set up with R.N. Dandekar, Pune, as the Chairman in the CSL to advise on the mark-up issues and other policy matters. (The Committee was reconstituted after one year, as Prof. Dandekar expressed his inability to take the strain of visiting Delhi due to old age and health reasons). One Research Assistant with sound knowledge of Sanskrit was appointed for coding mark-ups and data input with the 'Linguist' software package. It may be worth noting here that there was no other software package available locally, which could have been considered in January 1990. However, the situation has since changed. There are a few similar software packages available with *Devanāgarī* font variants. But switching to another software is not an easy task.

4. Issues: Language, Script and the Format

The *Mahābhārata* is a work of transition period. So all the trends and features in a transition period of language are clearly visible in the epic. The rigidity of *Pāṇinian* grammar was not strictly adhered to in the epic. The language was undergoing a constant change and was very near to the spoken language of the people as we see the variations in the following examples:

दृश्यति/पश्यति; त्वा/त्वाम्; अपश्यत/अपश्यत्; ददाहि/देहि

About ninety-five percent of the *Mahābhārata* is composed in *śloka* metre. Each *śloka* is usually having a specific quantitative pattern for the cadence, of each eight syllable (*Varṇas* line (*Pāda*) in *anuṣṭubh* metre form. Besides many other Vedic as well as classical metres were found in the epic. Two or three classical metres in a single verse were also used. e.g.

यमश्च सोमश्च महर्षयश्च <a साध्या विश्वे वालखिल्याश्च सर्वे <b

एतेऽपि यस्योद्विजन्ते प्रभावात् <c कस्मात्तस्मान्मादृशी नोद्विजेत (आदिपर्व)

<d/v39/c65

In this verse the first *pāda* is of *Upendravajrā* , second and fourth are of *Shālini* and the third one is *Vidhvaṅkamālā* metres. The verse (all the *padas* having 11 varnas each) is marked up as a *Triṣṭubh* metre. *Upajāti* metres are quite common throughout the text. Of all the various texts of the *Mahābhārata,* it was decided to take the Pune edition for the Pilot Project.

In creating a Sanskrit database the most crucial factors are to identify each word and syntax, and for that, all *padas* are to be coded separately and these are to be indicated by using standard mark-ups. The Technical Review Committee recommended the following codes and mark-ups for adoption as standards:

1. Beginning of the book : <b;
2. Beginning of the chapter: <c;
3. End of the chapter: >c;
4. End of the book: >b;
5. Prose : <p/(number);
6. Verse: <v/(number);

7. *Pādas* are coded with one alphabat - a, b, c, d, e, f, etc.;

8. Hemistich is not indicated ;

9. Printing mistakes if any in the text, are corrected from the critical edition;

10. Unit (phonetic unit) is taken as a standard for division in Sanskrit prosody;

11. Every metre, other than *Anuṣṭubh,* is indicated in each and every verse by M1, M2, etc.; (separate number is assigned to each metre);

12. Verses that are not being numbered, are indicated by unv/ms (e.g. un-numbered verse: *Maṅgala Śloka*);

13. *Samāsa* is not separated in a *pāda* unless it is essential to *indicate pādas* (indicated by a (-) hyphen e.g.

तांस्तथारूपवीर्यौजः संपन्नान्पौरसंमतान्
तांस्तथारूपवीर्यौजः– <a संपन्नान्पौरसंमतान् (आ. प.) <b/v7/c54;

14. ऋ(दी.) is used for the limitation of the font used ;

15. Where it was essential to separate *sandhis* (to break a *śloka* into *pādas*) . the grammatical ending is optionally admitted (क्=ग्, त्=द्, इ=य्, उ=व्, ए=अय्, ऐ=आय्, औ=आव्), म् is restored at the end of a *pāda* instead of an *Anuswāra* (अं) the neutral form of a word is indicated by an equal sign within parenthesis (=), where dissolution of *sandhi* is essential for indicating *pādas* i.e. first, third and fifth *pādas* of the verse e.g.

तस्या मार्गं सृतवतीं दृष्ट्वा तु सरितं तदा।
नाम तस्यास्तदा नद्याश्चक्रे लोकपितामहः।
वधूसरेति भगवांश्च्यवनस्याश्रमं प्रति।।
तस्या मार्गं सृतवतीम् <a दृष्ट्वा तु सरितं तदा <b/v7.1
नाम तस्यास्तदा नद्याश् (=:) <c चक्रे लोकपितामहः <d/v7.2
वधूसरेति भगवांश् (=वान्) <e च्यवनस्याश्रमं प्रति (आ.प.) <f/v7.3/m1/c6

16. *Visarga* (:) which admits both the forms as correct, i.e., स, सः; एष, एषः text form is retained ;

Following are a few examples of *sandhi*, which are being dissolutioned and netural form of the words are used to mark-up *pādas* :

श्रुत्वाहं ता विचित्रार्था महाभारतसंश्रिताः

श्रुत्वाहं ता विचित्रार्था (:) <a महाभारतसंश्रिताः (*आदिपर्व*) <b/v10/c1

जनमेजयस्य यां राज्ञो वैशंपायन उक्तवान्

जनमेजयस्य यां राज्ञो (=ज्ञः) <a वैशंपायन उक्तवान् (*आ. प.*)<b/v18/c1

छन्दोवृत्तैश्च विविधैरन्वितं विदुषां प्रियम्

छन्दोवृत्तैश्च विविधैर् (=:) <c अन्वितं विदुषां प्रियम्(*आ.प.*) <d/v26/c1

गान्धारराजसहितैश्छद्मद्यूतममन्त्रयत्

गान्धारराजसहितैश् (=:) <c छद्मद्यूतममन्त्रयत् (*आ.प.*)<d/v100/c1

शिष्टाचारे भवेत्साधू रागः शुक्ले च वाससि

शिष्टाचारे भवेत्साधू (धुः) <c रागः शुक्ले च वाससि (आरण्यक प.) <d/v68/c198

दिव्यौ सुपर्णौ विरजौ विमानावधिक्षियन्तौ भुवनानि विश्वा

दिव्यौ सुपर्णौ विरजौ विमानाव् <c अधिक्षियन्तौ भुवनानि विश्वा (*आ. प.*) <d/v60/c3

समयो यौवराज्यायेत्यब्रवीच्च शकुन्तलाम्

समयो यौवराज्यायेत्य् <c अब्रवीच्च शकुन्तलाम् (*आ. प.*) <d/v9/c68

जीर्णः शिशुवदादत्तेऽकालेऽन्नमशुचिर्यथा

जीर्णः शिशुवदादत्ते <a ऽ(=अ) कालेऽन्नमशुचिर्यथा (*आ.प.*) <b/v21/c79

दक्षो धृतव्रतो धीमाञ्शास्त्रे चारण्यके गुरुः

दक्षो धृतव्रतो धीमाञ् (=न्) <c शास्त्रे चारण्यके गुरुः (*आ.प.*) <d/v5/c4

न तु मर्त्यस्य धर्मात्मन्नायुरस्ति गतायुषः

न तु मर्त्यस्य धर्मात्मन् (=न्) <c आयुरस्ति गतायुषः (*आ.प.*) <d/v6/c9

यथा वा मन्यसे राजंस्तत्क्षिप्रं संविधीयताम्

यथा वा मन्यसे राजंस् (=जन्) <c तत्क्षिप्रं संविधीयताम् (*आ.प.*) <d/v28/c33

स ददर्श हतान्भ्रातॄँ (दी.) ल्लोकपालानिव च्युतान्

स ददर्श हतान्भ्रातॄँ (दी.) ल् (=तॄ(दी.) न्) <a लोकपालानिव च्युतान् (*आर.प.*)<d/v1/c297

स चापि तां प्राप्य मुदा युतोऽभवन्न चान्यनारीषु मनो दधे क्वचित्

स चापि तां प्राप्य मुदा युतोऽभवन् (=त्)<C न चान्यनारीषु मनो दधे क्वचित् (आ. प.)<d/v9/c40

न तां वध्रः परिणहेच्छतचर्मा महानणुः

न तां वध्रः परिणहेच् (=त्) <a छ (=श) तचर्मा महानणुः (*आ.प.*) <b/v19/c26

असंशयं त्रिदिवमियात्स पुण्यभाङ्महात्मनः पतगपतेः प्रकीर्तनात्

असंशयं त्रिदिवमियात्स पुण्यभाङ्(=क्)<c महात्मनः पतगपतेः प्रकीर्तनात् (आ.प.) <d/v22/c30

तथाति पुरुषानन्यान्त्सारुकौ यमजावुभौ

तथाति पुरुषानन्यान्त् (=यान्) <a सारुकौ यमजावुभौ (*आ.प.*) <b/v41/c123

भूतानामपरः कश्चिद्धिंसायां सततोत्थितः

भूतानामपरः कश्चिद् <a धिं (हिं) सायां सततोत्थितः (*आरण्यक प.*) <b/v10/c200

17. Colophone is abbreviated to Col ;

18. A different number is being used for each speaker - <S 1, 2, 3, etc. according to the sequence of the text. Where one speaker is referred to by different names or personalities, the same code number is being used to indicate the speaker. However, the most common name form is also mentioned in ( ). e.g., सूत उवाच <S1 इन्द्र उवाच <S19 शक्र (इन्द्र) उवाच <S19, ब्राह्मण (इन्द्र) उवाच <S19 etc. If a common name like ब्राह्मण, ब्राह्मणी, राक्षस, राक्षसी is used for a particular person, the proper name of that person is always mentioned within parenthesis( ).

5. A Few Thoughts

This article is an account of the scope and standardization of mark-up adopted in converting the *Mahābhārata* into machine-readable form. Mark-ups adopted so far, are by no means complete or exhaustive. There may be more of these as we go along the text. *ĀDIPARVA to UDYOGAPARVA* have been taken up thus far.

Most of modern Indo-European languages have the best part of their information available at the syntax level, whereas, Sanskrit, Pāli and other classical languages may very well be approached on word-level first. For this dissolution of *sandhi* and identification of verbal roots and other derivatives are basic requirements for creating a data bank of Sanskrit. Some Computer-literate Sanskritists are developing software packages, which would help in Sanskrit data processing much faster than has been possible under this pilot project.

We originally planned to complete data entry for the *Mahābhārata* within two years. Unfortunately it has been delayed due to a shortage of financial resources and various local factors. The sooner we complete the data entry job of the 4 volumes of the epic, the easier it will be to develop an appropriate software package, which would ultimately help in analysing the structure and the basic composition of Sanskrit literature.

REFERENCES

1. Brunner Theodore F., *Scholarly Communication*, No. 7, Winter, 1987.
2. Chaitanya K., *The Mahābhārata*, Clarion Books, Delhi 1985.
3. Chidbhavanand Swami, Mahābhārata. The Philosophy of Humanity, Shri Ramakrishna Tapovanam, Tiruchirapalli, 1973.
4. Chaitanya, *ibid*.
5. Mishra, K.C., Tribals in the Mahābhārata, National Publishing House, Delhi, 1987.
6. Suryavanshi, *Geography of the Mahābhārata*, Ramananda Vidya Bhawan, Delhi, 1986.
7. *Virāṭa Parva* 9.13.
8. Sharma R.K., Elements of the Poetry in the Mahābhārata, Motilal Banarasidas, 1988.

Adapting Technologies for Library Processing Projects : Africa, Asia, and South America

ANTON R. PIERCE

Planning and administering automation projects for the Library of Congress' overseas field offices involves dealing with unique processing requirements, desperate backgrounds of host country staff, multiple alphabets and scripts, poor telecommunications infrastructure, and frequent power outages. A series of nine strategies are given which have helped implementing automation in the Library's overseas offices.

1. INTRODUCTION TO THE LIBRARY OF CONGRESS' OVERSEAS OPERATIONS

The Library of Congress isn't just located in Washington, D.C., U.S.A. For 30 years the Library has operated its *Special Foreign Acquisitions* program run from overseas field offices which provide acquisitions and cataloging services. These services are performed in offices that are very different from the Capitol Hill setting. They are currently located in Cairo, Egypt; Jakarta, Indonesia; Karachi, Pakistan; Nairobi, Kenya; New Delhi, India; and Rio de Janeiro, Brazil. The automation of these offices presents a difficult set of challenges involving telecommunications facilities, electrical power stability, hardware repair and parts inventories, and even time zones.

In the following paper, after introducing the overseas offices' operations, I want to describe the Library of Congress' progress towards the development of a consistent overseas office automation policy under these desperate conditions and requirements. I have listed a set of *strategies* that have emerged to help us meet our situation and which may apply to other organizations as well involved in the introduction of information technology in remote locations.

In addition to collecting materials for the Library of Congress itself, the overseas field offices also collect for participants in the program. Over time, the program evolved and is now known as the Overseas Acquisitions Program. Program participants are drawn from several major research and special libraries located in the United States and in other countries. Since 1962, the program has grown to include participants from 87 institutions in the United States and around the world. Exchange and gift materials and spot purchases made during acquisition trips form the heart of the acquisitions process.

2. A FIRST AUTOMATION STEP IN THE OVERSEAS OFFICE : OVERSEAS DATA ENTRY

The application of computer technology to processing in the overseas field offices began in New Delhi with the introduction of the *Overseas Data Entry* or ODE project about 10 years ago. The purpose of ODE was two-fold : 1) to create MARC compatible machine readable data for uploading cataloging data into the mainframe computer in Washington and 2) to create printed catalog cards and proof sheets. Once uploaded in Washington the MARC records are distributed by the Library's Catalog Distribution Service (CDS) to bibliographic utilities and other institutions in the United States and around the world. ODE-produced catalog cards are included with items sent to program participants.

ODE capitalized in large measure on the local language skills of host country staff which allows the office to analyse and provide cataloging data for use by the Library of Congress, by program participants, and, by virtue of national bibliographic networks, to libraries around the world. These cataloging data also provide the basis for publication of the *South Asian Accessions List*. one of five regional *Lists* which frequently supplement or sometimes serve as substitute for the national bibliography in some countries.

The ODE project was an early and perhaps the first example of a system that could create MARC records and cards on a microcomputer; provide a degree of interactive data validation; and honor the full character set required by MARC as implemented by the Library of Congress. It is remarkable that the Terak microcomputers used have only 64Kb of memory. The system was designed by Library staff in Washington and New Delhi with a good deal of the programming being done by contract staff.

As successful as the ODE installation in New Delhi proved to be, it was not exported to the other five offices. Rapid changes in the world of microcomputers such as the introduction of IBM's PC employing an "open" architecture brought the DOS operating system to the fore and rendered the ODE hardware and software platforms obsolete only a couple of years after the project's attainment of production-level status in 1984. The ODE project, as excellent as it was, was therefore frozen.

3. A SECOND GENERATION OF AUTOMATION IN THE OVERSEAS OFFICES

The opportunities offered by the PC "revolution" provided the impetus to seek to automate additional functions in the offices. Cost and availability of staff around the would led us away from seeking a mainframe solution: it would have been expensive to buy and support remotely big machines and difficult to find staff to run and maintain them. The PC/DOS revolution provided a direct and immediate way to provide relatively powerful computing at low unit cost in a widely understood operating system. Thus, our expansion efforts after the ODE project were based on the utilization of PC/DOS technology. Another advantage of using PCs overseas was that it became easier to provide a stable electrical environment with the use of relatively compact and widely available uninterruptable power supplies which we provide for each PC in the field. After the introduction of these UPSs data losses and equipment failure due to electrical problems were a thing of the past. These considerations lead to our first strategy:

Strategy I : Use of PCs and DOS and not a mainframe computer as the basis for computer development

Shared Software Applications

It became clear that as we distributed PCs to the offices spread around the world, steps would have to be taken to introduce a degree of standardization of systems and supporting hardware. It was also evident that unless a degree of centralized control were present the solution of each office's problems would require a new set of skills to be learned. Remote trouble shooting from Washington is difficult and error prone. Time differences force Washington staff to be resourceful at 05:00 (which is just 15:30 in New Delhi or 17:00 in Jakarta--after they have gone home!) That's possible if all are using the same set of hardware, software, and applications.

Strategy II : Standardize Hardware and Software

Integrated Order, Accounting, and Distribution System

The next major system was also developed in the New Delhi office and was written under contract. It is known as the *Integrated Order, Accounting, and Distribution* system or IODA. IODA's basic task is to provide processing support for items ordered for the Library of Congress and, especially, for program participants. IODA does this by matching a participant's profile against codes for subject, country, and language assigned to the title. The assignment is usually made after a review copy has been obtained from a local dealer or acquired on a field trip. The participant profile can be very rich, having about 2,000 topical entries possible in the New Delhi profile.

After the successful introduction of IODA in the New Delhi office, it was clear that IODA would provide useful capabilities in the other offices. Moreover, the introduction of IODA in other offices would be major step forward in the implementation of strategy II, software standardization.

A meeting involving several offices was held in New Delhi to review IODA and further refine it to meet their requirements. In December 1988 version 2.0 was installed in the Cairo and Karachi offices. This marked the first time a specially developed application was running in multiple offices. Later IODA was expanded to the other offices and is now running as version 2.23 with an additional major enhancement (IODA 2.30) expected in March of 1993.

Strategy III : Introduction in a Step Wise Fashion.

CD-MARC

Another big problem the offices faced was access to the whole Library of Congress' catalog. Such access would provide answers to questions such as "Has this title already been acquired?" or "What other works has this author written ?" Access to the Library's bibliographic and name and series data is required to provide consistent cataloging data. In the past microfiche bibliographic and name files distributed by the Library's Cataloging Distribution Service (CDS) were the sources of these data. As effective as this microfiche product was, it nevertheless was difficult to use. Furthermore, several microform issues had to be consulted to ensure an exhaustive search had been made. This was especially true for names, where it is difficult to narrow a search by time period.

The introduction of CDS' CD-MARC product changed the picture dramatically. One major objective of this project was to provide the overseas offices with a better means of accessing bibliographic, name, and subject data. Several features required by the offices were included in its design, e.g., retrieval by country of publication or language. Complete cumulations issued quarterly means there is only a single issue to check. In addition to the efficiencies introduced by having a single cumulation, the product offers the advantages afforded by the superior retrieval capabilities of computer-based searching, such as key word. Offices report a major gain in efficiency using the product. Thus, even though the offices are geographically remote, they have immediate access to the Library of Congress catalog.

ODE, Phase II

Even though we decided not to implement the Terak-based ODE system in other offices, the *concept*, point-of-acquisitions cataloging, remains valid. Thus, we looked for, in essence, a "MARC record making machine" which would run on a PC (i.e., under DOS) and create correct USMARC records with local extension required by the Library for its internal processing. Rather than developing the ODE-2 system ourselves (as was the case for the original ODE) we reviewed the marketplace and found an acceptable system.[1] The selected system offered a good mix between online data validation (e.g., instant alert if an operator tries to key an undefined field) and the ability to add fields as required by additions to USMARC.

Strategy IV : If at All Possible, Buy or Obtain Existing Shared Software Rather than Develop Your Software In-House

The adaptation of the selected commercial software to the requirements of ODE-2 has not been easy, but this is a consequence of using a "mass produced" product and not a custom made product and accepting some compromises. Nevertheless, ODE-2 software is now installed in all offices and being used in "start-up" mode with production slated to begin in a few weeks. This has been accomplished faster and at less cost than if the software for ODE-2 were custom made.

Strategy V : Accept a few Compromises in Order to Use Bought/Shared Software Effectively.

Local Software Developments

Systems staff in each offices have made their own contributions and written several applications for use in their local settings. These applications supplement the functions provided by the shared or common systems such as IODA or ODE-2 Some of the offices also correspond in non-Roman scripts (e.g., Arabic or Thai) and use a variety of PC (i.e. DOS) based multi-lingual word processors.

These auxiliary applications are based on the use of dBase III or IV (and the functionally similar Fox Base/ Fox Propackages); Lotus 123 for spread sheet applications; the ask Sam textual database management system; and the Pro cite package for generation of bibliographies. These are all well supported, standardized, software packages, a tent of Strategy II. In some offices of function, such as an in-process database, may be implemented using dBase or in others using askSam. This is to be expected, given the diverse backgrounds of staff in different offices and the relatively loose control from Washington.

Strategy VI : Encourage Independent Work in Each Office so that Highly Motivated Staff will Know they Are Making Real Contributions.

In-House and Contract Development

If an acceptable existing system can not be obtained, either as a shared system (e.g., MINISIS) or through purchase, then one enters the difficult and complex area of system development. (This was the case for IODA given the unique acquisitions requirements the offices faced n running the participant programs.) Perhaps the not difficult thing about development is deciding what is to be accomplished. There are many ways to decide but all effective ways should include:

(a) Consultation with potential systems users at all levels

(b) Development of a *Requirements Document* to refine user input and, ultimately, to act as a check list for the delivered system

Both in-house development and contracted development (by an external source, e.g., a software house, by an "NGO", or Non-Governmental Organisation, or by a private contractor) require monitoring by someone other than the person responsible for developing the system. This is needed to provide the requisite checks and balances to ensure the desired system is what is actually delivered.

We have frequently found it useful to state requirements of the proposed contract in terms of "mandatory" and 'desirable" features. For example:

> (Mandatory) The XYZ system shall ignore diacritic marks for sorting purposes. (Desirable) It is desirable that the XYZ system provide the capability for the user to alter the default sorting order.

Stating the requirements this way forces the debate to focus on the essentials of the system. It is, however, *not* an easy process and one should expect several drafts before arriving at a satisfactory version. This format also allows the library or information center to select from multiple proposals if the system is being "put out to bid". The proposal reviewers can weigh various proposals in terms of absolutely critical items and "nice-but-less-than-critical" items. A rule of thumb is that no more than half of the requirements should be in the mandatory category.

Strategy VII : Invest a Major Effort in Defining the System's Requirements *with* Your Potential System Users *Prior* to Building the System

4. SYSTEM INTEGRATION

An important concept in data processing is the principle of the non-redundancy of data. One example of this could be having the serial check-in part of a system derive its title data from the title entry defined in the cataloging part of the system. This usually implies that different system functions are integrated : otherwise, the check-in function couldn't easily or gracefully draw upon the data resources of the cataloging function. In terms of practical computer applications, functional integration implies a multi-user, interactive system, with minimal reliance on batch or off-line processing.

Functional integration adds greatly to the overall value of the system and offers major advantages :

> Users have a single, authoritative, and up-to-date place to check. Data is only entered once, into only one part of the system. Workflow becomes more efficient because users can obtain immediately needed data from any unit of the enterprise.

The Library of Congress wants to extend serials check-in, for example, more fully into the field offices, thus relieving some of the processing load from Washington. Thus, overseas field offices are now starting the process of obtaining an integrated system which would provide this functionality as well as a host of other functions. While the offices engage in several traditional library functions they also engage in several unique activities and consequently it is not expected that any "off-the-shelf" library software could offer all the required capabilities. But rather than build the system in-house we have gone to the marketplace and are now reviewing proposals from system vendors and software houses to meet this set of requirements. These proposals will probably be a mix of existing capabilities and program enhancements needed to meet the unique requirements. The strategies derived in this paper are basic to this process of obtaining the new integrated system.

Role of Standards in System Development

We are all familiar with national and international standards and indeed IFLA and the associations represented here have labored to develop a host of important standards at both levels. And these standards have been adapted by several commercial and shared systems. However, unless enterprise or in-house standards exist and *are keyed to national' international* standards the options for picking up and using an existing system are more limited. Further, it is more difficult, if not impossible, to contribute to and to utilize external data resources, such as computer-based union catalogs and bibliographies. In our case, standards permit the overseas offices to create records which fit smoothly into the Washington database.

By the same measure, if various unit in the enterprise are not adhering to common standards then it may be impossible to transform existing machine readable data into that required by available systems.

Strategy VIII : Adhere Rigorously to Any and All Appropriate National/International Standards

In the development of the Library's Integrated Field Office System (IFOS) we have specified the following existing and developing standards as relevant to the system:

USMARC Bibliographic, Name, and Holding Formats

ANSI Z39.42, covering the display of serials holdings

USMARC Arabic character set so as to process extended Arabic script on RLG's RLIN system

ANSI Z39.50: *Information retrieval service definition and protocol specifications for library applications.*

Outline of the IFOS

In order to keep the IFOS project to manageable size it has been divided into two phases expected about a year apart. Some of the major functions required are given below.

Phase I:

Distribution of documents to participants and calculating participant cost.

Ability to search and import MARC records to create portions of order and for catalog control purposes.

Creation of a transaction database which will support time series analysis allowing comparison of different time periods.

User defined report generation capability based on data elements from transaction log.

Non-serial item receiving and tracking.

Major Phase II features include :

Output of USMARC Bibliographic, Name, Subject, and Holdings data.

Serial and continuation receiving (Check-in)

Control of Binding and Microform handling.

The ability to process extended Arabic script is also a "highly desirable" feature.

Given the round-the-world nature of the Library of Congress' overseas field offices, we have also emphasized how well the bidders can provide software corrections and enhancements. Given also the remarkable improvements in telecommunications in several of the host cities where the overseas offices operate, it is possible that fixes and upgrades may be transmitted directly to the offices using international gateways linked to local PTT facilities. (We do not use private satellite channels given the current cost of these facilities.)

5. TECHNOLOGY COLLABORATION

The Library of Congress' overseas offices also work with host country and regional organizations in computer-based collaborative projects. Such projects, in addition to addressing the goals of the project itself, help strengthen good relations with library, scholarly, and publishing sectors in the region.

The National Bibliography of Indian Literature (NBIL) or Kesavan project is one example of such a technology collaboration. The project consists of 1) building a database of titles cited in the NBIL and 2) creating preservation microfilm of the items identified in the the bibliography. The problem addressed by the project is that a multitude of important materials are decaying and will be lost. Preservation filming now can save these unique materials. The project was proposed by James H. Nye, University of Chicago, and utilize funds from the United Sates-India Fund (USIF). The New Delhi office is acting as project host site but also provided technical administrative support at the project's inception.

The concept was straightforward and is almost a replication of Mr. Nye's highly successful preservation project for Sanskrit series run at the University of Chicago in cooperation with Harvard. The key move is to build a database to describe the items using USMARC and then to use the database as a tool to locate the items to be filmed and track their progress through the filming process. NBIL is an accepted reference source and copies exist in libraries around the world. The bibliographic data of the database is exportable as USMARC records and could therefore be distributed to bibliographic resources databases and networks. We close with the "use whatever works" strategy :

Strategy IX : Whenever possible, Buy Beg, Borrow, or Adapt an existing Application.

---

1. The software is known as "Minaret" and is developed by Geoff Mottram at Cactus Software in Morristown N.J. U.S.A.

Index